U0560286

"行业英语（ESP）微环境应用研究（2011）"横向课题成果

浙江农业商贸职业学院

绍兴禹庄开元酒店管理有限公司　联合修订

技术顾问（主审）

尉宵宵　绍兴禹庄开元酒店管理有限公司　人事总监

主　编

王　群　浙江农业商贸职业学院　教授

尉宵宵　绍兴禹庄开元酒店管理有限公司　人事总监

浙江省高职院校"十四五"重点教材

HOTEL ENGLISH:
MANAGEMENT &
OPERATIONS

酒店管理与经营

 英汉对照 第3版

王　群　尉宵宵 / 主　编
杨　骞　李雨霖 / 副主编

ZHEJIANG UNIVERSITY PRESS
浙江大学出版社
·杭州·

图书在版编目（CIP）数据

酒店管理与经营 ：英汉对照 / 王群，尉宵宵主编
. -- 3版. -- 杭州 ： 浙江大学出版社，2023.1
ISBN 978-7-308-23117-6

Ⅰ．①酒… Ⅱ．①王… ②尉… Ⅲ．①饭店－经营
管理－教材－英、汉 Ⅳ．①F719.2

中国版本图书馆CIP数据核字(2022)第181273号

酒店管理与经营（英汉对照·第3版）

JIUDIAN GUANLI YU JINGYING

王　群　尉宵宵　　主编

责任编辑	陈丽勋
责任校对	陶　杭
封面设计	春天书装
出版发行	浙江大学出版社
	（杭州市天目山路148号　　邮政编码　310007）
	（网址：http://www.zjupress.com）
排　　版	杭州林智广告有限公司
印　　刷	杭州高腾印务有限公司
开　　本	787mm×1092mm　1/16
印　　张	23.25
字　　数	560千
版 印 次	2023年1月第3版　2023年1月第1次印刷
书　　号	ISBN 978-7-308-23117-6
定　　价	65.00元

版权所有　翻印必究　　印装差错　负责调换

浙江大学出版社市场运营中心联系方式：0571-88925591；http://zjdxcbs.tmall.com

■ 本书介绍

旅游业的快速发展带来了酒店业发展的突飞猛进，也使得酒店从业人员的数量激增。酒店业的国际化需要国际化的管理与服务，这就要求员工掌握系统的酒店管理与服务的专门英语知识，具备更强的专门英语应用能力。当前，在我国酒店从业人员中，具备较高的酒店行业专门英语理论水平和较强的专门英语应用能力的员工的比例还很低，行业专门英语的教育和教学还不能很好地满足酒店行业各种微环境的需要。因此，"行业英语（ESP）微环境应用研究"课题应运而生。作为该课题的重要研究成果之一，《酒店管理与经营（英汉对照）》的出版得到了浙江大学出版社的鼓励、支持和帮助。

本书本着"必需、实用、应用"的原则，对酒店微环境进行深入调研，基于整个酒店经营与管理的过程，把专业理论知识和专门英语运用于岗位工作的各个环节，旨在以专业理论指导解决岗位工作中的实际问题。本书在体现实用性的同时，还注意一定的系统性，也反映了国内外酒店业的新观点和新经验。

本书是横向课题项目研究成果，凝聚了企业专家的智慧和心血，他们的贡献保证了教学内容的科学性、针对性和应用性，因而本书是一本真正意义上的校企合作教材，适合专科院校相关专业学生使用。本书还是酒店从业人员的良师益友，适合酒店管理人员和服务人员使用，可用作酒店企业的内部培训教材或员工工作手册，也可用作相关在职人员岗位培养、自学进修用书。

《酒店管理与经营（英汉对照·第3版）》是浙江省高职院校"十四五"重点教材建设立项项目。本书的修订结合课程知识特点，隐显结合地丰富了大量的课程思政元素，便于教师开展课程思政教育，并开辟了"二十大精神学习专栏"，以切实推动党的二十大精神进教材、进课堂、进头脑。本书的编排采用英汉对照方式，为酒店专业开展双语培训提供便利；本书配置了大量的学习资源，形式多样，有利于学生开展自主学习和教师进行混合式教学。

■ 第3版前言

　　《酒店管理与经营（英汉对照 ·第3版）》是浙江省高职院校"十四五"重点教材建设立项项目。本书第1版问世，就受到了一些学校相关专业师生的青睐，获得了较好的评价，连续数次重印。根据有关使用学校的意见和浙江大学出版社的建议，我们围绕教学需要，改编出版了第2版教材，进一步得到了许多学校师生的深切关怀与厚爱，收到了许多中肯的批评意见和宝贵的修订建议。在此，我们谨向关心本教材的读者表达最诚挚的谢意和最崇高的敬意。为了更好地服务酒店专业英语课程教学，更好地支撑酒店管理专业建设，我们根据课程思政教育、职业教育"三教"改革、职业教育教材"双元"开发等相关要求，开展了本教材第3版的修订工作。经过两年多的辛勤劳动，我们汲取经验、总结教训、采纳建议，终于使教材以全新的面貌展现在广大师生面前，希望新版教材能为酒店英语课程建设做出更大贡献。

　　1. 教材特色

　　（1）"双元"合作更深入。本次教材修订工作坚持"行业指导、企业参与"的原则，吸收了更广泛的社会力量参与。他们中有专业带头人、酒店企业培训专家、酒店企业服务人员、一线骨干教师等。他们的参与保证了本教材紧跟行业发展趋势，满足行业人才需求，充分地反映岗位职业能力要求，从而保证教学内容的科学性、实用性和针对性。

　　（2）编写理念更新颖。本次教材修订基于内容型教学法(Content-Based Instruction, CBI)理念，把内容课程与语言课程紧密结合，将语言技能教学融于特定专业知识教学，把语言作为工具或媒介来传授专业知识，使学生通过专业知识的学习提升英语语言能力，并在英语语言活动中获得专业知识，提高思维能力。本教材的材料选取基于课程思政教育理念和要求，将思政教育的理论知识、价值理念及精神追求等元素融入教学内容之中，潜移默化地对学生的思想意识、价值观念和行为举止等产生影响。本教材的教学设计基于混合式教学理论，把传统学习方式的优势和网络学习的优势结合起来，注重学生直接经验体验和间接经验体验的获得。本教材的课堂设计基于"翻转教学"方法，开展自主学习，发展学生利用各种学习工具或资源自主发现、分析和解决问题的能力，同时开展小组学习，让学生学会协作和分享，培养学生团队协作精神。

1

（3）实用特色更鲜明。本次修订对接岗位职业能力要求，重视学生的职业能力培养和职业素质养成。本教材内容的选取以"必需、实用"为原则，减少了理论知识，更加贴近岗位工作需要，基于典型工作任务选取实践性的教学内容，突出培养学生在岗位工作中应用行业英语的能力，教材的实用性特色更加鲜明。

（4）内容设置更科学。深入酒店企业开展"行业英语(ESP)微环境应用研究"，为我们更准确、科学地设置教学内容提供了有力保证。在此横向课题研究的基础上，经过细致分析、反复讨论和广泛征询意见，确定本教材设置酒店基础英语(English for Hospitality Basics)和酒店服务英语(English for Hotel Services)两个内容板块。前者以酒店专业知识学习和酒店专业文献阅读能力培养为目的，根据具体酒店微环境管理与经营的实际工作需要，兼顾专业知识的系统性，具体包括酒店基础(Hospitality Basics)，服务指南(Service Guide)，酒店管理(Hospitality Management)，房务部(Rooms Division)，餐饮部(Food & Beverage Division)，会议服务、康乐服务与投诉处理(Convention, Recreation, and Complaints)等；后者以酒店服务英语的口语实践能力培养为目标，基于岗位工作过程，反映典型工作任务，把专业知识和英语知识运用于岗位工作的各个环节，具体包括基本交际用语(General Expressions)、情景交际用语(Situational Expressions)、酒店应用表单(Hotel Application Forms)和酒店餐饮菜单(Food & Beverage Menus)等。专业知识体系的系统性增强，使本教材的内容组织更加科学，满足了课程目标的要求，从而为专业人才培养目标提供有力支撑。

（5）教学资源更丰富。本教材努力开发配套的在线课程，打造"立体化"教材，同步丰富课程资源。我们将提供课程标准、教学设计、电子教案、演示文稿、微课视频、线上互动社区以及题库、试卷库等课程资源，利教利学，更好地服务师生，助力信息化教学改革。

2. 教材使用建议

（1）关于教学内容取舍。本教材旨在培养学生的酒店专业英语应用能力，依据酒店管理与经营各岗位工作需要的英语技能，设置了酒店基础英语、酒店服务英语两部分内容。两部分内容独立设置，有利于分别开展有针对性和系统性的读、说能力训练，避免了以往教材"融合"式设计的非系统性，使得学生在读、说技能两方面都能得到较充分的训练。本教材内容按4个学分进行教学课时设计，可供一学期或两学期使用。建议各学校根据学生学情学力、课程目标和学时学分安排，对本教材内容进行合理取舍。"剩余"内容，包括附录部分，可供延伸性学习使用，建议组织学生利用在线课程资源开展自主学习。

（2）关于词汇设计。由于各地各校学生英语基础各异，本教材根据反馈意见以1000词的词汇基础设计词汇表，供教学使用。建议把第一部分的词汇学习要求设定在认知层面，即学生在日后岗位工作中，能够借助工具书阅读本专业文献或其他工作需要即可。对于第二部分的词汇学习，可适用"四会"（听、说、读、写）要求。专业术语作为必须掌握的内容，安排在各单元的题库中。

（3）关于教学侧重。本教材根据专业及课程目标进行设计，侧重专业英语读、说能力培养，围绕能力目标依托教材文本设计了内容丰富、形式多样的题库。建议教学时不要按照英语精读课或综合英语课的模式进行课文教学，而应侧重组织各种学习活动，使学生通过完成题库作业达成课程目标。

（4）关于课堂组织。本教材的教学设计基于"混合式""翻转"教学理念，倡导基于团队的自主学习，使学生逐渐养成自主学习习惯和团队协作意识。在教学中，应当着眼于学生学而非教师教，应当重视学生直接学习过程体验和直接学习经验获得；应当鼓励提问、质疑和答辩，多引导、多启发、耐心帮助，不可急于求成；应当摒弃"对错"观，变标准答案为参考答案，表扬和鼓励发表不同意见，促进学生发散性思维发展。建议课前由学生通过自主学习方式，完成词汇自主学习资源和课文自主学习资源的学习，并完成相关的自主学习自测；课中先由教师对学生课前自主学习成果进行点评、答疑和成绩记录，接着让学生跟着教师或课堂教学视频开展学习，然后通过小组学习方式，完成课堂练习（练习成绩可实时记录），接着组织学生分享、提问、质疑和答辩，最后由教师进行评价和总结。

（5）关于课程考核。建议课程考核重视形成性过程考核，以出勤、小组参与度、课堂活跃度、作业完成量为主要考核指标，在线课程资源学习量不足60%者不能参加课程考试。期末考试建议以题库为纲采用开卷或闭卷形式。

（6）关于课程思政。教材是知识和技术的传播载体，更是政治、思想、文化、价值观的传播载体，教材的思想性影响着课程思政教育的方向和效果。在本次教材修订中，我们根据酒店英语课程的知识特点，基于"隐显结合，润物无声"的原则，从单词和短语的选择、释义、造句及翻译到课文内容的选取，再到学习活动(Learning Activities)内容的设计，尽最大可能地丰富了思政元素，涉及价值观念、精神追求、职业道德等诸多方面。为了方便教师开展课程思政，我们把相关的德育元素进行了整理，放在课程标准和教案中。建议以"浸润"为主要方式，让学生耳濡目染、潜移默化、润物细无声地接受教育和启迪，可以有意识地围绕"思政元素"教学内容，适度拓展和讨论。更为突出的是，根据国家教材委员会、浙江省教育厅等相关部门的部署，本次教材修订结合英语学科和酒店专业的特点，选取恰当内容，开辟了"二十大精神学习专栏"，以切实推动的党的二十大精神进教材、进课堂、进头脑。

（7）关于课程资源。本教材配备了大量的多类型、多形式的课程教学资源。有Word、PowerPoint和视频等形式的词汇及课文学习资源，可供学生进行自主学习和自主测试；有Word、PowerPoint和视频等形式的课堂教学与练习资源，可供教师开展课堂教学使用；更有可供教师教学参考使用的课程标准、授课计划、教案、课件、题库、试题库等教学文件。

本教材在写作及修订过程中，参考了国内外出版的部分酒店管理方面的专业图书、国内外网络资料，以及部分酒店的宣传资料和信息，得到了绍兴咸亨大酒店原经理陈宝根先生、绍兴禹庄开元酒店管理有限公司人事总监尉宵宵女士等在整个研究过程中给予的辛勤指导和无私帮助，接受了浙江越秀外国语学院王书侠副教授、浙江农业商贸职业学院张文莲副教授、浙江经贸职业技术学院胡爱娟教授等老师的理论与实践指导。在此，谨向相关作者、单位及个人表示诚挚的感谢。由于作者经验不足和水平所限，本教材难免有欠缺，也恳请同行和读者批评指正。

为了方便老师们的教学交流，我们建了一个酒店专业英语教学交流QQ群（群号：585142849），欢迎进群领取各类教学资源，参与教学讨论和交流教学资料。

编者于世纪东街770号

2022年12月

CONTENTS
目　录

Part One　English for Hospitality Basics
第一部分　酒店基础英语

English for Hospitality Basics
酒店基础英语

Chapter One

Hospitality Basics
酒店基础

思政园地／二十
大精神学习专栏

Learning Objectives

· *To get familiar with hotel functions, hotel categories, hotel ratings, hotel organization, and hotel operating models;*

· *To understand hotel guests, guest cycle, and hotel services;*

· *To master the new words and professional terms concerned;*

· *To improve reading ability through learning the text;*

· *To develop team spirit and self-study ability through learning activities;*

· *To receive education in ideological and political theories through course learning.*

Teaching Arrangements

节次	教学内容	自主学习资源	自主学习自测	课堂教学视频	课堂练习
L 1	1.1 Functions, Categories, and Ratings	词汇、课文资源	词汇、课文自测	微课	课堂练习
L 2	1.2 Hotel Organization	词汇、课文资源	词汇、课文自测	微课	课堂练习
L 3	1.3 Hotel Operating Models	词汇、课文资源	词汇、课文自测	微课	课堂练习
L 4	1.4 Hotel Guests, Guest Cycle, and Hotel Services	词汇、课文资源	词汇、课文自测	微课	课堂练习

The word "hotel" comes from French, meaning "country villa," in which noblemen *entertained* their *distinguished* guests. It was at the end of the 18th century or the beginning of the 19th century that the word got its present meaning of "hotel" (*jiudian*), meaning a kind of *labor-intensive hospitality enterprise* with its *functional* and *corporate* elements up to *established* standards, making profit by offering services like *lodging*, *catering*, shopping, and *recreation* to business people and other types of guests.

A hotel should *equip* itself with safe and comfortable rooms, different restaurants with a wide selection of local foods and *superb cuisines*, business conference halls *furnished* with modern equipment and office *communication* system for business activities, recreational *facilities* to meet guests' demands like swimming pool and fitness room, shopping areas like *arcade* and gift & *souvenir* store, and business center offering bank service, postal service, bookstore, flower shop, beauty *salon*, etc. Meanwhile, a hotel should build a group of good-quality *personnel* that can offer *tip-top* service to guests.

1.1 Functions, Categories, and Ratings

1.1.1 Hotel Functions

The hospitality industry, which is the basic element of *tourism* supplies and the *indispensable* material condition in social-economic activities,

"酒店"一词源于法语，指贵族在乡间招待贵宾用的别墅。大约在18世纪末或19世纪初，它才具有现代"酒店"之意。酒店是指其功能要素和企业要素都达到规定的标准，能够接待商务及其他类型的宾客，并为他们提供住宿、饮食、购物、娱乐及其他服务来获取经济效益的劳动密集型服务企业。

一个酒店应设有舒适安全的客房，可供应多种风味佳肴的各式餐厅，具备商务活动所需的现代化的会议设备和办公通信系统的商务会议厅，满足宾客所需要的游泳池、健身房等各种康乐设施，商品部、礼品部等购物场所和能够提供银行服务、邮局服务，设有书店、花店、美容院等的商务中心，同时应具备一支能够向宾客提供一流服务的素质良好的服务人员队伍。

酒店的功能

酒店业是旅游供给的基本构成要素，是社会经济活动不可或缺的物质条件，是所在地对外交往、社会交

serves as the center of *external* contact and social *interaction* for local people and the base camp for travelers at the tourist *destination*, and also makes an important *contribution* to tourism *earnings*, especially foreign *exchange* earnings. As far as the hotel functions are concerned, it can: 1) provide guests with safe and comfortable rooms; 2) provide guests with various *delicious* cuisines; 3) provide a wide selection of places for parties, *gatherings*, *banquets*, conferences, and other business activities; 4) provide *specialized venues* for cultural activities such as training, lectures, *performances*, *exhibitions*, concerts, and other similar things; 5) provide *fitness* facilities for guests' *leisure* activities; 6) offer guests services of health medical *treatment*, health care *consultation*, *hairdressing*, etc.

1.1.2 Hotel Categories

Hotels can be *categorized* by location, *ownership*, price, and other factors, such as service, guestroom *format*, or *clientele*.

Some of the most generally *recognized* hotel-location categories are: center-city, *resort*, *suburban*, highway, and airport. The majority of center-city hotels attract mostly business travelers, and most guests who stay in city-center hotels are corporate individuals or *convention* guests. Most of center-city hotels are full-service facilities, including rooms, a coffee shop, restaurants, at least one bar, room service, *laundry* and *valet* services, a business center, a *newsstand* and gift shop, and a health club. Resort

际活动的中心，是旅游者在目的地的大本营，也是创造旅游收入，特别是外汇收入的重要部门。就酒店业的功能而言，主要有以下几个方面：1) 住宿功能，为客人提供舒适安全的客房；2) 餐饮功能，向客人提供各式餐饮；3) 会议接待功能，能够提供各种场所举行聚会、集会、宴会、会议及其他商业活动；4) 文化服务功能，能够提供场地举行各种培训、讲座、表演、展览、音乐会等文化传播活动；5) 运动休闲功能，能够提供各种健身设施使客人享受运动休闲服务；6) 健康服务功能，能够为客人提供健康医疗、保健咨询、美发等服务。

酒店的类型

酒店可根据其所在地、所有权、收费价格进行分类，也可根据其服务水平、客房格局和客户群特点等其他因素进行分类。

最为普遍的是，酒店按其所在位置可分为：市中心酒店、度假酒店、城郊酒店、高速公路沿线酒店和近机场酒店。大多数的市中心酒店主要招揽的是商务旅行者，住在市中心酒店的客人也大多是企业的个人或会议客人。大多数市中心酒店提供全方位服务设施，包括客房、咖啡店、餐厅、至少一个的酒吧、客房服务、洗衣及代客服务、

hotels are generally found in destinations that are *desirable* vacation spots. It is not unusual for resorts to have *elaborately landscaped* grounds with hiking *trails* and gardens as well as *extensive* sports facilities such as golf *courses* and tennis *courts*. Successful resorts *achieve* higher *occupancy* and higher sales per room than other categories of hotels. Business travelers make up nearly half of the resort lodging market for large resort hotels that have conference and convention facilities. Suburban hotels tend to be *somewhat* smaller than *downtown* hotels, with 250 to 500 rooms and limited banquet facilities. Their major *source* of *revenue* is from business-meeting and convention *attendees* and from individual business travelers. Highway hotels offer the same facilities found in downtown and suburban hotels, but with a *distinct identity* of their own—plentiful parking space, informal *atmosphere*, lower number of employees per room, and lower total sales per room. Airport hotels *address* the need for guestrooms near airports and enjoy some of the highest occupancy rates in the lodging industry. They have been changing to hotels that can *accommodate* the needs of business travelers who may plan to stay more than one night and might require meeting space.

Hotels, by ownership, can be categorized as independent hotels and chain hotels.

Another way of categorizing hotels is by the prices they charge. Three *broad* hotel categories *distinguished* by price are limited service, mid-price, and first-class / luxury.

Other hotel categories include all-*suite*

商务中心、报刊亭与礼品店以及康乐中心。度假酒店通常位于理想的度假胜地，除了设有高尔夫球场和网球场等宽广的体育设施，常常还拥有精心设计的园林景观，内有徒步小径和花园。与其他类型的酒店相比，度假酒店的入住率更高，单房销售额更高。在拥有各种会议设施的大型度假酒店，近一半的住宿客人是商务旅行者。城郊酒店往往较市中心酒店稍小一些，客房数在250～500间，宴会设施有限，主要收入来源于商务会议、与会者以及商务旅行者。高速公路沿线酒店提供的各种设施与市中心酒店和城郊酒店相同，但有着自己的独特之处——充足充裕的停车场地、随和友好的氛围、较少的房单员工数，以及较低的房单销售总额。近机场酒店满足了机场附近的客房需求，获得住宿行业最高的入住率，它们已经或正在转型成为满足商务旅客住宿需求的酒店，这些旅客可能住宿不止一晚，而且可能需要会议场地。

酒店根据其所有权可以分为独立酒店与连锁酒店。

还有一种酒店分类的方法是按其收费价格。以价格分类的三大酒店类型是：有限服务酒店、普通服务酒店、豪华酒店。

其他酒店类型有：全套房酒店、

hotels, conference centers, *timeshare properties*, *condominium* hotels, and *seniors housing*.

In addition, *eco-tourism* is becoming more popular, so eco-hotels have become more common. Eco-hotels, similar to resort hotels, are usually located close to or in a beautiful natural area such as beaches, mountains or forests. The difference between resorts and eco-hotels is that eco-hotels stress low or no *impact* on the natural *environment*.

According to the *statistics* about China's tourist hotels, the hotel-scale categories fall into five types: those with rooms over 499, 300 to 499, 200 to 299, 100 to 199 and under 100. The hotel-feature categories could be business hotels, resort hotels, extended-stay hotels, convention hotels, *economy / budget* hotels, suites hotels, *casino* hotels, and bed & breakfast hotels.

1.1.3　Hotel Ratings

Different systems for *rating* hotels are *applied* in different countries and regions, with the purpose of making a sound development of hospitality industry, *facilitating* the trade management and *supervision*, protecting guests' benefits, and *enhancing* staff's sense of responsibility and sense of honor. A hotel is *graded* by certain standards or requirements concerning its location, environment, facility, service, and management. The rating of a hotel must be made public with a certain sign. The rating systems currently applied in the world are: the Stars system with "five stars" as the top rating, the Letters system with "A" the highest and "E" the

会议中心酒店、分时度假酒店、公寓酒店和养老公寓酒店。

另外，随着生态旅游的发展，环保酒店也开始普遍起来。环保酒店与度假酒店类似，都建在海滨、高山或森林等环境优美的自然风景区附近。两者的区别在于，环保酒店的经营理念是将对自然环境造成的影响控制在最小范围内。

根据有关中国旅游酒店的统计，酒店规模分为500间及以上、300～499间、200～299间、100～199间和99间及以下五类。按市场特点，有商务酒店、度假酒店、长住酒店、会议型酒店、经济型酒店、全套房酒店、博彩酒店及B+B家庭酒店等。

酒店的等级

为了促进酒店业的健康发展，便于行业管理与监督，保护宾客的利益，增强员工的责任感和荣誉感，不同的国家和地区采取了不同的酒店等级评定的方式。根据酒店的位置、环境、设施、服务及管理等情况，按照一定的标准和要求，对酒店进行分级，并用某种标志告知公众。目前，国际上采用的酒店等级制度有：星级制，以"五星"为最高级；字母表示法，"A"为最高级，"E"为最低级；数字表示法，"豪华"表示最高级，接下来依次由

lowest, the Numbers system with the top "Luxury," followed by 1, 2, 3, and 4 from high to low, and the *Diamonds* system with "five diamonds" at the top and "one diamond" at the bottom. The system for rating hotels used in many Asian countries including China is the Stars system, in which, from the lowest to the highest, hotels are rated at one star, two stars, three stars, four stars, and five stars. In China the system is *administered* by the *Ministry* of Culture and Tourism. The Diamonds system, used in the US, Canada, Mexico, UK, and other *Commonwealth* countries, follows basically the same pattern as the Stars system.

The rating systems are used by *organizations* to help hotel guests know what to expect from a hotel and help hotels focus their efforts on standard levels of service. This helps hotels *compete* in the market. Most hotels of higher star or diamond ratings provide *well-equipped* facilities. The hotels with luxury or world-class service are rated at four or five stars, the ones with mid-range service at three, and the ones with economy service at one or two. But the rating of a hotel includes more than the standard of rooms and facilities, and the key factor is the personnel in the hotel who deal directly with the guests. Levels of service, as well as *target* markets, vary as much as the ratings of hotels. High-level *executives*, movie stars, and *politicians* are the target *clients* of world-class luxury hotels. Budget travelers are the target clients of economy hotels.

高到低为1、2、3、4级；钻石表示法，最高级为五钻，最低级为一钻。包括中国在内的许多亚洲国家都采用了酒店星级制评定系统。从低到高依次是一星级、二星级、三星级、四星级和五星级。在中国，星级评定由文化和旅游部负责管理。在美国、加拿大、墨西哥、英国及其他英联邦国家通常使用钻石制，其形式和星级系统基本相同。

等级评定系统被机构用来帮助宾客了解一个酒店可以提供什么样的服务，同时也帮助酒店努力提供与其等级相应的服务。这有利于酒店在市场上的竞争。星、钻级别越高的酒店，就会有越好的服务设施。拥有豪华顶级服务设施的酒店属于四星级或五星级，提供中等服务的是三星级，经济实用的则是一星级或二星级酒店。但酒店档次不仅仅指酒店房间和设施的标准，关键因素是那些直接面对宾客的员工。酒店的不同等级决定了不同的消费对象，也决定了不同等级的酒店服务。顶级豪华的五星级酒店的消费对象通常是高级职员、电影明星及政客。自助旅行的宾客通常会选择经济型酒店。

Vocabulary

entertain /ˌentəˈteɪn/ v. 招待

distinguished /dɪˈstɪŋgwɪʃt/ adj. 尊贵的

labor-intensive /ˈleɪbə(r) ɪnˈtensɪv/ adj. 劳动密集型的

hospitality /ˌhɒspɪˈtæləti/ n. 酒店管理

enterprise /ˈentəpraɪz/ n. 企业

functional /ˈfʌŋkʃnl/ adj. 功能的；职能的

corporate /ˈkɔːpərət/ adj. 公司的

established /ɪˈstæblɪʃt/ adj. 制定的；规定的

lodging /ˈlɒdʒɪŋ/ n. 住宿

catering /ˈkeɪtərɪŋ/ n. 餐饮服务

recreation /ˌrekriˈeɪʃn/ n. 娱乐

equip /ɪˈkwɪp/ v. 给……提供装备

superb /suːˈpɜːb/ adj. 极佳的

cuisine /kwɪˈziːn/ n. 菜肴

furnish /ˈfɜːnɪʃ/ v. 给……提供家具

communication /kəˌmjuːnɪˈkeɪʃn/ n. 通信

facility /fəˈsɪləti/ n. 设施

arcade /ɑːˈkeɪd/ n. 购物中心

souvenir /ˌsuːvəˈnɪə(r)/ n. 纪念品

salon /ˈsælɒn/ n. 美容院；沙龙

personnel /ˌpɜːsəˈnel/ n. 职员

tip-top /tɪptɒp/ adj. 最好的；第一流的；头等的

tourism /ˈtʊərɪzəm/ n. 旅游业；观光业

indispensable /ˌɪndɪˈspensəbl/ adj. 不可缺少的

external /ɪkˈstɜːnl/ adj. 外部的

interaction /ˌɪntərˈækʃn/ n. 互动交流；交际

destination /ˌdestɪˈneɪʃn/ n. 目的地

contribution /ˌkɒntrɪˈbjuːʃn/ n. 贡献

earnings /ˈɜːnɪŋz/ n. 收入

exchange /ɪksˈtʃeɪndʒ/ n. 兑换

delicious /dɪˈlɪʃəs/ adj. 美味的；可口的

gathering /ˈgæðərɪŋ/ n. 聚会

banquet /ˈbæŋkwɪt/ n. 宴会

specialized /ˈspeʃəlaɪzd/ adj. 专门的

venue /ˈvenjuː/ n. 会场；场地

performance /pəˈfɔːməns/ n. 表演

exhibition /ˌeksɪˈbɪʃn/ n. 展览

fitness /ˈfɪtnəs/ n. 健康

leisure /ˈleʒə(r)/ n. 休闲

treatment /ˈtriːtmənt/ n. 治疗

consultation /ˌkɒnslˈteɪʃn/ n. 咨询

hairdressing /ˈheədresɪŋ/ n. 美发

categorize /ˈkætəgəraɪz/ v. 分类

ownership /ˈəʊnəʃɪp/ n. 所有权

format /ˈfɔːmæt/ n. 样式

clientele /ˌkliːənˈtel/ n. 客户（总称）

recognize /ˈrekəgnaɪz/ v. 承认

resort /rɪˈzɔːt/ n. 度假胜地

suburban /səˈbɜːbən/ adj. 城郊的

convention /kənˈvenʃn/ n. 会议

laundry /ˈlɔːndri/ n. 洗衣

valet /ˈvæleɪ/ n.（照顾客人私人衣物的）服务员

newsstand /ˈnjuːzstænd/ n. 报摊

desirable /dɪˈzaɪərəbl/ adj. 令人满意的

elaborately /ɪˈlæbərətli/ adv. 精巧地

landscape /ˈlændskeɪp/ v. 美化景观

trail /treɪl/ *n.* 小径

course /kɔːs/ *n.* 场地

achieve /əˈtʃiːv/ *v.* 完成；达到；实现

somewhat /ˈsʌmwɒt/ *adv.* 稍微；有些

source /sɔːs/ *n.* 来源

attendee /əˌtenˈdiː/ *n.* 出席者

identity /aɪˈdentəti/ *n.* 特征

address /əˈdres/ *v.* 设法解决

broad /brɔːd/ *adj.* 一般的

suite /swiːt/ *n.* 套房

timeshare /ˈtaɪmʃeə(r)/ *n.* 分时使用度假房的方法

property /ˈprɒpəti/ *n.* 地产；花园住宅；庄园；房屋及院落

condominium/ˌkɒndəˈmɪniəm/ *n.* (独立产权的) 公寓

senior /ˈsiːniə(r)/ *n.* 年长者；老年人

eco-tourism /ˈiːkəʊˈtʊərɪzəm/ *n.* 生态旅游

impact /ˈɪmpækt/ *n.* 影响

statistics /stəˈtɪstɪks/ *n.* 统计数据

budget /ˈbʌdʒɪt/ *adj.* 廉价的；不贵的

rate /reɪt/ *v.* 定等级

facilitate /fəˈsɪlɪteɪt/ *v.* 使容易；使方便

enhance /ɪnˈhɑːns/ *v.* 提高；增强

diamond /ˈdaɪəmənd/ *n.* 钻石

ministry /ˈmɪnɪstri/ *n.* (政府的) 部

organization /ˌɔːgənaɪˈzeɪʃn/ *n.* 机构

well-equipped /ˈwel ɪˈkwɪpt/ *adj.* 装备精良的

target /ˈtɑːgɪt/ *n.* 目标

politician /ˌpɒləˈtɪʃn/ *n.* 政客

extensive /ɪkˈstensɪv/ *adj.* 宽广的；广阔的

court /kɔːt/ *n.* 球场

occupancy /ˈɒkjəpənsi/ *n.* 入住率

downtown /ˌdaʊnˈtaʊn/ *adj.* 市中心的

revenue /ˈrevənjuː/ *n.* 收入；所得

distinct /dɪˈstɪŋkt/ *adj.* 独特的

atmosphere /ˈætməsfɪə(r)/ *n.* 氛围

accommodate /əˈkɒmədeɪt/ *v.* 迎合

distinguish /dɪˈstɪŋgwɪʃ/ *v.* 区分

housing /ˈhaʊzɪŋ/ *n.* 住宅

environment /ɪnˈvaɪrənmənt/ *n.* 环境

economy /ɪˈkɒnəmi/ *adj.* 经济的；廉价的

casino /kəˈsiːnəʊ/ *n.* 娱乐场；赌场

apply /əˈplaɪ/ *v.* 应用

supervision /ˌsjuːpəˈvɪʒn/ *n.* 监督；管理

grade /greɪd/ *v.* 分级

administer /ədˈmɪnɪstə(r)/ *v.* 管理；执行

commonwealth /ˈkɒmənwelθ/ *n.* 联邦

compete /kəmˈpiːt/ *v.* 竞争

executive /ɪgˈzekjətɪv/ *n.* 主管

client /ˈklaɪənt/ *n.* 客户

Useful Expressions

make profit by doing sth. 通过……获取经济效益

equip ... with ... 给……配置……　　a wide selection of ... 多种多样的……

furnish ... with ... 给……配备……

make a ... contribution to ... 对……做出……贡献

as far as ... be concerned 就……来说

provide ... with ... 为……提供……

be categorized by ... 根据……进行分类

make up ... 组成……

tend to do sth. 倾向于做某事

with the purpose of ... 以……为目的

make ... public 把……公之于众

focus efforts on ... 致力于……

词汇、课文资源　　　　词汇、课文自测　　　　微课　　　　课堂练习

1.2　Hotel Organization

1.2.1　Hotel Organization

Hotel organization is a *complicated combination* of different functional *departments* and different *administrative* levels. In order to meet its *operation* goals, a hotel should get all the business activities arranged into different levels or types, which are then arranged into various *posts*. The *coordination* among posts, as well as the responsibilities and *authorities* for each post, should be properly and *unambiguously delineated*. The *structure* of these posts is just called the hotel organization.

Every hotel, regardless of its size and *amenities*, has an organizational structure, but there is no standard organizational structure for all hotels. In fact, structures differ from hotel to hotel based on the size and category of the property. For instance, all hotels have a rooms *division* to

酒店组织

　　酒店组织是一个不同职能部门和不同职权层次组合而成的复杂系统。为了达到经营的目标，酒店把必须要做的各项业务活动进行分层分类，形成各种职位，恰当而又明确地规定各个职位的责任与权限以及相互间的协调关系。这个职位结构就是酒店的组织结构。

　　每一个酒店，不论其大小和设施条件，都有一个组织结构。对于所有酒店而言，没有一个标准的组织结构。事实上，酒店的组织结构因资产的规模和类型的不同而不同。例如，所有酒店都设有管理客

manage guestrooms. The rooms division *handles reservations*, check-in and check-out activities, *housekeeping* tasks, *uniformed* service activities, and *telecommunications* service. At a small hotel, these functions are performed by personnel who report to and take their *instructions* from the general manager. At a large hotel, rooms personnel report to a rooms division manager.

1.2.2 Organizational Structure

A hotel's organizational structure should be *designed* to clearly delineate the responsibilities of the management, an individual or a department in meeting the hotel's *overall* goals.

The divisions in a hotel can be categorized as revenue centers, which *generate income* for the hotel through the sale of services or products to guests, and cost centers, which support the proper functioning of revenue centers.

The two main hotel revenue centers are the rooms division and the food & *beverage* division. Other revenue centers include the telecommunications department; *concessions*, *rentals*, and *commissions*; and fitness and *recreational* facilities. The cost centers of a hotel include divisions like *marketing* and sales, *engineering*, *accounting*, human *resources*, and *security*.

In a hotel, either big or small, the rooms division has four departments or functions: front office, reservations, housekeeping, and uniformed service. With the food & beverage division, the food & beverage manager reports to the general manager and takes charge of departments like *kitchen*, dining

房的房务部，负责预订、入住和结账、客房管理、制服服务及电信服务。在小型酒店，这些职能是由报告并接受总经理指令的员工来执行。在大型酒店，房务员工向房务部经理报告。

组织结构

酒店组织结构的设计应当明确规定管理机构、个人及部门在实现酒店总体目标过程中所要履行的职责。

酒店各部门可以归为两类：一类是营收中心，通过向客人销售服务或产品为酒店带来收入；另一类是成本中心，支持营收中心的正常运作。

房务部和餐饮部是酒店的两个主要营收部门。其他的营收部门还有话务部、特许、租赁与代办和康乐设施。酒店的成本中心包括市场推广与销售、工程、会计、人力资源和安保等部门。

在酒店中，不论大小，房务部都下设四个部门：前厅、预订、客房管理和制服服务。在餐饮部，餐饮经理向总经理报告，负责厨房、餐厅、酒吧、宴会、客房服务等部门。

room, *bartender*, *catering*, and room service.

In most hotels, the marketing and sales division is headed by a director of marketing and sales, to whom a sales manager, an *advertising* and public relations director, and a convention sales manger will report. The engineering division is responsible for the hotel's physical plant and energy-controlling costs, and also responsible for heating and air-conditioning systems and the systems that *distribute* electricity, *steam*, and water throughout the property. The accounting division is responsible for keeping track of the business *transactions* that occur in the hotel. The human resources division is responsible for *recruiting*, *hiring*, *orienting*, training, *evaluating*, *motivating*, *rewarding*, *disciplining*, developing, *promoting*, and communicating with all the employees of the hotel. The security division is to ensure the safety of guests, employees, personal property, and the hotel itself.

1.2.3 Structure Mode

Structure is the best way to *channel* employees' efforts toward *productive* ends. Whether the *set-up* of a hotel is good or not mainly depends on whether or not it can improve work *efficiency* and make sure that all kinds of work are in perfect operation. Any hotel should determine an appropriate set-up in line with its own feature. Currently adopted in most hotels in China is the *linear* functional system, in which all divisions or departments of a hotel fall into two major groups: *operational* and administrative. The operational group, which is of a linear type, is

在大多数酒店中，营销部由一名营销主管领导，销售经理、广告与公共关系主管，以及会议销售经理向营销主管报告情况。工程部负责酒店的设备及能控成本，并负责供暖与空调系统，以及整个酒店的配电、供气、供水系统。会计部门负责记录酒店内发生的各种业务事项。人力资源部门负责招聘、聘用、定岗、培训、评估、激励、报酬、纪律、发展、晋升及员工沟通。安保部门确保客人和员工的人身安全，以及个人和酒店的财产安全。

结构模式

组织结构是让员工通力协作提高工作效率的最佳途径。酒店组织结构的优劣主要是看其能否提高酒店组织的工作效率，保证各项工作的运行协调有序。不同的酒店必须根据自身的特点确定合适的酒店组织模式。目前，中国酒店普遍采用的组织形式是直线职能制。这种组织形式是把酒店所有的机构和部门分为业务部门和职能部门两大类。业务部门是直线的，包括房务部、

generally *split* further into the rooms division, the food & beverage division, the *merchandise* division, and the recreation division, each handling its own specific business. The administrative group works supporting the operational group. Any function that does not involve constant interaction with guests or impact on service level goes into this group. It may include such divisions as human resources, security, *finance*, and engineering. Both the two groups should report to the general manager.

A hotel's structure varies depending on the type of hotel. An economy hotel or motel might *outsource* many of its functions and have a limited structure made up of front desk staff and small *maintenance crew*. Limited-service hotels with small staff usually consist of the front desk, the housekeeping, the maintenance, and the sales & *auditing*. Full-service or large hotels with a large structure include divisions of the rooms, the food & beverage, the human resources, the sales & marketing, and the accounting. The rooms division and the food & beverage division are the most complicated. The rooms division can include the reservations, the front office, the housekeeping, and the laundry. The food & beverage division may include the *culinary*, the restaurants, the room service, the beverage, and the *banqueting*. Resort hotels have the most complicated structure, because they are generally *spread* out over a much bigger area and include many more features and amenities for guests, such as golf courses and specialized venues.

餐饮部、商品部、康乐部等，各自有自己特定的业务内容。职能部门为业务部门服务，任何一个不与宾客持续打交道或不影响服务水平的职能都归为此类，它包括人力资源部、安保部、财务部、工程部等。职能部门和业务部门都要向总经理报告。

酒店的类型不同，其组织结构也不同。经济型酒店或者是汽车旅馆可能会把许多职能外包，有限的组织结构仅包括前台和一个小型维修组。有限服务的酒店通常有少量的员工，包括前台、客房部、维修部、销售与审计部。全方位服务的酒店或大型酒店有庞大的组织结构，包括房务部、餐饮部、人力资源部、市场销售部和会计部。最复杂的是房务部和餐饮部。房务部可以有预订、前厅、客房、洗衣等部门；餐饮部可有厨房、餐厅、送餐服务、酒水及宴会等部门。度假型酒店的组织结构最为复杂，因为它们通常占地范围广，给宾客提供了更多特色的服务和设施，如高尔夫球场、各式各样的专用会场。

Vocabulary

complicated /ˈkɒmplɪkeɪtɪd/ *adj.* 结构复杂的

combination /ˌkɒmbɪˈneɪʃn/ *n.* 结合在一起的人或事物

department /dɪˈpɑːtmənt/ *n.* 部门；处；局

administrative /ədˈmɪnɪstrətɪv/ *adj.* 行政的；管理的

operation /ˌɒpəˈreɪʃn/ *n.* 经营   post /pəʊst/ *n.* 职位

coordination /kəʊˌɔːdɪˈneɪʃn/ *n.* 协调；协作

authority /ɔːˈθɒrəti/ *n.* 权力；职权；权限

unambiguously /ˌʌnæmˈbɪɡjuəsli/ *adv.* 清楚地；清晰地；不含糊地

delineate /dɪˈlɪnieɪt/ *v.* 描绘；叙述   structure /ˈstrʌktʃə(r)/ *n.* 结构

amenity /əˈmiːnəti/ *n.* 便利设施   division /dɪˈvɪʒn/ *n.* 部门

handle /ˈhændl/ *v.* 处理；操作   reservation /ˌrezəˈveɪʃn/ *n.* 预订

housekeeping /ˈhaʊskiːpɪŋ/ *n.* 管家   uniformed /ˈjuːnɪfɔːmd/ *adj.* 穿制服的

telecommunication /ˌtelikəˌmjuːnɪˈkeɪʃn/ *n.* 电信

instruction /ɪnˈstrʌkʃn/ *n.* 指令   design /dɪˈzaɪn/ *v.* 设计

overall /ˌəʊvərˈɔːl/ *adj.* 总体的   generate /ˈdʒenəreɪt/ *v.* 产生

income /ˈɪnkʌm/ *n.* 收入   beverage /ˈbevərɪdʒ/ *n.* 饮料

concession /kənˈseʃn/ *n.* （摊位）特许经营权

rental /ˈrentl/ *n.* 租借   commission /kəˈmɪʃn/ *n.* （业务）代办

recreational /ˌrekriˈeɪʃənl/ *adj.* 娱乐的；消遣的

marketing /ˈmɑːkɪtɪŋ/ *n.* 营销推广   engineering /ˌendʒɪˈnɪərɪŋ/ *n.* 工程

accounting /əˈkaʊntɪŋ/ *n.* 会计   resource /rɪˈsɔːs/ *n.* 资源

security /sɪˈkjʊərəti/ *n.* 安全   kitchen /ˈkɪtʃɪn/ *n.* 厨房

bartender /ˈbɑːtendə(r)/ *n.* 酒保   catering /ˈkeɪtərɪŋ/ *n.* 承办酒席

advertising /ˈædvətaɪzɪŋ/ *n.* 广告   distribute /dɪˈstrɪbjuːt/ *v.* 分配；分布

steam /stiːm/ *n.* 蒸汽   transaction /trænˈzækʃn/ *n.* 事务；事项

recruit /rɪˈkruːt/ *v.* 招聘   hire /ˈhaɪə(r)/ *v.* 雇用

orient /ˈɔːrient/ *v.* 定岗   evaluate /ɪˈvæljueɪt/ *v.* 评估

motivate /ˈməʊtɪveɪt/ *v.* 激励   reward /rɪˈwɔːd/ *v.* 给报酬

discipline /ˈdɪsəplɪn/ *v.* 惩戒；纪律约束

promote /prəˈməʊt/ v. 晋升

channel /ˈtʃænl/ v. 集中（精力）；引导

productive /prəˈdʌktɪv/ adj. 有成效的；多产的

set-up /set ʌp/ n. 安排；组织

efficiency /ɪˈfɪʃnsi/ n. 效率

linear /ˈlɪniə(r)/ adj. 线性的

operational /ˌɒpəˈreɪʃənl/ adj. 经营的；运营的

split /splɪt/ v. 使分成若干部分

merchandise /ˈmɜːtʃəndaɪs/ n. 商品

finance /ˈfaɪnæns/ n. 财务

outsource /ˈaʊtsɔːs/ v. 外包

maintenance /ˈmeɪntənəns/ n. 维修；保养

crew /kruː/ n. 一组工作人员

auditing /ˈɔːdɪtɪŋ/ n. 审计

culinary /ˈkʌlɪnəri/ adj. 烹饪的

banquet /ˈbæŋkwɪt/ v. 设宴

spread /spred/ v. 扩散到大面积

Useful Expressions

arrange … into … 把……分成……

regardless of … 无论……；不管……

take charge of … 负责……

keep track of … 记录……

channel efforts to … 使专注于……

in perfect operation 完善运行

in line with … 符合……

fall into … 分成……

split … into … 把……分成……

be made up of … 由……组成

consist of … 由……组成

spread out 散布（开）

词汇、课文资源

词汇、课文自测

微课

课堂练习

1.3 Hotel Operating Models

The operating models which are commonly adopted in modern hospitality industry are: *franchising* operations, *cooperative* operations, *leased* operations, management *contract*, and wholly-owned operations.

Many hotels are *affiliated* with others in a chain

现代酒店业常见的经营模式有五种：特许经营模式、合作经营模式、租赁经营模式、合同管理模式和自主经营模式。

许多酒店通过管理合同或所有

through management or ownership agreements. Independent hotels do not have any *affiliation*. Affiliations are valuable in marketing, *branding*, sales, purchasing supplies, operational *procedures*, and management *expertise*. All of these are increasingly important in today's *competitive* market place.

Chains operate in two main ways, either according to a management contract or as a franchise. Management contracts usually require the owner of the property to keep the financial and *legal* responsibility. The management company operates the hotel, pays *expenses*, and receives a fee for their management services. Franchising is a leasing arrangement that requires the hotel operator to pay a fee for the use of plans, procedure *manuals*, and advertising materials. In return, he is *granted* a license to operate a business in the name of the parent corporation. The *franchisee* puts up the *capital*, but he gets a standardized operation method and a well-known sales *potential*. Of course, he can also get a great deal of help from the licensing corporation in establishing his operation and then in solving problems that *arise* after it has opened. In such a model, the *franchiser* grants *access* to software for sales and operations, central purchasing contracts with *vendors* at low prices, and *pooled* advertising. If the local franchisee operates according to the procedures, he keeps going as a franchisee. If he does bad things or does not follow the procedures as set down in the franchise agreement, his *license* may be *terminated*.

权证明与其他酒店共同加盟某一连锁集团。独立经营的酒店间不存在加盟关系。加盟对市场营销、品牌推广、销售、物资采购、运营程序和管理技术等非常重要。所有这些在当今激烈的市场竞争中显得日益重要。

连锁酒店有两个主要的运营方式。一是按照管理合同，一是特许经营。管理合同通常让酒店的业主承担财务和法律上的责任。管理公司负责酒店的运营，支付费用，并为自己所提供的管理服务收取费用。特许经营是一种租借安排，要求酒店的经营者支付一笔费用，以便能使用该连锁的计划、规程手册和广告材料，并获得以母公司名义经营业务的许可。取得特许的经营者付出了一笔投资，但是得到了标准化的经营方法和因声誉带来的销售潜力。在建立酒店和解决开业后出现的问题方面，他当然还能得到特许经营授权商的许多帮助。在特许经营模式中，特许经营授权商提供销售和运营软件、与供应商的低价中央采购合同以及联合广告。如果本地特许经营加盟商遵守运营程序，就能继续保持其加盟商地位，如果有不良行为或违反规定程序，则可能被终止特许经营权。

The chains *expand* in a number of other ways. One way is through direct *investment*. This means that the *headquarters* corporation itself puts up the necessary money to build and operate a new hotel or to buy and *refurbish* an old one. Another way to expand is by establishing management contracts with the actual owners of the hotel. The chain, in effect, takes over an empty building and operates it according to its own operating procedures for a fee or for a *percentage* of the profits. This method is frequently used when the chain expands into a foreign country, since it *eliminates* the risk that the organization will lose its investment because of political *upheaval*. A somewhat similar method is the *joint venture*, a *partnership* in which both the chain and local *investors* put up part of the capital that is necessary for new *construction* or the purchase of an existing building.

The hotel chains have several competitive *advantages* over individually owned and operated *establishments*. One of the most important advantages is having resources to spend more money on advertising. Television advertising, for example, is too expensive for most individual hotel *operators*. The chains, on the other hand, can have the cost shared by all of their member units. Another advantage comes from the *standardization* of equipment and operating procedures. The chains *publish detailed* manuals that *specify* procedures to be *followed*. Even when the different hotels in the chain are not tightly controlled by a central office, it is *customary* to have an *inspection* system in order

连锁酒店还通过其他一些方式得到扩展。一种方式是直接投资。这是指由总公司出资兴建并经营新酒店，或者买下旧酒店加以整修。另一种方式是与酒店的实际业主签订经营合同。连锁酒店实际上是接管一座空楼，然后按照自己的经营方式进行营运，从中收取一笔费用或一定比例的利润。连锁酒店向国外扩展通常采用这一方式，以免一旦发生政治动乱，该连锁有丧失投资的风险。还有一种类似的方式是合资经营，即连锁酒店和当地投资者合资建设新酒店或买下现成的建筑物。

同自主经营的酒店相比，连锁酒店在竞争力方面有几种优势。最大的优势之一是它花得起更多的钱做广告。比如，电视广告对大多数自主经营的酒店来说未免过于昂贵，而连锁酒店却可以把上述费用分摊给所有成员。另一个优势是设备和营运的标准化。连锁酒店印发内容详尽的工作手册，规定必须遵守的工作规程。即便这个连锁酒店下属的各家酒店不受总店的严密控制，一般还是设有一个监督系统，以保证各店的营运能符合总的服务标准。结果是，连锁酒店系统的各

to *guarantee* that the overall standards are being followed. This results in a very *visible* degree of *uniformity* among the hotels in the chain, which gives the guests an excellent idea of what kind of *accommodations* to expect. The most important and most *obvious* advantage is the increased efficiency in making and controlling reservations. A guest at one hotel, for instance, can receive *confirmation* of a *vacancy* at another in a couple of minutes. The chains also make it easy to reserve a room by telephone. The telephones are *tied* in to computer systems, which make it possible to confirm whether there is any *spare* room while the caller is still on the phone.

酒店间实现了一种显而易见的高度一致。这种一致性使宾客能清楚地预先知道能够享受到什么样的膳宿服务。最重要也是最明显的优势是连锁酒店在预订和控制预订房间方面的效率得到提高。例如，顾客到了一家酒店可以在几分钟之内立即得到能否在另一家酒店找到房间的确切答复。有了连锁酒店，就便于通过电话预订房间；这些电话是和电脑连接在一起的，打电话的人不用放下耳机就可以立刻了解到是否有空余客房。

Vocabulary

franchising /ˈfræntʃaɪzɪŋ/ *n.* 特许；出卖产销权

cooperative /kəʊˈɒpərətɪv/ *adj.* 合作的；协作的

leased /liːst/ *adj.* 租用的 　contract /ˈkɒntrækt/ *n.* 合同

affiliate /əˈfɪlieɪt/ *v.* 使隶属于 　affiliation /əˌfɪliˈeɪʃn/ *n.* 加盟关系

branding /ˈbrændɪŋ/ *n.* 品牌推广 　procedure /prəˈsiːdʒə(r)/ *n.* 程序

expertise /ˌekspɜːˈtiːz/ *n.* 专门技术（知识）

competitive /kəmˈpetətɪv/ *adj.* 有竞争力的

legal /ˈliːgl/ *adj.* 法律的 　expense /ɪkˈspens/ *n.* 费用；支出

manual /ˈmænjuəl/ *n.* 手册 　grant /ɡrɑːnt/ *v.* 授予；许可

franchisee /ˌfræntʃaɪˈziː/ *n.* 特许经营人

capital /ˈkæpɪtl/ *n.* 资本 　potential /pəˈtenʃl/ *n.* 潜力

arise /əˈraɪz/ *v.* 出现；发生 　franchiser /ˈfræntʃaɪzə(r)/ *n.* 授予特许者

access /ˈækses/ *n.* 使用……之权利 　vendor /ˈvendə(r)/ *n.* 供应商

pooled /ˈpuːld/ *adj.* 合并的；联合的

terminate /ˈtɜːmɪneɪt/ *v.* 终止

investment /ɪnˈvestmənt/ *n.* 投资

refurbish /ˌriːˈfɜːbɪʃ/ *v.* 整修

eliminate /ɪˈlɪmɪneɪt/ *v.* 消除

joint /dʒɔɪnt/ *adj.* 联合的；共同的

partnership /ˈpɑːtnəʃɪp/ *n.* 合伙经营

construction /kənˈstrʌkʃn/ *n.* 建筑（物）

establishment /ɪˈstæblɪʃmənt/ *n.* 酒店

standardization /ˌstændədaɪˈzeɪʃn/ *n.* 标准化

publish /ˈpʌblɪʃ/ *v.* 印发

specify /ˈspesɪfaɪ/ *v.* 规定

customary /ˈkʌstəməri/ *adj.* 惯例的

guarantee /ˌɡærənˈtiː/ *v.* 保证

uniformity /ˌjuːnɪˈfɔːməti/ *n.* 一致性

obvious /ˈɒbviəs/ *adj.* 显著的

vacancy /ˈveɪkənsi/ *n.* 空房

spare /speə(r)/ *adj.* 闲置的

license /ˈlaɪsns/ *n.* 许可证

expand /ɪkˈspænd/ *v.* 扩张

headquarters /ˌhedˈkwɔːtəz/ *n.* 总部

percentage /pəˈsentɪdʒ/ *n.* 比例

upheaval /ʌpˈhiːvl/ *n.* 动乱

venture /ˈventʃə(r)/ *n.* 企业（项目）

investor /ɪnˈvestə(r)/ *n.* 投资者

advantage /ədˈvɑːntɪdʒ/ *n.* 优势

operator /ˈɒpəreɪtə(r)/ *n.* 经营者

detailed /ˈdiːteɪld/ *adj.* 详细的

follow /ˈfɒləʊ/ *v.* 遵守

inspection /ɪnˈspekʃn/ *n.* 检查；监督

visible /ˈvɪzəbl/ *adj.* 显而易见的

accommodation /əˌkɒməˈdeɪʃn/ *n.* 膳宿（服务）

confirmation /ˌkɒnfəˈmeɪʃn/ *n.* 确认

tie /taɪ/ *v.* 连接

Useful Expressions

be affiliated with ... 与……有关系

in the name of ... 以……名义

grant access to ... 授权使用……

take over ... 接管……

in return 作为回报

put up 出（资）

in effect 实际上

result in ... 导致……

词汇、课文资源

词汇、课文自测

微课

课堂练习

1.4　Hotel Guests, Guest Cycle, and Hotel Services

1.4.1　Hotel Guests

Hotels are in the business of *attracting* guests. The most important guest *segments* that *constitute* the market for the hotel industry are corporate individuals, corporate groups, convention and *association* groups, leisure travelers, and long-term stay guests.

Corporate individuals are hotel guests who are traveling for business purposes and are not part of any group. They usually stay one or two nights. The top six factors that determine the hotels they select are location, *previous* experience with the hotel, price / value, room rate, previous experience with the hotel chain, and *recommendation* of friend or associate. Business travelers want clean, functioning rooms and friendly, *efficient* service.

Corporate groups travel *purely* for business purposes but, unlike individual corporate travelers, they are usually attending a small conference or meeting at their hotel, and their rooms are *booked* in *blocks* by their company or a travel *agency*. These travelers usually stay from two to four days. Corporate groups favor hotels that offer *intimate* meeting rooms and *private* dining facilities.

Convention and association groups, different from other corporate groups, have a larger size, which can run well into the thousands. Convention groups usually share rooms and stay three to four days. They prefer hotels offering *extremely* competitive rates.

客人类型

酒店职责在于招揽顾客。酒店行业最重要的客户群体由企业个人、企业团客、会议与协会团客、休闲旅行者及长住客人组成。

企业个人是指那些商务旅行的酒店客人，不属于任何团体，通常会住一两个晚上。决定他们选择酒店的前六个因素分别是酒店位置、以往的酒店体验、价格／价值、房价、以往的连锁酒店体验，以及朋友或同事的推荐。商务旅行者想要的是干净、实用的房间，以及友好、高效的服务。

企业团客纯粹出于商业目的旅行，但不同于企业个体旅行者的是，他们通常是在酒店参加小型会议，房间由他们的公司或旅行社统一预订，通常要住2～4天。企业团客更喜欢酒店提供温馨的会议室和专用的用餐设施。

与其他企业团客不同，会议与协会团客规模更大，人数可达数千人。会议团客通常共住房间，一般住宿3～4天。他们更喜欢价格极具竞争力的酒店。

Leisure travelers often travel with their families on *sight-seeing* trips, or on trips to visit friends or *relatives*. They *typically* stay only one night at the same hotel and prefer a room for a *couple* as well as one or more children, but because they typically travel during *peak* season, they usually pay high rates.

Long-term stay guests are *primarily* individuals or families *relocating* to an area and requiring lodging until *permanent* housing can be found. Their needs include limited cooking facilities and more living space than is *available* in a typical hotel room. They prefer a room which has twice the size of an *average* hotel room typically with a living area, a bedroom, extra *closet* space, and a small kitchen.

1.4.2　Guest Cycle

The guest cycle *describes* the activities that each guest passes by from the moment he / she calls for a reservation *inquiry* till he / she *departs* from the hotel. It is made up of three *stages* guests go through: before they arrive, while they stay, and after they leave. Typically these stages are described as contact / pre-arrival, check in / arrival, occupancy, and check out / *departure*. The hospitality industry is competitive, so it is important for a hotel to have a strong system for handling efficiently all the contact and *paperwork* in the whole guest cycle. It is worth *mentioning* that reservation, once considered one of the main stages in the guest cycle, has become an *anachronism* today. Nowadays, in order to book a hotel, clients use services of major tour operators. Online booking through the *numerous* tourist online

休闲旅行者常常是全家人一起观光旅行，或走亲访友，通常在同一家酒店只住一晚，比较喜欢能供夫妻及一个或多个孩子住宿的房间，但他们通常是在旺季出行，常常要支付很高的价格。

长住客人主要是搬迁到某一个地方的个人或家庭，他们需要一直住到找到常住房屋为止。他们需要有限的烹饪设施，需要比典型的酒店客房更大的生活空间。他们比较喜欢有普通酒店客房 2 倍大小的房间，通常兼具客厅、卧室、特大储物空间和一个小型厨房的功能。

住店流程

住店流程指的是一个宾客从他 / 她开始来电咨询预订到离店时所经过的所有活动环节，包括宾客从到店前、入店直到离店的每个阶段。这些阶段一般分为联系或到店前、入住登记或到店、入住、退房或离店。酒店业的竞争很激烈，因此，拥有一个高效快速的系统来处理整个住店流程中所有对客联系和文书的工作是非常重要的。值得一提的是，预订曾经被认为是宾客住店流程中的主要环节之一，如今已成为一种过去式。现在宾客可以通过大的旅游公司订房。通过大量的旅游在线服务进行网上预订正越来越流行。下面描述的是住店流程中

services is getting increasingly popular. Below is a *description* of activities *undertaken* at each stage of the guest cycle.

Information

At this stage, a guest decides to use the services of a hotel, and *explores* which hotel might be the best *choice*.

Contact

At this stage, a guest contacts the hotel through the telephone, fax, or Internet, and asks questions that help him / her to make a decision.

Reservation

At this stage, a guest makes a reservation or booking, checking the details of his / her stay with a hotel.

Check-In

At this stage, a guest registers his / her personal information, and arranges a *deposit* when he / she arrives at the hotel.

Occupancy

At this stage, a *registered* guest stays in a hotel. He / She may *incur* extra charges for services during this stage. Sometimes, a guest may be asked *survey* questions.

Check-Out / Departure

At this stage, a guest receives an *accurate statement* of charges, pays the bill, and gets a *receipt* and sometimes a thank-you note.

In the recent one or two *decades*, the computer *technology* has been applied in the operation and administration of the hospitality industry. Many hotels have got their guest cycles fully *automated*.

每个阶段所进行的各项活动。

搜集信息阶段

在这一阶段，宾客决定要享用酒店服务，并考察住哪家酒店才是最好的选择。

联系咨询阶段

在这一阶段，宾客通过电话、传真或互联网与酒店取得联系，询问各种问题以便做出决定。

预订阶段

在这一阶段，宾客向酒店预订房间，确定入住细节。

到店阶段

在这一阶段，宾客到店，登记信息并交付押金。

入住阶段

在这一阶段，宾客登记后入住酒店。在此期间，有可能产生额外的服务费用。有时，宾客还会被请求做调查问卷。

退房 / 离店阶段

在这一阶段，宾客拿到消费明细单，付账并取得发票，有时还会得到一张感谢卡。

近一二十年，计算机技术被广泛应用于酒店业的经营与管理。许多酒店的住店流程都已经完全自动化。以下是一份《完全自动化的宾

Below is a "Guest Cycle under Fully-Automated Systems."

Pre-arrival Activities

At this stage, the reservation department is equipped with a software *package*, which is *interfaced* and connected with one or more central reservation offices. Moreover, the reservation department can automatically generate letters of confirmation, produce requests for guest deposits, handle pre-registration activities for all types of guests, and generate daily expected arrival lists, occupancy, and revenue *forecast* lists ...

Arrival Activities

At this stage, *various* reservation *records* can be *transferred* to front office department. Moreover, hotels might be equipped with online *credit* authorization *terminals* for *timely* credit card *approval*, and / or self check-in / check-out terminals. Lastly, all guest charges and payments are saved in *electronic* guest *folios*. As far as *walk-ins* are concerned, all registration activities should be *initiated* from the very beginning.

Occupancy Activities

At this very stage, guest *purchases* at different revenue outlets are *electronically* transferred and *posted* to *appropriate* guest *accounts*. Moreover, the front office department can run and process continuous *trial balances* and, therefore, save the *tedious* work for the night *auditor*.

Departure Activities

At this stage, *cashiers* can automatically produce *bills* to be sent to various guests with direct *billing*

客住店流程》。

到店前

在这个阶段，预订部配备一个软件包，与一个或更多的预订中心相连接。而且，预订部还能自动生成确认信，要求宾客交付押金，并能为各类宾客进行预登记，还能生成每天预期到店宾客名单、入住单和收入预报单……

到店

在这个阶段，各种预订记录可以转送至前厅部。而且，酒店可能装有用于即时信用卡审批的在线信用授权终端、自动到店 / 离店终端。最后，宾客的所有消费都保存在宾客的电子账单上。对于未预订的宾客，所有登记手续都要从头做起。

住店

在这一阶段，宾客在各种营收店的购买消费通过电子方式转记到宾客的账户。而且前厅部还能够连续运行和处理试算平衡表，免去夜间账目审计员的繁重工作。

离店

在这一阶段，收银员按程序生成票据，发送给各类有直接结算权

privileges and create electronic guest history records.

1.4.3　Hotel Services

Hotel services are all the *lines* of business that hotels offer. A hotel may have a very wide range of services available. Typically, the basic hotel services include *reception*, room service, catering service, restaurants, and security. Other services offered to guests are the laundry service, *massage* room, fitness *gyms*, conference rooms, *valuables deposit*, and many others. Typical guest services available for no charge or a small charge include communication services like mail service, receiving faxes, telephone calls, voice mail, and email. Another group of free *conveniences* include wake-up calls, cashing checks, booking tickets, and free items in the room. Fee-based services include the business center and all the associated services such as *photocopy*, fax, computers, the Internet, and meeting rooms. These services can be included in the price of the room or paid separately.

The *varieties* of hotel services, along with the amount of personnel *engaged* in them, depends on the size of the hotel as well as on its *status*. In general, the main service of a hotel is lodging, and other major facilities attracting guests include restaurants and bars. In addition to these, travel services are usually busy selling tickets for in-city travel, beauty salons and health clubs help people feel good and *relax*, and hotel stores offer *sundries*. Even some hotels may have art *galleries* and provide facilities for activities like golf, sailing, swimming, and *sauna*.

限的宾客，并生成电子客史记录。

酒店服务

酒店服务是指酒店所提供的一切服务范畴。酒店提供的服务非常广泛。通常情况下，酒店的基本服务有宾客接待、客房服务、餐饮服务、各式餐厅及安保。其他服务有干洗服务、按摩室、健身房、会议室、贵重物品存管处等。向宾客提供的免费或收取少量费用的服务项目有通信服务，如邮寄服务，接收传真、电话、语音留言和电子邮件等。另一组免费的便利服务有叫醒服务、支票兑现、订票及客房里的免费物品。收费服务包括商务中心及复印、传真、电脑、互联网和会议室等其他关联服务。这些服务可以计入房费，也可单付。

酒店服务的种类及相关服务人员的数量取决于酒店的规模和档次。一般而言，酒店的主要服务是提供住宿，餐厅和酒吧是另一种吸引宾客的主要场所。此外，酒店内的旅行服务通常是销售市内观光票。美容厅和健身俱乐部使宾客心情愉悦、放松。酒店内商店提供各种日用品。有些酒店还可能有艺术走廊，以及高尔夫、帆船、游泳和桑拿等服务。

Vocabulary

attract /əˈtrækt/ *v.* 吸引

constitute /ˈkɒnstɪtjuːt/ *v.* 组成

previous /ˈpriːviəs/ *adj.* 以往的

recommendation /ˌrekəmenˈdeɪʃn/ *n.* 推荐；建议

efficient /ɪˈfɪʃnt/ *adj.* 高效的

book /bʊk/ *v.* 预订

agency /ˈeɪdʒənsi/ *n.* 代理机构

private /ˈpraɪvət/ *adj.* 私用的

sight-seeing /ˈsaɪtˌsiːɪŋ/ *n.* 观光

typically /ˈtɪpɪkli/ *adv.* 通常地

peak /piːk/ *n.* 顶峰

relocate /ˌriːləʊˈkeɪt/ *v.* 搬迁

available /əˈveɪləbl/ *adj.* 可得到的

closet /ˈklɒzɪt/ *n.* 衣帽间；储物间

inquiry /ɪnˈkwaɪəri/ *n.* 查询；询问

stage /steɪdʒ/ *n.* 阶段

paperwork /ˈpeɪpəwɜːk/ *n.* 日常文书工作

anachronism /əˈnækrənɪzəm/ *n.* 不合潮流的人或事物

numerous /ˈnjuːmərəs/ *adj.* 为数众多的

undertake /ˌʌndəˈteɪk/ *v.* 进行

choice /tʃɔɪs/ *n.* 选择

registered /ˈredʒɪstəd/ *adj.* 注册过的

survey /ˈsɜːveɪ/ *n.* 调查

statement /ˈsteɪtmənt/ *n.* 明细单

decade /ˈdekeɪd/ *n.* 十年

automate /ˈɔːtəmeɪt/ *v.* 使自动化

interface /ˈɪntəfeɪs/ *v.* （界面）接合

various /ˈveəriəs/ *adj.* 各种各样的

transfer /trænsˈfɜː(r)/ *v.* 转移，转送

terminal /ˈtɜːmɪnl/ *n.* 终端

segment /ˈsegmənt/ *n.* 部分

association /əˌsəʊʃiˈeɪʃn/ *n.* 协会；社团

purely /ˈpjʊəli/ *adv.* 纯粹地

block /blɒk/ *n.* 团体；一组

intimate /ˈɪntɪmət/ *adj.* 舒适怡人的

extremely /ɪkˈstriːmli/ *adv.* 极其

relative /ˈrelətɪv/ *n.* 亲戚

couple /ˈkʌpl/ *n.* 夫妇

primarily /praɪˈmerəli/ *adv.* 主要地

permanent /ˈpɜːmənənt/ *adj.* 永久的

average /ˈævərɪdʒ/ *adj.* 普通的

describe /dɪˈskraɪb/ *v.* 表述

depart /dɪˈpɑːt/ *v.* 离开

departure /dɪˈpɑːtʃə(r)/ *n.* 出发；离开

mention /ˈmenʃn/ *v.* 提及；说起

description /dɪˈskrɪpʃn/ *n.* 描述（内容）

explore /ɪkˈsplɔː(r)/ *v.* 考察

deposit /dɪˈpɒzɪt/ *n.* 押金

incur /ɪnˈkɜː(r)/ *v.* 招致；带来；引起

accurate /ˈækjərət/ *adj.* 明确的；精确的

receipt /rɪˈsiːt/ *n.* 收据

technology /tekˈnɒlədʒi/ *n.* 技术

package /ˈpækɪdʒ/ *n.* 软件包

forecast /ˈfɔːkɑːst/ *n.* 预报

record /ˈrekɔːd/ *n.* 记录

credit /ˈkredɪt/ *n.* 信用

timely /ˈtaɪmli/ *adj.* 及时的；即时的

approval /əˈpruːvl/ *n.* 审批

folio /ˈfəʊliəʊ/ *n.*（记账）本

initiate /ɪˈnɪʃieɪt/ *v.* 开始

electronically /ɪˌlekˈtrɒnɪkli/ *adv.* 通过电子手段

post /pəʊst/ *v.* 登入（账）

account /əˈkaʊnt/ *n.* 账户；账目

balance /ˈbæləns/ *n.* 结余

auditor /ˈɔːdɪtə(r)/ *n.* 审计员

bill /bɪl/ *n.* 票据；账单

privilege /ˈprɪvəlɪdʒ/ *n.* 特权

reception /rɪˈsepʃn/ *n.* 接待

gym /dʒɪm/ *n.* 健身房

deposit /dɪˈpɒzɪt/ *n.* 寄存

convenience /kənˈviːnjəns/ *n.* 便利设施；便利品

photocopy /ˈfəʊtəʊkɒpi/ *n.* 复印

engage /ɪnˈɡeɪdʒ/ *v.* 雇佣；使从事

relax /rɪˈlæks/ *v.* 休闲；放松

gallery /ˈɡæləri/ *n.* 美术馆；画廊

electronic /ɪˌlekˈtrɒnɪk/ *adj.* 电子的

walk-in /ˈwɔːk ɪn/ *n.* 未经预约的来客

purchase /ˈpɜːtʃəs/ *n.* 购买（物）

appropriate /əˈprəʊpriət/ *adj.* 合适的

trial /ˈtraɪəl/ *n.* 试用；试算

tedious /ˈtiːdiəs/ *adj.* 单调乏味的

cashier /kæˈʃɪə(r)/ *n.* 收银员

billing /ˈbɪlɪŋ/ *n.* 结账；记账；编制账单

line /laɪn/ *n.* 种类

massage /ˈmæsɑːʒ/ *n.* 按摩

valuables /ˈvæljuəblz/ *n.* [pl.] 贵重物品

variety /vəˈraɪəti/ *n.* 种类

status /ˈsteɪtəs/ *n.* 状态

sundry /ˈsʌndri/ *n.* 杂物；日用品

sauna /ˈsɔːnə/ *n.* 桑拿（浴）

Useful Expressions

be in the business of ... 职责在于……；从事……

in blocks 成批地

transfer ... to ... 将……转送……

be busy doing sth. 忙于做某事

run into ...（费用或数量）高达……

a wide range of ... 许多种类的……

词汇、课文资源

词汇、课文自测

微课

课堂练习

Service Guide
服务指南

思政园地 / 二十
大精神学习专栏

Learning Objectives

· *To get familiar with the structure and contents of the Service Guide, and the writing of hotel profile, welcome speech, and environment commitment;*

· *To understand the hotel rules and regulations, and all the services the hotel offers;*

· *To master the new words and professional terms concerned;*

· *To improve reading ability through learning the text;*

· *To develop team spirit and self-study ability through learning activities;*

· *To receive education in ideological and political theories through course learning.*

Teaching Arrangements

节次	教学内容	自主学习资源	自主学习自测	课堂教学视频	课堂练习
L 1	2.1 Hotel Profile, Welcome Speech, and Environment Commitment	词汇、课文资源	词汇、课文自测	微课	课堂练习
L 2	2.2 Hotel Rules and Regulations	词汇、课文资源	词汇、课文自测	微课	课堂练习
L 3	2.3 Front Office Services	词汇、课文资源	词汇、课文自测	微课	课堂练习
L 4	2.4 Housekeeping Services	词汇、课文资源	词汇、课文自测	微课	课堂练习
L 5	2.5 Food and Beverage Services	词汇、课文资源	词汇、课文自测	微课	课堂练习
L 6	2.6 Conference and Recreation Services	词汇、课文资源	词汇、课文自测	微课	课堂练习

The services that a modern hotel, especially a *deluxe* hotel, provides for its guests are getting more and more extensive and *sophisticated*. Thousands of hotels all around the world compete with one another in adding new *temptations* to the already *dazzling array* of services. Travelers have never been *accommodated* so comfortably, *luxuriously*, and conveniently, served so *meticulously*, and entertained so happily. A present-day traveler can have all the comfort of his / her home throughout his / her trip and in most cases even find himself / herself more comfortable and *pampered*. Luxurious hotels have become, in a very real sense, more comfortable "homes away from home."

What a guest most wants to know about a hotel after going through the registration *formalities* is nothing more than what services a hotel provides, how much they are charged, when they are open, and what he / she must pay attention to while staying over. Typically, he / she will find in his / her room a smooth and *elaborate brochure*, containing all the main service items the hotel offers and all affiliated information about them. This brochure is used as the service guide. What is included in the service guide varies from hotel to hotel. But in general, it may include hotel *profile*, welcome speech, environmental *commitment*, fire safety tips, front office services, housekeeping services, food & beverage services, conference services, recreation services, consultation services, friendly *reminders*, etc.

现代酒店，尤其是豪华酒店向宾客提供的服务越来越多、越来越高档。全球有成千上万家酒店，它们的服务本已琳琅满目，还竞相推出各式新的诱人服务。旅客从来没有像现在这样，住得如此舒适、豪华和便捷，享受着如此精心的服务，玩得如此开心。今天的旅客能够在整个旅程中享受到家一样的舒适，甚至有时比在家里更舒服、更受宠。很现实地讲，豪华酒店已经成了更加舒适的"家外家"。

宾客入住后最想了解的莫过于酒店所能提供的各种服务内容、收费情况、营业时间及各种注意事项等。通常情况下，酒店会在客房里放上一本精美的小册子，里面汇集了酒店所提供的主要服务项目及相关信息，供宾客自己浏览。这本小册子就是服务指南。不同的酒店，其服务指南的内容也不尽相同，但一般来说，它主要包括酒店简介、欢迎辞、环保倡议、消防安全须知、前厅服务、客房服务、餐饮服务、会议服务、康乐服务、咨询服务和友情提醒等。

2.1 Hotel Profile, Welcome Speech, and Environment Commitment

2.1.1 Hotel Profile

The ×××Hotel

Sitting *atop* 12 *acres* of *lush, fragrant* gardens, the hotel offers the *ambience* of a city resort with 210 guestrooms, including 38 suites and 21 *bungalows*. Special *features* include the *palm*-lined pool and *cabanas*, the Hotel Spa, beautifully *appointed* guest rooms with *marble* bathrooms, and public areas *reminiscent* of *timeless* Hollywood *glamor*.

The×××Singapore Hotel

Centrally located in the *fashionable* Orchard Road area, the×××Singapore Hotel has a *welcoming* atmosphere that *emphasizes* friendly and *hospitable* service. The hotel has excellent facilities as well as comfortable guestrooms and public areas.

Relax by the *rooftop* pool and *savor* views of *bustling* Orchard Road at the×××Singapore Hotel. *Feast* on fresh *oysters* at the *award-winning Harbor Grill* and Oyster Bar, work out in the fitness center, and *indulge* in a massage. The hotel has an executive *lounge*, and all rooms have wireless Internet access and city views. Go offsite for a night *safari* or a shopping *spree* in the nearby malls.

Just 20 minutes from Changi Airport, the×××Singapore Hotel has 11 meeting rooms

酒店简介

×××酒店

酒店坐落在12英亩葱郁芳香的花园之巅，是人们城市度假之胜地，共有客房210间，其中套房38间，平房21间。酒店的特色有棕榈环抱的游泳池和帐篷小屋，酒店水疗中心，具有精美的大理石浴间套房，以及展现永恒好莱坞魅力的公共区域。

新加坡×××大酒店

新加坡×××大酒店位于新加坡乌节路闹市区的中心位置，竭诚为宾客提供热情友好的服务。酒店拥有舒适的客房、公共区间及一流的设施。

在新加坡×××大酒店，您可以在屋顶泳池拥有怡然自得的感觉，并尽情享受乌节路闹市区的繁华景象。您可以在一流的海港烧烤店和牡蛎吧享用新鲜美味的牡蛎餐，可以在健身中心健身，更可以享受按摩服务。酒店有高级行政人员休息厅，所有房间都有无线网络接入，并能一览城市景色。您还可以去店外夜游，或去附近购物中心尽享疯狂购物之乐趣。

新加坡×××酒店，距离樟宜机场仅20分钟的路程，有11个

for 18,550 people and 2 business centers.

The hotel is part of an international chain of deluxe hotels, and recommended for executives, corporate or leisure clients.

2.1.2 Welcome Speech

The ×××San Francisco Financial District

Welcome to the ×××San Francisco Financial District. Business travelers, family *vacationers*, and couples looking for that perfect *romantic getaway* will be drawn to our recently *renovated* downtown hotel that raises the bar on luxury lodging.

Experience spacious, amenity-rich guestrooms and suites, first-rate service, and *upscale extras* for the *utmost* in comfort. Join our ×××Honors *program*.

The ×××Hotel of Xishuangbanna

Dear friend,

Welcome to the winter resort—Xishuangbanna, and we are happy to have you with us.

Our hotel, under the management of ×××Hotel Management Co. Ltd., is a five-star hotel, with 439 rooms, 8 restaurants, and 12 meeting rooms. The hotel *abides* by the *principles* of "*sincere* service, warm service, and friendly service." The hotel's software and hardware both take the lead in the hospitality *sector* of Xishuangbanna.

You will be *intoxicated* with the *harmony* between man and nature, and deeply *impressed* by our colorful *folk* cultures. Our hotel is just the

会议厅，可容纳 18550 人，还有 2 个商务中心。

新加坡×××酒店是国际豪华酒店连锁集团成员，是广大行政人员、商务旅行者或休闲度假者的理想住宿之选。

欢迎辞

旧金山金融区 ××× 酒店

欢迎来到旧金山金融区 ××× 酒店。我们的市中心酒店最近经过全面翻新，为商务旅行者、举家度假者及追求完美浪漫之旅的良朋知己提供豪华的住宿服务。

快来体验我们宽敞、完备的客房及套房，享受最贴心的服务，以及享用极为舒适的各种高档设施。请即加入我们 ××× 荣誉客会计划。

西双版纳 ××× 酒店

亲爱的朋友：

欢迎您来到避寒胜地——西双版纳，下榻我们 ××× 酒店！

我们酒店是由 ××× 酒店管理有限公司管理的一家五星级酒店，共有客房439 间，餐厅8 个，会议室 12 个。酒店秉承"真情、热情、友情"的服务原则。无论是硬件还是软件在西双版纳酒店业都处于领先地位。

朋友，在西双版纳，您会为人与自然的和谐音符所陶醉，为多姿多彩的民俗文化所折服。我们的

epitome of Xishuangbanna—*graceful* Dai girls *shuttling* in the *coconut* trees. In××× Hotel, your "home away from home," you will be *greeted* with Dai's welcoming teams playing elephant-foot *drums* and *splashing holy*, lucky, and happy water, and you will be treated with Dai's delicious pineapple rice, Aini bamboo chicken ...

We are *earnestly* looking forward to your staying with us.

2.1.3 Environmental Commitment

Dear Guest,

It is probable that you have been experiencing the fact that the environment we are living in is becoming more and more *deteriorating*. Water *pollution* has made it difficult for us to find any lakes or rivers suitable for fishing and swimming, and the greenhouse *effect* has made it stranger and stranger to us that "a timely snow *promises* a good harvest."

In order to protect our living environment, we are, in *response* to the government's *appeal*, running a *campaign* for "green hotel," and have been providing a series of "green services" and "green products" in the areas of the hotel.

When dining in restaurants, please order no more than or as much as you need, and take home what you have left *uneaten*. We are always at your service to pack food or keep wine. We will never provide any dishes made from the *wildlife* in protection. We will recommend to you better green foods for your health.

酒店就是西双版纳的缩影——婀娜多姿的傣族少女穿梭于椰林。打起鼓，敲起铓，洒着圣洁、吉祥、幸福水的傣家迎宾队伍，恭候您到"×××，您西双版纳的家"，品尝香味四溢的傣家菠萝饭、傻尼竹筒鸡……

恭候您的光临！

环保倡议

尊敬的贵宾：

或许您已经亲身感受到我们生存的环境正变得越来越令人担忧。水域污染使您可以垂钓、游泳的湖泊与河流已难以找到，而温室效应将使"瑞雪兆丰年"成为一句日益陌生的谚语。

为了保护我们的生存环境，我们响应政府号召，开展"创建绿色酒店"活动，并且已在酒店区域推出了一系列"绿色服务"和"绿色产品"。

在餐厅就餐时，请您适量点菜，并将剩余的菜食带回家，我们将为您提供打包和存酒服务。本酒店不提供以野生保护动物为原料的菜肴。为了您的健康，餐厅将向您推荐绿色食品。

In order to reduce pollution, please reduce the use of those one-use items. We will not add them before they are used up, and will no longer *replace* the room amenities that can be reused during your stay. Please contact the express service center if you need them to be added or replaced.

When leaving your room, please turn off the power *switch* and air conditioner so as to save *energy*.

Please drop the used *batteries* into the collecting-box in the *lobby* for safe *disposal*.

Green *consumption* is more a *concept* and a way of life than a *slogan* and a topic to *comment* on. A better environment depends on your *participation*, as well as that of the government and experts.

We have only one earth. Let's make a joint effort to work for a better future.

为了减少污染，请您减少一次性消耗用品的使用，在未用完之前，我们将不再添加。您在店期间，我们也将不再更换可重复使用的房间物品。需要添加或更换时，您可致电快捷服务中心。

离开客房时请您关闭客房的电源开关和空调，以减少能源的消耗。

请您将废电池放入大堂废电池收集箱，以便我们进行安全处理。

绿色消费不仅仅是一句口号、一个话题，它更是一种理念、一种生活方式。环境保护不但需要政府和专家的参与，更需要您的参与。

我们只有一个地球，让我们一起努力，共同营造一个美好的未来。

Vocabulary

deluxe /dəˈlʌks/ *adj.* 豪华的；高级的

sophisticated /səˈfɪstɪkeɪtɪd/ *adj.* 尖端的；高级的

temptation /tempˈteɪʃn/ *n.* 诱惑　　dazzling /ˈdæzlɪŋ/ *adj.* 令人眼花缭乱的

array /əˈreɪ/ *n.* 一系列；一连串；大量　　accommodate /əˈkɒmədeɪt/ *v.* 供给住宿

luxuriously /lʌgˈʒʊəriəsli/ *adv.* 豪华地；奢侈地

meticulously /məˈtɪkjələsli/ *adv.* 仔细地；一丝不苟地

pampered /ˈpæmpəd/ *adj.* 娇惯的　　formality /fɔːˈmæləti/ *n.* 程序；手续

elaborate /ɪˈlæbəreɪt/ *adj.* 精美的　　brochure /ˈbrəʊʃə(r)/ *n.* 小册子

profile /ˈprəʊfaɪl/ *n.* 简介　　commitment /kəˈmɪtmənt/ *n.* 承诺

reminder /rɪˈmaɪndə(r)/ *n.* 提醒；提示　　atop /əˈtɒp/ *prep.* 在……顶上

acre /ˈeɪkə(r)/ n. 英亩

lush /lʌʃ/ adj. 苍翠繁茂的；茂盛的

fragrant /ˈfreɪɡrənt/ adj. 芳香的

ambience /ˈæmbiəns/ n. 气氛

bungalow /ˈbʌŋɡələʊ/ n. 有凉台的房间；小屋

feature /ˈfiːtʃə(r)/ n. 特色

palm /pɑːm/ n. 棕榈

cabana /kəˈbɑːnjɑː/ n. 平房小屋

appoint /əˈpɔɪnt/ v. 配备

marble /ˈmɑːbl/ n. 大理石

reminiscent /ˌremɪˈnɪsnt/ adj. 使人联想的

timeless /ˈtaɪmləs/ adj. 永恒的

glamor /ˈɡlæmə(r)/ n. 魅力

fashionable /ˈfæʃnəbl/ adj. 流行的

welcoming /ˈwelkəmɪŋ/ adj. 热情的；欢迎的

emphasize /ˈemfəsaɪz/ v. 重点突出

hospitable /hɒˈspɪtəbl/ adj. 热情好客的

rooftop /ˈruːftɒp/ n. 屋顶

savor /ˈseɪvə(r)/ v. 欣赏

bustling /ˈbʌslɪŋ/ adj. 繁华的

feast /fiːst/ v. 享受；享用

oyster /ˈɔɪstə(r)/ n. 牡蛎

award-winning /əˈwɔːd ˈwɪnɪŋ/ adj. 应获奖的；一流的

harbor /ˈhɑːbə(r)/ n. 海港

grill /ɡrɪl/ n. 烧烤店

indulge /ɪnˈdʌldʒ/ v. 沉湎于；纵情于

lounge /laʊndʒ/ n. 休息室

safari /səˈfɑːri/ n. 游览

spree /spriː/ n. 狂欢

district /ˈdɪstrɪkt/ n. 行政区

vacationer /vəˈkeɪʃənə(r)/ n. 休假者

romantic /rəʊˈmæntɪk/ adj. 浪漫的

getaway /ˈɡetəweɪ/ n. 短假

renovate /ˈrenəveɪt/ v. 翻新

experience /ɪkˈspɪəriəns/ v. 体验

spacious /ˈspeɪʃəs/ adj. 宽敞的

upscale /ˌʌpˈskeɪl/ adj. 高档的；高端的

extra /ˈekstrə/ n. 额外的事物；另收费的东西

utmost /ˈʌtməʊst/ n. 极限；最大可能

program /ˈprəʊɡræm/ n. 计划；方案

abide /əˈbaɪd/ v. 遵守；坚持

principle /ˈprɪnsəpl/ n. 原则

sincere /sɪnˈsɪə(r)/ adj. 真诚的

sector /ˈsektə(r)/ n. 部分

intoxicate /ɪnˈtɒksɪkeɪt/ v. 使陶醉

harmony /ˈhɑːməni/ n. 和谐

impress /ɪmˈpres/ v. 使有印象

folk /fəʊk/ adj. 民间的

epitome /ɪˈpɪtəmi/ n. 缩影；典范

graceful /ˈɡreɪsfl/ adj. 优雅的

shuttle /ˈʃʌtl/ v. 穿梭移动

coconut /ˈkəʊkənʌt/ n. 椰子

greet /ɡriːt/ v. 迎接；恭候

drum /drʌm/ n. 鼓

splash /splæʃ/ v. 洒水

holy /ˈhəʊli/ adj. 圣洁的

earnestly /ˈɜːnɪstli/ adv. 热情地

deteriorate /dɪˈtɪəriəreɪt/ v. 恶化

pollution /pəˈluːʃn/ n. 污染

effect /ɪˈfekt/ *n.* 效应

response /rɪˈspɒns/ *n.* 响应

campaign /kæmˈpeɪn/ *n.* 运动；活动

wildlife /ˈwaɪldlaɪf/ *n.* 野生动植物

switch /swɪtʃ/ *n.* 开关

battery /ˈbætəri/ *n.* 电池

disposal /dɪˈspəʊzl/ *n.* 处理；处置

concept /ˈkɒnsept/ *n.* 理念

comment /ˈkɒment/ *v.* 评论

promise /ˈprɒmɪs/ *v.* 预示

appeal /əˈpiːl/ *n.* 呼吁；号召

uneaten /ʌnˈiːtn/ *adj.* 没吃的；剩下的

replace /rɪˈpleɪs/ *v.* 替换

energy /ˈenədʒi/ *n.* 能量；能源

lobby /ˈlɒbi/ *n.* 大堂

consumption /kənˈsʌmpʃn/ *n.* 消费（耗）

slogan /ˈsləʊgən/ *n.* 口号

participation /pɑːˌtɪsɪˈpeɪʃn/ *n.* 参与

Useful Expressions

an array of ... 一排；一批；一群

stay over 过夜；住宿；待过

feast on ... 尽情欣赏；尽情享受；大吃大喝

indulge in 尽情享受

abide by ... 遵守……

be intoxicated with ... 陶醉于……

look forward to ... 期盼……

in response to ... 为了响应……

use up 用完

in a very real sense 现实地讲

be reminiscent of ... 展现……；回忆起……

work out 健身

raise the bar on ... 提升了……

take the lead in ... 领先于……

be greeted with ... 受到……的接待

be suitable for ... 适合于……

be at service to do sth. 提供……服务

make an effort to do sth. 努力做某事

词汇、课文资源

词汇、课文自测

微课

课堂练习

2.2　Hotel Rules and Regulations

2.2.1　Fire Safety Tips for Hotel Guests

The following *regulations formulated* according to the Fire Control Law of the People's Republic of China and *Interim Provisions* on the Hospitality Industry Management of ×× *Municipal* Public Security Bureau shall be *executed* in the purpose of ensuring the hotel's *normal* order and *safeguarding* the guest's personal security.

1) A guest shall *produce* his / her ID card when checking in. A foreigner, an overseas Chinese, or a *compatriot* from Hong Kong, Macao, or Taiwan shall produce his / her passport, home-visit *permit* or any other *relevant identification document*.

2) A guest shall use his / her specified room and specified bed. Any visitor or *imposter* shall not be allowed to stay overnight in the guestroom. A guest shall be allowed in by key card only, and shall not be allowed to receive visitor(s) in the guestroom without *permission*.

3) Valuables, cash money, and luggage shall be stored in the *depository* of the hotel in case of loss or theft.

4) *Flammable, explosive, poisonous, radioactive,* and other *hazardous* materials shall be strictly *prohibited* in the hotel. *Firearms* and *ammunition* that *military,* police, *judicial* officers carry due to public *affairs* shall all be deposited in the public security *organs* or the military unit in the *locality* of the hotel.

宾客消防安全须知

为了确保酒店的正常秩序，保障宾客的人身安全，依据《中华人民共和国消防法》和 ×× 市公安局《关于酒店业管理的暂行规定》，必须遵守下列规定：

1) 宾客住宿必须持有能够证明其身份的居民身份证。外国人、华侨、港澳台同胞凭护照、回乡证或其他有关证明。

2) 宾客应按照指定客房和床位住宿。不准私自留宿客人或冒名顶替住宿。宾客仅可凭房卡进入，未经同意，不得私自在客房会客。

3) 宾客携带的贵重物品、现金和行李应托酒店代为保管，谨防遗失或被窃。

4) 严禁将易燃、易爆、剧毒、有放射性的及其他危险物品带入酒店。军、警、司法人员等因公携带的枪支弹药应一律交由酒店所在地的公安机关或军事部门寄存。

5) *Excessive* drinking, fighting, *gambling*, drug-taking, *prostitution*, or any other *illegal* activities including *dissemination* of *reactionary* or *obscene* books and periodicals, photos, *audio* and *video recordings*, shall be strictly prohibited in the hotel.

6) Smoking in bed and use of high-power *appliances* like *irons* and *stoves* shall be prohibited.

7) The hotel management shall *reserve* the right to *question* any guest who *violates* these rules and regulations. A guest shall *forwardly* produce his / her identification document, while the police are carrying out *routine* room checks.

8) A guest shall *consciously* abide by the laws of the People's Republic of China. When finding some illegal activity, he / she shall report to the public security organs, protect the *scene*, and wait for the *investigation* by the public security organs.

Those who violate the above rules and regulations shall be given, by the public security organs, *criticism*, *disciplinary warning*, *penalty*, administrative *detention* or *punishment* as a *crime*, in *accordance* with the *seriousness* of the *case* and Interim Provisions on the Hospitality Industry Management of ×× Municipal Public Security Bureau and relevant laws.

2.2.2 Lodging Regulations

1) Upon entering the hotel, please *complete* check-in formalities at the Front Desk.

2) For the sake of safety, inflammable, explosive and *toxic articles* or articles with

5) 严禁在酒店内酗酒、斗殴、赌博、吸毒、嫖宿，以及传播反动、淫秽的书刊、照片、录音和录像等违法活动。

6) 不准在客房床上吸烟。严禁在酒店内擅自使用电炉、电熨斗等大功率家用电器。

7) 自觉遵守酒店规章制度，接受酒店管理人员的查询。公安人员查房时，应主动出示证件，接受检查。

8) 自觉遵守中华人民共和国的法律，如发现违法犯罪活动，要向公安机关检举揭发，保护现场，等候公安机关查处。

上述规定如有违反者，视情节轻重，由公安机关根据××市《关于酒店业管理的暂行规定》和相关法律，分别给予批评、警告、罚款、行政拘留直至追究刑事责任。

入住规定

1) 阁下进店时，请先在前台办理入住手续。

2) 为了安全起见，请勿将易燃、易爆、剧毒和气味难闻物品携

nauseating odors are prohibited from being carried into the *premises*; valuables and large *sums* of cash money shall be stored in the depository of the hotel.

3) The hotel is fully air-conditioned. Please don't open windows unless it is necessary.

4) Excessive drinking, terrible noises, and *annoying disturbances* are prohibited in the purpose of keeping a quiet environment.

5) Guestrooms are used for nothing but lodging. No illegal activities such as gambling are allowed in any area of the hotel.

6) Do not smoke in bed.

7) In order to keep the guestroom clean and quiet, you are prohibited from bringing in pets or *snack* boxes.

8) Visitors to guestroom shall register at the Service Desk and leave before 23:00.

9) Please do not *disclose* any information such as your room number or open door to any stranger except the hotel staff in uniform. Contact assistant manager at Extension 28 for *assistance* when in *doubt*.

10) If you are not in good health, please contact the Front Desk for a quick help.

2.2.3　Room *Tariff*

1) The hotel provides the following types of rooms: standard room, business single room, deluxe double room, deluxe single room, business suite, extra bed, etc.

2) All room rates include service charge.

3) Breakfast is not included.

入本店。贵重物品、大宗现金须交由酒店代为保管。

3) 酒店内全部使用空调，请尽量少开窗户。

4) 为保证环境的安静，请勿酗酒、喧哗和打扰别人。

5) 客房仅供睡眠或休息所用，请勿用作其他用途。店内任何地方均不允许有赌博等违法现象发生。

6) 请不要在床上吸烟。

7) 为了保持客房的整洁和安宁，请勿将宠物和快餐盒带入房内。

8) 访客须在服务台登记，并须在 23 点前离开。

9) 除身着制服的酒店员工外，勿向陌生人透露房号等信息或为陌生人开门。如有疑问，请致电分机 28 联系大堂副理。

10) 如您感到身体不适，请通知前台，我们将努力提供帮助。

房费规定

1) 酒店提供的房型如下：标准间、商务单人间、豪华双人间、豪华单人间、商务套间、加床间等。

2) 所有房费均包括服务费。

3) 不含早餐。

4) All the rooms in Business Floor (non-smoking) have a personal computer and 24-hour Internet access.

5) Group rates are available.

6) Check-out time is 12:00 p.m. 50% room rate will be charged for checking-out before 6:00 p.m., and a full day rate will be charged after 6:00 p.m.

7) Reservations not guaranteed will be automatically canceled at 6:00 p.m.

8) As the *policy* of the hotel, room *prepayment* or deposit is required when you are checking in.

9) The hotel reserves the right to change the above room rates without *prior* notice.

2.2.4　Breakfast Coupon

1) *Complimentary buffet* breakfast is available to the *coupon* holder at our specific restaurant.

2) Please present this coupon to our staff before dining.

3) The coupon is non-*refundable* and can't be used for room service.

4) There is no *compensation* for loss, and it is *invalid* after the specified time.

5) Breakfast is not available to half-day room users.

4) 商务层（无烟房）所有房间配有个人电脑和24小时网络接入。

5) 有团体房价。

6) 退房时间为中午12点，中午12点至下午6点退房加收50%房费，下午6点以后退房收整天房费。

7) 无担保预订房在下午6点自动取消。

8) 按酒店规定，入店登记时，需要预付或押金。

9) 酒店改变上述房价，无须预先通知。

早餐券规定

1) 凭此券在指定餐厅享用早餐一份。

2) 用餐前，请向服务员出示此券。

3) 此券不能兑换现金，不可用于客房送餐服务。

4) 遗失不补，过期作废。

5) 半天房客不享受早餐。

Vocabulary

regulation /ˌreɡjuˈleɪʃn/ *n.* 规章

interim /ˈɪntərɪm/ *adj.* 暂行的；暂时的

municipal /mjuːˈnɪsɪpl/ *adj.* 市的

normal /ˈnɔːml/ *adj.* 正常的

produce /prəˈdjuːs/ *v.* 出示

permit /ˈpəmɪt/ *n.* 许可证

identification /aɪˌdentɪfɪˈkeɪʃn/ *n.* 身份证明

document /ˈdɒkjumənt/ *n.* 文件

permission /pəˈmɪʃn/ *n.* 允许；许可

flammable /ˈflæməbl/ *adj.* 易燃的

poisonous /ˈpɔɪzənəs/ *adj.* 有毒的

hazardous /ˈhæzədəs/ *adj.* 危险的

firearm /ˈfaɪərɑːm/ *n.* 枪支

military /ˈmɪlətri/ *adj.* 军队的

affair /əˈfeə(r)/ *n.* 事务

locality /ləʊˈkæləti/ *n.* 当地；本地

gambling /ˈɡæmblɪŋ/ *n.* 赌博

illegal /ɪˈliːɡl/ *adj.* 非法的

reactionary /riˈækʃənri/ *adj.* 反动的

audio /ˈɔːdiəʊ/ *adj.* 有声的；音频的

recording /rɪˈkɔːdɪŋ/ *n.* 录音（像）制品

iron /ˈaɪən/ *n.* 熨斗

reserve /rɪˈzɜːv/ *v.* 保留

violate /ˈvaɪəleɪt/ *v.* 违反

routine /ruːˈtiːn/ *adj.* 常规的；例行的

scene /siːn/ *n.* 现场

criticism /ˈkrɪtɪsɪzəm/ *n.* 批评

warning /ˈwɔːnɪŋ/ *n.* 警告

detention /dɪˈtenʃn/ *n.* 拘留

crime /kraɪm/ *n.* 犯罪

formulate /ˈfɔːmjuleɪt/ *v.* 制订

provision /prəˈvɪʒn/ *n.* 规定

execute /ˈeksɪkjuːt/ *v.* 执行；实行

safeguard /ˈseɪfɡɑːd/ *v.* 保卫；保障

compatriot /kəmˈpætriət/ *n.* 同胞

relevant /ˈreləvənt/ *adj.* 相关的

imposter /ɪmˈpɒstə(r)/ *n.* 冒名顶替者

depository /dɪˈpɒzɪtri/ *n.* 存储处

explosive /ɪkˈspləʊsɪv/ *adj.* 爆炸的

radioactive /ˌreɪdiəʊˈæktɪv/ *adj.* 放射性的

prohibit /prəˈhɪbɪt/ *v.* 禁止

ammunition /ˌæmjuˈnɪʃn/ *n.* 弹药

judicial /dʒuˈdɪʃl/ *adj.* 司法的

organ /ˈɔːɡən/ *n.* 机关；机构

excessive /ɪkˈsesɪv/ *adj.* 过多的

prostitution /ˌprɒstɪˈtjuːʃn/ *n.* 卖淫

dissemination /dɪˌsemɪˈneɪʃn/ *n.* 传播

obscene /əbˈsiːn/ *adj.* 淫秽的

video /ˈvɪdiəʊ/ *n.* 视频；录像

appliance /əˈplaɪəns/ *n.* 电器

stove /stəʊv/ *n.* 炉子

question /ˈkwestʃən/ *v.* 询问

forwardly /ˈfɔːwədli/ *adv.* 主动地

consciously /ˈkɒnʃəsli/ *adv.* 自觉地

investigation /ɪnˌvestɪˈɡeɪʃn/ *n.* 调查

disciplinary /ˈdɪsəplɪnəri/ *adj.* 惩戒的；纪律的

penalty /ˈpenəlti/ *n.* 处罚

punishment /ˈpʌnɪʃmənt/ *n.* 惩罚

accordance /əˈkɔːdns/ *n.* 一致；符合

seriousness /ˈsɪəriəsnəs/ *n.* 严重性

complete /kəmˈpliːt/ *v.* 完成

article /ˈɑːtɪkl/ *n.* 物品

odor /ˈəʊdə(r)/ *n.* 气味

sum /sʌm/ *n.* 一笔款项

disturbance /dɪˈstɜːbəns/ *n.* 混乱

disclose /dɪsˈkləʊz/ *v.* 透露

doubt /daʊt/ *n.* 疑问

policy /ˈpɒləsi/ *n.* 政策；制度

prior /ˈpraɪə(r)/ *adj.* 在先的

buffet /ˈbʊfeɪ/ *n.* 自助餐

refundable /rɪˈfʌndəbl/ *adj.* 可退的

invalid /ɪnˈvælɪd/ *adj.* 无效的

case /keɪs/ *n.* 案件

toxic /ˈtɒksɪk/ *adj.* 有毒的

nauseating /ˈnɔːzieɪtɪŋ/ *adj.* 令人作呕的

premise /ˈpremɪs/ *n.* 室内；场地

annoying /əˈnɔɪɪŋ/ *adj.* 悚人的

snack /snæk/ *n.* 快餐

assistance /əˈsɪstəns/ *n.* 帮助

tariff /ˈtærɪf/ *n.* 价目表

prepayment /ˌpriːˈpeɪmənt/ *n.* 预付（款）

complimentary /ˌkɒmplɪˈmentri/ *adj.* 免费赠送的

coupon /ˈkuːpɒn/ *n.* 票券；优惠券

compensation /ˌkɒmpenˈseɪʃn/ *n.* 赔偿

Useful Expressions

in the depository of ... 由……代管

in the locality of ... 在……当地

for the sake of ... 为了……起见

large sums of ... 大量的……

in good health 身体好

in case of ... 万一……

reserve the right to do sth. 有权做某事

prohibit ... from doing sth. 阻止……做某事

nothing but 无非；只有

 词汇、课文资源 词汇、课文自测 微课 课堂练习

2.3 Front Office Services

Assistant Manager/Guest Service Manager

We are delighted to have you with us during your travel here. If you have any questions, please call 8828. The assistant manager or guest service

大堂副理 / 客服经理

很高兴您在旅行期间入住我们酒店。如有什么问题，请致电8828。大堂副理或客服经理将随时

manager will be at your service any time. We ensure that you will be content and comfortable through our hospitality and service.

Front Desk

Check-in, check-out, and enquiry service are available all day at the front desk. *Extension* 8506.

Concierge Desk
(Service hours: 7:00–23:30)

Such services as enquiry, airport transfer, letter and parcel mailing, luggage *storage*, tourism information, and *limousine* rental are available at the *concierge* desk at the *entrance*. Extension 8510.

Business Center
(Service hours: 8:00–20:00)

Service items of Chinese and English typing, copying, fax sending and receiving, ticket booking, DDD and IDD calls, and Internet access are provided at the business center on the left side of the lobby. Extension 8866.

Room Reservation

24-hour room reservation service is offered at the room reservation. Extension 8855. You can reserve rooms either in our hotel or in nation-wide hotels.

Wake-Up Service

Please contact the express service at extension 8806 for wake-up calls.

Currency Exchange
(Service hours: 7:00–23:00)

Foreign *currency* exchange is available at the front office cashier. Extension 0879. Currencies to be exchanged are British pounds, HK dollars, US

为您服务。您定将对我们的接待和服务感到满意。

前台

前台 24 小时办理入店登记、退房离店手续及咨询服务，分机 8506。

礼宾部
（服务时间：7:00—23:30）

酒店入口处的礼宾部为您提供问讯、机场接送、递送信件包裹、行李寄存、旅游信息、租车代理等服务，分机 8510。

商务中心
（服务时间：8:00—20:00）

大堂左侧的商务中心提供中英文打字、复印、收发传真、票务、国内长途电话、国际长话直拨及互联网等服务，分机 8866。

客房预订

预订部提供 24 小时客房预订服务，分机 8855。您可以预订本店房间，也可以预订全国各酒店的房间。

叫早服务

如需叫早服务，请拨分机 8806，与便捷服务处联系。

货币兑换
（服务时间：7:00—23:00）

货币兑换在前厅出纳处，分机 0879。可兑外币有英镑、港元、美元、日元和欧元。最高限额不超过

dollars, Yen, and Euros, with the *maximum* sum of 3,000 RMB.

3000 元人民币。

Safety Deposit Box

Safety deposit box is available free of charge at the front office cashier counter. Extension 9879. You are advised not to leave valuables in the guestroom.

保险箱服务

在前厅出纳处设有免费的保险箱，分机 9879。建议宾客不要把贵重物品放在客房里。

Service for the Disabled

Fee-based vehicles for the disabled are available at the concierge desk. The hotel is equipped with a toilet for the disabled only at the right end on each floor.

无障碍服务

酒店在礼宾部设有收费的无障碍轮椅车，在每一层的右尽头配有无障碍专用洗手间。

Cashier's Counter

The cashier's counter is located next to the reception counter. Domestic credit cards such as Dragon card, Peony card, and Great Wall card, and foreign credit cards such as American Express, Master, Visa, Diners, and JCB are accepted. Check-out time is not later than 12:00 at noon. An additional charge will be applied for an extended stay. For late check-out, please contact the reception desk at extension 8678.

收银处

收银处在接待处旁边。本酒店结账可接受龙卡、牡丹卡、长城卡等国内信用卡和美国运通卡、万事达卡、维萨卡、大来卡和日财卡等国外信用卡。退房时间不迟于中午 12 点，超过时间要加收房费。若需延迟退房，请拨分机 8678 与接待处联系。

Message Service

Word and voice message services are both available to someone paying a visit to the guest who is out. Messages can be accepted at the information desk. When the message lamp on your phone is lit, please call extension 5161 for your message.

留言服务

宾客不在房间时，有人来访，可以使用文字留言或语音留言。有留言可在问讯处获取。当话机上的留言灯亮起时，拨打分机 5161 获取留言。

Elevators

Elevators are for your comfort and convenience. Please don't use them if there is a fire. If *trapped* in the elevator, please call extension 5533.

电梯

电梯给您提供了舒适与方便，但遇火情时，请不要使用电梯。如遇困于电梯，请拨分机 5533。

Telephone *Directory*

Please refer to the telephone guide or contact the operator at extension 5501 for any assistance.

After completing your direct dial call, please ensure the receiver is properly placed for *disconnection*. The hotel will reserve the right to charge any call *duly* caused by *misplacement*.

As new destinations are added from time to time, we only list up those in common use. If the country or city code you wish to reach cannot be connected, please kindly call the hotel operator (dial 5501) to check. He / She is always at your service.

Phone charges are automatically recorded to your account together with the *surcharge* or handling charge. If you want to make a collect call, please consult the operator (dial 5501) or ask the operator to dial for you.

The *discount* of international or *domestic* calls will be permitted according to the regulations of the Ministry of Industry and Information Technology.

Ways of dialing:

Room to Room Call: Dial room number.

Local Call: Please dial "0" for local call.

Domestic Direct Dial Call: "0"+Area Code+Telephone Number.

International Direct: "0"+Country Code+Area Code+Telephone Number.

电话簿

请参阅电话指南或拨分机 5501 向酒店接线员查询。

打完直拨电话以后，请正确放回听筒，确保线路切断。如果因听筒放置不当而未及时切断线路，酒店有权收取所耗费用。

由于长途电话接通地时有增加，我们只列出常用的新增地点名。如果阁下想通话的国家或城市号码接不上，请联系酒店接线员（拨 5501）核查，他们很乐意为您服务。

电话费用及相关服务费会自动记录在阁下的账单上。如果需拨打对方付费电话，请拨 5501，向酒店接线员查询或让其为您代拨。

国际国内电话的话费折扣情况按工信部的规定执行。

拨打方法：

房间电话，直接拨房间号码。

市话，请先拨 "0"。

国内直拨电话，"0" ＋区号 ＋电话号码。

国际直拨电话，"0" ＋国家代码 ＋区号 ＋电话号码。

Vocabulary

extension /ɪkˈstenʃn/ *n.* 电话分机

limousine /ˈlɪməziːn/ *n.*（用于接送的）中型客车

concierge /ˈkɒnsieəʒ/ *n.* 礼宾

entrance /ˈentrəns/ *n.* 入口处

maximum /ˈmæksɪməm/ *adj.* 最大数的

directory /dəˈrektəri/ *n.* 名录；指南

duly /ˈdjuːli/ *adv.* 适当地；相应地

surcharge /ˈsɜːtʃɑːdʒ/ *n.* 附加费

domestic /dəˈmestɪk/ *adj.* 国内的

storage /ˈstɔːrɪdʒ/ *n.* 保管

currency /ˈkʌrənsi/ *n.* 货币

trap /træp/ *v.* 使陷入；使困在

disconnection /ˌdɪskəˈnekʃn/ *n.* 断开

misplacement /mɪsˈpleɪsmənt/ *n.* 错放

discount /ˈdɪskaʊnt/ *n.* 折扣

Useful Expressions

be delighted to do sth. 很高兴做某事

refer to 参考；查阅

pay a visit to ... 访问……

be in use 在使用

词汇、课文资源　　　词汇、课文自测　　　微课　　　课堂练习

2.4 Housekeeping Services

The hotel has guestrooms of different styles, consisting of business rooms, luxury rooms, executive rooms, and suites, all with full equipment and with free high-speed Internet access, which makes the hotel an *ideal* choice for businessmen and travelers.

Room Amenities

During your stay, for the purpose of saving water and reducing pollution, we will not replace the room amenities such as towel, tooth brush, and

酒店拥有商务房、豪华套房、行政房、套房等风格各异的各种客房。所有房间的设施配套齐全并提供免费高速上网，是商旅人士的理想选择。

客房用品

在您住店期间，为了节约用水和减少污染，我们将不替换毛巾、牙刷、肥皂等可以重复使用的物

soap that can be reused, and will no longer change the bed *linens* as a daily routine. If you do need a replacement or change, please dial extension 8855. We are always at your service.

品，也不再每天更换床上的棉制用品。如果确有需要更换，请拨打分机 8855。我们随时为您提供服务。

Air Conditioning & Heating

The hotel is fully air-conditioned. You can *adjust* the room *ventilation* and the temperature by turning the *thermostatic* control switch *installed* in each room.

空调系统

酒店全部装有空调系统，转动客房里的温控开关可以调节房间内的通风和温度。

Electricity

A multi-functional *socket* is installed in the wall against the desk. The hotel has a supply of electricity with 220 V, 50 Hz. The use of heating or cooking appliances is prohibited in the guestrooms.

电源

靠桌子的墙上装有多功能插座。酒店所供电源是 220 伏特、50 赫兹。客房内禁止使用加热器或厨房电器。

Master Switch

The guestroom is equipped with a master switch, which is located beside the room entrance. It is automatically turned on when your *magnetic* key card is *inserted* into the *slot*, and automatically turned off when the magnetic key card is *removed*.

总开关

客房的入口旁装有总开关装置。当磁性房卡插入槽中，电源自动接通。当磁性房卡被取出时，电源则自动切断。

Hairdryer

Hairdryer is placed under the *washbasin*. Please use it only for hair drying.

吹风机

洗发吹风机放在洗面盆下面，请勿用作其他用途。

Television

Programs from CCTV, Beijing TV, Dragon TV, Zhejiang TV, and many other channels including Channel V and Phoenix Chinese Channel are available.

电视

可以收看到中国中央电视台、北京卫视、东方卫视、浙江卫视，以及包括星空卫视音乐台、凤凰卫视中文台在内的许多其他电视台的节目。

VOD System

Internal Movie Theater is available. Each movie will be charged for 15 to 25 yuan.

视频点播

酒店为您提供了内部影院视频点播系统。点播一部影片收费

15 ～ 25 元。

Clothes Line

Each bathroom is equipped with a *retractable* clothes line for your washing convenience.

Housekeeping

For extras, turn-down service, room cleaning, or any additional service, please contact housekeeping department at extension 8655.

Laundry Service

Dry cleaning, wet wash, and ironing are available in the hotel. Laundries are collected before 10:00 a.m. and returned before 7:00 p.m. Laundries collected after 10:00 a.m. are returned before 5:00 p.m. on the following day. For our 4-hour *express* service, a 100% of *urgent* fee will be charged.

Drinking Water

Hot and cold drinking water is available in each room. Please contact the housekeeping for *replenishment* at extension 8655.

Mini Bar

All items in the mini bar are for sale. Please call extension 8655 for any immediate replenishment or additional requirements. The service charge on each item is included in its price, and we will automatically *count* when you open.

Shoeshine Service

Shoeshine service is available free of charge. Please place your shoes inside the shoe basket in your wardrobe or contact the service center at extension 8657.

晾衣绳

浴间里都装有可伸缩的晾衣绳，方便洗浴。

客房服务

如需额外用品、开夜床服务、打扫房间或任何其他服务，请拨分机 8655，与客房部联系。

干洗服务

酒店提供干洗、水洗和熨烫服务。上午 10 点之前收的衣物会在下午 7 点之前送回。上午 10 点以后收的衣物要在次日下午 5 点之前送回。酒店还提供 4 小时加急干洗服务，收取 100% 的加急费。

饮用水

每个房间里都有可饮用的冷、热水。需要充装，请拨分机 8655，与客房部联系。

迷你酒吧

消费迷你酒吧里的所有物品，都是要收费的。如需立即添补或其他需要，请拨分机 8655。所有物品价格均包含服务费。如不消费，请勿打开包装，否则按消费计算。

擦鞋服务

免费提供擦鞋服务。请把您要擦的鞋子放在壁橱里的鞋筐里或拨打内线 8657 与服务中心联系。

Newspaper Service

The hotel has many local newspapers and some English newspapers available. They will be delivered to your room immediately when your order comes at extension 8866.

Children's Service

Cribs and high chairs are available free of charge. If you need a *babysitter*, please contact the service center 4 hours in *advance*.

Visitors

Visitors are not allowed in guestrooms unless *accompanied* by registered guests. All visitors are requested to leave guestrooms by 23:00.

Pet-Caring Service

No pets are allowed in guestrooms. Only medium-size pets with a maximum weight of 20 kilograms can be *trusted* to the hotel's care at a daily price of 100 yuan.

No-smoking Rooms

No-smoking rooms are available for non-smokers.

DND

When you don't like to be disturbed, please put the "DND" card on the *knob* outside the door.

Lost and Found

Lost and Found items will be kept in the hotel for three months. *Perishable* items will be *retained* for one day only. The hotel reserves the right to *dispose* of the items not *claimed* within the specified period.

报纸服务

酒店有多种地方报纸和一些英文报纸。如需要，请拨分机8866。一接到您的订阅电话，马上就会送到您的房间。

儿童服务

婴儿床和高脚儿童椅可免费使用。如需临时儿童保姆，请提前4个小时与服务中心联系。

访客

无店客陪同，访客不许进入客房。所有访客请在23点之前离开客房。

宠物寄养服务

禁止宠物进入客房。只有体重不超过20千克中等体型的宠物方可托付店方寄养，每天收费100元。

无烟房

酒店有供不吸烟者使用的无烟房。

免打扰

当您不想被打扰时，请把"请勿打扰"牌挂在房门的外门柄上。

失物招领

遗失物品将由酒店保管三个月，易变质物品仅保留一天。规定期限内无人认领的物品，酒店有权处置。

Vocabulary

ideal /aɪˈdiːəl/ *adj.* 理想的	linen /ˈlɪnɪn/ *n.* 棉织品；亚麻制品
adjust /əˈdʒʌst/ *v.* 调节	ventilation /ˌventɪˈleɪʃn/ *n.* 通风
thermostatic /ˌθɜːməˈstætɪk/ *adj.* 温度调节装置的	
install /ɪnˈstɔːl/ *v.* 安装	socket /ˈsɒkɪt/ *n.* 插座
master /ˈmɑːstə(r)/ *adj.* 总的；主要的	magnetic /mægˈnetɪk/ *adj.* 有磁性的
insert /ɪnˈsɜːt/ *v.* 插入	slot /slɒt/ *n.* 卡槽
remove /rɪˈmuːv/ *v.* 移除	hairdryer /ˈheədraɪə(r)/ *n.* 吹风机
washbasin /ˈwɒʃbeɪsn/ *n.* 洗面盆	retractable /rɪˈtræktəbl/ *adj.* 可伸缩的
express /ɪkˈspres/ *adj.* 快捷的	urgent /ˈɜːdʒənt/ *adj.* 紧急的
replenishment /rɪˈplenɪʃmənt/ *n.* 补充；再填充	count /kaʊnt/ *v.* 计算
shoeshine /ˈʃuːʃaɪn/ *n.* 擦鞋	crib /krɪb/ *n.* 婴儿小床
babysitter /ˈbeɪbisɪtə(r)/ *n.* 临时照看孩子的保姆	advance /ədˈvɑːns/ *n.* 事先
accompany /əˈkʌmpəni/ *v.* 陪同	trust /trʌst/ *v.* 托付
knob /nɒb/ *n.* 门把手	
perishable /ˈperɪʃəbl/ *adj.* 易腐烂的；易变质的；易枯萎的	
retain /rɪˈteɪn/ *v.* 保持；保留	dispose /dɪˈspəʊz/ *v.* 清除；解决；处理掉
claim /kleɪm/ *v.* 认领	

Useful Expressions

in advance 提前	trust ... to ... 把……托付给……
dispose of 处置	

词汇、课文资源

词汇、课文自测

微课

课堂练习

2.5 Food and Beverage Services

The hotel provides all kinds of local *specialties* and delicious cuisines of the northern and southern

酒店美食集地方特色，南北风味，由专业厨师主理。典雅的用餐

styles, all prepared in charge of professional chefs. The *elegant* environment, as well as *exquisite* cuisine, brings a great *enjoyment* to your dining here.

Banquet Hall

The banquet hall, located on the ground floor, has a total of 400 seats. You and your *honorable* guests can enjoy the Chinese banquets in the *landscape* of lakes and mountains. Reservation: 88887777.

Chinese Restaurant

There is no doubt that the hotel is where you'll find some of the most *tantalizing* meals, and where there is no *shortage* of types of cuisine. We are sure that our *incomparable authentic* Chinese cuisine will give you a good *appetite*. Open Hours: 6:30–21:30. Contact: 88886666.

Western Restaurant

Buffet breakfast, Western foods, and *à la carte* foods are available in the half-open Western restaurant, which, located in the *backyard* of the lobby, is a place where all Western foods meet. Your dining here is just like enjoying birds' singing in a *vernacular* house of Jiangnan style. Service Hours: 6:30–21:30. Tel.: 88885577.

Café

Café serves a *diverse* buffet with an array of salads, *spaghetti*, and fruits. The *dynamic* open kitchen *incorporates* eight stations, *showcasing* the quality of *ingredients* that go into every dish and the whole culinary process of each dish. In addition to the buffet, an à la carte menu is also available.

环境，精致的菜肴，给你一个迥然不同的美食享受。

宴会大厅

宴会大厅位于一楼，共有座位400个。您和您的贵宾可以在这湖光山色之美景中获得中式宴会的享受。预订电话：88887777。

中餐厅

勿庸置疑，您在这里会享受到最诱人的餐饮。各式菜系，应有尽有。我们相信各式无可比拟的纯正中餐一定会使您胃口大开。营业时间6:30—21:30。联系电话：8888666。

西餐厅

半开放式的西餐厅，位于大堂后院，各式西餐荟萃，可供应自助早餐、西餐和零点美食。在这里用餐，犹如闲坐江南民居，聆听鸟鸣一般。营业时间6:30—21:30。电话：88885577。

咖啡苑

咖啡苑提供各式自助餐，包括沙拉、意大利面和水果。活力十足的开放式厨房由八张工作台组成，展示了每道菜所用原料的质量及烹饪过程。除自助餐外，咖啡苑还有零点菜单供选择。

Gourmet Corner

Gourmet Corner is an excellent gourmet *takeaway outlet* in the West Wing of the hotel, with sandwiches, salads, and an array of *confectionery* and chocolates. It's a great spot to pick up a *bite* before a day on the go.

Summer Palace

Summer Palace combines the *classic* Cantonese cuisine with the *creative* Huaiyang cuisine, and places a strong emphasis on Chinese tea culture as well as French Bordeaux *vintages*. Summer Palace also serves a daily lunch with an array of popular *dim sums*. Six elegant private dining rooms are available for a higher level of *personalized* service. Summer Palace's wide selection of Chinese *premium* teas and culinary *condiments* make ideal gifts.

Lobby Lounge

With live classical music nightly, the Lobby Lounge is an ideal venue for a business meeting, a cup of tea, or an elegant evening *cocktail*. The Sunday's afternoon High Tea features a *sublime* buffet accompanied in *splendor* by a *magnificent orchestra*.

Room Service

Fresh and delicious Chinese and Western dishes are available for the room service between 7:00 and 24:00. Extension 8777.

美食店

美食店位于酒店西楼，是一家极好的外卖店。有三明治、面食、沙拉和各种甜点、巧克力。美食店是每次外出前购买随身食物的好地方。

夏宫餐厅

夏宫餐厅结合经典传统粤菜和创新淮扬美食，专注于历史悠久的中国茶文化以及法国波尔多葡萄酒。夏宫餐厅每日中午还推出品种多样的美味点心。六个独立雅间带给您私密专属服务。夏宫的众多中式茗茶及厨房调味品是馈赠亲朋的理想佳品。

大堂酒廊

大堂酒廊每晚都有古典音乐现场演奏，是商务洽谈、品茶和夜饮鸡尾酒的理想场所。星期天的下午茶伴有管弦乐演奏，让您享受美妙绝伦的自助餐的同时，沉醉在华丽的气氛之中。

送餐服务

从 7 点至 24 点，为您提供新鲜美味的中、西菜肴。分机 8777。

Vocabulary

specialty /ˈspeʃəlti/ *n.* 特色（菜）

exquisite /ɪkˈskwɪzɪt/ *adj.* 精致的

honorable /ˈɒnərəbl/ *adj.* 尊贵的；体面的

tantalizing /ˈtæntəlaɪzɪŋ/ *adj.* 诱人的

incomparable /ɪnˈkɒmprəbl/ *adj.* 无可比拟的

appetite /ˈæpɪtaɪt/ *n.* 胃口

backyard /ˌbækˈjɑːd/ *n.* 后院

diverse /daɪˈvɜːs/ *adj.* 各式各样的

dynamic /daɪˈnæmɪk/ *adj.* 有活力的

showcase /ˈʃəʊkeɪs/ *v.* 展示

gourmet /ˈɡʊəmeɪ/ *n.* 美食（家）

outlet /ˈaʊtlet/ *n.* 店口；商店

bite /baɪt/ *n.* （少量）食物

creative /kriˈeɪtɪv/ *adj.* 创新的

dim sum /ˌdɪm ˈsʌm/ *n.* 点心

premium /ˈpriːmiəm/ *adj.* 优质的

cocktail /ˈkɒkteɪl/ *n.* 鸡尾酒

splendor /ˈsplendə(r)/ *n.* 壮丽

orchestra /ˈɔːkɪstrə/ *n.* 管弦乐队

elegant /ˈelɪɡənt/ *adj.* 优雅的；典雅的

enjoyment /ɪnˈdʒɔɪmənt/ *n.* 享受

landscape /ˈlændskeɪp/ *n.* 风景

shortage /ˈʃɔːtɪdʒ/ *n.* 缺少

authentic /ɔːˈθentɪk/ *adj.* 纯真的；纯正的

à la carte /ə lɑː kɑːt/ *n.* （照菜单）零点

vernacular /vəˈnækjələ(r)/ *adj.* 民间风格的

spaghetti /spəˈɡeti/ *n.* 意面

incorporate /ɪnˈkɔːpəreɪt/ *v.* 合并组成

ingredient /ɪnˈɡriːdiənt/ *n.* 成分；原料；配料

takeaway /ˈteɪkəweɪ/ *n.* 外卖（食品）

confectionery /kənˈfekʃənəri/ *n.* 糕点；甜点

classic /ˈklæsɪk/ *adj.* 经典的

vintage /ˈvɪntɪdʒ/ *n.* 葡萄（酒）

personalized /ˈpɜːsənəlaɪzd/ *adj.* 个性化的

condiment /ˈkɒndɪmənt/ *n.* 调味品；佐料

sublime /səˈblaɪm/ *adj.* 美妙的

magnificent /mæɡˈnɪfɪsnt/ *adj.* 极好的

Useful Expressions

in charge of ... 负责……

on the go 忙碌地

place an emphasis on ... 专注于……

have a total of ... 总数达……

combine ... with ... 把……与……结合起来

词汇、课文资源

词汇、课文自测

微课

课堂练习

2.6 Conference and Recreation Services

2.6.1 Conference Services

The hotel has meeting rooms and multi-function rooms of various styles, furnished with pieces of advanced meeting equipment such as *portable* stage, multi-microphone system, *interpretation* facilities, LCD *projector*, slide projector, AV equipment, full-range lighting sets, *laser* beam pointer, and high-speed Internet access, which makes an ideal place to stage all types of events.

The Magnolia Hall, magnificent and elegant, covers an area of 500 square meters with no *pillars*, can serve up to 400 persons for a banquet, and makes an ideal choice for the superior meetings and banquets.

Orchid Room, full of *oriental charm*, covers an area of 153 square meters including an independent sitting room, and can serve up to 100 persons at maximum.

Peony Room, modern and *splendid*, covers an area of 45 square meters and can serve up to 16 persons for *board* meeting.

Lotus Room, full of oriental charm and fashion design, covers an area of 108 square meters and can serve up to 80 persons at maximum.

The *experienced* and *dedicated* convention team, together with *secretaries*, *interpreters*, and service *professionals*, will help make the event a success.

会议服务

酒店拥有多个风格各异的会议厅和多功能厅，先进的活动舞台、多重麦克风设备、口译设施、LCD投影仪、幻灯机、音响设备、全方位的照明设备、激光笔、高速网络接入等会议设施，一应俱全，是举办各类大型宴会的理想选择。

玉兰厅，富丽堂皇，方正大气，面积500平方米，无立柱，能同时容纳400人，是举办各类高端会议及宴会的理想选择。

兰花厅，东方典雅，有独立的会客区。面积153平方米，能容纳多至100人宴会或活动。

牡丹厅，时尚现代，面积45平方米，可容纳16人的董事会议。

莲花厅，富有东方气息，雍容雅致。面积108平方米，能容纳多至80人的会议或活动。

经验丰富和兢兢业业的会务组，以及秘书、口译和专业服务人员，将有助于活动取得圆满成功。

2.6.2　Recreation Services

The hotel has a number of recreational facilities like KTV *entertainment* center, beauty salon, chess room and spa, which let you enjoy your leisure time during your travel. The *boutique* sells a variety of high *quality* goods at low prices, including brand-name products, famous wines and cigarettes, *handicrafts*, souvenirs, and so on, which facilitates your travel or business activity.

Bar

In the bar, located on the west side of the second floor, you can sip tea or coffee while enjoying a good night view of the harbor. Open Hours: 19:00–2:00 (next day). Extension 8734.

KTV (*Karaoke*)

In the KTV rooms, located on the third floor, you can enjoy many kinds of *amusements* including excellent floor shows. Open Hours: 12:00–24:00.

Mahjong Room

24-hour *mahjong* room, located on the ground floor, is equipped with automatic mahjong machines.

Beauty Salon

On the southeast corner of the ground floor is a beauty salon, where experienced professionals will offer you a full set of service. Open Hours: 8:00–22:00. Extension 5566.

Sauna Center

Sauna Center, located in the basement, offers you a full set of service by professionals, including sauna, footbath, massage, etc. Open Hours: 8:00–22:00. Extension 6655.

康乐服务

酒店设 KTV 娱乐中心、美容美发、棋牌室、水疗馆等多个康乐设施，为您的旅途增添休闲时光。精品商店经营多种名牌商品、名烟名酒、工艺品、纪念品，这些商品质优价廉，品种繁多，为您的旅游和商务活动增添便利。

酒吧

在二楼左侧的酒吧里，您可以一边品尝茶或咖啡，一边欣赏港湾的夜景。营业时间：19:00—2:00（次日）。分机 8734。

KTV（卡拉 OK）

KTV 在三楼，在那里您可参与许多娱乐节目，包括精彩的歌舞表演。营业时间：12:00—24:00。

麻将室

麻将室在一楼，24 小时营业，配有自动麻将机。

美容厅

美容厅在一楼的东南角，有经验丰富的专业人员为您提供全套美容服务。营业时间：8:00—22:00。分机 5566。

桑拿中心

桑拿中心在地下室，有专业技师为您提供桑拿、足浴、按摩等全套服务。营业时间：8:00—22:00。分机 6655。

Boutique

Located on the ground floor, the boutique offers a great variety of quality goods, gifts, souvenirs, and *tobaccos* at reasonable prices. Open Hours: 8:00–22:00. Extension 5588.

精品商场

精品商场在一楼，有各种优质商品、礼品、纪念品和烟草等优价供应。营业时间：8:00—22:00。分机 5588。

Vocabulary

portable /ˈpɔːtəbl/ *adj.* 移动式的

projector /prəˈdʒektə(r)/ *n.* 投影灯

pillar /ˈpɪlə(r)/ *n.* 立柱

charm /tʃɑːm/ *n.* 魅力

board /bɔːd/ *n.* 董事会

dedicated /ˈdedɪkeɪtɪd/ *adj.* 兢兢业业的；专注的

secretary /ˈsekrətri/ *n.* 秘书

professional /prəˈfeʃənl/ *n.* 专业人士

boutique /buːˈtiːk/ *n.* 精品店

handicraft /ˈhændɪkrɑːft/ *n.* 手工艺品

amusement /əˈmjuːzmənt/ *n.* 娱乐（节目）

mahjong /mɑːˈdʒɒŋ/ *n.* 麻将

interpretation /ɪnˌtɜːprɪˈteɪʃn/ *n.* 口译

laser /ˈleɪzə(r)/ *n.* 激光；镭射

oriental /ˌɔːriˈentl/ *adj.* 东方的

splendid /ˈsplendɪd/ *adj.* 辉煌的；壮观的

experienced /ɪkˈspɪəriənst/ *adj.* 经验丰富的

interpreter /ɪnˈtɜːprɪtə(r)/ *n.* 口译人员

entertainment /ˌentəˈteɪnmənt/ *n.* 娱乐

quality /ˈkwɒləti/ *adj.* 优质的

karaoke /ˌkæriˈəʊki/ *n.* 卡拉 OK

tobacco /təˈbækəʊ/ *n.* 烟草

Useful Expressions

cover an area of ... 占地……

a full set of ... 一整套……

at maximum 至多

词汇、课文资源

词汇、课文自测

微课

课堂练习

Chapter Three

Hospitality Management
酒店管理

思政园地／二十
大精神学习专栏

Learning Objectives

· *To get familiar with all the five divisions of the hotel cost centers;*

· *To understand the management, functions, tasks, goals, and practices of each of the five divisions;*

· *To master the new words and professional terms concerned;*

· *To improve reading ability through learning the text;*

· *To develop team spirit and self-study ability through learning activities;*

· *To receive education in ideological and political theories through course learning.*

Teaching Arrangements

节次	教学内容	自主学习资源	自主学习自测	课堂教学视频	课堂练习
L 1	3.1 Hotel Management	词汇、课文资源	词汇、课文自测	微课	课堂练习
L 2	3.2 Hotel Human Resources Management	词汇、课文资源	词汇、课文自测	微课	课堂练习
L 3	3.3 Hotel Finance Management	词汇、课文资源	词汇、课文自测	微课	课堂练习
L 4	3.4 Hotel Engineering Management	词汇、课文资源	词汇、课文自测	微课	课堂练习
L 5	3.5 Hotel Security Management	词汇、课文资源	词汇、课文自测	微课	课堂练习
L 6	3.6 Hotel Marketing Management	词汇、课文资源	词汇、课文自测	微课	课堂练习

The traditional *definition* of management is *planning*, leadership, management, and control of personnel and resources to achieve the goals of a company or other organizations. The hospitality management provides planning, leadership, management skills, and control functions for the hotel. In general, it is a combination of *technical* skills such as communications technology, *interpersonal* skills, sales and marketing skills, finance and *accountancy* skills, and the very latest *practices* and *theories* in top hospitality management. So, the divisions with management function are mainly dealt with in this chapter.

管理的传统定义是策划、领导、管理与控制人员和资源，以完成公司或其他组织机构的目标。酒店管理就是在酒店发挥策划、领导、管理技巧和控制职能。一般说来，它是一种多技能的结合，包括交流技巧、人际沟通技巧、销售营销技巧、财务与会计技能，以及最新的酒店高层管理方面的实践与理论。本章主要讲解酒店的管理部门。

3.1　Hotel Management

Hotel managers work by guiding and *regularly* reporting on the general state of a hotel, and hold responsibility for the efficient and *profitable* operation of their establishments. They work within their own divisions and across all divisions, *supervise* the work of others, and ensure that all plans are carried out and all goals reached. Specifically, their duties include planning, organizing, *coordinating*, *staffing*, *directing*, controlling, and evaluating the hotel's procedures and personnel; their goals are mainly to return a profit to the owners and to ensure that the staff of all divisions *satisfies* guests' *expectation* by offering quality services.

酒店管理层负责指导和定期汇报酒店的总体情况，并负责各自部门的高效、盈利化运营。他们的工作涉及自己的部门和其他所有部门，对他人的工作进行指导，以确保所有的计划和目标都能够完成。具体地说，他们的职责就是策划、组织、协调、人事、指导、控制以及评估酒店的程序和人事；他们的目标主要是向业主返利和确保各部门的员工都提供优质服务，满足宾客的期望。

The executive manager in a hotel can be called by different names as general manager,

酒店的行政经理有各种称谓，如总经理、总裁或驻店经理等。他／

managing director, or *resident* manager. He / She directs hotel operations by planning and leading other departments, which should meet owners', employees', and guests' needs. The general manager controls the affairs including finance, establishment of service *norms*, housekeeping, food quality, *interior decor*, etc. Assistant managers supervise the day-to-day operations of all divisions. Resident managers, in some large hotels, *resolve* problems round the clock. A manager-on-duty often *assumes* overall *managerial* responsibility when both the general manager and resident managers are *off-site*.

In a small hotel, the executive manager may be the owner or *co-owner*. In a larger hotel, he / she may be a professional *hotelier*. An executive manager, in charge of a complicated business with many divisions, should know sales and *promotion*, accounting, tax and business law, and public relations in addition to the common services and functions offered by the hotel itself. He / She may be called in to lead in a situation that lower-level managers cannot handle at any time.

In seeing that all the activities of a hotel run *smoothly* and efficiently, the general manager carries out routine spot checks of different aspects of the hotel, often on a daily basis, and deals with unusual problems whenever they occur. In a large *complex* operation that directly deals with the public, there are hundreds of problems that range from the *comic* to the *tragic*. In a large hotel, the general manager coordinates the work of those division managers who supervise housekeeping, advertising

她通过策划和领导其他部门来指导酒店的运营，以满足业主、员工和宾客的需求。总经理主管财务、建立员工服务规范、房务、食品质量及内设等事务。副经理监督各部门的日常运作。大型酒店有驻店经理全天候处理各种问题。如果总经理和驻店经理都不在，值班经理通常要承担起所有的管理职责。

在小型酒店内，行政经理可能由业主或合伙人担任。在较大的酒店里，可能是一名专业的酒店经理人。行政经理掌管着由许多部门组成的复杂企业，除酒店本身的各项业务和功能，还必须懂销售与推广、会计、税法与商法及公共关系等。任何时候，如果出现下级经理无法解决的情况时，就会请行政经理前来领导局势。

为了确保酒店一切工作顺利有效地进行，总经理通常每天都对酒店内的各方面工作做例行现场检查，处理一些突发的特殊问题。在工作繁复又是直接与公众打交道的大型酒店，总会出现许多令人高兴或令人沮丧的问题。在大型酒店，总经理协调各部门负责人的工作。他们分管客房服务、广告宣传、食品供应和其他业务。他 / 她同各部

and promotion, food services, and the rest of the operation. His / Her working relationship with these people *contributes significantly* to the smooth functioning of the hotel.

In big hotels, each division operates by itself, but they are all linked to each other *tightly*. The division managers work under the supervision and *guidance* of the top management. They work hard to make their own departments function well. So, to take a department head seat, one must understand the functions, goals, and practices of the department completely.

The way to *attain* the *position* of manager is through education and experience. In earlier times, experience alone, in as many departments of a hotel as possible, was considered the *appropriate background*. Today, however, two main reasons for many people going into the hotel management are *career opportunities* and *advancement*. If they keep learning and working hard, they can advance quickly. For example, a front office manager may move up to be a general manager. If the hotel belongs to a chain, then another step up would be a *regional* manager, which might be followed by a vice *president* or a corporate level job. At each step up, salary and benefits increase but so does *pressure* and responsibility.

门负责人的工作关系对于酒店业务能否顺利开展关系重大。

在大型酒店里，各个部门虽然独立运作，但紧密关联。各部门经理的工作要接受高管的监督与指导。他们的工作就是努力使自己的部门良好地运行。想坐部门经理的位子，就必须完全懂得该特定部门的职能、目标及工作方式。

获得经理职位的途径是凭借知识和经验。以前，只有具有酒店内尽可能多部门的经验被视为特定的背景条件。然而现如今，事业机会与晋升是很多人踏入酒店管理层的两个主要原因。他们如果坚持学习且努力工作，就会很快获得晋升。例如，前厅部经理可能会被提升为总经理。如果酒店是连锁的，那么下一步就可能是区域经理，随后就可能是副总裁或集团总部级别的职位。随着每一级的提升，薪水和福利就会增加，但压力和责任也会更大。

Vocabulary

definition /ˌdefɪˈnɪʃn/ *n.* 定义

technical /ˈteknɪkl/ *adj.* 技术的

interpersonal /ˌɪntəˈpɜːsənl/ *adj.* 人际关系的；人与人之间的

accountancy /əˈkaʊntənsi/ *n.* 会计工作

theory /ˈθɪəri/ *n.* 理论

profitable /ˈprɒfɪtəbl/ *adj.* 有利可图的；有益的

supervise /ˈsuːpəvaɪz/ *v.* 指导

staff /stɑːf/ *v.* 员工安排；配置员工

satisfy /ˈsætɪsfaɪ/ *v.* 使满足

resident /ˈrezɪdənt/ *adj.* 常住的

interior /ɪnˈtɪəriə(r)/ *adj.* 内部的

resolve /rɪˈzɒlv/ *v.* 解决

managerial /ˌmænəˈdʒɪəriəl/ *adj.* 管理的

co-owner /ˈkəʊ ˈəʊnə(r)/ *n.* 共同所有者

promotion /prəˈməʊʃn/ *n.* 推广

complex /ˈkɒmpleks/ *adj.* 复杂的

tragic /ˈtrædʒɪk/ *adj.* 悲剧的

significantly /sɪɡˈnɪfɪkəntli/ *adv.* 意义深远地；重大地

tightly /ˈtaɪtli/ *adv.* 紧密地

attain /əˈteɪn/ *v.* 获得

appropriate /əˈprəʊpriət/ *adj.* 相称的

career /kəˈrɪə(r)/ *n.* 职业；生涯

advancement /ədˈvɑːnsmənt/ *n.* 晋升

president /ˈprezɪdənt/ *n.* 总裁

planning /ˈplænɪŋ/ *n.*（制订）规划

practice /ˈpræktɪs/ *n.* 做法

regularly /ˈreɡjələli/ *adv.* 有规律地；定期地

coordinate /kəʊˈɔːdɪneɪt/ *v.* 协调；一致

direct /dəˈrekt/ *v.* 指导

expectation /ˌekspekˈteɪʃn/ *n.* 期望

norm /nɔːm/ *n.* 规范；标准

decor /ˈdeɪkɔː(r)/ *n.* 陈设；布置

assume /əˈsjuːm/ *v.* 承担

off-site /ˈɒf ˈsaɪt/ *adj.* 不在现场的

hotelier /həʊˈteliə(r)/ *n.* 旅馆经营者

smoothly /ˈsmuːðli/ *adv.* 顺利地；平稳地

comic /ˈkɒmɪk/ *adj.* 喜剧的

contribute /kənˈtrɪbjuːt/ *v.* 贡献

guidance /ˈɡaɪdns/ *n.* 指导

position /pəˈzɪʃn/ *n.* 职位

background /ˈbækɡraʊnd/ *n.* 背景

opportunity /ˌɒpəˈtjuːnəti/ *n.* 机会

regional /ˈriːdʒənl/ *adj.* 区域的

pressure /ˈpreʃə(r)/ *n.* 压力

Useful Expressions

hold responsibility for ... 对……负责　　round the clock 夜以继日地

see that ... 务必……；确保……　　on a ... basis 以……为基础

deal with ... 处理……　　range from ... to ... 从……到……的范围内变化

be linked to ... 与……关联　　under the supervision of ... 在……监督下

belong to ... 属于……

词汇、课文资源　　词汇、课文自测　　微课　　课堂练习

3.2　Hotel Human Resources Management

A hotel is a service enterprise, in which the staff directly deals with guests during their participation in offering various service products. An increasing number of guests desire to be provided with *considerate*, *humane*, and *customized* services. So, the human resources management should be laid on as a special emphasis in hotels. The human resources division *exercises* its administrative function under the leadership of the HR manager. The division works by making plans of human resources, recruiting and hiring employees, training and developing human resources, and establishing the hotel's perfect *performance appraisal* system, salary system, and *benefits* system. The human resources division is one of the most important divisions of any hotel. A good HR division can help a hotel meet guests' expectations by putting the right people in the right jobs. So, it can be said that proper

酒店是提供服务产品的企业，员工参与服务生产过程，向宾客提供面对面的服务。越来越多的宾客需要体贴入微、富有人情味和个性化的服务。所以酒店应特别重视人力资源的管理。人力资源部在人力资源经理的领导下行使其管理职能，其内容包括制订人力资源计划，招聘和录用员工，加强人力资源的培训和开发，建立完善的绩效考评、薪酬和福利体系。人力资源部是任何一个酒店里最重要的部门之一。出色的人力资源部能够通过选择合适的人员担任合适的工作来帮助酒店满足宾客的期望。所以，可以这么说，酒店经营好坏的区别在于是否有高效的人力资源管理。

human resources management can be used to tell a well-run hotel from a poorly-run one.

There are several different areas in which human resources management is very important. One of these areas is for newly-hired employees. Employees can really *alter* the quality of service and the whole atmosphere of a hotel. It is the job of the HR manager to ensure that good people are chosen and those people who do want to work and meet the post requirements are employed. In a business where *courtesy* is one of the major services, the *personality*, experience, and expertise of every employee in a hotel are a matter of importance. The *references* given by job *applicants* must be carefully checked, and a *watchful* eye must be kept on their performance after they have been hired.

Another big question for the HR management is the *retention* of employees. That is because many hotel employees do not have hotel work as their ending career goals, and also because some other employees may have to be *dismissed* due to poor work *ethics* or other *issues*. Managers should provide good training and *incentive programs* to cause employees to work longer. A clear *progression* plan to advance to higher levels can also be a good incentive for employees to *stick* around.

The importance of the HR management in a hotel also lies in the area of employee services. If the employees know they can come to the HR manager whenever they have a problem or issue, then it is easier for them to work in good *conscience*. Many services, such as *babysitting*, or park day every

有几个方面可以体现出人力资源管理的重要性，其中之一就是新聘员工。酒店员工可以真正改变服务质量和酒店整体氛围。人力资源部经理的工作就是选择优秀的员工，即选择那些真正想干而又适合岗位的员工。在这个十分讲究举止礼貌的服务行业，每个酒店职工的人品、经验和专门知识都至关重要。对于求职者自报的情况必须仔细加以核实，职工录用后必须严格考察其工作表现。

人力资源管理的另一大职责就是留住员工。那是因为有很多员工并不想终身从事酒店职业，又因为有些员工会因为职业道德或其他问题而不得不被解雇。经理们应当给员工提供良好的培训，制定激励措施，让员工能够在酒店长期工作。一个明确的晋升发展计划也能使员工愿意在酒店长期工作。

服务员工也是酒店人力资源管理的一个重要方面。如果员工知道他们有事就能找人力资源经理，他们就更容易用心工作。人力资源部经理可以用很多服务来鼓舞员工，例如提供保姆服务或每年举办一次

year, can be used by an HR Manager to *inspire* and *encourage* employees. Little services make happy employees. And happy employees make happy hotels and happy customers.

The employee progression and promotion is another important area for the hotel industry. What is very important to the retention of employees is that the hotel should provide ways for employees to advance, and provide training for them to gain skills necessary for advancement. It is very easy for a hotel to *implement* such services, and the expense in doing so is *negligible compared* to that necessary for constantly finding new employees.

In order to maintain the standards of the establishment, *in-house* training programs, either formal or informal, are customary in large hotels. Training usually falls into two parts. One is about the organization; the other is about the specific post-based skills. Generally, the training process consists of four main steps. First is to prepare for training by working out training *objectives* and lesson plans, deciding training methods, and arranging time, place, and materials. Second is to *conduct* the training by getting the *trainers* and the *trainees* at one place at the same time. Third is to *measure* the effect of training by giving a post test. Fourth is to give *feedback* to the trainees, to give *on-the-job coaching*, and to make *progress evaluation*.

In brief, according to Rocco M. Angelo and Andrew N. Vladimir, a *sound* human resources program typically *contains* caring about employees, *defining* the job, establishing *productivity* standards,

公园日活动。细微的服务能够让员工感到快乐，而幸福快乐的员工又能够使酒店满意宾客开心。

酒店业另一大问题就是员工的发展和晋升。为了挽留员工，酒店应为员工提供职位晋升的通道，以及提供培训以帮助其获得职位晋升所需的必要技能，这是非常重要的。推行这样的服务是很容易的，且比起不断寻找新员工所花费的费用来说，其费用是微不足道的。

为了保持酒店的服务水平，大型酒店通常都不断举办正规的或非正规的店内职工培训。培训通常分两方面：一是有关公司的培训；二是特定的岗位技能培训。培训过程一般分四步：第一，培训准备，制订培训目标和课程计划，确定培训方法，安排培训时间、地点和材料；第二，开展培训，把培训师与学员集中起来，在同一时间和地点实施培训；第三，通过课后测试衡量培训效果；第四，向学员提供反馈，进行在职辅导和进展评估。

简单来讲，根据罗科·M. 安吉洛和安德鲁·N. 弗拉基米尔的理论，一个优秀的人力资源计划通常包括关心员工，明确工作内容，建立工

recruiting suitable *candidates*, selecting the best applicants, implementing *continual* training and career development programs, motivating and retaining employees, offering competitive benefits, and evaluating employees.

作效率标准，招聘合适者，选择最佳应聘者，持续实施培训和职业发展规划，激励和留住员工，提供具有竞争力的福利，以及评估员工。

Vocabulary

considerate /kənˈsɪdərət/ *adj.* 考虑周到的

customize /ˈkʌstəmaɪz/ *v.* 使个性化

performance /pəˈfɔːməns/ *n.* 绩效

benefit /ˈbenɪfɪt/ *n.* 奖金；福利

courtesy /ˈkɜːtəsi/ *n.* 举止礼貌

reference /ˈrefrəns/ *n.* 提及的事情

watchful /ˈwɒtʃfl/ *adj.* 警惕的；注意的

dismiss /dɪsˈmɪs/ *v.* 开除

issue /ˈɪʃuː/ *n.* 问题

program /ˈprəʊɡræm/ *n.* 方案；措施

stick /stɪk/ *v.* 坚持；固守

babysitting /ˈbeɪbisɪtɪŋ/ *n.* 当临时保姆

encourage /ɪnˈkʌrɪdʒ/ *v.* 鼓励

negligible /ˈneɡlɪdʒəbl/ *adj.* 可以忽略的；微不足道的

compare /kəmˈpeə(r)/ *v.* 比较

objective /əbˈdʒektɪv/ *n.* 目标

trainer /ˈtreɪnə(r)/ *n.* 培训师

measure /ˈmeʒə(r)/ *v.* 测量

on-the-job /ˈɒn ðə ˈdʒɒb/ *adj.* 在职的

progress /ˈprəʊɡres/ *n.* 进步；进展

sound /saʊnd/ *adj.* 充分的；完好的

define /dɪˈfaɪn/ *v.* 明确

humane /hjuːˈmeɪn/ *adj.* 有人情味的

exercise /ˈeksəsaɪz/ *v.* 行使

appraisal /əˈpreɪzl/ *n.* 评估

alter /ˈɔːltə(r)/ *v.* 改变

personality /ˌpɜːsəˈnæləti/ *n.* 人品；个性

applicant /ˈæplɪkənt/ *n.* 申请人

retention /rɪˈtenʃn/ *n.* 留住

ethic /ˈeθɪk/ *n.*（职业）道德规范

incentive /ɪnˈsentɪv/ *n.* 激励

progression /prəˈɡreʃn/ *n.* 发展；晋升

conscience /ˈkɒnʃəns/ *n.* 凭良心

inspire /ɪnˈspaɪə(r)/ *v.* 鼓舞

implement /ˈɪmplɪment/ *v.* 执行；推行

in-house /ˌɪn ˈhaʊs/ *adj.* 机构内部的

conduct /kənˈdʌkt/ *v.* 实施；开展

trainee /ˌtreɪˈniː/ *n.* 学员；实习生

feedback /ˈfiːdbæk/ *n.* 反馈

coaching /ˈkəʊtʃɪŋ/ *n.* 训练；辅导

evaluation /ɪˌvæljuˈeɪʃn/ *n.* 评估

contain /kənˈteɪn/ *v.* 包含

productivity /ˌprɒdʌkˈtɪvəti/ *n.* 生产效率

candidate /ˈkændɪdət/ *n.* 求职者

continual /kənˈtɪnjuəl/ *adj.* 连续的

Useful Expressions

tell ... from ... 把……与……区分开来

stick around 继续留职

give feedback to ... 向……反馈

care about ... 关心……

keep a watchful eye on ... 严格考察……

in good conscience 凭良心地

in brief 简单来说

词汇、课文资源

词汇、课文自测

微课

课堂练习

3.3　Hotel Finance Management

The hotel finance management is carried out by the finance division. It involves the *financing* management, investment management, cost control, revenue management, and profit *distribution* management. The finance division operates with the chief *financial* officer (CFO) at the top, *accountants* and *bookkeepers* at the mid-level, and cashiers in all operating departments. The CFO is able to give managers advice on how to increase profits and *smooth* out cash *flow*, to provide *options* with which managers solve *current* specific financial problems, and to offer managers financial data on which to make decisions. The accountants and bookkeepers are responsible for entering, posting, keeping, and checking. The cashiers work directly with guests for bill payment.

酒店财务管理由财务部负责实施。其内容包括酒店筹资管理、投资管理、成本控制、营收管理及利润分配管理。财务部门的运作由财务总监负责，中间层是会计师和记账人员，还有各营业部门的出纳员。财务总监能够建议经理如何提高利润和缓和现金流，为经理们提供解决当前特定财务问题的方案，并为其提供财务数据供决策参考。会计记账员负责入账、过账、记账和审账等。出纳员直接面对宾客为他们结算账单。

The finance division, one of the most important divisions of the hotel management, is responsible for all the financial transactions of a hotel, including *issuing invoices*, collecting bills, paying expenses, and preparing managerial accounting information for staff managers and financial accounting information for tax and government agencies.

Issuing and collecting are key functions of the finance division. Accounts *receivable* is prepared daily, weekly, monthly, and often *quarterly*. An invoice or bill is issued telling the guest what he / she has to pay the hotel, and then the guest is given a receipt upon paying the bill.

Paying bills and expenses is another big part of the monthly and weekly *cycle* of hotels. A good record of Accounts Payable is an important tool in cash flow management for hotel managers. A lot of money comes in and goes out every month, so to manage the balance is of *critical* importance to *profitability*.

In addition, the finance team provides financial accounting reports to tax bureaus and government agencies, which are also key in generating budgets, and bringing budget *estimates* into line with actual market prices and conditions. This helps the hotel with purchasing and cost estimates for each department.

According to Angelo and Vladimir, the responsibilities of the accounting division include *forecasting* and budgeting; managing what the hotel owns and what money is due from guests; controlling cash; controlling costs in all areas of the

财务部是酒店管理最重要的部门之一，主要负责酒店所有的财务事项，如开具发票、收取账款、支付费用，以及准备人事经理所需的管理会计信息和税务及其他政府机构所需的财务会计信息。

开具账单和收账是财务部的主要职责。应收账款每天、每周、每月、每季度（通常）要做一次。发票或账单的开出通知宾客应付款额，然后在宾客付账后开具收据。

支付账单和费用是酒店每月或每周工作的另一大部分。记录好的应付款是酒店经理用于现金流量管理的重要工具。酒店每个月都有大量的钱进出，所以控制平衡对于酒店的盈利而言至关重要。

另外，财务人员要向税务机关和政府部门提交财务报表。对于做预算并使之符合实际的市场价格和情况而言，这些报表同样非常重要。这有助于酒店各个部门的采购和成本估算。

根据安吉洛和弗拉基米尔，会计部门的职责包括财务预报预算；管理酒店资产和宾客服务收入；控制现金流；控制酒店各部门的成本；如食品饮料、客房用品和家具

hotel; purchasing, receiving, storing, and issuing operating and capital *inventory* such as foods and beverages, housekeeping supplies, and *furniture*; and keeping records, preparing financial statements and daily operating reports, and *interpreting* these statements and reports for management.

Hotel's accounting has many *distinctive* features because guests' bills must be kept up-to-date. 1) All charges that a guest *incurs* must be entered, or posted on his or her account as soon as possible. In addition to the charge for the guest's room, there may also be charges resulting from the use of the telephone, the laundry service, the restaurant, and room service. 2) All the charges must also be entered on other *ledgers* or financial records. In many hotels, these *postings* are done by *computerized* accounting machines, but in smaller operations, they are still done by hand. 3) All the financial transactions not only must be posted, but also must be checked for *accuracy*. This is usually the job of a night auditor, who goes through this mass of figures on the night *shift*, when there is little activity in the hotel.

等的采购、收货、储存并填报经营和资本存量表；记录账簿，准备财务报表和营业日报，并向管理层解释报表。

酒店的会计工作有许多特点，因为顾客的账单必须及时结算。1) 顾客应付的各项费用必须尽快记入或过入其账户，其中除顾客的房费，可能还有电话费、洗熨费、用餐费和房内服务费等。2) 须将所有费用另行记入分类账或其他账务账簿。许多酒店的这些过账工作是由电脑控制的记账机来完成的；但在较小的酒店，过账工作仍须靠人来做。3) 各项财务收支不仅必须过账，而且必须审核，以求准确无误。这项工作通常由夜班审计员完成。他在夜班，利用酒店工作清闲的机会来审核这大批的数字。

Vocabulary

finance /ˈfaɪnæns/ *v.* 融资；提供资金

financial /faɪˈnænʃl/ *adj.* 财务的

bookkeeper /ˈbʊkiːpə(r)/ *n.* 记账员

smooth /smuːð/ *v.* 消除（问题）；克服（困难）

distribution /ˌdɪstrɪˈbjuːʃn/ *n.* 分配

accountant /əˈkaʊntənt/ *n.* 会计人员

flow /fləʊ/ n. 流；持续供应

current /ˈkʌrənt/ adj. 当前的

invoice /ˈɪnvɔɪs/ n. 发票

quarterly /ˈkwɔːtəli/ adv. 按季度地

critical /ˈkrɪtɪkl/ adj. 关键的；紧要的

estimate /ˈestɪmeɪt/ n. 估算

inventory /ˈɪnvəntri/ n. 库存；存量表

interpret /ɪnˈtɜːprət/ v. 解释

distinctive /dɪˈstɪŋktɪv/ adj. 独特的；与众不同的

incur /ɪnˈkɜː(r)/ v. 引致；带来

posting /ˈpəʊstɪŋ/ n. 过账

computerize /kəmˈpjuːtəraɪz/ v. 使计算机化

accuracy /ˈækjərəsi/ n. 准确性；精准度

option /ˈɒpʃn/ n. 可供选择的方案

issue /ˈɪʃuː/ v. 开具（发票）

receivable /rɪˈsiːvəbl/ adj. 应收的

cycle /ˈsaɪkl/ n. 循环；周期

profitability /ˌprɒfɪtəˈbɪləti/ n. 盈利能力

forecast /ˈfɔːkɑːst/ v. 预测；预报

furniture /ˈfɜːnɪtʃə(r)/ n. 家具

ledger /ˈledʒə(r)/ n. 分类账

shift /ʃɪft/ n. 轮班；班次

Useful Expressions

smooth out ... 缓和……

bring ... into line with ... 使……与……相符

be key in doing sth. 对做某事很重要

result from ... 缘于……

词汇、课文资源

词汇、课文自测

微课

课堂练习

3.4 Hotel Engineering Management

Two *supports* are a must for a hotel to provide quality services. One is the hardware, and the other is the software. The hotel's hardware mainly refers to the equipment and facilities. The *scientific* management of facilities has a direct impact on the hotel's revenue, as well as the hotel's service quality. According to Angelo and Vladimir, the physical

　　酒店要提供优质服务，就必须有硬件和软件两方面的支持。酒店的硬件主要是指酒店的设备设施。做好酒店设备的科学管理，直接关系到酒店的服务质量和经济效益。根据安吉洛和弗拉基米尔，对建筑物、家具、固定物件和设备进行物

upkeep of the building, furniture, *fixtures*, and equipment is *essential* to slowing a hotel's physical *deterioration*, *preserving* the *original* hotel *image*, keeping revenue-producing areas operational, keeping the property comfortable for guests and employees, preserving the safety of the property for guests and employees, and creating *savings* by keeping repairs and equipment *replacements* to a *minimum*.

The engineering division is in charge of the management of facilities. Therefore, the hotel engineering management is just that of facilities. The hotel's facilities can be *classified* by system into power, water, heating, *refrigeration*, air *conditioning*, communications, audio, *elevators*, and fire *alarm*. The hotel engineering management includes equipment-*asset* management, equipment operation and maintenance, and energy management.

A hotel is a *plant encompassing* a *myriad* of facilities and services, and it is *imperative* that all those *elements* work smoothly to ensure that the guests have a comfortable and safe stay. Although hidden behind the scenes, a hotel's engineering division performs an *invaluable* role in the *equation*. The responsibility of such a division is to maintain the hotel building and its assets, from walls, *ceiling*, fixtures, *electrical* distribution to the hotel's *sewage* and water system, fire-alarm system, air conditioning, heating and ventilation, elevator, kitchen and laundry equipment, sound and *lighting* system, and so on.

The engineering division has categorized their

理维护保养的重要性在于，减缓酒店的自然损耗折旧，保持原本的酒店形象，保持各营收部门正常运营，保证酒店客人与员工获得舒适感，保证客人与员工的财产安全，以及把维修与设备更换的开支降到最低。

酒店设备设施的管理由工程部负责，因此酒店的工程管理就是酒店设备管理。酒店的设备按系统可分为供电、供水、供热、制冷、空调、通信、音响、电梯、消防报警等。酒店工程管理的内容主要有设备资产管理、设备的使用与维护以及酒店的能源管理。

酒店是一座拥有大量设施和服务的工厂，所有这些设施都必须运转正常，以保证宾客住得舒适安全。酒店的工程部虽然隐藏在幕后，但同样起着不可估量的作用。酒店工程部的职责是酒店大楼所有资产的维护，包括墙壁、天花板、固定器具、配电系统、给排水系统、消防报警系统、空调、暖气和通风、电梯、厨房和洗衣设备、音响和灯光系统等。

工程部的工作分为两类：预防

work in two ways: *preventive* maintenance and *scheduled* maintenance. In preventive maintenance, the division sees to the security and safety from any electrical *leaks* and fires, timely inspection of the *machinery*, and *periodically* shutting down guestroom *blocks* and other areas for *refurbishment* in the purpose of ensuring that all guestroom areas and the *utilities* operate properly. With scheduled maintenance, the division sees to servicing wall paintings, air conditioning plants and *boiler* rooms.

The engineering division performs scheduled maintenance work and is on-call to take care of urgent problems. The scheduled maintenance refers to the *servicing* and landscaping of all the equipment. Special *projects* include adding new equipment or repairing existing equipment for special events, adding more rooms, *redecorating* rooms, or installing new equipment. All these require the *oversight* of the engineering division, even though they may not do all the work themselves.

The chief engineer *oversees* the work of the engineering staff. They should make sure that routine checks are done every day and that they walk through the entire hotel premises on regular basis for inspection and attention and keep good records. They should also be on call 24 hours of the day. In case of any repair or maintenance, the chief engineer is expected to be informed by the heads of other divisions.

The *existence* of the hotel depends on the engineering division. The staff of the said division works *unnoticed* on *strenuous* and *tiring* jobs

性维护和定期维修。在预防性维修时，工程部负责排查电器泄漏和火灾隐患，及时检查机械，定期对客房及其他地方进行关停整修，以确保所有的客房区与公共设施的正常运行。在定期维修时，要对墙壁画、空调设备和锅炉房进行检修。

工程部按照日程安排表开展维修工作，同时也随时待命解决紧急问题。日常维护指的是对各种装置设备的维护及美化。特殊项目包括为举办特殊活动而添加新设备或对酒店已有设备进行修缮，也有可能是增加房间、重新布置房间或安装新的设备。这一切都需要他们监督管理，尽管并不一定要他们亲自完成所有工作。

总工程师负责监督工程人员的工作。每天要做例行检查，定期巡查整个酒店大楼，并做好记录。他们必须做到24小时随时待命。如需修理或维护，酒店其他部门的主管应当告知总工程师。

酒店的存在有赖于工程部门。该部门的员工所干的活艰苦而劳累，且不为人所知，为的是确保宾

to ensure that the guest could stay comfortably without any *mishap* or *misadventure*. The staff of the engineering division should be *commended* for their *commitment*, and their work *appreciated*. The beauty and comfort of the hotel is entirely due to their *untiring* efforts.

客能够住得舒适，免遭意外与不幸。工程部员工的奉献应该受到表扬，他们的工作应该得到赞赏。酒店的美丽舒适全靠他们的不懈努力。

Vocabulary

support /səˈpɔːt/ *n.* 支持

upkeep /ˈʌpkiːp/ *n.* 维护；保养

essential /ɪˈsenʃl/ *adj.* 重要的

preserve /prɪˈzɜːv/ *v.* 保持

image /ˈɪmɪdʒ/ *n.* 形象

replacement /rɪˈpleɪsmənt/ *n.* 更换

classify /ˈklæsɪfaɪ/ *v.* 分类；归类

condition /kənˈdɪʃn/ *v.* 调节

alarm /əˈlɑːm/ *n.* 警报

plant /plɑːnt/ *n.* 工厂

myriad /ˈmɪriəd/ *n.* 极大数量

element /ˈelɪmənt/ *n.* 要素

invaluable /ɪnˈvæljuəbl/ *adj.* 无价的；非常珍贵的

equation /ɪˈkweɪʒn/ *n.* 相等

electrical /ɪˈlektrɪkl/ *adj.* 电的

lighting /ˈlaɪtɪŋ/ *n.* 照明

scheduled /ˈʃedjuːl/ *adj.* 预定的；预先安排的

leak /liːk/ *n.* 泄漏

periodically /ˌpɪəriˈɒdɪkli/ *adv.* 定期地

refurbishment /ˌriːˈfɜːbɪʃmənt/ *n.* 整修

scientific /ˌsaɪənˈtɪfɪk/ *adj.* 科学的

fixture /ˈfɪkstʃə(r)/ *n.* 固定物

deterioration /dɪˌtɪəriəˈreɪʃn/ *n.* 折旧

original /əˈrɪdʒənl/ *adj.* 原有的

saving /ˈseɪvɪŋ/ *n.* 节省开支

minimum /ˈmɪnɪməm/ *n.* 最小量

refrigeration /rɪˌfrɪdʒəˈreɪʃn/ *n.* 制冷

elevator /ˈelɪveɪtə(r)/ *n.* 电梯

asset /ˈæset/ *n.* 资产

encompass /ɪnˈkʌmpəs/ *v.* 包含

imperative /ɪmˈperətɪv/ *adj.* 必需的；必要的

ceiling /ˈsiːlɪŋ/ *n.* 天花板

sewage /ˈsuːɪdʒ/ *n.* 污水

preventive /prɪˈventɪv/ *adj.* 预防的

machinery /məˈʃiːnəri/ *n.* 机械（总称）

block /blɒk/ *n.* 区；区域

utility /juːˈtɪləti/ *n.* 公共设施

boiler /ˈbɔɪlə(r)/ *n.* 锅炉房	service /ˈsɜ:vɪs/ *v.* 维护
project /ˈprɒdʒekt/ *n.* 项目	redecorate /ˌriːˈdekəreɪt/ *v.* 重新装饰
oversight /ˈəʊvəsaɪt/ *n.* 监管	oversee /ˌəʊvəˈsi:/ *v.* 监管
existence /ɪɡˈzɪstəns/ *n.* 存在	unnoticed /ˌʌnˈnəʊtɪst/ *adj.* 不为人所知的
strenuous /ˈstrenjuəs/ *adj.* 费力的，艰苦的	
tiring /ˈtaɪərɪŋ/ *adj.* 累人的；令人疲劳的	
mishap /ˈmɪshæp/ *n.* 意外；不幸	misadventure /ˌmɪsədˈventʃə(r)/ *n.* 不幸；灾难
commend /kəˈmend/ *v.* 嘉奖	commitment /kəˈmɪtmənt/ *n.* 奉献
appreciate /əˈpriːʃɪeɪt/ *v.* 欣赏	untiring /ʌnˈtaɪərɪŋ/ *adj.* 不懈的；不知疲倦的

Useful Expressions

have an impact on ... 对……有影响	keep ... to a minimum 保持……最低
a myriad of 大量的	behind the scenes 在幕后
perform a ... role in ... 在……中起……作用	in the equation 同样地
see to ... 负责……	be on-call to do sth. 待命做某事
be expected to do sth. 应当做某事	be commended for ... 因……而受表扬

词汇、课文资源

词汇、课文自测

微课

课堂练习

3.5 Hotel Security Management

The hotel security management is carried out by the security division. The head of the security division supervises the security staff performing their duties and reports to the on-duty manager or the general manager. The security division ensures the safety and security of guests, staff, and property in the hotel. The job of the security division is to *reduce threats* by keeping *unwelcome* individuals

　　酒店的安全管理工作由安保部承担。安保部经理监督安保人员的工作并向当班经理或总经理汇报。安保部的职责是确保酒店内宾客、员工以及财产的安全。安保部的工作主要是禁止不受欢迎的人入内以减少威胁，以及在发生事故时抓住肇事者。安保人员常用的方法是对

from entering, and to ensure that the one responsible for a problem is caught when it occurs. The security personnel can usually *patrol* the property regularly and keep the hotel premises under *surveillance* by video camera. The security personnel in hotels are mostly off-duty policemen, former army personnel, or those who have gone through security training programs. A *qualified* security worker should be a person who has *obtained* the *certification* through training in crime *prevention*, personal *combat*, and crime *detection*.

Most of the illegal activities or crimes in a hotel are *theft*, *robbery*, *rape*, prostitution, gambling, or *murder*. The security or other personnel must be able to recognize these *criminal* activities and stop them from happening on the grounds of the hotel. Big crimes in hotels mostly come from external threats. Recently, more emphasis has been laid on the detection and prevention of *terrorism*, so security personnel should be familiar with common *terrorist* threats and methods. There are also some other threats coming from nature, like fires, *earthquakes*, and *floods*. In general, all response procedures for those possible threats should be made known to all personnel in the hotel. For example, the front desk *clerks* should know who has keys; *suspicious* people should be reported and watched; and *emergency* exits should be *cleared*.

Two things are to be done in order to ensure the safety and security of guests and their *belongings*. One is to ensure all the personnel are *vigilant*. *Non-residents* cannot be served *alcohol* outside

酒店财产进行定时巡查或通过录像进行监控。安保人员通常由退伍警察、退伍军人或接受过安保培训的人员组成。一个称职的安保人员应当经过预防犯罪、个人搏击及犯罪侦察等培训，持证上岗。

酒店内的违法或犯罪活动大多数是偷盗、抢劫、强奸、卖淫、赌博或谋杀等。安保人员和酒店其他人员必须能够识别这些犯罪活动，并制止其在酒店范围内发生。酒店内发生的大型犯罪大多数是来自外部的威胁。最近，人们更加重视恐怖活动的侦查和防范，安保人员要熟悉常见的恐怖威胁行为和方式。其他还有一些来自自然的威胁，如火灾、地震和水灾等。一般而言，所有的酒店工作人员都应了解所有关于这些可能威胁的应对程序。例如，前台职员要知道钥匙在谁手里，遇可疑人员要报告并实行监视，紧急通道要保持畅通。

为保证宾客的人身和财产安全，必须做好以下两件事：第一，确保全体员工具有高度的警惕性。例如，在规定时间之外（地方性法

of licensing hours (local laws do apply). *Conflicts* might be caused due to someone drinking too much. The hotel staff can refuse to serve alcohol to anyone who is either *intoxicated* or under age. It is the bar staff's duty to stop any *unruly*, *offensive*, or *drunken behavior*, and it is a good habit for them not to serve alcohol without checking a person's hotel registration card or key card. *Diplomacy* is often used by the hotel security staff in dealing with these individuals. They can ask him / her if he / she is a resident, and for his / her name in a *calming* voice. The other is to ensure that the hotel has basic security requirements. It is suggested that the hotel should install CCTV systems, access control, *perimeter* security control, electronic keys for bedrooms, and storage areas designed to protect cash and valuables belonging to members of staff and residents. It is a best practice to install security cameras in lobby areas, opposite to lifts, and all over *corridors*, and improve the design of *architectural ironmongery* for doors, window, fire exits, and entrances under the supervision of security professionals.

In general, according to Angelo and Vladimir, a *comprehensive* security program, includes all of the following elements: security officers make regular *rounds* of the hotel premises, observe suspicious behavior and take appropriate action, investigate *incidents*, and cooperate with local law *enforcement* officials; security equipment includes two-way radios, closed-*circuit* television and *motion sensors*, smoke *detectors* and fire-alarm systems,

规适用）不能向非店客侍酒。醉酒可能会引发冲突。酒店服务人员有权拒绝向任何醉酒的或不到法定年龄的人侍酒。酒吧的工作人员有义务制止不法的、攻击性的或醉酒的行为。他们要养成一个良好的习惯，必须在检查酒店登记卡或客房钥匙后方可侍酒。酒店安保人员应对这些人需要一些策略。用镇定平静的声音问他 / 她是不是店客，也可以问他 / 她叫什么名字。第二，确保酒店拥有基本的安全设施。建议安装闭路电视系统、通道控制、周边安全监控、电子客房钥匙，以及用以保护员工及宾客的现金和贵重物品安全的储存区域。最佳做法是把酒店里的安保摄像机安装在大堂里、电梯对面，覆盖全部走道，并在安全专家的督导下改进门、窗、消防通道、出入口等建筑五金的设计。

概括来讲，根据安吉洛和弗拉基米尔，全面的安保计划包括以下各要素：安保人员定期巡视酒店场所，观察可疑行为，采取适当措施，调查偶发事件，并与当地执法人员展开合作；安全设备包括双向无线对讲机、闭路电视和运动传感器、烟雾探测器和火灾报警系统、消防设备及足够的内外部照明设

fire-fighting equipment, and *adequate* interior and exterior lighting; security officers should be able to gain access to guestrooms, store-rooms, and offices at all times with master keys; all employees should be familiar with *evacuation* plans in case of fire, bomb threats, terrorism, or some other emergency; every employee should be issued an identification card with his or her photo.

备；安保人员应能够随时使用主钥匙进入客房、储藏室和办公室；所有员工都应熟悉在发生火灾、炸弹威胁、恐怖活动或其他紧急情况下的疏散计划；应该给每个员工发放贴有照片的身份证件。

Vocabulary

reduce /rɪˈdjuːs/ *v.* 减少

unwelcome /ʌnˈwelkəm/ *adj.* 不受欢迎的；讨厌的

patrol /pəˈtrəʊl/ *v.* 巡逻；巡查

qualified /ˈkwɒlɪfaɪd/ *adj.* 有资格的；称职的

certification /ˌsɜːtɪfɪˈkeɪʃn/ *n.* 证书

combat /ˈkɒmbæt/ *n.* 搏击；搏斗

theft /θeft/ *n.* 盗窃

rape /reɪp/ *n.* 强奸

criminal /ˈkrɪmɪnl/ *adj.* 违法犯罪的

terrorist /ˈterərɪst/ *adj.* 恐怖主义的

flood /flʌd/ *n.* 水灾

suspicious /səˈspɪʃəs/ *adj.* 可疑的

clear /klɪə(r)/ *v.* 使畅通

vigilant /ˈvɪdʒɪlənt/ *adj.* 警惕的

non-resident /ˌnɒn ˈrezɪdənt/ *n.* 非住店客人

alcohol /ˈælkəhɒl/ *n.* 酒（精）

intoxicated /ɪnˈtɒksɪkeɪtɪd/ *adj.* 喝醉的

unruly /ʌnˈruːli/ *adj.* 不法的；无法无天的

offensive /əˈfensɪv/ *adj.* 攻击性的

threat /θret/ *n.* 威胁

surveillance /sɜːˈveɪləns/ *n.* 监视

obtain /əbˈteɪn/ *v.* 获得

prevention /prɪˈvenʃn/ *n.* 预防

detection /dɪˈtekʃn/ *n.* 侦查

robbery /ˈrɒbəri/ *n.* 抢劫

murder /ˈmɜːdə(r)/ *n.* 谋杀

terrorism /ˈterərɪzəm/ *n.* 恐怖行动

earthquake /ˈɜːθkweɪk/ *n.* 地震

clerk /klɑːk/ *n.* 职员

emergency /ɪˈmɜːdʒənsi/ *n.* 突发情况

belonging /bɪˈlɒŋɪŋ/ *n.* 财产；所有物

conflict /ˈkɒnflɪkt/ *n.* 冲突

drunken /ˈdrʌŋkən/ *adj.* 喝醉的

behavior /bɪˈheɪvjə(r)/ *n.* 行为

calming /ˈkɑːmɪŋ/ *adj.* 镇定的

corridor /ˈkɒrɪdɔː(r)/ *n.* 走廊

architectural /ˌɑːkɪˈtektʃərəl/ *adj.* 建筑的

ironmongery /ˈaɪənmʌŋgəri/ *n.* 五金；铁器

comprehensive /ˌkɒmprɪˈhensɪv/ *adj.* 全面的

incident /ˈɪnsɪdənt/ *n.* 偶发事件

circuit /ˈsɜːkɪt/ *n.* 电路

sensor /ˈsensə(r)/ *n.* 传感器

adequate /ˈædɪkwət/ *adj.* 充足的

diplomacy /dɪˈpləʊməsi/ *n.* 手腕（段）

perimeter /pəˈrɪmɪtə(r)/ *n.* 周围；周边

round /raʊnd/ *n.* 巡视

enforcement /ɪnˈfɔːsmənt/ *n.* 执（法）

motion /ˈməʊʃn/ *n.* 运动

detector /dɪˈtektə(r)/ *n.* 探测器

evacuation /ɪˌvækjuˈeɪʃn/ *n.* 撤离；疏散

Useful Expressions

keep sb. from doing sth. 保护某人做某事

stop sb. from doing sth. 阻止某人做某事

in a ... voice 以……语气

gain access to sth. 获得使用……权利

go through 经历；接受

lay emphasis on ... 重视……

make rounds of ... 巡查……

词汇、课文资源

词汇、课文自测

微课

课堂练习

3.6　Hotel Marketing Management

The hotel marketing management *involves* conducting marketing *research*, developing marketing *strategy*, implementing corporate image strategy, and perfecting marketing management system.

Today, the marketing of services is a major *aspect* of the hotel management. The hotel marketing management is carried out by the sales &

　　酒店营销管理的主要任务包括开展市场调研，制定营销策略，实施企业形象战略和完善营销管理系统。

　　如今，服务营销是酒店管理的一个主要方面。酒店的营销管理是由市场部实施的，它主要负责掌

marketing division, which works to *identify* the needs of *prospective* customers and sell rooms and services to major customers, such as travel agencies, conventions, exhibitions, and large business groups. The activities of the sales & marketing division include business promotions, public relations, contact with the media for advertising, and website operations. Every hotel distinguishes itself from others, and every hotel has its own target customer groups. The marketing staff's work is to make them known to the public. They *assess* their SWOT (*strengths*, *weaknesses*, opportunities, and threats), choose their target customers, carry out market researches, and then develop advertising strategies to increase their brand *recognition*. Besides, they have to arrange *banner* advertisements and travel website partnership. Hotel marketing staff work in a competitive market, so they should have a high *sensitivity* of the market. They need to work with existing customers, as well as to seek for and fight for new business opportunities, for instance, to actively collect all kinds of information about major conventions, exhibitions, sports events, etc. to be held in their locality.

Another major administrative function is the promotion of the hotel. Promotion involves making the public *aware* of the hotel and trying to attract customers. Promotion is carried on by advertising, which is paid, or by making *publicity* and establishing good public relations, which are *unpaid*. Advertising for any hotel is *dictated* by such factors as the *nature* of the operation, its market, and

握目标客户的需求，向旅行社、会议、展览会及大型商务团体等大客户销售客房和各种服务。市场部的主要活动有业务推广、公共关系、媒体广告联系和网站管理等。每一家酒店有各自区别于其他酒店的特色，每一家酒店也有各自的目标客户群。市场部员工的工作就是要让公众了解这些。他们做SWOT（优势、劣势、机会、威胁）评估，选定目标客户，进行市场调研，然后制定广告策略来提升品牌知名度。此外，他们还得安排横幅广告及与旅游网站合作等事宜。酒店市场充满了激烈的竞争，所以市场部员工要有高度的市场敏感性。他们需要与老客户联系，也要寻找并夺得新的商机，例如，主动搜集各种将在本地举行的大型会议、展览、体育赛事等信息。

酒店的宣传是另一项主要的管理工作，包括提升酒店知名度和吸引顾客。宣传既可通过广告这种付费的方式进行，也可通过公众宣传和建立良好的公共关系这些免费的方式进行。任何酒店的宣传广告工作都应依酒店性质、市场情况和拥有的各种广告媒介等因素而定。一

the different advertising media that are available. In general, resort hotels do more direct advertising than other kinds of hotels. They try to *advertise* in the area from which most of their customers come. The media used for advertising may range from *matchbooks* or *ashtrays* that guests take home with them, to advertisements in magazines and newspapers, and to radio campaigns. Television advertising is so expensive that it is generally *restricted* to the major international chains.

Publicity involves getting *press*, radio, or television *coverage* for events that occur at the hotel and events that will enhance the hotel's image. The publicity may be in the form of pictures of a *celebrity* who is a guest at the hotel, or it may be a news story about a political meeting in the hotel that attracts national or even international attention. A television *shot* of a speaker that also shows the name of the hotel would be considered excellent publicity.

In many hotels, the sales & marketing division has public relations management as its *partial* work. That is the management of the hotel's public image, which includes promotions, advertising, events, *charitable donations*, *community* work, and *damage* control. Public relations, an unpaid promotion, should *focus* mainly on the establishment and protection of the hotel's *positive* image. But sometimes good hotels also have trouble with some bad things like food *poisoning*, rude *treatment*, or other *accidents*. The public relations team will have to do damage control, to reduce the impact

般来说，度假酒店的直接广告比其他类型的酒店多，它们尽可能在大多数顾客的来源地进行广告宣传。广告媒介包括顾客可随身带回家的纸板火柴或烟灰缸，以及报刊广告和电台广告。电视广告过于昂贵，所以一般只限于主要的国际连锁酒店。

公共宣传可以让报纸、电台和电视台报道在酒店发生的事件，报道那些能提高酒店形象的事件。这种公共宣传可以采用图片形式，刊登该酒店某知名人士顾客的照片，或者采用新闻报道形式，报道在本酒店召开的为全国乃至世界瞩目的某次政治会议的情况。在映出会议发言人的电视画面上同时也显示出酒店的名称，堪称是出色的宣传。

在许多酒店，公共关系管理属于市场部的部分职能，指的是酒店的公众形象管理，包括宣传、广告、赛事活动、慈善捐助、社区活动及损害控制等。公共关系是一种免费的宣传，其重点在于酒店正面形象的树立与维护。但有时声誉良好的酒店也会遇到不良事件的麻烦，如食物中毒、待客粗鲁或其他事故等。这时公关团队就要启动损害控制，减少不良消息的影响与传播。这种事情的解决有赖于与社

and *spread* of bad news. This can be done by maintaining a good relationship with the community, the authority, and the media. There is also a *negative* aspect to hotel public relations. This often takes the form of preventing stories that may be *harmful* to the hotel from reaching the news media.

区、政府及媒体的良好关系。酒店的公共关系工作还在于处理负面内容，就是防止把可能对酒店有害的情况泄露给新闻媒体。

Vocabulary

involve /ɪnˈvɒlv/ v. 包含

strategy /ˈstrætədʒi/ n. 策略

identify /aɪˈdentɪfaɪ/ v. 发现；找到

assess /əˈses/ v. 评估

weakness /ˈwiːknəs/ n. 劣势

banner /ˈbænə(r)/ n. 横幅

aware /əˈweə(r)/ adj. 意识到的；明白的

unpaid /ˌʌnˈpeɪd/ adj. 没有报酬的

nature /ˈneɪtʃə(r)/ n. 类型；种类

matchbook /ˈmætʃbʊk/ n. 纸板火柴

restrict /rɪˈstrɪkt/ v. 限制

coverage /ˈkʌvərɪdʒ/ n. 新闻报道

shot /ʃɒt/ n. 镜头；画面

charitable /ˈtʃærətəbl/ adj. 慈善的

community /kəˈmjuːnəti/ n. 社区

focus /ˈfəʊkəs/ v. 使集中；使聚焦

poisoning /ˈpɔɪzənɪŋ/ n. 中毒

accident /ˈæksɪdənt/ n. 事故；意外

negative /ˈnegətɪv/ adj. 消极的；负面的

research /rɪˈsɜːtʃ/ n. 调查；研究

aspect /ˈæspekt/ n. 方面

prospective /prəˈspektɪv/ adj. 预期的；未来的

strength /streŋθ/ n. 优势

recognition /ˌrekəgˈnɪʃn/ n. 认知度；知名度

sensitivity /ˌsensəˈtɪvəti/ n. 敏感性；感受性

publicity /pʌbˈlɪsəti/ n. 宣传

dictate /dɪkˈteɪt/ v. 影响；决定

advertise /ˈædvətaɪz/ v. 做广告；宣传

ashtray /ˈæʃtreɪ/ n. 烟灰缸

press /pres/ n. 报刊

celebrity /səˈlebrəti/ n. 社会名流

partial /ˈpɑːʃl/ adj. 部分的

donation /dəʊˈneɪʃn/ n. 捐赠

damage /ˈdæmɪdʒ/ n. 损害

positive /ˈpɒzətɪv/ adj. 正面的；积极的

treatment /ˈtriːtmənt/ n. 对待

spread /spred/ n. 传播

harmful /ˈhɑːmfl/ adj. 有害的

Useful Expressions

distinguish ... from ... 使……不同于……   have a sensitivity of ... 对……敏感

seek for ... 寻求……   make ... aware of ... 使……意识到……

restrict ... to ... 使……限于……   in the form of ... 以……形式

have trouble with ... 有……麻烦

maintain a(n) ... relationship with... 与……保持……关系

take the form of ... 表现为……形式   be harmful to ... 对……有害

词汇、课文资源

词汇、课文自测

微课

课堂练习

Chapter Four

Rooms Division
房务部

思政园地／二十
大精神学习专栏

Learning Objectives

· To get familiar with the most important operation of the hotel revenue centers—the rooms division;

· To understand the staff, tasks, standards, goals, and requirements of each of its departments;

· To master the new words and professional terms concerned;

· To improve reading ability through learning the text;

· To develop team spirit and self-study ability through learning activities.

Teaching Arrangements

节次	教学内容	自主学习资源	自主学习自测	课堂教学视频	课堂练习
L 1	4.1.1 Overview of Front Office Department	词汇、课文资源	词汇、课文自测	微课	课堂练习
L 2	4.1.2 Front Desk 4.1.3 Room Reservations Desk	词汇、课文资源	词汇、课文自测	微课	课堂练习
L 3	4.1.4 Reception Desk 4.1.5 Information Desk 4.1.6 Business Center	词汇、课文资源	词汇、课文自测	微课	课堂练习
L 4	4.1.7 Cashier's Counter 4.1.8 Concierge Desk	词汇、课文资源	词汇、课文自测	微课	课堂练习
L 5	4.1.9 Hotel Lobby 4.1.10 Telephone Operator	词汇、课文资源	词汇、课文自测	微课	课堂练习
L 6	4.2.1 Overview of Housekeeping Department	词汇、课文资源	词汇、课文自测	微课	课堂练习

Continued

节次	教学内容	自主学习资源	自主学习自测	课堂教学视频	课堂练习
L 7	4.2.2 Housekeeping Center 4.2.3 Laundry, Linen, and Public Areas	词汇、课文资源	词汇、课文自测	微课	课堂练习
L 8	4.2.4 Room Description 4.2.5 Room Cleaning	词汇、课文资源	词汇、课文自测	微课	课堂练习

The rooms division of a hotel, typically consisting of the front office department and the housekeeping department, acts as the most important division, usually producing the most revenue for a hotel. The rooms division has the most *frequent* contact with guests, which can give guests a direct *impression* of the hotel's service quality and public image, so the staff must be well trained in languages and *etiquettes*. In recruiting, a hotel should have a higher demand for work experience, formal education, general knowledge, previous training, physical condition, communication ability, and equipment skills. The rooms division is where many managers start their hospitality industry careers. Front desk agents today might become managers tomorrow.

酒店的房务部由前厅部和客房部组成，是酒店最重要的部门，通常为酒店带来最大的收入。房务部员工与宾客的接触最为频繁，会使宾客对酒店服务质量和公众形象留下直接印象，所以房务部的员工必须接受良好的语言与礼仪培训。招聘时，对员工的工作经历、正规教育、通识、以前的培训、健康状况、沟通能力和设备使用技能等方面有着较高的要求。许多经理都是从房务部开始他们的酒店职业生涯的，今天的前台员工很有可能就是明天的经理。

4.1 Front Office Department

4.1.1 Overview of Front Office Department

The front office department is usually considered as one of the most important departments in a hotel because that is where the most interaction with hotel guests takes place. The front office department, typically *composed* of reservation desk,

前厅部概述

人们通常认为，前厅部是酒店里最重要的部门之一，因为那是与酒店宾客接触最多的地方。前厅部一般由客房预订处、礼宾处、接待处、问讯处、收银处、电话总

concierge desk, reception desk, information desk, cashier's counter, telephone operator, business center, lobby manager or assistant manager, *transportation* coordination, and public areas in the lobby, is always *located* in the lobby, the public entrance area that gives access to the guestrooms, restaurants, bars, shops, and other facilities in the hotel.

The major functions conducted by the front office department are: selling guestrooms, *registering* guests, assigning guestrooms, coordinating guest services, providing information concerning hotel services, outer markets, and inner management, *updating* accurate room status, maintaining and *settling* guest accounts, *fulfilling* concierge services, like guest shuttling, baggage, mail, information, and business support, and creating guest history records. The routine work of the front office department includes doorman and baggage, operator, business center, information, message, mail, valuables deposit, etc.

The *sole priority* of the rooms division shall be ensuring guest satisfaction, which happens when guest expectations *match* what the hotel provides. In order to achieve guest satisfaction, the front office department shall prepare a front office organization *chart*, which shall be carefully designed according to its functions. Doing so not only enhances the control the front office department has over its operations, but also provides guests with more specialized services. In addition, frequent and *consistent* communication among front-office functions is critical. The reservation desk, for instance, must

机、商务中心、大堂经理/大堂副理、车队及大堂公共区域等机构组成，总是设在酒店的大堂，即通向客房、餐厅、酒吧、商店和酒店其他设施的共同入口处。

前厅部的职能包括推销客房，办理入住登记，分配客房，协调对客服务，提供酒店服务信息、外部市场信息及内部管理信息，准确更新客房销售状态，建立客账并完成财务结算，提供迎送、行李、邮件、问讯及商务支持等各类前厅礼宾服务，以及建立宾客档案。前厅的日常工作内容包括门童行李服务、总机、商务服务、问询服务、留言服务、邮件服务、贵重物品保管服务等。

房务部的首要目标就是保证宾客满意，而只有在酒店提供的服务与宾客的期望相匹配时，宾客才会满意。为了使宾客满意，前厅应当依据它的功能精心设置前厅组织机构。这样，不仅能够加强前厅对其运作的控制，而且还能向宾客提供更专业的服务。此外，前厅各部门间的频繁一致的沟通是至关重要的。例如，预订处必须每天与前台交流预售房间数；前台必须与客房部员工进行沟通，告知他们宾客

communicate with the front desk each day about the number of rooms that have been pre-sold. The front desk must communicate with housekeeping staff members to let them know when guests check out. Management for all front-office departments must *stress* consistent and frequent communication to ensure a smooth-running operation.

The front-office management consists of the front office manager, the *assistant* manager, the lobby manager, and heads of all *subordinate sections*. The front office manager, directly responsible to the *deputy* general manager-in-charge or the rooms director, is at the top of the front-office management, with overall responsibilities for all items of work, including the communication and coordination between the front office and other hotel departments, the quality and efficiency of the services offered by the front office, and the *maximization* of room sales. The assistant manager, directly responsible to the front office manager, assists with the daily management of front-office work, and acts in the manager's place to ensure the normal operation of the front office while the manager is not on duty. The lobby manager, also named the on-duty manager, working at a desk in the lobby near the reception area, is directly responsible to the front office manager, assisting him / her to check and supervise the work of all the subordinates, or to inspect the work of various hotel departments, listen to guest comments and handle *complaints* on *behalf* of the general manager. In big luxury hotels, there is a guest relations *dean*, who works right under the lobby manager, holds special responsibility for establishing

何时离店。前厅各部门的管理必须强调频繁一致的沟通，以确保平稳运作。

前厅部管理层由前厅部经理、前厅部副经理、大堂副理和各下属部门主管组成。前厅部经理是前厅部的最高管理者，直接对分管副总或房务总监负责，全面负责前厅部的各项工作，保证前厅与酒店其他部门间的沟通和协调，确保前厅的服务质量和工作效率，努力争取客房销售的最大化。前厅部副经理，直接对前厅部经理负责，协助前厅部经理管理前厅部日常工作；前厅部经理不在时代行其职，确保前厅部工作的正常运转。大堂副理，也叫值班经理，通常在门厅接待处旁设有办公桌，直接对前厅部经理负责，协助前厅部经理检查和督导各下属部门的服务工作，代表总经理检查巡视酒店各部门工作，听取宾客意见，处理宾客投诉。大型豪华酒店设有宾客关系主任一职，直接向大堂副理负责，专门负责建立和维护良好的宾客关系，协助欢迎贵宾及安排临时性团客的特别要求。

and maintaining good relationship with guests, and assists welcoming guests and handling special requirements of *temporary* group guests.

Vocabulary

frequent /ˈfriːkwənt/ *adj.* 频繁的

etiquette /ˈetɪkət/ *n.* 礼仪

transportation /ˌtrænspɔːˈteɪʃn/ *n.* 交通车辆

register /ˈredʒɪstə(r)/ *v.* 登记

settle /ˈsetl/ *v.* 结算

sole /səʊl/ *adj.* 唯一的

match /mætʃ/ *v.* 匹配

consistent /kənˈsɪstənt/ *adj.* 一致的

assistant /əˈsɪstənt/ *adj.* 副的；辅助的

subordinate /səˈbɔːdɪnət/ *adj.* 下级的；次要的

section /ˈsekʃn/ *n.* 部门

maximization /ˌmæksɪmaɪˈzeɪʃn/ *n.* 最大化

behalf /bɪˈhɑːf/ *n.* 代表

temporary /ˈtemprəri/ *adj.* 临时的

impression /ɪmˈpreʃn/ *n.* 印象

compose /kəmˈpəʊz/ *v.* 组成

locate /ləʊˈkeɪt/ *v.* 使坐落

update /ˌʌpˈdeɪt/ *v.* 更新；升级

fulfil /fʊlˈfɪl/ *v.* 履行

priority /praɪˈɒrəti/ *n.* 重点；优先

chart /tʃɑːt/ *n.* 图表

stress /stres/ *v.* 强调

deputy /ˈdepjuti/ *n.* 副手

complaint /kəmˈpleɪnt/ *n.* 投诉

dean /diːn/ *n.* 主任

Useful Expressions

act as ... 充当……；作……用

be considered as ... 被认为是……

be composed of ... 由……组成

have control over ... 对……控制

act in sb.'s place 代……行其职

be responsible to sb. 对……负责

have contact with ... 与……有接触（联系）

take place 发生

give access to ... 准许进入……

assist with ... 帮助……

be on duty 值班

词汇、课文资源　　　词汇、课文自测　　　微课　　　课堂练习

4.1.2　Front Desk

The most visible part of the front office area is of course the front desk. It can be a counter or an actual desk where a guest can sit down and register. In small hotels, the front desk is the counter where guests register, pick up their keys and mails, request information, deposit their valuables, and pay their bills. In larger hotels, the front desk is located in the lobby of the hotel, and is divided into several sections. One section is for guests to register or sign in; another is for guests to pick up their keys, mails, and messages; the third is for guests to ask for information or make local travel arrangements; the fourth is for the cashiers to receive payment from guests, cash checks, make change, and exchange foreign currency. In some luxury hotels, there is no front desk, and such jobs are clearly defined and are separately in the charge of several sections, like the reservation desk, the reception desk, the information desk, the concierge desk, the cashier's desk, the operator, and the business center.

The front desk operates under the leadership of the *captain*, who, led by the front office manager, is in charge of planning and training of the section, inspecting and supervising the subordinate staff offering services to guests, *appraising* the staff's performances, and ensuring the normal work of the

前　台

前厅区域最明显的地方当属前台。前台可以是一个工作台，抑或是一张供客人坐下来进行入住登记的办公桌。在小型酒店，前台是指顾客登记、领取钥匙和邮件、问讯、寄存贵重物品和付账的柜台。在较大型酒店，前台设在酒店大堂，分为以下几部分：第一部分是供顾客登记或办理入住手续；第二部分是顾客领取钥匙、邮件和留言的地方；第三部分是顾客问讯或安排当地旅行的地方；第四部分供出纳员向顾客收费，兑换支票、外币和找零。在豪华酒店一般不设前台，这些工作分工明确，分别由几个部门负责，如预订处、接待处、问讯处、礼宾处、收银处、电话总机和商务中心等。

前台设有主管，接受前厅部经理领导，负责本部门的计划与培训，检查和督导下属员工的对客服务工作，考核员工工作表现，确保前台各项工作的正常开展。

front desk.

The front desk mainly deals with check-in registrations, information enquiries, valuables storage, and accounts *settlement*. Specifically, the duties of front desk agents include: greeting guests, registering guests, *establishing* a method of payment for the guestroom (credit card, cash, or direct billing), *assigning* guestrooms that are *unoccupied* and have been cleaned, assigning guestroom keys to guests, informing guests about their room location and special hotel facilities, and answering questions about the property and the *surrounding* community, and calling a bellman to assist guests with their luggage. Another important duty performed at the front desk is the night *audit*. The purpose is to *reconcile* the charges or postings to each guest account with the income of each department.

Currently, computerized property management systems have *simplified* check-in. Guests with reservations are greeted personally at the door by an employee, who then *escorts* them to a special *rack* with a *packet* containing a room key and an already-filled registration card, and checks to confirm that the information is correct before offering to escort the guests to their rooms. In some hotels, self-service *kiosks* in the lobbies provide an even more simplified check-in and check-out system.

Front desk employees, in most cases, *represent* the first and last contact the guest has with hotel personnel. Their ability to make guests feel at home has a *tremendous* impact on the quality of a guest's experience. Therefore, the front desk agents should

前台的工作主要是办理入住登记、提供问讯服务、贵重物品保管和收银等。具体来说，前台员工的工作职责有：迎客、入住登记、确定房费支付方式（信用卡支付、现金支付或直接账单）、分配清洁空房、派发客房钥匙、讲解客房位置和酒店特殊设施、回答客人有关酒店及附近社区的询问以及呼叫门童帮提行李等。夜审是前台的另一项重要任务，其目的是使各个客账的收费或过账与各部门的收入相符。

当前，计算机化的酒店管理系统简化了客人入住流程。预订客人会有员工在门口亲自迎接，然后陪同他们来到一个特别的资料架，取一个装有房间钥匙和已填写的注册卡的资料袋，检查确认信息正确之后，再主动陪送客人去房间。在一些酒店，设在大堂的自助服务亭使得入住和结账更加简便。

在大多数情况下，客人第一次和最后一次接触的酒店员工都是前台员工。他们让客人感觉宾至如归的能力对客人的住店体验质量有巨大的影响。因此，前台员工应当训

be well-trained and morale should be kept high so that interactions with guests are always positive.

4.1.3　Room Reservations Desk

The reservations desk operates under the leadership of the captain, who is directly responsible to the front office manager, and for ensuring the normal work of the reservation desk.

Reservations staff should be familiar with the procedures and *related* knowledge concerning reservation, sales, and reception, should have a good *command* of *written* and *verbal* communications, should be able to write business letters and produce documents, and should be able to make *dialogues* in one or several foreign languages.

Reservationists should be skilled *telemarketing* personnel who are able to accept reservations over the phone, answer questions about the hotel and its facilities, and *quote* guestroom rates and available dates. They also have to *process* reservations that arrive through a computer reservation system or through third parties such as travel agents, hotel *representatives*, tour operators, *independent* reservation systems, *airlines*, *cruise* lines, and other transportation companies, who typically contact hotels by telephone or on the Internet. Most hotels have their own *websites* where guests can make reservations directly.

The reservations desk *chiefly* deals with the room sales (typically, selling rooms to large group customers is in the charge of sales & marketing division, while selling rooms to small groups

练有素，保持昂扬的精神风貌，与客人始终保持积极的互动。

客房预订处

客房预订处由预订处主管领导，主管直接对前厅部经理负责，保证预订处的各项工作正常开展。

预订员要熟悉酒店预订、销售、接待程序及相关知识，有良好的书面和口头表达能力，能独立撰写商业函件和文稿，能用一门以上的外语进行会话。

预订人员应该是熟练的电话营销人员，能够通过电话接受预订，回答有关酒店及其设施的问题，并对客房价格和可预订日期进行报价。他们还必须处理来自计算机预订系统或旅行代理人、酒店代表、旅游承办商、独立预订系统、航空公司、邮轮公司和其他运输公司等第三方的预订，他们通常通过电话或互联网联系酒店。大多数酒店都有自己的网站，供客人直接预订。

预订处主要负责销售客房（大型团体的客房销售一般由市场部负责，小型团体或散客的客房销售由预订处销售）和办理各种预订。客

or individuals is in the charge of the reservation desk) and the processing of reservation requests. Room reservations can be made by telephone, the Internet, face-to-face talk, fax, or letter. Nowadays, reservations are most popularly made on the Internet, and seldom by telephone.

In general, the reservation process falls into six stages: to receive reservation requests through communication *links*, to make sure of guest requirements and fill in reservation *applications*, to check the room status and accept or *decline* reservations (with technology development, the reservation desk can, on real time, be *informed* of the number and types of rooms available, various room rates, and *furnishings*, along with the various facilities existing in the hotel), to confirm reservations and create reservation records, to *revise* reservations, and to make necessary *preparations* for *arrivals*. Concerning large group reservations, there should be close communication with the sales & marketing division.

房预订的方式多种多样，有电话预订、网络预订、面谈预订、传真预订、信函预订等。现在网络预订非常流行，而电话预订已不多见了。

一般来说，酒店的客房预订程序有以下六个阶段：通过通信线路接受预订请求，明确宾客要求并填写客房预订单，查看客房状态并受理或婉拒预订（随着技术的发展，预订处能够实时地获悉有关可售房间的数量、房型、房费、陈设及酒店现有的各种设施等信息），确认预订并建立预订记录，修改预订和抵店准备。关于大型团客预订，预订处应与市场部保持密切联系。

Vocabulary

captain /ˈkæptɪn/ *n.* 领班；主管

settlement /ˈsetlmənt/ *n.* 结算

assign /əˈsaɪn/ *v.* 分配

unoccupied /ˌʌnˈɒkjupaɪd/ *adj.* 空闲的；没人住的

surrounding /səˈraʊndɪŋ/ *adj.* 周围的；附近的

audit /ˈɔːdɪt/ *n.* 审计；查账

appraise /əˈpreɪz/ *v.* 考核；鉴定

establish /ɪˈstæblɪʃ/ *v.* 确定

reconcile /ˈrekənsaɪl/ *v.* 使一致（相符）

simplify /'sɪmplɪfaɪ/ *v.* 使简化；使简单

rack /ræk/ *n.* 架子

kiosk /'kiːɒsk/ *n.* 亭子

tremendous /trə'mendəs/ *adj.* 巨大的

command /kə'mɑːnd/ *n.* 掌握

verbal /'vɜːbl/ *adj.* 口头的；用言语的

reservationist /ˌrezə'veɪʃnɪst/ *n.* 预订人员

telemarketing /'telimɑːkɪtɪŋ/ *n.* 电话推销

quote /kwəʊt/ *v.* 报价

representative /ˌreprɪ'zentətɪv/ *n.* 代表

airline /'eəlaɪn/ *n.* 航空公司

website /'websaɪt/ *n.* 网站

link /lɪŋk/ *n.* 通信手段；交通路线

application /ˌæplɪ'keɪʃn/ *n.* 申请表格；申请单

inform /ɪn'fɔːm/ *v.* 告知

revise /rɪ'vaɪz/ *v.* 修改；修正

preparation /ˌprepə'reɪʃn/ *n.* 准备（工作、措施）

escort /'eskɔːt/ *v.* 护送；陪同

packet /'pækɪt/ *n.* 小袋

represent /ˌreprɪ'zent/ *v.* 相当于

related /rɪ'leɪtɪd/ *adj.* 相关的

written /'rɪtn/ *adj.* 书面的

dialogue /'daɪəlɒg/ *n.* 会话；对话

process /'prəʊses/ *v.* 处理

independent /ˌɪndɪ'pendənt/ *adj.* 独立的

cruise /kruːz/ *n.* 乘船游览

chiefly /'tʃiːfli/ *adv.* 主要地

decline /dɪ'klaɪn/ *v.* 婉拒

furnishing /'fɜːnɪʃɪŋ/ *n.* 陈设

arrival /ə'raɪvl/ *n.* 抵达者

Useful Expressions

be divided into ... 被分成……

inform sb. of/about sth. 告知某人某事

escort sb. to sp. 护送某人去某地

make sure of ... 明确……；确定……

on real time 实时地

sign in 办理入住；签到

reconcile ... with ... 使……与……相符

feel at home 宾至如归

fill in/out ... 填（表）……

词汇、课文资源

词汇、课文自测

微课

课堂练习

4.1.4　Reception Desk

The reception desk is also called the registration desk. The employee here who checks in arriving guests and assigns them rooms is the room clerk. When a guest arrives, the room clerk checks his / her reservation or the *availability* of rooms if the guest does not have a confirmed reservation. When the room clerk has confirmed the availability of the accommodations, the guest fills out a registration form with his / her name, home address, and any other *pertinent* information. The room clerk fills in the room number, the rate the guest will pay, and the way in which payment is made. In many countries, the guest's passport or identification card must also be checked or held for a short period of time due to the police regulations. When the registration is completed, the room clerk hands over the key card or welcome card to the guest, and calls a bellman to escort the guest to his or her room. What is to be done next by the room clerk is create relevant forms or documents, produce the room rack *slip*, and transfer the guest's check-in information to the closely related departments like the operator, the information desk, the bell service, and the housekeeping center.

In detail, the registration procedures include greeting guests, confirming reservations and room availability, filling in applications, deciding how payment is made, producing key card, transferring check-in information to the housekeeping, and creating guests' accounts. A bellman takes guests and their baggage to their rooms, tells them where

接待处

接待处，也叫登记处。在这里为来宾办理入住手续并为他们安排房间的是客房登记员。来宾抵达酒店时，由客房登记员核查其是否曾预订房间，如果来宾未预订房间，则由客房登记员安排空闲客房。客房登记员查明有空闲房间后，请顾客在登记表上填好姓名、家庭住址和其他有关情况。客房登记员则填写房间号、房费和支付方式等信息。在许多国家，按治安条例还必须检验护照或身份证，或将这些证件留存一小段时间。入住和登记的所有手续办妥，客房登记员要把房卡或欢迎卡交给宾客，并唤来应接员，送顾客到客房。紧接着，客房登记员要建立相关表格资料，制作客房状况卡条，将来宾的入住信息尽快传递给密切相关的总机、问讯处、大厅服务处和客房中心。

具体地讲，办理住宿登记的程序包括：问候、确认预订信息和空房情况、填写登记表、确定付款方式、出房卡、向客房部通报来宾的入住信息、制作宾客账单。应接员陪送宾客并把行李送到客房，向其指明电灯开关和其他设备的位

to locate light switches and other equipment, shows them how to operate air conditioners, television sets, and other appliances in their rooms, and also runs *errands* for them. Some luxury hotels separate the functions of bellmen and *porters*. In such cases, the baggage is turned over to a porter at the entrance and brought to the room by him rather than a bellman.

4.1.5 Information Desk

The information clerk takes messages, provides *directions* to guests, and maintains mails. He / She should be able to introduce to guests the hotel's internal and external conditions, assist visitors to find the in-hotel guests, answer questions about all the services offered by the hotel, such as the service hours of laundry, restaurants, and room service, handle messages and mails from or to guests, and sometimes keep key cards for guests.

In detail, the information clerk is responsible for answering any question from guests, helping them with any problem that they may have, answering telephones and taking messages for guests, handling complaints from guests, receiving and *dispatching cables* and *telexes*, preparing guest folios, distributing Whitney slips, and explaining the hotel's services to guests or informing guests of where they can find information about the hotel's service themselves.

4.1.6 Business Center

The business center, typically located in the public area nearby the lobby, provides various services under the supervision of its captain, who

置，说明如何使用空调、电视机以及房内其他设备，此外还帮宾客做些杂事。在一些豪华酒店，应接员的工作同行李员的工作是分开的。在此情况下，行李在门口就交给行李员，由行李员而非应接员送至客房。

问讯处

问讯员的职责是收发信息、给宾客指路、处理邮件等。要能够向宾客介绍酒店的内、外部情况，帮助访客查找住客，回答有关酒店服务事项的所有问题，诸如洗衣、餐厅及客房服务的时间等，为宾客收发留言和邮件以及代为管理客用钥匙。

具体地说，问讯员负责回答宾客的问讯，帮助他们解决可能遇到的问题，替宾客接电话、记录留言，处理宾客投诉，收发电报和电传，记录客房账目，分发房间状态指示单以及向宾客介绍酒店的各项服务或告诉宾客哪里可以自行了解酒店服务项目。

商务中心

商务中心一般设在大堂附近的公共区域内，在主管的领导下，完成对客服务。商务中心主管直接

is directly responsible to the front office manager. Secretaries of the business center should have a better command of skills of communicating and reading in foreign language(s), and a great *proficiency* in using various *devices* of the business center. What is worth *mentioning* is that secretaries should transfer the received faxes or other documents to guests in time, and make sure that guests receive *notifications* of new messages.

The business centers of different hotels provide various services, ranging from *secretarial* service, to *translation* service, to business support of computer, *printer*, *scanner*, high-speed Internet access, and *photocopying* & faxing machine, and to services of 24-hour *multilingual* concierge, *flight* booking, and direct-dial multi-line telephone with voice mail, speaker, and data *port*.

对前厅部经理负责。商务中心秘书必须具有较好的外语表达与阅读能力，能熟练操作商务中心的各种设备。值得一提的是，秘书一定要把接收的传真等文件及时转送至宾客手中，确保宾客收到新的留言通知。

不同的酒店，其商务中心所提供的服务也是多种多样的，有秘书服务和翻译服务，电脑、打印机、扫描仪、高速网络接入以及复印和传真设备等商务支持，24 小时多语种礼宾服务，预订航班服务，还配置有语音信箱、扬声器和数据端口的直拨多线电话等。

Vocabulary

availability /əˌveɪləˈbɪləti/ *n.* 可用性

slip /slɪp/ *n.* 纸条

porter /ˈpɔːtə(r)/ *n.* 行李员

dispatch /dɪˈspætʃ/ *v.* 派遣；派件

telex /ˈteleks/ *n.* 电传

device /dɪˈvaɪs/ *n.* 设备

notification /ˌnəʊtɪfɪˈkeɪʃn/ *n.* 通知

translation /trænzˈleɪʃn/ *n.* 翻译

scanner /ˈskænə(r)/ *n.* 扫描仪

multilingual /ˌmʌltiˈlɪŋgwəl/ *adj.* 使用多种语言的

flight /flaɪt/ *n.* 航班

pertinent /ˈpɜːtɪnənt/ *adj.* 相关的

errand /ˈerənd/ *n.* 杂事；差事

direction /dəˈrekʃn/ *n.* 方向；指路

cable /ˈkeɪbl/ *n.* 电报

proficiency /prəˈfɪʃnsi/ *n.* 熟练；精通

mention /ˈmenʃn/ *v.* 提起；提及

secretarial /ˌsekrəˈteəriəl/ *adj.* 秘书的

printer /ˈprɪntə(r)/ *n.* 打印机

photocopy /ˈfəʊtəʊkɒpi/ *v.* 影印；复印

port /pɔːt/ *n.* 端口

Useful Expressions

hand over ... to ... 把……交给……

turn sth. over to sb. 把某物交给某人

have a great proficiency in ... 熟练掌握……

in detail 具体地讲

词汇、课文资源

词汇、课文自测

微课

课堂练习

4.1.7　Cashier's Counter

The cashier's counter is responsible for handling daily guest accounts, auditing and *consolidating* guest bills transferred by cashiers from different operations, exchanging foreign currencies, receiving payments, preparing various accounting statements, and reporting business operations to the management in time.

At the cashier's counter, cashiers close folios and properly check out guests, money *changers* are *commissioned* by the Bank of China to exchange foreign currencies and cash traveler's checks or credit cards, accounts receivable clerks post charges in correct guest folios and update folios' *outstanding* balances, and night auditors control the work of accounts receivable clerks and prepare daily reports to the management, such as occupancy report and revenue report.

Settling payment is the final part of providing quality service to guests. Cashiers should keep postings on the room accounts up-to-date in order

收银处

收银处负责处理每日客账，核算和整理各业务部门收银员转来的宾客消费账单，兑换外币，办理收银，编制各种财务报表，及时反映酒店的营业活动情况。

在收银处，收银员办理宾客结账离店手续，兑换员受中国银行委托为宾客收兑外汇现钞、旅行支票及信用卡，应收款文员把各种费用准确地过入客账，更新客账余额，夜审员查验应收款文员的工作，为管理层编制日报表，例如入住率报表和收入报表。

结账是为宾客提供高质量服务的最后一个环节。收银员应把宾客的住房账目及时登记过账，以便

to *expedite* the check-out procedure. The bill should be presented in a bill *folder* and must be completely correct. Every item served should be clearly shown along with any taxes and service charges for guests to *examine*. After settling the bill, the guest gives the key back to the cashier or puts it in the key *drop*.

Another service in the charge of the cashier is safety deposit box, a kind of complimentary service offered to guests who have to deposit their valuables. The Box is usually placed behind the cashier's counter or in a *secluded* room beside it. Each box is equipped with two keys, one master key for all boxes, kept by the cashier, and one sub-key, kept by the *depositor* himself / herself. When offering service, the cashier should become aware of the storage requirements, fill out valuables forms, and *remind* guests of relevant *conditions*.

If the guest settles his / her account in traveler's check, make sure that he / she *countersigns* the check in front of you. Do not accept checks that have already been countersigned. Then compare the two *signatures* carefully. When a traveler's check is *suspected* to be a *counterfeit* one, first look at the check closely and see if the *portraits* and *patterns* are clearly printed, and then feel the check with your hand. If it is a Thomas Cook traveler's check, the *fringe* should be printed in *relief*. With American Express traveler's check, if you hold it with face down and *rub* the face-value spot on the left part of the check back with a wet finger, the blue ink on the the face-value spot comes off. With other traveler's checks, the cashier can look for *watermarks* by holding the check against the light

加快结账手续。递交账单时应将其放入账单夹，而且账单必须完全正确，所有的服务项目以及税和服务费一一列明，以便宾客检查账单。付完账后，宾客将钥匙还给收银员或放进专门的钥匙箱中。

收银处还有一项服务——保险箱服务，这是酒店为宾客提供的一种免费的贵重物品保管服务。保险箱一般放在总台收银处后侧或旁边一个僻静的房间。每个箱子都备有两把钥匙，一把为总钥匙，可开启所有保险箱，由收银员保管；另一把为分钥匙，由宾客自己保管。寄存时，收银员要弄清楚寄存的要求，填写贵重物品寄存单，并向宾客介绍相关注意事项。

如果宾客用旅行支票结账，必须让其当面在支票上签字。切勿接受事先加签好的支票。仔细比较支票上的两个签名。如果一张支票有伪造的嫌疑，首先仔细地看一下这张支票，查看一下上面的头像和花纹印得是否清晰；然后用手摸支票，如是托迈酷客旅行支票的话，花边就应该是凸纹的。美国运通旅行支票正面朝下拿着的时候背面左边印有面值的地方用湿手搓，上面的蓝油墨就掉下来。其他的旅行支票，把支票对着灯光看，看看里面是否有水印图案或者把支票放在紫外灯光下，看支票上有无特殊颜色的油

or look for the special ink color by putting the check under an *ultraviolet* light.

In cases when the guest pays bills by credit card, the cashier should always follow the procedures below:

1) Check and see if the card is still valid.

2) *Imprint* the card onto a sales *voucher* and then write out on it the transaction amount and the transaction date.

3) Make sure that the amount of sales does not go beyond the authorized credit limit.

4) Ask the cardholder to sign in the *designated* space and then compare the signature with the one in the signature *panel* on the back of the card.

5) Give the cardholder's copy to the guest, keep the establishment's copy in your files for one year, and mail the *remaining* copy, along with a *summary sheet*, to the credit card company within specified number of days.

4.1.8 Concierge Desk

The concierge desk, also named the bell service, provides guest shuttling, baggage handling, and some other valet services under the leadership of the head concierge, who, led by the front office manager, is responsible for planning and training of the section, inspecting and supervising the subordinate staff offering services to guests, appraising the staff's performances, and ensuring the normal work of the concierge team.

Employees in this department include door *attendants*, bellpersons, concierges, and transportation

墨出现。

如果宾客使用信用卡付账，收款员一定要遵循下列步骤：

1) 查看信用卡是否有效。

2) 把信用卡压印在一份收款单上，然后把收款额和收款日期填写上。

3) 务必要注意收款金额不超过信用额度。

4) 请持卡人在指定的空白处签名，然后比对宾客的签名和信用卡背面签名栏里的签名字迹。

5) 把收款三联单中的顾客联交给顾客，把酒店联存档保留一年，把剩下的一联附上一份汇总单在规定的日数内寄给信用卡公司。

礼宾处

礼宾处，也叫大厅服务，在礼宾处主管的领导下为宾客提供迎送服务、行李服务和代办服务。礼宾处主管接受前厅部经理领导，负责本部门的计划与培训，检查和督导下属员工完成对客服务工作，考核员工工作表现，确保礼宾处各项工作的正常开展。

本部门的员工包括应接员、行李员、礼宾员、交通服务员或代客

or valet-parking employees. Door attendants move luggage from cars or *taxicabs* into the hotel. Bell persons move guest luggage to and from guestrooms, escort guests to their rooms, inspect guestrooms while *rooming* the guest, and explain the features of the room and the hotel to guests. The concierge is the main source of information about the hotel and the local area. Transportation services include valet parking either in the hotel's own *garage* or a nearby facility, and airport shuttling, if provided.

In fact, in many hotels nowadays, the concierge desk includes many more services than those above. Besides concierges assisting guests by answering questions about the hotel's services, providing information about local entertainment, sports events, and *sights* of interest, getting *theater* tickets, making restaurant reservations, recommending secretarial services and copying centers, ordering limousines, and performing small *chores* for guests, such as mailing letters and packages, the concierge consists of representatives-at-the-airport shuttling guests to and from the airport, bell attendants depositing luggage as well as moving luggage from the lobby to guestrooms, door attendants providing luggage service and ensuring traffic control at or outside the hotel entrance, valet parking attendants parking *automobiles* for guests, and transportation personnel providing transportation services for guests from and to the hotel. While serving guests, all these attendants wear elaborate uniforms, which gives a hotel an elegant note. So all the services offered by these uniformed attendants can be called "Uniformed Services."

泊车员。应接员把行李从汽车或出租车搬到酒店。行李员将客人的行李搬到或搬离客房，陪送客人到房间，在客人入住时检查房间，并向客人解释房间和酒店的特点。礼宾部是酒店及当地相关信息的主要来源。交通服务包括在酒店自己的车库或附近设施代客停车及机场接送服务。

事实上，现在很多酒店的礼宾服务已经超出上述内容。除礼宾员回答客人关于酒店服务的问讯，提供当地的娱乐活动、体育赛事和风景名胜等相关信息，订购影票，预订餐厅，推荐秘书服务和复印中心，订购接送车服务以及代客做一些寄信件和包裹这样的杂事，礼宾部还有驻机场代表负责在机场迎送宾客，行李员负责大堂至客房间的行李服务和行李寄存，门厅应接员负责酒店入口处的行李服务和交通控制，代客泊车员负责向宾客提供泊车服务，车队人员负责宾客来往酒店的交通服务。这些人员在提供服务时都身穿考究的酒店制服以体现酒店的高级品位，所以可把这些礼宾服务统称为"穿制服的服务"。

Vocabulary

consolidate /kənˈsɒlɪdeɪt/ *v.* 整理（成一体）	changer /ˈtʃeɪndʒə(r)/ *n.* 兑换员
commission /kəˈmɪʃn/ *v.* 委托	outstanding /aʊtˈstændɪŋ/ *adj.* 未支付的
expedite /ˈekspədaɪt/ *v.* 加快	folder /ˈfəʊldə(r)/ *n.* （票）夹
examine /ɪgˈzæmɪn/ *v.* 检查	drop /drɒp/ *n.* 投信口
secluded /sɪˈkluːdɪd/ *adj.* 隐蔽的；僻静的	depositor /dɪˈpɒzɪtə(r)/ *n.* 寄存者
remind /rɪˈmaɪnd/ *v.* 提醒	
condition /kənˈdɪʃn/ *n.* 条件；规定（事项）	
countersign /ˈkaʊntəsaɪn/ *v.* 会签	signature /ˈsɪgnətʃə(r)/ *n.* 签名
suspect /səˈspekt/ *v.* 怀疑；嫌疑	counterfeit /ˈkaʊntəfɪt/ *adj.* 假冒的
portrait /ˈpɔːtreɪt/ *n.* 肖像	pattern /ˈpætn/ *n.* 花纹；图案
fringe /frɪndʒ/ *n.* 饰边；花边	relief /rɪˈliːf/ *n.* 浮雕（方法）
rub /rʌb/ *v.* 搓；擦	watermark /ˈwɔːtəmɑːk/ *n.* 水印
ultraviolet /ˌʌltrəˈvaɪələt/ *adj.* 紫外线的	imprint /ɪmˈprɪnt/ *v.* 使有印痕
voucher /ˈvaʊtʃə(r)/ *n.* 凭证	designated /ˌdezɪgneɪtɪd/ *adj.* 指定的
panel /ˈpænl/ *n.* 方格；方框	remaining /rɪˈmeɪnɪŋ/ *adj.* 剩余的
summary /ˈsʌməri/ *n.* 一览	sheet /ʃiːt/ *n.* 单张（纸）
attendant /əˈtendənt/ *n.* 侍者	taxicab /ˈtæksikæb/ *n.* 出租汽车
room /ruːm/ *v.* 给……提供留宿	garage /ˈgærɑːʒ/ *n.* 车库
sight /saɪt/ *n.* 风景	theater /ˈθɪətə(r)/ *n.* 影院
chore /tʃɔː(r)/ *n.* 琐事	automobile /ˈɔːtəməbiːl/ *n.* 汽车

Useful Expressions

report sth. to sb. 向某人汇报某事
commission sb. to do sth. 委托某人做某事
remind sb. of sth. 提醒某人某事　　　　　　　　compare ... with ... 把……与……比较
come off 掉下来

词汇、课文资源

词汇、课文自测

微课

课堂练习

4.1.9　Hotel Lobby

The hotel lobby is the entrance of a hotel, the focus of transportation to and from the hotel, and the central area for guests arriving, checking-in, checking-out, and departing. In this area, there are a series of front office sections, like the bell service, the front desk, the business center, and the telephone department, offering various services to guests, such as transportation, baggage, shopping, and business support.

The hotel lobby has a baggage area where a guest's luggage is placed as soon as he / she arrives or right before he / she leaves. A guest, while checking in, can relax and feel *confident*, with his / her baggage taken care of in the baggage area. When a guest checks out, he / she will call for the porter to bring his / her luggage downstairs. While paying the bill, he / she also stores his / her baggage in the baggage area. As soon as the taxi arrives, he / she can pick up his / her baggage and leave.

The hotel lobby also has a meeting area, where guests can meet with their friends, family, or business *associates*, so typically there is a small bar or cafe that charges for coffee, tea, drinks, and light snacks. Besides, the meeting area serves as a center for business activities, where business people meet each other, have informal meetings, get to know each other over coffee, and *eventually conclude deals*.

In addition to the front desk area, the baggage area, and the meeting area, it is typical that the hotel

酒店大堂

酒店大堂是酒店的入口，是来去酒店的交通中心，也是宾客抵店、登记入住和退房离店的中心区域。在这里有行李部、前台、商务中心、话务部等前厅部门为宾客提供交通、行李、购物及商务支持等各种服务。

酒店大堂设有一个行李区，是宾客刚抵店或即将离店暂放行李的地方。宾客办理入住手续时，可以放心地将行李放在行李区。宾客离店时，会叫行李员把行李拿到楼下。结账时，行李也存放在行李区。出租车一到，宾客便可拿上行李离开。

大堂还设有一个会客区，宾客可以在这里会见朋友、家人或商务伙伴，所以这里常设有一个小型的大堂吧或咖啡厅，提供付费咖啡、茶、饮料或点心。除此之外，会客区还是一个商务活动中心，商务人士在这里进行会晤，召开非正式会议，一边喝咖啡一边相互了解，最终促进生意的达成。

酒店大堂除了前台区、行李区、会客区以外，一般还设有一个

lobby has a shopping area, where many kinds of *retail* outlets are open to the public, for example, the sundry store selling personal-care items like *shampoos* and shaving *creams*, media items like newspapers and magazines, and travel conveniences like batteries and snacks, the domestic-product store selling goods which are sold in most *supermarkets* or department stores, the local-item store selling locally-produced handicraft items or items with local *themes* and cultural *influence*, and the luxury-product store selling luxury-brand goods like clothing, luggage, pens, watches, jewelry, alcohol, and tobacco products. These outlets sell items at high prices, but do a good business. That is because the guests shopping in these outlets don't care too much about price; on the contrary, they regard it as a story worth showing off. These hotel outlets not only make shopping convenient for guests but also help promote local culture, advertise local products, and, meanwhile, make up part of the revenue *stream* of the hotel.

4.1.10　Telephone Operator

The telephone operator provides guests with such services as call distributions, international or domestic long-distance calls, wake-up calls, inquiry calls, and IDD (international direct dial). The telephone operator ensures quick, accurate, and efficient telecom services under the leadership of the captain, who is directly responsible to the front office manager.

The telephone operator serves as the window

购物区。在这里有各种各样的向公众开放的零售店，例如：日用品商店，出售洗发液和剃须膏等个人护理品、报纸杂志等媒体刊物、电池及小食品等旅行便利品等；家庭用品商店，销售大多数超市和百货商店有售的商品；地方特产店，销售当地生产的工艺品或有当地风格和文化影响的小商品；奢侈品店，销售高档名牌产品，供应服装、行李、钢笔、手表、首饰和烟酒等。这里销售的商品价格不菲，但依然生意火爆，因为酒店宾客在这些商店购物并不太在意商品的价格，反而认为值得炫耀一番。酒店商场不仅方便了宾客购物，而且宣传了地方文化，推广了地方产品，同时也增加了酒店的收入。

电话总机

酒店总机为宾客提供电话转接、国际国内长途电话、叫早电话、查询电话、IDD（国际直拨电话）等多项服务。电话总机主管在前厅部经理的直接领导下，确保迅速、准确、高效地完成各项电信服务。

电话总机是酒店对外联系的窗

of a hotel's external contacts, and its service as a hotel's service standard. So, a telephone operator should have a sweet and *articulate* voice, have a quick dictation skill and a good memory, have a strong ability of English listening and speaking, have a good command of computer skills and communication skills, have a good *grasp* of knowledge and information about hotel services, scenic spots, and entertainments, and have a duty of protecting guest *privacy*.

The operators are in charge of managing the *switchboard*, answering or distributing calls to the appropriate extensions, placing wake-up calls, *monitoring automated* systems, and coordinating emergency communications.

口，体现着酒店的服务水准，因此，要求话务员音质甜美，口齿清晰，听写迅速，记忆力强，有较强的英语听说能力、较熟练的计算机操作技术和较强的沟通能力，较好掌握酒店服务、旅游景点及娱乐等知识与信息，并严守话务机密。

总机话务员负责管理总机，接听电话或转接分机，设置叫早电话，监控自动化系统，协调应急通信。

Vocabulary

confident /ˈkɒnfɪdənt/ *adj.* 自信的

eventually /ɪˈventʃuəli/ *adv.* 最终

deal /diːl/ *n.* 交易；生意

shampoo /ʃæmˈpuː/ *n.* 洗发剂

supermarket /ˈsuːpəmɑːkɪt/ *n.* 超市

influence /ˈɪnfluəns/ *n.* 影响

articulate /ɑːˈtɪkjuleɪt/ *adj.* 发音清晰的

privacy /ˈprɪvəsi/ *n.* 隐私

monitor /ˈmɒnɪtə(r)/ *v.* 监控

associate /əˈsəʊsieɪt/ *n.* 伙伴

conclude /kənˈkluːd/ *v.* 达成协议

retail /ˈriːteɪl/ *n.* 零售

cream /kriːm/ *n.* 面霜；膏

theme /θiːm/ *n.* 主题

stream /striːm/ *n.* 流

grasp /grɑːsp/ *n.* 理解；把握

switchboard /ˈswɪtʃbɔːd/ *n.* 电话总机

automated /ˈɔːtəmeɪtɪd/ *adj.* 自动化的

Useful Expressions

a series of 一系列

meet with sb. 和某人会面；偶遇某人

get to know 初认识；了解到

do a good business 生意兴隆

on the contrary 相反地

be worth doing（某事）值得做

have a grasp of ... 掌握……

be open to sb. 向某人开放

care ... about ... 在乎；介意

regard ... as ... 把……看成……

show off 炫耀

词汇、课文资源

词汇、课文自测

微课

课堂练习

4.2 Housekeeping Department

4.2.1 Overview of Housekeeping Department

A hotel requires cleaning and maintenance on a very large *scale*. The department in charge of such work is the housekeeping department, which is responsible for cleaning the hotel's guestrooms, lounges, lobby, public areas, etc., ensuring room safety, and maintaining room facilities. The housekeeping department is an especially important department of the rooms division, for a comfortable, clean, quiet, and *well-appointed* room with a large, soft bed is what every traveler looks for at the end of his / her journey or a day's *sightseeing*. Even such *trivial* carelessness as an unemptied ashtray or waste basket, an *improperly* cleaned bath *tub*, or an *unthoroughly* dried bed sheet can *upset* a *frazzled* guest and thus affect his / her impression of the hotel.

The housekeeping department, commonly

管家部概述

酒店有大量的清洁、维保工作。负责这种工作的部门叫作管家部，负责清洁客房、休息室、大堂、公共区域等场所，保证客房安全以及维护客房设备物品。管家部是房务部的一个尤其重要的部门，因为一个又大又松软的床铺，舒适、安静、陈设齐全的房间是所有刚刚结束了长途旅行或者一整天观光游览的宾客所渴望的。哪怕是一个没有倒净的烟灰缸或废纸篓，一个没有刷洗干净的浴缸或者是一条没有彻底烘干的床单都可能使一位疲惫的宾客感到不快，从而影响其对酒店的印象。

管家部通常由客房服务中心、

consisting of the housekeeping center, the public areas, the linen room, and the laundry room, functions under the supervision of the executive housekeeper, who is directly responsible to the deputy general manager-in-charge or rooms director just as the front office manager does. He / She has the responsibility for the daily affairs of his / her own department, like ensuring that guestrooms, meeting rooms, banquet rooms, and public areas are clean, *orderly* and well-maintained, training staff, *scheduling* and supervising their work, inspecting rooms, and controlling large inventories of linens, supplies, and equipment, and, what's more, he / she has responsibility for the communication and coordination with other departments.

The housekeeping department has the largest staff in most hotels. The employees under the executive housekeeper are an assistant housekeeper, room *inspectors*, room attendants, a linen room *supervisor* and attendants, laundry employees, and, in some hotels, *painters*, *plumbers*, general maintenance men, and window washers.

Room inspectors supervise room attendants. Room attendants are responsible for inspecting rooms before they are available for sale, cleaning occupied, *vacant* rooms, and public areas according to specified procedures, and communicating the status of guestrooms to the front office department. Linen attendants are responsible for cleaning and *pressing* the hotel's linens and towels, and maintaining *recycled* and non-recycled inventory items. Laundry employees are in charge of cleaning

公共区域、布草房和洗衣房等部门组成，行政管家督导该部门的工作。和前厅经理一样，行政管家直接对副总或房务总监负责。他／她负责自己部门的日常事务，如确保客房、会议宴会厅和公共场所的清洁、整齐和完好，培训员工，安排和督导他们的工作，检查客房，以及管控布草、客房必需品和设备的库存，而且还要负责与其他部门之间的联络协调。

在大多数酒店，管家部员工是最多的。在行政管家管理下的员工有管家助理、客房检查员、客房服务员、布草房主管及服务员、洗衣房员工等，在有些酒店里还配有油漆工、水暖工、维修工和玻璃清洁工。

客房检查员督导客房服务员工作，客房服务员负责待售房的检查，按规定程序清扫占用房、空置房及公共区域，并向前厅部报告房态。布草房员工负责清洗或熨烫酒店的布草和毛巾等，并保养与维护循环用品和一次性用品的库存。洗衣房员工则负责清洗客人的衣物（按定价收费），也负责清洗酒店员工制服。

guest clothing (for a *predetermined* fee) and employee uniforms as well.

The assistant housekeeper, also called housekeeping *coordinator*, offers administrative support to the housekeeping department. He / She is usually the first to *respond* to a guest's request through the telephone. The coordinator will usually answer the telephone (as *stipulated* in a hotel, all calls should be answered within three rings), issue guests' requests to the other staff concerned in the housekeeping department, *log* all calls in the message book, and follow up to make sure tasks are *accomplished* quickly. Other *assignments* for the coordinator include assisting the supervisor to *track attendance* and work through *payroll* procedures, maintaining accurate records of the room status and reporting it to proper departments, *securing* keys, and taking lost and found calls.

管家助理又叫作管家部协调员，为管家部提供行政支持。他 / 她通常是第一个在电话中答复客人要求的人员。协调员接听电话（根据一般酒店的规定，铃响三声内接听电话），并将客人相关要求传递给管家部相关人员，将所有的电话记录在留言簿上，并追踪确保任务能够迅速完成。此外，协调员还要协助主管考勤、结算工资，维护准确的房态记录并向有关部门报告房态，保管钥匙，接听失物招领电话等。

Vocabulary

scale /skeɪl/ *n.* 规模

well-appointed /ˌwel əˈpɔɪntɪd/ *adj.* 设备完善的；配备齐全的

sightseeing /ˈsaɪtsiːɪŋ/ *n.* 观光；游览

improperly /ɪmˈprɒpəli/ *adv.* 不正确地

unthoroughly /ʌnˈθʌrəli/ *adv.* 不彻底地

frazzled /ˈfræzld/ *adj.* 疲惫的

schedule /ˈʃedjuːl/ *v.* 安排；预定

supervisor /ˈsuːpəvaɪzə(r)/ *n.* 主管人

plumber /ˈplʌmə(r)/ *n.* 管道工

trivial /ˈtrɪviəl/ *adj.* 琐碎的；不重要的

tub /tʌb/ *n.* 浴盆

upset /ˌʌpˈset/ *v.* 使心烦

orderly /ˈɔːdəli/ *adj.* 有秩序的；整齐的

inspector /ɪnˈspektə(r)/ *n.* 检查员

painter /ˈpeɪntə(r)/ *n.* 油漆工

vacant /ˈveɪkənt/ *adj.* 空置的

press /pres/ *v.* 熨烫

predetermined /ˌpriːdɪˈtɜːmɪnd/ *adj.* 预定的

respond /rɪˈspɒnd/ *v.* 回应；响应

log /lɒg/ *v.* 记入（日志）

assignment /əˈsaɪnmənt/ *n.* 任务

attendance /əˈtendəns/ *n.* 出勤（情况）

secure /sɪˈkjʊə(r)/ *v.* 妥善保管

recycle /ˌriːˈsaɪkl/ *v.* 循环；再利用

coordinator /kəʊˈɔːdɪneɪtə(r)/ *n.* 协调员

stipulate /ˈstɪpjuleɪt/ *v.* 规定

accomplish /əˈkʌmplɪʃ/ *v.* 完成；实现

track /træk/ *v.* 跟踪进展情况

payroll /ˈpeɪrəʊl/ *n.* 工资单

Useful Expressions

on a large scale 大量地

respond to ... 响应……

log ... in ... 把……记录在……

what's more 而且

issue ... to ... 把……发送给……

follow up 追踪

词汇、课文资源

词汇、课文自测

微课

课堂练习

4.2.2　Housekeeping Center

The housekeeping center, functioning as the information center and the *liaison* & coordination center of the housekeeping department, carries out all face-to-face guest services under the leadership of the captain. The housekeeping center undertakes no task of receiving guests. When a room attendant is needed, the guest can *dial* the extension call of the center, and the center will *notify* the room attendant in the workroom nearest to the guest's room.

The housekeeping center works around the clock, controlling staff's attendance, carrying out face-to-face guest services, managing the floor master key, communicating with the front office,

客房服务中心

客房服务中心是管家部的信息中心和联络协调中心，在中心主管的领导下，开展面客服务工作。客房服务中心不承担接待宾客的任务。宾客需要找客房服务员时，可以拨打内线电话通知客房服务中心，由其通知离宾客房间最近的工作间的服务员。

客房服务中心实行 24 小时值班制，控制员工出勤，开展面对面的对客服务，管理楼层万能钥匙，与前厅部联系，处理投诉和失物，

handling complaints and lost property, keeping records, reporting maintenance to the engineering department, and coordinating with other departments.

While guests stay in the hotel, room attendants not only ensure clean and comfortable rooms but also provide face-to-face services, that is, offer guests all kinds of services face to face to meet guests' *reasonable* requirements. Room attendants should be healthy and hard-working, and should have a nice and good *appearance*, a polite and *restrained attitude* towards guests, a *refined* behavior, and a certain level of a foreign language. *Emphasis* should be laid on utmost *sincerity*, high efficiency, and good *manners* when services are offered.

The face-to-face guest services can be placed into five categories: 1) to get to know something relevant about the guest, get ready various guest *consumables*, and inspect room facilities and amenities before the guest arrives; 2) to meet and show the guest into the room, make an *introduction* of the room facilities, and serve tea or water to the guest the moment the guest checks in; 3) to provide services like room-cleaning, floor-safeguarding, *parlor*, convention, laundry, shoeshine, beverage, item-renting, *infant* care, and lost items while the guest stays in; 4) to make sure of the guest's accurate check-out time, check bills, remind the guest of his / her baggage, and *bid farewell* to the guest as the guest leaves; 5) to check the room, deal with something left undone, clean up the room, and complete the housekeeping report after the guest

保管档案，向工程部申报工程维修，以及协调与其他部门的关系。

在宾客住店期间，客房服务人员不仅要保证客房清洁、舒适，还要提供面对面的对客服务，即面对面地为宾客提供各种服务，满足宾客提出的各种合理的要求。对客服务员要求身体健康，能吃苦耐劳，仪表仪容美观大方，待人有礼有节，言谈举止规范，有一定的外语水平。对客服务重点是要做到真诚服务、讲求效率和礼貌待客。

面对面对客服务的内容可以分为五个部分：1) 宾客抵店前，了解宾客的相关情况，准备各种客用消耗品，检查设备和用品；2) 宾客抵店时，迎接宾客并引领入房，介绍房间设备和端茶送水；3) 宾客住宿期间，提供房间整理、楼面保安、会客、会议、洗衣、擦鞋、饮料、对客租借、托婴及遗失物品处理等服务；4) 宾客离店时，掌握宾客离店的准确时间，检查账单，提醒宾客检查行李，送别宾客；5) 宾客离店后，检查房间，处理遗留事项，整理清洁客房和填写房务报表。此外还包括向宾客提供的个性服务或定向服务。

leaves. In addition, guests are also provided with some personalized services or *targeted* services.

4.2.3 Laundry, Linen, and Public Areas

The laundry room, the linen room, and the public areas are the three subordinate functions of the housekeeping department in addition to the housekeeping center.

The laundry room, under the leadership of the captain, provides laundry service to guests, and is responsible for cleaning and pressing the hotel's linen products and the staff's uniforms. The laundry staff should have all laundries collected, cleaned, and stored, and have laundry lists filled out according to the procedures and requirements stipulated in the laundry management rules of the housekeeping department.

The linen room, led by the captain, is in charge of the replacement and distribution of after-wash linens and uniforms. In detail, the work of the linen room includes collecting and distributing, *sorting*, making *periodic* inventories, cleaning and saving, mending, replacing, and supplying of all linens from the housekeeping department and the food & beverage division.

The public areas, under the supervision of the captain, does the cleaning and maintenance work of the public areas, including, in detail, carpet cleaning, marble maintenance, public area cleaning, equipment maintenance, and so on.

洗衣房、布草房及公共区域

洗衣房、布草房及公共区域是管家部除客房服务中心以外的三个下属部门。

洗衣房在领班的督导下为宾客提供洗涤服务，并承担酒店布草用品和员工制服的洗熨工作。洗衣房员工要按管家部洗衣管理办法进行衣物的收集、洗涤、保存，以及洗衣单的填写。

布草房由其领班领导，负责酒店所有布草、制服洗涤后的交换、发送业务。具体来讲，布草房的工作包括客房和餐饮部布草的收发、分类、定期盘点、洗涤储存、修补、更新和供应等。

公共区域部在领班的领导下，负责酒店公共区域的清洁保养工作，具体包括地毯洗涤、大理石养护、公共区域的清洁卫生及设备养护等。

Vocabulary

liaison /liˈeɪzn/ *n.* 联络

notify /ˈnəʊtɪfaɪ/ *v.* 通知；报告

appearance /əˈpɪərəns/ *n.* 相貌

attitude /ˈætɪtjuːd/ *n.* 态度

emphasis /ˈemfəsɪs/ *n.* 重点

manners /ˈmænəz/ *n.* 礼貌

introduction /ˌɪntrəˈdʌkʃn/ *n.* 介绍

infant /ˈɪnfənt/ *n.* 婴儿；幼儿

farewell /ˌfeəˈwel/ *n.* 告别

sort /sɔːt/ *v.* 分类

dial /ˈdaɪəl/ *v.* 拨号

reasonable /ˈriːznəbl/ *adj.* 合理的

restrained /rɪˈstreɪnd/ *adj.* 有节制的

refined /rɪˈfaɪnd/ *adj.* 优雅的

sincerity /sɪnˈserəti/ *n.* 真诚

consumable /kənˈsjuːməbl/ *n.* 消费品

parlor /ˈpɑːlə(r)/ *n.* 会客室

bid /bɪd/ *v.* 告别

target /ˈtɑːgɪt/ *v.* 定向

periodic /ˌpɪəriˈɒdɪk/ *adj.* 定期的

Useful Expressions

undertake no task of ... 不承担……任务

make an introduction of ... 介绍……

face to face 面对面地

bid farewell to ... 为……送行

词汇、课文资源

词汇、课文自测

微课

课堂练习

4.2.4　Room Description

When a guest checks in, an important item of the guest service is to get him / her to know something about the room product and relevant services, like room design, room type, and room amenities. Specifically, a guest should be informed of the type, design, and interior amenities of the room he / she is staying in, and which amenities are complimentary or room extras. The most important thing is that a guest should be made familiar with

客房介绍

宾客入住时，对客服务的一个重要内容就是让宾客了解客房产品及相关服务，如客房设计、客房类型和客房用品等。具体讲，要让宾客了解其所入住的客房的类型、设计和设施，哪些设施是免费的以及哪些是要额外付费的。最重要的是让宾客知道如何使用客房设施，包括如何打电话订客房送餐服务，如

how to use the room amenities, including how to call to order room service, how to *lock* the *safe*, how to use the TV set and his / her *remote controller*, how to connect the Internet, how to set the alarm clock, and, above all, how to contact someone if he / she needs any help at all.

In the hospitality industry, guestrooms are a hotel's *infrastructure*, the *basis* on which a hotel exists, and also an important *symbol* of the quality level of a hotel's services. In China, the area of a hotel's guestrooms usually accounts for over 60% of its total construction area. Guestrooms are the products a hotel sells for guests to rest and sleep in. Guests often *base* their choices upon the most basic requirements: clean, comfortable, convenient, and safe. In star hotels, as a rule, a standard room has a net area of not less than 14 *square* meters (bathroom excluded, which is not less than 4 square meters), and a net height of not less than 2.7 meters. A guestroom must be equipped with bed, *carpet*, TV set, telephone, air conditioner, other pieces of furniture, and, in addition, with guest consumables and rental amenities. And certainly it is a must to make sure that guestrooms are clean, safe, and in normal operation.

Guestrooms are the main places for guests to live in during their stay in the hotel. So we should follow the principles below while designing rooms: 1) human-*oriented*, to have in mind the needs of guests; 2) function *foremost*, to provide guests with comfortable places for them to rest and sleep in; 3) security ensuring, to prevent fire and protect

何锁住保险箱，如何操作电视机及遥控器，如何连接互联网，如何设置闹钟等，尤其是，宾客需要帮助时如何与相关人取得联系。

在酒店业，客房是酒店的基本设施，是酒店赖以存在的基础，也是酒店服务水平的重要标志。在我国，酒店客房的建筑面积一般占酒店总面积的60%以上。客房是酒店出售的主要满足宾客休息、睡眠需要的产品。清洁、舒适、方便、安全是宾客选择酒店的最基本要求。按规定，星级酒店的标准间客房净面积（不含卫生间）不小于14平方米，卫生间面积不小于4平方米，房间净高度不低于2.7米。客房必须配置床、地毯、电视、电话、空调及家具等，还要配备客用消耗用品、客用租借用品等。当然，客房还必须保证卫生、安全和正常运转。

客房是宾客在酒店逗留期间的主要生活场所，所以客房设计必须遵循以下原则：1) 以人为本，以满足宾客的需求为出发点；2) 功能第一，满足宾客休息和睡眠的需要；3) 保证安全性，注重火灾预防和隐私保护；4) 追求舒适性，房间大小、

privacy; 4) comfort *pursuing*, to take into account the *sensory* enjoyment of guests in such things as room size, interior designs, furniture *arrangements*, room amenities, interior color and light, and in-door *houseplants* and *decorations*.

A hotel should accommodate guests of different types or grades by providing them with appropriate guestrooms according to the hotel's type and location. Guestrooms of a hotel can be put into the following categories: *single* room, with only a single bed, appropriate for single guests traveling for business; *double* room, with a double bed, suitable for traveling couples; *twin* room (or standard room if it has a bath), with two single beds, usually used to accommodate tour groups or convention groups; *triple* room (also *economic* room), with three single beds, or two single beds plus a *rollaway* bed; standard suite, generally with one bedroom and one living room; deluxe suite, with a living room, a bedroom, and a dining or conference room; *presidential* suite, with seven or eight rooms, accommodating heads of the states or anyone else who can *afford* it; special room, specially designed for a particular type of guests; special floor, like business floor, executive floor, ladies' floor, designed on the same floor for guests of a kind.

A hotel *stocks* guestrooms with charge-based or non-charge-based amenities, which are available either with the room or on request. Charge-based amenities include *contents* in the mini-bar, and other

室内设计、家具摆放、房间用品、室内色彩光线、室内绿化饰品等都要考虑人体感官的享受。

酒店要适应不同类型或档次宾客的需求，考虑酒店的类型和所处的位置，设置相应类型和档次的客房。酒店的客房可以做如下分类：单人间，只有一张单人床，适合商务旅行的单身宾客住用；大床间，配备一张双人床，适合夫妻旅游者居住；双人间，放置两张单人床，带卫生间的双人间，称为标准间，一般用来安排旅游团队或会议宾客；三人间，也叫经济间，放置三张单人床或两张单人床加一张可移动的折叠床；标准套间，有一间卧室和一间起居室；豪华套间，有两间做起居室和卧室，还有一间或做餐室或做会议室；总统套间，一般由七八个房间组成，并不是只有国家元首才能住，只要付得起房费谁都可以入住；特殊客房，为某一类人特别设置；特色楼层，如商务楼层、行政楼层、女士楼层，由酒店在同一楼层上面向同类消费宾客设置。

酒店客房内配有收费的和免费的客用品，这些有随房配好的，也有应宾客要求提供的。收费客用品有迷你吧物品，以及避孕套、短

items with price marked on, like condoms, shorts, *compressed* towels, bath robes, and movie channels. Non-charge-based amenities include the items in the bathroom: toothbrush, toothpaste, soap, shampoo, hair conditioner, bath salt, *emery* board, cotton balls, and *lotion*; those in the bedroom: an iron, ironing board, extra *blankets* or *pillows*, cable TV, a safe, and a *digital* alarm clock; those as gifts for guests: *envelopes*, postcards, gift bags, and sewing *kits*; and those *reusable* items that can't be taken away, like linens, ashtrays, and wine sets.

4.2.5 Room Cleaning

Room cleaning, one of the major tasks of the housekeeping department, includes three things: *sanifying* rooms to keep a clean and fresh environment; replacing and adding amenities to make guests a comfortable and convenient "home"; and maintaining rooms to ensure rooms of high quality.

Room codes are often used in housekeeping to update the status of a room. They can help the housekeeping staff know which rooms to service first, and also help the front desk personnel know the room status. The room codes include Early Cleaning, VIP, Reserved, Vacant, Vacant and Dirty, Stay-Over, Late Checkout, DND (Do Not *Disturb*), and No-Service. Upon finishing the room cleaning, room attendants should keep a record of their work by writing "OC" for occupied clean rooms and "VC" for vacant clean rooms.

While cleaning occupied rooms, room attendants should *observe* the following: do not disturb or

裤、压缩毛巾、浴袍、电影频道等其他标有价格的物品。免费客用品包括浴室里的牙刷、牙膏、肥皂、洗发液、护发素、浴盐、指甲锉、棉球和洗浴剂；卧室里的熨斗、熨衣板、加毯或枕头、有线电视、保险箱和数字闹钟；供馈赠宾客的信封、明信片、礼品袋和针线包；不能让宾客带走的可重复使用的客用品，如布草、烟灰缸、酒具等。

客房清洁

客房清洁是管家部的主要任务之一。其任务一是搞好清洁卫生，以保持客房清新的环境，二是更换添补客房用品，为客人提供一个舒适、方便的"家"，三是维护保养，满足客人对客房产品的质量要求。

客房部经常用房间代码来更新房态。这些代码有助于客房部的员工了解哪些房间应先做服务，同时也有助于前台员工了解房态。代码包括：早晨清洁要求、贵宾房、预留房、空房、空脏房、过夜房、迟退房、"请勿打扰"房、无须服务房等。客房服务员打扫完之后要做好记录，干净的占用房标注"OC"，干净的空房标注"VC"。

在对住客房进行清扫作业时，客房服务员要做到：不要干扰客人，

interfere with guests, knock at the door before entering, clean with no guest in and with door open, respect guests' living habits, protect the environment, and turn off the lights and lock the door before leaving. As to check-out rooms, room attendants should give them a *thorough* cleaning as soon as possible to ensure that they are normally for rent.

The first thing for room attendants to do upon entering is check whether there is anything left by guests and whether there is any damage on or loss of the room facilities or furniture. If anything above is found, they should immediately report it to the captain and make a record of it. Below are the procedures specified for room attendants to follow while doing room cleaning: removing *soiled* linen and towels and replacing them with fresh ones, checking the bed and blankets for damage, making the beds, emptying trash, checking the guestroom for broken appliances, damaged *shades* or *blinds*, and *leaky faucets*, cleaning the guestroom and bathroom, replacing bathroom towels and amenities, and in some hotels, *replenishing* guest consumables.

进房前先敲门，无客时作业，开着门作业，尊重客人生活习惯，注意环境保护，离开时关灯锁门。对于走客房，客房服务员应尽快进行彻底清扫，以保证客房的正常出租。

客房服务员进入房间后，应首先检查房内是否有客人遗落下来的物品，房间的设备和家具有没有损坏或丢失。如发现以上情况，立即报告领班，并进行登记。清洁客房时，客房服务员必须遵循以下指定程序：移除弄脏的布草和毛巾并换上新的布草和毛巾，检查床铺和毯子是否有损坏，整理床铺，倒空垃圾，检查客房电器、窗帘或百叶窗是否损坏，水龙头是否漏水，清洁客房和浴室，更换浴室毛巾及设施，在有些酒店里客房服务员还必须补充客用消费品。

Vocabulary

lock /lɒk/ *v.* 锁

remote /rɪˈməʊt/ *adj.* 远程的

infrastructure /ˈɪnfrəstrʌktʃə(r)/ *n.* 基础设施

symbol /ˈsɪmbl/ *n.* 象征；标志

square /skweə(r)/ *n.* 平方

oriented /ɔːrientɪd/ *adj.* 以……为方向（目的）的

safe /seɪf/ *n.* 保险箱

controller /kənˈtrəʊlə(r)/ *n.* 遥控器

basis /ˈbeɪsɪs/ *n.* 基础

base /beɪs/ *v.* 把……建立在

carpet /ˈkɑːpɪt/ *n.* 地毯

foremost /ˈfɔːməʊst/ *adj.* 最重要的

pursue /pəˈsjuː/ *v.* 追求

arrangement /əˈreɪndʒmənt/ *n.* 布置

houseplant /ˈhaʊsplɑːnt/ *n.* 盆栽植物；室内植物

decoration /ˌdekəˈreɪʃn/ *n.* 装饰品

double /ˈdʌbl/ *adj.* 双人的

triple /ˈtrɪpl/ *adj.* 三人的

economic /ˌiːkəˈnɒmɪk/ *adj.* 节约的；经济的

rollaway /ˈrəʊləweɪ/ *adj.* 滚动的；移动的

afford /əˈfɔːd/ *v.* 花费得起

content /ˈkɒntent/ *n.* 所容纳之物

emery /ˈeməri/ *n.* 金刚砂

blanket /ˈblæŋkɪt/ *n.* 毛毯

digital /ˈdɪdʒɪtl/ *adj.* 数字的

kit /kɪt/ *n.* 成套工具

reusable /ˌriːˈjuːzəbl/ *adj.* 可（多次）重复使用的

sanify /ˈsænəfaɪ/ *v.* 使卫生

observe /əbˈzɜːv/ *v.* 遵守；做到

soiled /sɔɪld/ *adj.* 污染的；弄脏的

blind /blaɪnd/ *n.* 百叶窗帘

faucet /ˈfɔːsɪt/ *n.* 水龙头

sensory /ˈsensəri/ *adj.* 感官的

single /ˈsɪŋgl/ *adj.* 单人的

twin /twɪn/ *adj.* 双人的

presidential /ˌprezɪˈdenʃl/ *adj.* 总统的

stock /stɒk/ *v.* 配备

compressed /kəmˈprest/ *adj.* 压缩的

lotion /ˈləʊʃn/ *n.* 洗液

pillow /ˈpɪləʊ/ *n.* 枕头

envelope /ˈenvələʊp/ *n.* 信封

disturb /dɪˈstɜːb/ *v.* 打扰

thorough /ˈθʌrə/ *adj.* 彻底的

shade /ʃeɪd/ *n.* 帘

leaky /ˈliːki/ *adj.* 有裂缝的；泄漏的

replenish /rɪˈplenɪʃ/ *v.* 补充；再装满

Useful Expressions

account for ... 占……

be in normal operation 正常运转

take ... into account 考虑……

on request 一经请求

interfere with ... 打扰……

as a rule 按规定

have ... in mind 想

stock ... with ... 给……配备

keep a record of ... 记录……

词汇、课文资源

词汇、课文自测

微课

课堂练习

Chapter Five

Food & Beverage Division
餐饮部

思政园地／二十
大精神学习专栏

Learning Objectives

· *To get familiar with the major operation of the hotel revenue centers—the Food & Beverage division;*

· *To understand the staff, tasks, standards, goals, and requirements of each of its departments;*

· *To master the new words and professional terms concerned;*

· *To improve reading ability through learning the text;*

· *To develop team spirit and self-study ability through learning activities;*

· *To receive education in ideological and political theories through course learning.*

Teaching Arrangements

节次	教学内容	自主学习资源	自主学习自测	课堂教学视频	课堂练习
L 1	5.1.1 Food & Beverage Management 5.1.2 Food & Beverage Facilities	词汇、课文资源	词汇、课文自测	微课	课堂练习
L 2	5.2.1 Food Service Management 5.2.2 Food Service Cycle	词汇、课文资源	词汇、课文自测	微课	课堂练习
L 3	5.2.3 The Chinese Food 5.2.4 The Western Food	词汇、课文资源	词汇、课文自测	微课	课堂练习
L 4	5.3.1 Beverage Service Department 5.3.2 Catering Department	词汇、课文资源	词汇、课文自测	微课	课堂练习
L 5	5.3.3 Room Service Department 5.3.4 Culinary Department 5.3.5 Purchasing Department	词汇、课文资源	词汇、课文自测	微课	课堂练习

The food & beverage division, which operates under the supervision of the food & beverage manager, is a major part in hotel operations, and a *principal* revenue-*earning* division of a hotel. A *considerable* income can be *derived* from the services provided by the food & beverage division, and almost a half of the total revenue in China's tourism hotels comes from their food & beverage services. The food & beverage manager, directly responsible to the general manager, supervises his / her own staff's work, and ensures a good relationship between the food & beverage division and other divisions, like the front office, the sales & marketing, the purchasing, the finance, and the engineering.

餐饮部在餐饮部经理的督导下运作，是酒店经营的重要组成部分，是酒店的主要营收部门。餐饮部可创造可观的经济效益。在我国旅游酒店里餐饮收入约占酒店总收入的近二分之一。餐饮部经理直接向酒店总经理负责，管辖餐饮部全体员工，并负责与前厅部、销售部、采购部、财务部和工程部之间的联系。

5.1 Overview of Food & Beverage Division

5.1.1 Food & Beverage Management

The food & beverage division can be complex, covering the traditional food & beverage facilities like restaurants and bars, and the entertainment facilities like karaoke bars, dance halls, and cafes, and even conference facilities in some hotels, each with its own unique decor, menu, and style of service. Whether or not the food & beverage division has a reasonable organization chart directly affects its production forms and ability to accomplish tasks, and its work efficiency, product (service) quality, *informative* communication, and authority *execution*.

餐饮部管理层

餐饮部门结构复杂，管辖范围一般包括各类餐厅、酒吧等传统餐饮设施，还有歌厅、舞厅、茶座等娱乐设施，甚至有些酒店里还管理各种会议设施，各有自己独特的装饰、菜单和服务风格。餐饮部组织机构是否合理，直接关系到生产的形式和完成生产任务的能力，关系到工作效率、产品（服务）质量、信息的沟通和职权的履行。

It is common that the food & beverage division includes such departments as the food service, the beverage service, the culinary, the catering, the room service, the *stewarding*, and the purchasing. All *subdivision* managers, *respectively* responsible to the food & beverage manager, supervise the work of their own staff. For example, the food service and the beverage service are responsible for eating and drinking, the culinary for providing food for various hotel functions, and the catering for selling banquets and conventions to companies and the public, and for the management of banquets and events.

The food & beverage division is made up of the food & beverage manager who directs the work of the division, the purchasing steward who buys, receives, and stores foods and beverages, the executive *chef* who decides on the items on the menus and coordinates preparation of the food and beverage, the chief steward who is in charge of *sanitation*, the *headwaiter* who is responsible for serving foods and beverages to guests, and the food & beverage controller who maintains control over the system, prepares *statements* for the management and *analyzes* all stages of the food and beverage operation. Under these people are *storekeepers*, *pantry* men, *icemen*, chefs, chef assistants, *butchers*, *pastry* men, *bakers*, waiters and waitresses, busboys, bartenders, porters and bar boys.

The food & beverage staff, especially waiters and waitresses in restaurants, offers face-to-face services to guests. Whether good or poor the food &

一般情况下，餐饮部主要有餐厅部、酒水部、厨房部、宴会部、客房送餐部、管事部和采购部等下属部门。所有下属部门经理都分别对餐饮部经理负责，并督导各自部门员工的工作。例如，餐厅部和酒水部负责饮食，厨房部向酒店各部门提供食物，宴会部向公司或公众出售宴会和会议服务，并负责宴会和活动管理。

餐饮部有下列人员：餐饮部经理、采购组长、厨师长、卫生监督员、服务员领班和监查员。经理领导整个餐饮部的工作，采购组长负责食品和饮料采购、购进和储藏，厨师长负责决定菜单的内容和协调食品的烹制和饮料的配制，管事长负责卫生状况，服务员领班负责给客人上食品和饮料，监查员负责监督全盘工作，向管理层报告餐饮部的情况和对餐饮部各阶段的工作进行分析。上述人员分管以下人员的工作：贮藏员、食品管理员、制冰工、厨师、助理厨师、切肉师、糕点师、面包师、男女服务员、助理服务员、吧台配酒员、杂务员和酒吧服务员。

餐饮部工作人员，特别是餐厅服务人员为客人提供面对面的服务。餐饮服务的好坏直接影响餐饮

beverage service is will have a direct impact on the hotel's revenue and even the hotel's image and *reputation*. So, the personnel of the food & beverage division must have a professional and *ideological* quality of a higher level, a good service attitude of being *initiative*, *enthusiastic*, *patient*, and *thoughtful*, a wide range of service basics and job *knowledge*, and certain *capabilities* like *eloquence*, *resilience*, marketing, *self-discipline*, and *collaboration*. What's more, the personnel are required to have a good health and a strong *physique*. Good service should meet the "SERVICE" standards: S (sincere), E (efficient), R (ready to serve), V (valuable), I (*individualized*), C (*courteous*), and E (excellent).

5.1.2 Food & Beverage Facilities

The food & beverage facilities in big hotels are listed as below.

Chinese restaurants, with the Chinese themes *highlighted* in their decoration, provide Chinese-style services. In Chinese restaurants, where only lunch and dinner meals are provided, the Chinese dishes, including cuisines of Sichuan, Cantonese, Shandong, and Huaiyang, are generally available.

Cafes, *chiefly* of Western-themed decoration, provide a convenient Western-style food and beverage service to guests in non-dining time. Simple Western foods, local fast foods, and self-service foods are commonly available.

Western restaurants, *characteristic* of luxury, *elegance*, *romance*, and live music, commonly provide French and Italian cuisines to those high

部及酒店的经济效益，更直接影响酒店的形象和声誉。所以，餐饮服务人员必须具备较高的专业、思想素质，具备主动、热情、耐心和周到的服务态度，具备较为宽泛的服务基础知识和岗位专业知识，具备一定的语言、应变、推销、自律和协作等能力，还需要有健康的身体和健壮的体格。优质餐饮服务的标准应当是"SERVICE"，即真诚的（S）、高效的（E）、即时的（R）、物有所值的（V）、个性化的（I）、礼貌的（C）和完美的（E）。

餐饮设施

大型酒店主要有如下餐饮设施。

中餐厅，装饰主题突出中式风格，采用中式服务，主要经营川菜、粤菜、鲁菜、淮扬菜等中式菜肴。一般仅提供中餐、晚餐服务。

咖啡厅，装饰主题以西式风格为主，采用西式服务，方便宾客非用餐时段的餐饮消费，一般提供简单西餐、当地风味快餐或自助餐。

西餐厅，豪华的布置、幽雅的环境、浪漫的情调、现场音乐演奏，满足部分高消费者的需求，一

consumers.

Multi-function halls, the largest venues of the Catering, are fully equipped and furnished for large-scale events like Chinese banquets, Western banquets, buffet receptions, cocktail parties, press conferences, news *releases*, *fashion* shows, and *academic* conferences.

Small banquet halls, also called private rooms, are designed for smaller-size events with one to three tables. Private rooms have their own names each, and *vary* in their decoration styles by their names.

Special restaurants, or theme restaurants, such as *seafood* restaurants, Thai restaurants, Japanese restaurants, and Korean *barbecue* restaurants, are designed for people who pursue personalized life, enjoy *exotic* cultures, and satisfy *curiosities*. A theme restaurant, in *essence*, sells a certain cultural theme, to add to ordinary dining activities a specific *geographical* culture, a time-and-space culture, a *historical* culture, a local culture, or an *urban* culture, and to show the theme culture by creating a certain special atmosphere and *reproducing* a certain life scene. A clearly-themed restaurant has an interior design full of *imagination*. It has its own target market, where it establishes a good relationship with guests on the basis of themed activities, and where it enables guests to enjoy special experiences while dining. The theme characteristics of restaurants can be *deepened* by organizing food *festivals* and themed events.

Buffet restaurants are currently popular,

般可提供法式或意式菜肴。

多功能厅，功能齐全，是宴会部最大的活动场所，可以举办大型中西餐宴会、冷餐酒会、鸡尾酒会、记者招待会、新闻发布会、时装展示会、学术会议等。

小宴会厅，又叫包间，一般可以满足 1～3 桌小型餐饮活动的需求。每个小宴会厅都有自己的名称，装饰风格因厅名而异。

特色餐厅，即主题餐厅，如海鲜餐厅、泰国餐厅、日本料理餐厅、韩国烧烤餐厅等，切合人们追求个性化生活、品味异域文化和满足好奇心的需求。主题餐厅的实质就是销售一种主题文化，赋予普通的就餐活动以特殊的地域文化、时空文化、历史文化、乡土文化或都市文化等，并通过特殊气氛的营造和生活场景的重现展现主题文化。主题餐厅主题鲜明，装潢设计充满想象，拥有自己的目标市场，借助主题活动与宾客建立良好关系，让人们在进餐过程中体验特殊经历。主题餐厅可以通过举办美食节活动、主题庆祝活动来深化其主题特色。

自助餐厅，当前较为流行。自助

offering self-service foods to individual or group guests. Differently, buffet receptions receive catering guests in a self-service way. Buffet service is characteristic of *affordable* price, full variety, quick service, easy access, and themed decoration.

Room service, another food & beverage facility, also called private dining, provides, as *requested*, some type of food service to guests in their rooms or any designated places.

餐厅不同于冷餐会。自助餐厅接待散客或团客，而冷餐会接待宴会宾客，是一种以自助形式提供的宴会服务。自助餐的特点是价格实惠、品种丰富、节省时间、方便宾客、主题装饰等。

送餐服务是另一种餐饮设施，也叫私人用餐服务，一种按客人要求，到客房或指定地点提供餐饮服务的形式。

Vocabulary

principal /ˈprɪnsəpl/ *adj.* 首要的；主要的

considerable /kənˈsɪdərəbl/ *adj.* 可观的；相当大的

derive /dɪˈraɪv/ *v.* 获得

execution /ˌeksɪˈkjuːʃn/ *n.* 执行；履行；实施

subdivision /ˌsʌbdɪˈvɪʒn/ *n.* 下属部门

chef /ʃef/ *n.* 主厨

headwaiter /ˈhedˈweɪtə(r)/ *n.* 服务生领班

statement /ˈsteɪtmənt/ *n.* 书面意见；（情况）说明

analyze /ˈænəlaɪz/ *v.* 分析研究

pantry /ˈpæntri/ *n.* 食品贮藏室

butcher /ˈbʊtʃə(r)/ *n.* 切肉师

baker /ˈbeɪkə(r)/ *n.* 面包师

ideological /ˌaɪdiəˈlɒdʒɪkl/ *adj.* 思想上的

enthusiastic /ɪnˌθjuːziˈæstɪk/ *adj.* 热情的

thoughtful /ˈθɔːtfl/ *adj.* 体贴的；周到的

capability /ˌkeɪpəˈbɪləti/ *n.* 能力

resilience /rɪˈzɪliəns/ *n.* 应变

earn /ɜːn/ *v.* 赚（钱）

informative /ɪnˈfɔːmətɪv/ *adj.* 传播信息的

steward /ˈstjuːəd/ *v.* 当管事

respectively /rɪˈspektɪvli/ *adv.* 各自地

sanitation /ˌsænɪˈteɪʃn/ *n.* （环境）卫生

storekeeper /ˈstɔːkiːpə(r)/ *n.* 仓库管理员

iceman /ˈaɪsmæn/ *n.* 制冰工

pastry /ˈpeɪstri/ *n.* 糕点

reputation /ˌrepjuˈteɪʃn/ *n.* 声誉

initiative /ɪˈnɪʃətɪv/ *adj.* 主动的

patient /ˈpeɪʃnt/ *adj.* 有耐心的

knowledge /ˈnɒlɪdʒ/ *n.* 知识；学问

eloquence /ˈeləkwəns/ *n.* 雄辩；口才

self-discipline /ˌself ˈdɪsəplɪn/ *n.* 自律

collaboration /kəˌlæbəˈreɪʃn/ *n.* 合作

individualized /ˌɪndɪˈvɪdʒuəlaɪzd/ *adj.* 个性化的

highlight /ˈhaɪlaɪt/ *v.* 突出

characteristic /ˌkærəktəˈrɪstɪk/ *adj.* 显示特色的

romance /rəʊˈmæns/ *n.* 浪漫氛围

fashion /ˈfæʃn/ *n.* 时尚

vary /ˈveəri/ *v.* 变化

barbecue /ˈbɑːbɪkjuː/ *n.* 烤肉；烧烤

curiosity /ˌkjʊəriˈɒsəti/ *n.* 好奇

geographical /ˌdʒiːəˈgræfɪkl/ *adj.* 地理上的

historical /hɪˈstɒrɪkl/ *adj.* 历史上的；与历史有关的

reproduce /ˌriːprəˈdjuːs/ *v.* 重现

deepen /ˈdiːpən/ *v.* 使浓烈；使强烈

affordable /əˈfɔːdəbl/ *adj.* 支付得起的；不算太贵的

request /rɪˈkwest/ *v.* 请求；要求

physique /fɪˈziːk/ *n.* 体格

courteous /ˈkɜːtiəs/ *adj.* 有礼貌的

chiefly /ˈtʃiːfli/ *adv.* 主要地

elegance /ˈelɪgəns/ *n.* 典雅

release /rɪˈliːs/ *n.* 发行；发表；发布

academic /ˌækəˈdemɪk/ *adj.* 学术的

seafood /ˈsiːfuːd/ *n.* 海味；海鲜

exotic /ɪgˈzɒtɪk/ *adj.* 异国的

essence /ˈesns/ *n.* 本质

urban /ˈɜːbən/ *adj.* 都市的

imagination /ɪˌmædʒɪˈneɪʃn/ *n.* 想象

festival /ˈfestɪvl/ *n.* 节日

Useful Expressions

be derived from ... 源自……

decide on ... 做……决定

be characteristic of 具有……特点

in essence 实质上

enable sb. to do sth. 使某人能够做某事

be made up of ... 由……组成

maintain control over ... 掌控……

vary by... 随……变化

full of imagination 充满想象的

词汇、课文资源

词汇、课文自测

微课

课堂练习

5.2 Food Service Department

5.2.1 Food Service Management

The food service department is a place where foods, beverages, and related services are sold to meet guests' *dietary* requirements, and a convenient and comfortable place where guests eat, meet friends, or have formal or informal meetings. The food service manager, reporting to the food & beverage manager, must see that guest service goes smoothly, that there is a *sufficient* number of food *servers* and buspersons on duty, and that all food service employees are *well-trained* and are meeting the hotel's service standards. The food service manager supervises the work of captains, reservationists, *greeters*, food servers, and buspersons, and ensures a good communication and coordination with the culinary department, the stewarding department, and some others. In some luxury hotels, reservationists take reservations, captains *seat* guests and take orders, buspersons *deliver* dishes from the kitchen to food servers, food servers serve orders, and cashiers receive cash payments or signed bills. When a guest wants to charge his / her bill to his / her room account, it must be reported to the finance division as soon as possible.

The food service is expected to be fast, polite, professional, and of top quality. Everything, from food *delicacy*, food taste, and food sanitation to wine *stocks*, and from serving skills, room decoration and atmosphere to even dining music and entertainment, must be on the first level among the

餐厅部管理

餐厅是通过出售食物、酒水及相关服务来满足宾客饮食需求的场所，也提供了一个方便、舒适的环境，供宾客就餐、会友或开正式或非正式会议。餐厅经理向餐饮部经理负责，必须确保对客服务顺利开展，确保有足够数量的当值上菜员和传菜员，确保所有餐厅员工都训练有素，符合酒店的服务标准。餐厅经理督导领班、预订员、迎宾员、餐厅服务员、传菜员等员工的工作，保持与厨房部、管事部及酒店其他部门的联系。在一些高级酒店里，预订员负责接受预订，领班负责引座和点菜，传菜员负责把菜肴从厨房端到餐厅交给服务员，服务员则负责上菜，出纳员负责收款或收宾客签名账单。当宾客要求把餐费记入酒店账户时，要尽快将该项账目通知财务部。

餐厅服务要求迅速、有礼貌、技术熟练和上乘的质量。从食品的精美度、风味、卫生到酒类的选配，从服务员的服务技术、餐厅的装潢到餐厅的气氛，甚至餐厅里的音乐和娱乐节目，所有一切都必须

dining establishments in the city. This is because a guest's experience with these outlets constitutes an important part of his / her overall experience with the property. Therefore, a guest usually demands that the service from the food & beverage division be on a *par* with that from other divisions in the hotel. If the service from the dining rooms fails to match that from other departments, it will fall short of the guest's expectation and *satisfactory* experience with the hotel.

5.2.2　Food Service Cycle

Successful restaurants are usually very busy that the only way to make sure of seats is by booking. Reservationists should be polite and efficient, and speak *briefly* with *confidence*. The most important thing to do is listen to guests *attentively* and write down guests' information *accurately*. This information should include: date and time of arrival, number of guests in the party, which room to use, smoking or non-smoking *preference*, any special seat arrangements, any *vegetarian* requirements, or any special *occasion* such as birthday or *anniversary*. And the last thing is to write down the guest's contact number. All reservations should be recorded in the booking *register*, the details of which are to be checked and *verified* by the dining room manager.

In top-class restaurants, a guest will not be shown directly to his / her table. He / She will be met by captain at the reception area, and then be guided to a seat in the bar area. The menu, as well as

达到所在城市一流餐厅的水准。因为这些餐饮销售点是宾客对酒店总体感受的一个重要组成部分。因此宾客常常要求餐饮服务的水平与酒店其他方面的服务水平一致。如果这些餐厅的服务水平低于其他部门的服务水平，就会使宾客感到失望，从而使宾客对酒店原有的良好印象大打折扣。

餐厅服务流程

成功的餐厅通常很热门，唯一能确保有座位的方法就是事先预订。预订员应当有礼貌、效率高、说话简明且有自信。最重要的是聆听并准确记录宾客信息，包括客到日期和时间、团体宾客人数、预订餐厅名称、是否有吸烟需求、有没有特别的座位安排、有没有素食要求以及是不是生日或周年庆典等特殊场合。最后，请宾客留下联系电话。所有的预订都记录在预订登记本上，供餐厅经理检查和核对。

高档餐厅一般不直接把宾客带到餐桌。餐厅领班在接待处接待宾客，再领他们去酒吧区域安排就座。服务员拿来菜单和酒水单让

the wine list, will be brought for him / her to study; and at the same time, beverages will be served.

Taking orders is usually in the charge of an experienced captain. He / She should be able to explain to guests what a dish is and how it is cooked, and should be able to make some timely suggestions to guests. The captain will have to write down the orders on a three-copy "Kitchen Order Ticket." One is used by the kitchen to prepare foods, another is used by the cashier to prepare the bill in advance, and the third is used by the waiter or waitress as a record of what has to be served.

After taking the order, the captain should read the order slowly and clearly for the guest to confirm, then have it taken to the kitchen as quickly as possible for the kitchen to prepare the *appetizer*, and ask the *sommelier* to come over to help select or recommend wines or other drinks to accompany the meal.

Only after everything is ready in the dining room and the kitchen will the captain invite guests to be seated at the table. Immediately, the waiter or waitress will deliver drinks to the table, assist guests with their *napkins*, and then be prepared to serve the *starter*. Only in this way should guests never feel that they are kept waiting nor feel that they are being hurried.

Table service is a *visual* display of the ability of the waiting staff. All kinds of services, such as serving orders, calling dish names, opening wine bottles, serving wines, serving towels, and replacing dishes, should be *standardized*. For example, order serving at the table is done on the guest's left hand side, and anything that has to be replaced

宾客研究菜单，同时向宾客提供饮料。

点菜一般由经验丰富的餐厅领班负责，他／她应能够向宾客介绍菜肴及其烹调方法，并适时地给出建议。领班要把宾客所点的菜写在三联式的厨房点菜单上，一联给厨房准备食品用，一联给收银员结账用，另一联给服务员记录餐桌服务内容用。

宾客点菜完毕后，领班要缓慢清楚地报菜以便宾客确认，再速送厨房，让厨房准备头道菜，安排酒水服务员过来帮助宾客选择或推荐配餐的酒水。

当餐厅和厨房一切就绪，领班带领宾客就座。服务员随后取来酒水饮料送至餐桌，并帮助宾客放餐巾，然后准备上头道菜。这样宾客就不会有等待的感觉，也不会感觉到匆匆忙忙。

餐桌服务是服务员展示能力的舞台。上菜、报菜、启酒、斟酒、递毛巾、撤换餐具等，都要做到规范服务。例如，上菜必须在宾客的左手方进行，而撤换餐具则要在宾客的右手方进行；开启酒瓶前，要向宾客展示没有开启过的酒瓶；得

or removed from the table should be done on the guest's right hand side; the unopened bottle should be shown to guests before it is opened; the bottle is opened in front of guests after they give permission; a small amount of the wine should be served first for guests to *sample* after the bottle is opened; a napkin should be used to wipe the neck of the bottle before *pouring*, and to *wrap* around the top of the bottle to stop wine from *dripping*.

Settling the payment is the final part of providing quality service to guests. When guests have decided to pay bills, they want a fast service. When the bill is presented, it should be kept in a bill folder. The bill should be completely correct, with every item served and its service charge clearly shown. The waiter or waitress should be ready to answer any question guests might ask. When the payment is made by credit card, the card must be checked by the cashier and returned to the holder, together with the credit slip, for signature. The slip with the bill together is the receipt for payment. When payment is made by cash, the receipt should be given together with the change.

到宾客允许后，方可当面打开；打开后，先给宾客少量酒试尝；倒酒前应先用餐巾擦拭酒瓶颈部，包住酒瓶上端，防止倒酒时酒往下流。

结账是为宾客提供高质量服务的最后环节。宾客决定买单时，希望得到快速服务。递交账单时要将其放入账单夹。账单必须完全正确，所有服务项目和服务费用必须一一列明。服务员要做好准备回答宾客有可能提出的任何问题。信用卡支付时，经收银员确认后，连同收款凭证一起交由持有人签字。凭证与账单一起作为付款收据。现金支付时，收据与零钱应一起给出。

Vocabulary

dietary /ˈdaɪətəri/ *adj.* 饮食的

server /ˈsɜːvə(r)/ *n.* 侍者

greeter /ˈɡriːtə(r)/ *n.* 迎宾员

deliver /dɪˈlɪvə(r)/ *v.* 传送

sufficient /səˈfɪʃnt/ *adj.* 足够的

well-trained /ˌwel ˈtreɪnd/ *adj.* 训练有素的

seat /siːt/ *v.* 使坐下

delicacy /ˈdelɪkəsi/ *n.* 精致；精美

stock /stɒk/ *n.* 存货　　par /pɑː(r)/ *n.* 同等

satisfactory /ˌsætɪsˈfæktəri/ *adj.* 令人满意的

briefly /ˈbriːfli/ *adv.* 简短地；简单地　　confidence /ˈkɒnfɪdəns/ *n.* 自信；信心

attentively /əˈtentɪvli/ *adv.* 注意地；留意地

accurately /ˈækjərətli/ *adv.* 准确地　　preference /ˈprefrəns/ *n.* 喜好

vegetarian /ˌvedʒəˈteəriən/ *adj.* 素食的　　occasion /əˈkeɪʒn/ *n.* 场合

anniversary /ˌænɪˈvɜːsəri/ *n.* 周年纪念日　　register /ˈredʒɪstə(r)/ *n.* 登记簿

verify /ˈverɪfaɪ/ *v.* 核实　　appetizer /ˈæpɪtaɪzə(r)/ *n.* 开胃菜

sommelier /səˈmelɪeɪ/ *n.* 斟酒服务员　　napkin /ˈnæpkɪn/ *n.* 餐巾

starter /ˈstɑːtə(r)/ *n.* 头道菜　　visual /ˈvɪʒuəl/ *adj.* 视觉的

standardize /ˈstændədaɪz/ *v.* 使标准化　　sample /ˈsɑːmpl/ *v.* 品尝

pour /pɔː(r)/ *v.* 倒；倾倒　　wrap /ræp/ *v.* 包起来

drip /drɪp/ *v.* 下滴

Useful Expressions

charge ... to an account 把……入账　　be on the first level 达到一流

be on a par with... 与……一致　　fall short of... 不足；达不到

with confidence 自信地　　guide sb. to a place 带某人去某地

词汇、课文资源

词汇、课文自测

微课

课堂练习

5.2.3 The Chinese Food

中　餐

China is a country with the largest *population*, where different *nationalities inhabiting* different geographical areas have developed different *customs*, different cultures, and a large variety of Chinese foods and dishes. Many guests will want to try different Chinese dishes while they are visiting China. The Chinese dishes, according to their

中国人口众多，不同地理环境下的不同民族形成了不同的习俗、不同的文化，也形成了众多的中式风味菜肴。许多宾客在访华期间想尝试各种不同的中式菜肴。根据地区、历史及风味等特点，中式菜肴主要有粤、川、鲁、淮扬等地方

regional distributions, histories, and *flavors*, can be categorized into local cuisines from Guangdong, Sichuan, Shandong, and Huaiyang, and others like *royal* cuisines, *feudal* official cuisines, vegetarian cuisines, and *ethnic* cuisines.

Various Chinese cooking methods include boiling, *stewing*, *braising*, *frying*, *stir-frying*, *quick-frying*, *deep-frying*, frying and *simmering*, *sautéing*, smoking, *roasting* / barbecuing, baking, *steaming*, *scalding*, and *candying*.

The Chinese restaurants are a place where domestic and foreign guests are made aware of Chinese food cultures and the service standards of a hotel. It is up to waiters or waitresses to explain to guests the different selections that are offered in the Chinese restaurants. They must, through *rigorous* and professional training, acquire skills of *tray upbearing*, table setting, napkin-flower folding, wine serving, and food serving, as well as skills of taking reservations, greeting guests, taking orders, serving towels, serving tea, laying down napkins, serving cigarettes, removing or replacing dishes, and settling bills.

5.2.4 The Western Food

The Western foods, prepared in Western ways and served according to Western customs, are popular with foreigners who want to eat foods that they are *familiar* with, and with people who like buffets. The Western foods mainly include the French food, the British food, the American food, the Russian food, and the Italian food. Among these, the French food is widely recognized as the

菜、宫廷菜、官府菜、素菜和少数民族菜等。

中式菜肴的烹调方法多样，有煮、炖、烩、煎、炒、爆、炸、扒、煸、煨、熏、烤、烘、蒸、灼和蜜汁等。

中餐厅是向国内外宾客宣传中国饮食文化和展示酒店服务水准的场所。向宾客讲解餐厅所供应的各式菜肴是中餐厅服务员的职责。他们必须接受严格和专业的训练，掌握托盘、摆台、餐巾折花、酒水服务和菜肴服务等各项技能，以及接受预订、迎宾、点菜、毛巾服务、茶水服务、铺餐巾、香烟服务、撤换餐具、结账等技能。

西　餐

西餐是根据西方国家饮食习惯烹制出的菜点以及根据西方习俗提供的服务，很受那些想吃自己熟悉的食物的外国宾客及喜好自助餐的宾客的欢迎。西餐主要有法式、英式、美式、俄式、意式等，其中法式料理被公认为西餐的代表。其特点是选料广泛，品种繁多，讲究烹

representative of the Western food, characteristic of wide choice of food materials, large variety of dishes, and great attention to cooking, *seasoning*, and *combining*.

Unique Western cooking methods include *grilling*, roasting, braising, deep frying, frying, sauteing, stewing, boiling, *broiling*, *pouching*, and baking.

Frequently-seen Western restaurants are cafe-style ones and top-class ones. The cafe-style Western restaurants, themed with traditional or *trendy* European & American cultures and arts, provide self-served foods around the clock, and give guests a dining experience with enjoyment at a lower cost. The top-class Western restaurants, also called "Grill Rooms," are characteristic of classic or romantic themes, luxurious enjoyment, and high-end consumption.

In Western restaurants, two waiters are required for one table, an experienced one responsible for seating guests, taking orders, serving wines, doing cooking in front of guests, and settling bills, and an assistant one responsible for pouring ice water, calling for dishes, delivering dishes, replacing dishes and *tableware*, clearing tables, and helping the waiter offer as much service as possible to guests. Western restaurant waiters should be able to identify all kinds of metal tableware, *porcelain* tableware, or *glassware*, have a good knowledge of how to use them, and set the table properly. They should also have a good command of how to combine dishes and beverages, and how to serve white wine, red

饪，注重调味，讲究搭配。

西餐的烹调方法也独具特色，主要有铁扒、烤、焖、炸、煎、炒、烩、煮、炭烧、汆、焗等11法。

常见的西餐厅有咖啡厅式西餐厅和高级西餐厅。咖啡厅式西餐厅以欧美传统或新潮的文化艺术为主题，采用24小时自助式服务。餐娱结合，消费比较经济。高级西餐厅，也叫"扒房"，突出经典浪漫的主题、豪华的享受和高档的消费。

西餐服务应由两名服务员共同为一桌宾客服务，一位是经验丰富的专业服务员，负责引座、点菜、服务酒水、客前烹制和结账；另一位是服务员助手，负责倒冰水、叫菜、传菜、换餐具、收台以及尽可能帮助服务员为宾客提供服务。西餐厅服务员要能够识别各种金属餐具、瓷器餐具和玻璃器皿，了解它们的用途，合理摆放餐台，还要掌握西餐菜肴与酒水的搭配规律以及白葡萄酒、红葡萄酒、香槟酒和菜肴等服务的规程和礼节。

wine, *champagne*, and food.

The service cycle in a Western restaurant, different from that in a Chinese restaurant, includes receiving reservation, setting table, greeting guest, serving *aperitif*, taking order, serving bread and butter, pushing table wine, serving table wine, serving appetizer, walking tables (to remove empty drink cups, light cigarettes, replace ashtrays, add ice water and table wine, etc.), serving second *course*, serving *entree*, serving *cheese* and *dessert*, serving coffee or tea, serving after-dinner cocktail or cigar, settling bill, seeing guests off, and cleaning table.

西餐厅的服务流程与中餐厅不同，包括接受预订、摆台、迎宾、服务餐前酒水、接受点菜、上黄油面包、推销佐餐酒、上佐餐酒、上头盘、巡台（撤下空的饮料杯，点烟，撤换烟缸，添加冰水、佐餐酒等）、上第二道菜、上主菜、上奶酪和甜点、上咖啡或茶、上餐后鸡尾酒或雪茄、结账、送客、清台等。

Vocabulary

population /ˌpɒpjuˈleɪʃn/ *n.* 人口

inhabit /ɪnˈhæbɪt/ *v.* 居住于

flavor /ˈfleɪvə(r)/ *n.* 风味

feudal /ˈfjuːdl/ *adj.* 封建的

stew /stjuː/ *v.* （用文火）炖

fry /fraɪ/ *v.* （油）煎

quick-fry /ˌkwɪkˈfraɪ/ *v.* 爆炒

simmer /ˈsɪmə(r)/ *v.* 煨

roast /rəʊst/ *v.* 烤

scald /skɔːld/ *v.* 灼

rigorous /ˈrɪgərəs/ *adj.* 严格的

upbear /ʌpˈbeə/ *v.* 托起；支起

season /ˈsiːzn/ *v.* 调味

grill /grɪl/ *v.* （在烤架上）烤；铁扒

pouch /paʊtʃ/ *v.* 汆

nationality /ˌnæʃəˈnæləti/ *n.* 民族

custom /ˈkʌstəm/ *n.* 习俗

royal /ˈrɔɪəl/ *adj.* 宫廷的

ethnic /ˈeθnɪk/ *adj.* 民族特色的

braise /breɪz/ *v.* 烩

stir-fry /ˈstɜː fraɪ/ *v.* 用旺火煸；炒

deep-fry /ˌdiːp ˈfraɪ/ *v.* 炸炒

sauté /ˈsəʊteɪ/ *v.* 快炒；煸

steam /stiːm/ *v.* 蒸

candy /ˈkændi/ *v.* 蜜汁；用糖煮

tray /treɪ/ *n.* 盘；托盘

familiar /fəˈmɪliə(r)/ *adj.* 熟悉的

combine /kəmˈbaɪn/ *v.* 搭配

broil /brɔɪl/ *v.* （用碳）烧

trendy /ˈtrendi/ *adj.* 流行的；时髦的

tableware /ˈteɪblˌweə(r)/ *n.* 餐具

porcelain /ˈpɔːsəlɪn/ *n.* 瓷

glassware /ˈglɑːsˌweə(r)/ *n.* 玻璃制品

champagne /ʃæmˈpeɪn/ *n.* 香槟（酒）

aperitif /əˈperətif/ *n.* 开胃酒

course /kɔːrs/ *n.* （一道）菜

entree /ˈɒntreɪ/ *n.* 主菜

cheese /tʃiːz/ *n.* 奶酪

dessert /dɪˈzɜːt/ *n.* 甜点

Useful Expressions

lay down 铺；摆

be popular with ... 受……欢迎

see off 送行

词汇、课文资源　　　　词汇、课文自测　　　　微课　　　　课堂练习

5.3　Other Subordinate Departments

5.3.1　Beverage Service Department

The beverage service department generally provides guests with drinks and live entertainment, with bars or lounges as main facilities for these activities. The beverage manager, also called head bartender, who is directly responsible to the food & beverage manager, oversees the operation of the bar or the lounge, supervises bartenders and beverage servers, and ensures a good coordination with the storehouse and the stewarding department. Bartenders work behind the bar *counter*, mixing drinks and serving them to guests at the bar counter. Beverage servers serve guests seating themselves at tables, and receive payment as cashiers do.

酒水部

酒水部主要为宾客提供酒水和现场娱乐表演。酒吧或酒廊是这些活动的主要设施。酒水部经理，也叫总调酒师，直接对餐饮部经理负责，监督酒吧或酒廊的运营，指导调酒员和酒吧服务员的工作，保证与仓库及管事部之间的良好协作。调酒员在柜台后面服务，配制饮料斟给柜台上的宾客。酒吧服务员为坐在餐桌旁的宾客服务，还像出纳员那样负责收款。

Bars are places in which for guests to relax, chat, and lift glasses together. Various bars include: the main bar, in which customers are seated at the counter facing towards bartenders; the lobby bar, located in one corner of the lobby, for guests to drink while having a short rest, meeting friends or waiting for guests; the *nightclub* lounge, located in the places of amusement; the service bar, providing beverage service for diners in the Chinese restaurant or the Western restaurant; the banquet bar, temporarily set for banquets; other bars like the swimming pool bar, tea bar, or mini guestroom bar.

5.3.2　Catering Department

Banqueting is a *grand* and *formal* dining activity held by *government* organs, social organizations, enterprises, public *institutions*, or individuals to meet their social needs of *expressing* welcomes, thanks, and *congratulations*, and to *celebrate* major festivals. Banquets can be categorized into Chinese banquets and Western banquets by cuisine, into state banquets, *institutional* banquets, gathering banquets, *wedding* banquets, birthday-celebrating banquets, and family banquets by type, and into traditional banquets, buffet receptions, cocktail parties, and self-service parties by dining style.

The department in charge of banqueting services is the catering department, which is not only the image-maker for the hotel but also the most profitable segment of the food & beverage division. Catering arranges and plans food & beverage

酒吧，是客人聚在一起休息、聊天、品味酒水的地方。各式酒吧包括可以直接面对调酒师的主酒吧，有设在大堂一侧供宾客小休、会友或候客时喝酒水的大堂吧，有设于酒店娱乐场所的夜总会酒廊，有设在中、西餐厅中为就餐宾客提供酒水的服务酒廊，有为宴会临时设立的宴会酒吧，其他的还有游泳池吧、茶座、客房小酒吧等。

宴会部

宴会是政府机关、社会团体、企事业单位或个人为了表示欢迎、答谢、祝贺等社会目的需要以及庆贺重大节日而举行的一种隆重、正式的餐饮活动。宴会按菜式分为中餐宴会和西餐宴会，按性质分为国宴、团体宴会、聚会、喜宴、寿宴、家宴等，按用餐方式分为传统宴会、冷餐会、鸡尾酒会和自助餐宴会等。

负责宴会服务的部门叫作宴会部，它不仅能够为酒店塑造形象，而且是餐饮部最赚钱的部门。宴会部负责安排和计划会议、较小规模的酒店团客，以及销售部预订的当

services for conventions and smaller hotel groups, and local banquets booked by the sales department. Catering sales can represent as much as 50% of a hotel's total food & beverage sales.

The catering manager, who is in charge of the catering sales and the food *production*, directly reports to the food & beverage manager, and maintains a good relationship with the culinary department, the stewarding department, and the beverage department. In big hotels, catering banquets, conventions, and events is already too big a task for the catering department in the food & beverage division. Therefore, the catering area's selling function is in the charge of the independent sales & marketing division of a hotel with the catering sales manager reporting to the director of sales or directly to the hotel's general manager, while the catering area's production and service function is in the charge of the banquet manager reporting to the food & beverage manager.

The selling of catered events includes advertising and promoting, receiving reservations, filling in reservation forms and daily arrangements book, signing banquet contracts, collecting deposits, making banquet confirmations and notifications, establishing banquet booking *files*, and conducting guest-satisfaction-tracking surveys.

The preparation work of the Chinese banquets, similar to that of the Western banquets, involves decorating halls, designing tables, arranging seats, studying menus, preparing dishes, setting up tables, preparing beverages, and doing before-banquet

地宴会的餐饮服务。宴会销售可以占到酒店餐饮总销售额的一半。

宴会部经理，负责餐饮销售及食物生产，直接对餐饮部经理负责，保持与厨房部、管事部和酒水部之间的联系。在大型酒店里，为宴会、会议和活动提供餐饮服务对于餐饮部下属的宴会部来说任务就过于重大，因此，宴会部的销售职能则由酒店独立的市场部来负责，宴会销售经理向销售总监负责或直接向总经理负责，而餐饮部的生产与服务功能则由宴会经理管理，向餐饮部经理负责。

宴会的预订销售工作包括广告宣传、接受预订、填写宴会预订单、填写宴会安排日记簿、签订宴会合同书、收取订金、确认和通知、建立宴会预订档案，以及进行客户满意度跟踪调查等。

中、西餐宴会的准备工作基本相似，包括宴会厅布置、台形设计、席位安排、熟悉菜单、餐具准备、摆台、酒水准备和宴前检查等。中、西餐宴会的服务流程有点

examinations. But the service procedures of the Chinese banquets are a bit different from those of the Western banquets. With the Chinese banquets, the procedure includes greeting guests, (serving before-banquet cocktails), seating guests, pouring wines, serving dishes, providing table services, settling bills, seeing off guests, and clearing tables, while the procedure of the Western banquets includes greeting guests, serving before-banquet cocktails, seating guests, serving appetizer, serving soups, serving fish dishes, serving meat dishes, serving desserts, serving beverages, settling bills, seeing off guests, and clearing tables.

The catering service is highly professional and *demanding* work in which dining *rituals* are strictly observed. A catering department must have employees with a broad range of abilities and knowledge, who *excel* in sales, menu planning, food & beverage service, food production, product knowledge, cost control, and *artistic talent*, and who have sound technical knowledge and skillful use of the hotel's facilities and equipment as well as correct attitude toward hospitality and good *occupational* habits.

不同。前者包括迎宾、（宴前鸡尾酒会）、入席、斟酒、上菜、巡台、结账、送客、清台等；后者包括迎宾、宴前鸡尾酒会、入席、上头盆、上汤、上鱼类菜肴、上肉类菜肴、上甜点、饮料服务、结账、送客和清台等。

宴会服务是专业性强、要求高和注重礼仪的一项工作。宴会部员工必须具有广泛的知识和能力，擅长销售、菜单制定、餐饮服务、食品制作、产品知识、成本控制、艺术才能。除了具备端正的从业态度和良好的职业习惯，还要掌握扎实的酒店设施相关技术，能够熟练使用各种酒店设施设备。

Vocabulary

counter /ˈkaʊntə(r)/ *n.* 柜台

grand /grænd/ *adj.* 隆重的

government /ˈɡʌvənmənt/ *n.* 政府

nightclub /ˈnaɪtˌklʌb/ *n.* 夜总会

formal /ˈfɔːml/ *adj.* 正式的

institution /ˌɪnstɪˈtjuːʃn/ *n.* 社会事业机构

congratulation /kənˌgrætʃəˈleɪʃn/ *n.* 祝贺

institutional /ˌɪnstɪˈtjuːʃənl/ *adj.* 机构的；团体的

wedding /ˈwedɪŋ/ *n.* 婚礼

file /faɪl/ *n.* 档案

demanding /dɪˈmɑːndɪŋ/ *adj.* 要求高的

excel /ɪkˈsel/ *v.* 善于

talent /ˈtælənt/ *n.* 才能

express /ɪkˈspres/ *v.* 表示；表达

celebrate /ˈseləˌbreɪt/ *v.* 庆祝

production /prəˈdʌkʃn/ *n.* 制作；生产

examination /ɪɡˌzæmɪˈneɪʃn/ *n.* 检查

ritual /ˈrɪtʃuəl/ *n.* 仪式

artistic /ɑːˈtɪstɪk/ *adj.* 艺术的

occupational /ɒkjuˈpeɪʃənl/ *adj.* 职业的

Useful Expression

excel in ... 擅长……

词汇、课文资源　　　　词汇、课文自测　　　　微课　　　　课堂练习

5.3.3　Room Service Department

Room service, or private dining, means that food servers deliver what in-hotel guests order for them to eat in their rooms. Guests order dishes through telephone or the door-knob menu card according to the menu placed in each room, order-takers receive orders, and food servers deliver orders to the guestrooms. Sometimes, the room service also provides fast foods and fast drinks for guests using the swimming pool and some other recreational facilities.

The room service department operates under the supervision of the room service manager, who directly reports to the food & beverage manager,

客房送餐部

客房送餐，也叫私人用餐，由送餐服务员把住店宾客所点的食品或饮料送至客房供宾客用餐。宾客根据房内菜单用电话或门把菜单卡点菜，订餐员负责接受订单，送餐服务员专门送餐至客房。有时，送餐服务还向在游泳池和其他一些游艺场所娱乐的宾客供应快餐或快饮。

客房送餐部在经理的领导下运作。客房送餐部经理直接向餐饮部经理负责，管辖送餐领班、订餐

supervises the work of the captain, order-takers, and food servers, and maintains coordination with the culinary department, the beverage service department, and the finance division. Food servers must know everything about the foods and beverages that are offered, and must be able to describe dishes to guests, as well as how they are prepared.

The room service is available for not less than 18 hours a day, providing breakfast, lunch, supper, *refreshments*, and beverages. In addition to the beverage service and food service, the room service offers special services like room cocktail parties. The procedures of the room service involve collecting door-knob menu cards or receiving orders by telephone, making preparations, examining and checking, delivering dishes to guestrooms, settling bills, saying goodbye to guests, and collecting dishes.

With room service, there are two main difficulties. One is that foods and beverages are served at great *distances* from production area, and the other is that the productivity of food servers is low. So many hotels charge higher prices for room service food and an additional charge per order for the service. To retain food quality, the food must be delivered to the room as quickly as possible and at the appropriate *temperature*. In most cases, to ensure a good efficiency, a hotel uses a door-knob menu that invites guests to order their breakfast the night before, *indicating* on the menu the items they want and the time they would like to be served. Guests then place the menus on the outside doorknobs of

员、送餐服务员等，保持与厨房部、酒水部和财务部之间的协作。送餐服务员必须了解供应的各种食物和饮品，能够向宾客描述菜品及其做法。

每天至少有 18 小时提供客房送餐服务。项目有早餐、午餐、晚餐、茶点和酒水等。除酒水服务和食品服务外，客房送餐服务还提供房间鸡尾酒会等特别服务。客房送餐服务流程包括收集门餐牌或接受电话订餐、餐前准备、检查核对、送餐至客房、结账、道别和收餐等。

客房送餐服务有两大困难：一是食物和饮料必须送到离制作区域很远的地方；二是送餐员的效率低下，所以许多酒店对送餐食物收费较高，并对每单服务加收附加费。为了保持食物质量，食物必须尽快送至客房，以保持合适的温度。通常为了保证高效率，酒店使用门把菜单，让客人在先一天晚上点早餐，在菜单上写明想要的食物和送达时间，然后将菜单放在房间外的门把上，以便服务员夜间收集菜单。

their rooms for *collection* during the night.

5.3.4 Culinary Department

The kitchen is almost a separate *kingdom* within the hotel. Even in big hotels with more than one restaurant, there is usually just one *central* kitchen. The special types of food served in the various restaurants are normally prepared by different chefs and cooks rather than in separate kitchens.

The executive chef, or head chef, is the boss of the culinary department. He / She directly reports to the food & beverage manager, supervises the work of chefs, *primary*-processing cooks, dish-*shredding* and dish-fixing cooks, *salad* cooks, dish-cooking cooks, and pastry cooks, and ensures coordination with the food service department, the room service department, the banqueting department, the stewarding department, and the purchasing department.

The executive chef is responsible for planning menus (the foods that are being served on a particular day), also plans, purchases, and frequently coordinates the operation of several restaurants. Cooks, under the supervision of the chef, cook foods and then place them on plates for buspersons to pick up. Under the cooks' supervision are kitchen helpers who, for example, collect food materials from the storehouse to the kitchen, do *peeling* work, cut up vegetables, and do dish-fixing work.

An important member of the chef's team is the chief *steward*, who reports to the executive chef, but

厨房部

厨房在酒店里几乎是一个独立王国。即便是有几个餐厅的大酒店，一般也只有一个中央厨房。各餐厅供应的各种特殊风味的食物往往并不是在不同的厨房里制作，而是出自不同的厨师长或厨师之手。

行政总厨或叫总厨是这里的负责人。他／她直接对餐饮部经理负责，管辖各点厨师长、初加工厨师、切配厨师、冷盘厨师、炉头厨师和点心师，保持与餐厅部、客房送餐部、宴会部、管事部和采购部之间的联系。

行政总厨负责设计菜单（某一天供应什么菜），制订计划，采购材料，还要经常协调各餐厅的工作。厨师在厨师长的督导下进行实际烹饪操作，并把菜肴盛入菜盘，让传菜员端走。在厨师监督下工作的是帮厨，他们主要是领取原料、削皮、切菜和配菜。

厨师团队中还有一个重要成员叫总管事，他向总厨负责，在有些

to the food & beverage manager in some hotels. He / She directs the kitchen steward, ware-washers, silver *polishers*, busboys, and storekeepers, makes sure all dining rooms, bars, and banquet rooms have sufficient inventories of clean china, glassware, and *silverware*, and manages the stocks of restaurant and kitchen supplies like tableware, linens, and paper supplies, the cleaning of furniture, fixtures, and all public areas of the food & beverage division, and the arrangement of equipment maintenance and repairs.

5.3.5 Purchasing Department

There is a support service, called the purchasing department, in the food & beverage division. It operates under the supervision of the purchasing manager, who is directly responsible to the food & beverage manager, and is responsible for buying all of the products used in the hotel, including items that are necessary for restaurants, bars, and kitchen.

The staff working under the leadership of the purchasing manager includes purchasing clerks, receiving clerks, and storeroom clerks. The purchasing manager maintains a good coordination with *suppliers*, the finance division, the culinary department, and the food service department, receiving clerks verify the number and quality of food and beverage items received, and storeroom clerks are responsible for properly storing and issuing items from the food & beverage storeroom. That is to say, all purchases are planned by the manager, bought by purchasing clerks, and stored or issued by storeroom clerks after the inspection and

酒店里向餐饮部经理负责。他 / 她指导厨房管家、洗碗工、擦银工、杂工和仓库保管员工作，确保所有餐厅、酒吧和宴会厅都有足够的清洁瓷器、玻璃器皿和银器，并负责餐具、布草和纸制品等餐厅和厨房必需品的存储，家具、固定物及餐饮部所有公共区域的打扫，以及设备的维修安排等。

采购部

在餐饮部有一个辅助服务部门，叫作采购部。它在采购经理的监督下运作，采购经理直接对餐饮部经理负责，购买酒店使用的所有物品，包括餐厅、酒吧及厨房所必需的各种物品。

采购部下属员工有采购员、收货员和仓库保管员等。经理与供应商、财务部、厨房部和餐厅部之间保持协作联系，收货员查验所收餐饮物品的数量与质量，仓库保管员负责妥善保存物品和仓库物品的发放。也就是说，采购部经理负责采购计划，采购员把物品采购回来后，经收验后，交由保管员保管或发放。

acceptance are made.

Because food can *spoil* quickly, ordering supplies is a daily activity. Usually, orders are given to the purchasing department by the chef, by the bar manager, or by the food & beverage manager. The purchasing department then seeks competitive bids from suppliers, and gives them *precise specifications* for each of the food and beverage items being ordered.

由于食品容易变质，所以订货是逐日进行的。通常情况是，订单会由总厨、酒吧经理或餐饮部经理发送给采购部，然后由采购部寻找出价具有竞争力的供应商，并明确地告知他们每一件所订餐饮物品的规格。

Vocabulary

refreshment /rɪˈfreʃmənt/ *n.* 茶点

temperature /ˈtemprɪtʃə(r)/ *n.* 温度

collection /kəˈlekʃn/ *n.* 取走

central /ˈsentrəl/ *adj.* 中央的

shred /ʃred/ *v.* 切丝

peel /pi:l/ *v.* 剥皮；削皮

polisher /ˈpɒlɪʃə(r)/ *n.* 擦拭工

supplier /səˈplaɪə(r)/ *n.* 供应商

spoil /spɔɪl/ *v.* 变质

specification /ˌspesɪfɪˈkeɪʃn/ *n.* 规格

distance /ˈdɪstəns/ *n.* 距离

indicate /ˈɪndɪkeɪt/ *n.* 写明

kingdom /ˈkɪŋdəm/ *n.* 王国

primary /ˈpraɪməri/ *adj.* 初步的；最初的

salad /ˈsæləd/ *n.* 冷盘

steward /ˈstju:əd/ *n.* 管事

silverware /ˈsɪlvəweə(r)/ *n.* 银餐具

acceptance /əkˈseptəns/ *n.* 接受

precise /prɪˈsaɪs/ *n.* 明确的；精确的

词汇、课文资源

词汇、课文自测

微课

课堂练习

Chapter Six

Convention, Recreation, and Complaints
会议服务、康乐服务与投诉处理

思政园地／二十
大精神学习专栏

Learning Objectives

· *To get familiar with the two special services of the hotel revenue centers—convention service and recreation service;*

· *To understand the staff, tasks, standards, goals, and requirements of the two services;*

· *To understand how to handle complaints;*

· *To master the new words and professional terms concerned;*

· *To improve reading ability through learning the text;*

· *To develop team spirit and self-study ability through learning activities;*

· *To receive education in ideological and political theories through course learning.*

Teaching Arrangements

节次	教学内容	自主学习资源	自主学习自测	课堂教学视频	课堂练习
L 1	6.1 Convention and Recreation	词汇、课文资源	词汇、课文自测	微课	课堂练习
L 2	6.2 Complaints	词汇、课文资源	词汇、课文自测	微课	课堂练习

In addition to guestroom service and food & beverage service, the two other special ones a hotel provides are convention service and recreation service, which are also important revenue centers of a hotel. Therefore, every star hotel, big or small, provides convention and recreation services.

Hotel staff, like people working in other service businesses, is *bound* to receive *compliments* and *commendations* from guests, as well as complaints and criticisms from them. The way for guests to express their complaints and criticisms is always complaining.

会议服务与康乐服务是酒店除房务和餐饮以外的两项重要的专门服务，也是酒店重要的营收部门。因此，各星级酒店，无论规模大小，都提供会议服务和康乐服务。

酒店员工跟其他服务性行业工作的员工一样，总要收到客人的称赞和表扬，也免不了受到客人的投诉和批评。客人表达批评和意见的途径往往就是投诉。

6.1 Convention and Recreation

6.1.1 Convention Service

会议服务

The convention business is very profitable for the hospitality industry. A convention guarantees a good occupancy rate for the hotel over a period of at least several days. In addition, the special exhibit and meeting areas are rented by the *sponsoring* organization for a fee, and the people attending the convention also generate more business in the hotel's restaurants, bars, and shops.

A convention is a meeting of members of a business or professional group. A typical convention includes business *sessions*, *workshops* and *seminars*, professional exhibits, and special events. Attendance at many conventions runs to a thousand or more people. In fact, a *figure* of three or four thousand is not unusual.

承办会议业务能给酒店业带来很高的利润。承办一次会议能保证酒店至少在几天的时期内具有很高的开房率。此外，专门用于展览和开会的场地出租给主办单位是要收费的。参加会议者还能为酒店的餐厅、酒吧和商店带来更多的生意。

会议是某一行业或某一专业团体的成员集会。典型的会议包括业务会议、专题讨论会和专业研讨会、专业展览以及专门安排的活动等。许多会议的出席人数多达1000或以上。实际上，三四千人的会议是屡见不鲜的。

Convention service is quite different from other services like the room service, or food & beverage service. Too many people attending the convention check in or out at the same time, and often have a longer stay in the hotel. The convention service involves almost as many management and operations as the hotel has. So, the whole convention service is a *systemic* project for a hotel. How to manage and operate the convention service varies from hotel to hotel. In some big hotels with full convention facilities and higher reception *capacity*, the common practice for saving *manpower* and increasing work efficiency is that the sales & marketing division is responsible for the sales of the convention service and that the *specific* work of the convention service is in the charge of a special convention division. Once the convention has been booked into the hotel, a management, made up of the managers from the rooms division, the food & beverage division, the convention division, the engineering division, the finance division, and the security division, is often specifically set up under the leadership of a vice general manager, who ensures communication and coordination with each division.

The convention manager supervises the work of the convention division, and is responsible for the communication and coordination with relevant divisions. The convention staff includes the captain, professionals, conference attendants, and busboys. Attendants should be familiar with all the conference halls, for example, their names, *locations*, sizes, and interior facilities, should be always *amiable*

会议服务较客房或餐饮等其他服务，有着很大的不同。出席会议的人数多，基本都在同一时间到达或离开，常常住店时间较长。会议服务几乎涉及酒店所有管理部门和经营部门。因此，整个会议服务对于酒店来说，是一个系统工程。不同的酒店对会议服务的管理与经营所采取的方式也不尽相同。在一些会议设施完备、会议接待能力较强的大型酒店里，为了节省人力、提高工作效率，一般做法是会议服务的销售由市场销售部负责，会议的具体工作由专门的会务部负责。在酒店决定承办某个大型会议时，往往会成立一个由客房部、餐饮部、会务部、工程部、财务部、安保部等各部门经理组成的管理机构，由酒店副总经理牵头负责各部门的沟通和协调。

会务部经理负责督导会务部的工作，并负责与相关各部门的联络与协作。会务部员工有领班、专业技术人员、会务服务人员及杂务员。服务人员要了解酒店所有会议厅室，如：它们的名称、位置、大小和内部设备情况，始终和善礼貌地指引宾客去会场及其他设施，能

and courteous in directing guests to the conference hall and other facilities, should be able to make reasonable seating arrangements according to the type of function, and should provide tea service during the meeting. Professionals should make the venue *layout* and every meeting device *accord* with the particular needs of the function, and ensure a successful event.

A hotel can *profit* not only from the rentals of conference facilities and other facilities of rooms, restaurants, shopping and recreation to the sponsoring party, but also from many *value-added* services provided by the convention division. They include professional and technical services, like venue layout, lighting and sound, *photography* and *video*, etiquette *model hosting*, visual design, music planning, video planning, flowers planning, and gifts & prizes planning, secretarial services like *simultaneous* interpretation and PR *presentation* writing, rental services of conference *vehicles* and conference devices, and other personalized services like babysitting.

6.1.2　Recreation Service

Recreational facilities, which are open not only to the in-hotel guests but also to the public, are another feature of many hotels. They can not only help guests relax and feel good but also meet guests' demand for high consumption, *reflect* and promote a hotel's level of service, and even bring in a huge revenue to the hotel.

Many large hotels are well equipped with

够根据会议类型合理安排座位，提供会间茶水服务。专业人员应根据各种不同会议的需要，布置好会场，装配调试好各种会议设备，以保证会议的顺利进行。

酒店除了通过向会议方出租会议设施及客房、餐饮、购物和康乐等其他设施赢利外，也可以由会务部提供许多增值服务，如场地布置、灯光音响、摄影摄像、礼仪模特主持、视觉设计、音乐策划、视频策划、鲜花策划、礼品奖品策划等专业技术服务，同声传译、公关文稿撰写等秘书服务，会议车辆、会议设备等租赁服务，以及托婴等个性化服务。

康乐服务

康乐设施是许多酒店的又一特色，它们不仅向住店宾客开放，也向社会公众开放。它们不仅可以帮助宾客放松身心、愉悦心情，满足高消费宾客的消费需求，体现和提升了酒店的服务档次，又能够给酒店带来丰厚的收入。

在许多大型酒店，康乐设施一

various recreational facilities, in which guests, without going outside, can enjoy high-quality fitness and entertainment services.

One particularly *popular* facility is the health and fitness center, in which a hotel guest can use the swimming pool, *aerobics* room, and *exercise* equipment without paying extra fees. Health services include exercise *courses*, special trainers, saunas or steam baths, massages, and beauty services, which are extra-pay services helping a guest feel good and relax after a day's hard work. Massage and sauna are two *relaxation* tools most popular with guests.

The recreation center is usually a busy place, in which there are always bars for guests to get together to enjoy drinks, music, and live performances after a long day of meeting or sightseeing.

Guests will often want to enjoy the local *nightlife* while visiting. The nightlife facilities can include dancing clubs, local snack bars, mini-cinemas, *bowling*, karaoke, various *chess* rooms, and game rooms. A few hotels include nightclubs as part of their operation, which are the responsibility of the food & beverage division or of a special staff, offering entertainment, such as dancing, singing, *band* playing, and floor shows, in addition to foods and drinks.

Other entertainment facilities include tennis courts and golf courses. Even in some resort hotels include facilities like *skiing* resorts, skating *rinks*, and horse-racing courses.

In general, the recreation division operates under the supervision of the recreation manager. The working

应俱全，五花八门，让宾客不用出酒店就能享受到自己想要的高档次健身娱乐服务。

特别受欢迎的一大设施就是健身中心。健身中心里有游泳池、有氧健身房及锻炼器材可供住店宾客免费使用。健身服务包括练习课程、专门教练、桑拿、按摩和美体等内容。这些有偿服务项目可帮助宾客愉悦身心、消除一天的疲劳。按摩和桑拿是深受宾客欢迎的两大热门项目。

康乐中心通常是很热闹的地方，在这里通常有酒吧供宾客在漫长的一日会议或观光之后来聚会畅饮，一起欣赏音乐，观看现场表演。

通常宾客都想在旅行期间充分享受一下当地的夜间娱乐生活。夜间娱乐设施通常有舞蹈俱乐部、风味餐厅、小型影院、保龄球馆、卡拉 OK、各种棋牌室、游戏厅等。有些酒店还有夜总会，由餐饮部或专门人员负责，除供应食品、酒水外，还提供娱乐项目，如跳舞、唱歌、乐队和节目表演等。

其他娱乐设施还包括网球场和高尔夫球场，甚至在有些度假酒店还推出滑雪场、滑冰场和马场等设施。

一般情况下，康乐部由康乐部经理负责，员工有各设施的领班、

staff includes the captains of all facilities, *coaches*, and attendants. All these recreational activities require the employment of additional personnel. For instance, workers are required for necessary maintenance of the swimming pool; golf courses must be carefully *tended* by a special staff of *groundskeepers*; and there have to be *grooms* to take care of horses. In addition, many resort hotels hire professional *athletes* to give lessons to guests in tennis, golf, and skiing, and employ riding *instructors*, *guides* for *hikers* and *campers*, and necessary *lifeguards* at swimming pools and *beaches*.

教练员和服务员等。这些康乐设施常常需要另雇员工。如，游泳池需要人手来做必要的维修保养工作，高尔夫球场必须由专门的场地管理员精心养护，马匹需要由马夫来照顾。此外，许多度假酒店雇用职业运动员向宾客传授网球、高尔夫球和滑雪技术，聘请骑术指导、为徒步旅行者及野营者当向导的人员，以及游泳池或海滩必备的救生员。

Vocabulary

bound /baʊnd/ *adj.* 极有可能；必定的

commendation /ˌkɒmenˈdeɪʃn/ *n.* 赞赏

session /ˈseʃn/ *n.* 会议

workshop /ˈwɜːkʃɒp/ *n.* 研讨会；讲习班

seminar /ˈsemɪnɑː(r)/ *n.* （大学）研讨班

systemic /sɪˈstiːmɪk/ *adj.* 系统的

manpower /ˈmænpaʊə(r)/ *n.* 人力

location /ləʊˈkeɪʃn/ *n.* 位置

layout /ˈleɪaʊt/ *n.* 安排；布置

profit /ˈprɒfɪt/ *v.* 得益；获利

photography /fəˈtɒɡrəfi/ *n.* 摄影

model /ˈmɒdl/ *n.* 模特

simultaneous /ˌsɪmlˈteɪniəs/ *adj.* 同步的

presentation /ˌpreznˈteɪʃn/ *n.* 展示文稿

vehicle /ˈviːəkl/ *n.* 车辆

popular /ˈpɒpjələ(r)/ *n.* 受欢迎的

compliment /ˈkɒmplɪmənt/ *n.* 恭维

sponsor /ˈspɒnsə(r)/ *v.* 主办

figure /ˈfɪɡə(r)/ *n.* 数字

capacity /kəˈpæsəti/ *n.* 能力

specific /spəˈsɪfɪk/ *adj.* 具体的

amiable /ˈeɪmiəbl/ *adj.* 友善的；和蔼的

accord /əˈkɔːd/ *v.* 与……相一致

value-added /ˈvæljuː ˈædɪd/ *adj.* 增值的

video /ˈvɪdiəʊ/ *n.* 录像

hosting /ˈhəʊstɪŋ/ *n.* 主持

reflect /rɪˈflekt/ *v.* 反映

aerobics /eəˈrəʊbɪks/ *n.* 有氧运动

exercise /ˈeksəsaɪz/ *n.* 锻炼

relaxation /ˌriːlækˈseɪʃn/ *n.* 消遣；放松

bowling /ˈbəʊlɪŋ/ *n.* 保龄球（运动）

band /bænd/ *n.* 乐队

rink /rɪŋk/ *n.* 溜冰场

tend /tend/ *v.* 照料；养护

groundskeeper /ˈɡraʊndzkiːpə(r)/ *n.* 运动场地管理员

groom /ɡruːm/ *n.* 马夫

instructor /ɪnˈstrʌktə(r)/ *n.* 教员；指导者

hiker /ˈhaɪkə(r)/ *n.* 徒步旅行者

lifeguard /ˈlaɪfɡɑːd/ *n.* 救生员

course /kɔːs/ *n.* 课程

nightlife /ˈnaɪtlaɪf/ *n.* 夜生活

chess /tʃes/ *n.* 棋

skiing /ˈskiːɪŋ/ *n.* 滑雪（运动）

coach /kəʊtʃ/ *n.* 教练

athlete /ˈæθliːt/ *n.* 运动员

guide /ɡaɪd/ *n.* 向导

camper /ˈkæmpə(r)/ *n.* 野营者

beach /biːtʃ/ *n.* 海滩

Useful Expressions

be bound to do sth. 必定会做某事

direct sb. to sp. 指引某人去某地

profit from ... 得益于……

give lessons to sb. 给某人上课

set up 建立；成立

accord with 与……相符合

bring in 赚（钱）

词汇、课文资源　　词汇、课文自测　　微课　　课堂练习

6.2　Complaints

Complaints occur when customers tell you why they are not *satisfied*. Although not all complaints are *justified*, businesses should welcome complaints, not *avoid* them. That is because it is cheaper for a hotel to keep existing customers rather than find new ones. Another reason for doing so is that complaints are like free market research. When you talk directly

投诉是指宾客告诉你他们不满意的原因。尽管并非所有的投诉都有道理，但酒店仍需要欢迎投诉，而不是逃避。这是因为对于酒店经营来说，维持现有客户的费用要比寻找新客户的费用低得多。此外，投诉就好比免费的市场调查，当你

to *complainers*, they will tell you what they want and what they are not satisfied with.

Complaints often include positive ones and negative ones. Positive complaints, always from customers who care about their own needs, can help a hotel *succeed* in its business. That is because they can tell the hotel what and where the *shortcomings* or *deficiencies* are, and tell how the hotel should improve its services. Close attention should be paid to positive complaints, and quick actions should be taken to deal with them. When handled properly, they will make the hotel even stronger in the competitive marketplace. Negative complaints are just results of *fastidious* and difficult personalities. They are always made by *selfish*, "*parasite*" customers or by *competitors*, and may not be good for the hotel's business in the short run. In many cases, the hotel has to be more careful about negative complaints, because if handled poorly, they may do harm to the hotel.

Complaints may *occur* in any operation or any site where customers are served directly. For instance, in the lobby, guests may complain about being kept waiting; in the guestrooms, they may be *disappointed* with the service quality and the room amenities, and may complain that something is wrong with the *shower*, that it is too hot in the room, that the Internet *connection* doesn't work, that the music in the next room is too loud, and that they are *bothered* by *mosquitoes*; in the restaurants, complaints about the food or the service may be

和投诉人直接交谈时，他们会告诉你他们想要什么，他们对你的服务有哪些地方不满意。

投诉一般有正面和负面两种。正面投诉来自关心自己需求的宾客，能够帮助酒店在业务上取得成功，因为它们可以让酒店知道其服务工作中的不足和缺陷，以及如何去改进服务。对于正面的投诉，应当给予重视，尽快采取行动。妥善的处理能使酒店在竞争激烈的市场里变得更强。负面投诉是由于个别人生性挑剔、难以满足而产生的，一般来自自私的客人、"吃白食"的客人或竞争对手，会在短期内对酒店的生意造成不利。对于负面的投诉，在很多情况下，要加倍小心地对待，处理不好可能会对酒店带来损失。

在酒店里直接与宾客接触的各经营部门或场所都有可能发生投诉，如：在大厅，宾客可能抱怨等候时间长；在客房，宾客可能对服务质量和房间设施感到失望，他们可能抱怨淋浴器坏了，室内温度太高，互联网连接不上，隔壁房间的音乐太吵，有蚊子等；在餐厅，他们可能针对食物或服务进行投诉，如抱怨上错菜，抱怨菜太咸或太甜等。通常情况下，投诉发生在哪个

made, like the dish being wrongly served and the food being too *salty* or too sweet. As a rule, complaints should be dealt with in a timely, *prompt*, and proper way where they are made.

People who make complaints and criticism can be friendly and reasonable, or can be rude and *abusive*. No matter how the person *behaves*, the hotel staff should always try to be nice to them. An *argument* with the guest is the most *undesirable* thing that can happen to a staff member and the hotel. When complaints occur, employees should be prepared to handle them. In general, when handling complaints, the hotel staff should follow the basic model: to listen attentively to the guest, to confirm the guest's complaint, to *apologize* to the guest, (to report to the *superior*), to make *corrections* or *remedies*, (and to follow up). In detail, in handling complaints, the hotel staff should always be polite and helpful. He / She should always be ready to lend an *attentive* ear to what the guest has to say, and must not *interrupt* the guest unless necessary. He / She should then make a short *apology* and express his / her *understanding* of the guest's *situation* or *sympathy* with the guest. After that, the staff member should take actions quickly to remove the complaint, either by making polite, patient, and detailed *explanations*, or making *swift*, effective corrections and remedies, or reporting the complaint to a superior. But whatever he / she *intends* to do, he / she must keep the guest informed of the *measures* or actions he / she intends to take and when he / she will carry them out. In addition, it is also *advisable* for him / her to write down what the guest has said. Every complaint should

部门，就由哪个部门负责及时、快速、妥善地进行处理。

投诉的人可能很友好、在理；也可能粗暴无礼、出言不逊。无论提意见的人如何表现，酒店员工都要永远努力做到热情周到。对于酒店员工和酒店来说最不可取的事莫过于与宾客争吵了。发生投诉时，员工就要做好准备处理投诉。一般来讲，处理投诉遵循"倾听、确认、道歉、（报告）、改进或弥补、（追踪）"这一基本模式。具体地说，在处理投诉时，酒店员工应该坚持做到彬彬有礼，乐于助人，随时虚心听取宾客的意见，不到万不得已不要打断宾客说话。听完宾客的意见后，向宾客表达歉意，并对宾客的处境表示理解，或者对其表示同情。之后，要立即处理宾客的意见，或是做礼貌的耐心细致的解释，或是采取迅速有效的改正和补救措施，抑或是把宾客的意见向上级反映。但是无论如何打算，都必须让宾客知道下一步的计划，以及何时行动。另外，记录宾客提出的投诉是一个很可取的做法。所有的投诉都应记录下来，包括详细投诉者、投诉时间、投诉原因、如何处理投诉、宾客对处理结果是否满意等。

be logged with details about who complained, when and why the complaint was made, how the complaint was removed, and whether the customer was pleased.

It is not at all easy to be always nice to the guest, especially when the guest is *unfriendly* and rude, even abusive. But the success of any hotel in the hospitality industry depends on people-pleasers with good *training* and a lot of practical experience with guests. Just keep one thing in mind, that is, a *dissatisfied* guest means a loss of *potential* business in the future, while a pleased guest leaving with a warm *memory* of the hospitality he / she has enjoyed will be *inclined* to repeat his / her visit to the hotel.

时刻做到热情周到地待客绝非易事，尤其是遇上不友好、粗暴无礼甚至出言不逊的宾客时。但是在酒店业，任何一家酒店的成功，都得靠一批热忱的、经过良好训练的和具有广泛的实际待客经验的服务人员。请牢记：一位宾客扫兴而去，意味着失去了将来可能达成的一笔生意；一个满意而去的宾客则会因在酒店所受到的热情周到的服务的良好回忆而再次光顾。

Vocabulary

satisfied /ˈsætɪsfaɪd/ *adj.* 感到满意的

justified /ˈdʒʌstɪfaɪd/ *adj.* 合理的；有道理的

avoid /əˈvɔɪd/ *v.* 回避；避免

succeed /səkˈsiːd/ *v.* 成功

deficiency /dɪˈfɪʃnsi/ *n.* 缺陷

fastidious /fæˈstɪdiəs/ *adj.* 严谨的；一丝不苟的

selfish /ˈselfɪʃ/ *adj.* 自私的；利己的

competitor /kəmˈpetɪtə(r)/ *n.* 竞争对手

disappointed /ˌdɪsəˈpɔɪntɪd/ *adj.* 感到失望的

connection /kəˈnekʃn/ *n.* 连接

mosquito /məˈskiːtəʊ/ *n.* 蚊子

prompt /prɒmpt/ *adj.* 立即；及时的

abusive /əˈbjuːsɪv/ *adj.* 辱骂的；出言不逊的

complainer /kəmˈpleɪnə(r)/ *n.* 抱怨者

shortcoming /ˈʃɔːtkʌmɪŋ/ *n.* 不足；缺点

parasite /ˈpærəsaɪt/ *adj.* 吃白食的；寄生的

occur /əˈkɜː(r)/ *v.* 发生；存在；出现

shower /ˈʃaʊə(r)/ *n.* 淋浴

bother /ˈbɒðə(r)/ *v.* 打扰；烦扰

salty /ˈsɔːlti/ *adj.* 咸的

behave /bɪˈheɪv/ *v.* 表现；行为

undesirable /ˌʌndɪˈzaɪərəbl/ *adj.* 不想要的；不可取的

apologize /əˈpɒlədʒaɪz/ *v.* 道歉

correction /kəˈrekʃn/ *n.* 纠正；改正

attentive /əˈtentɪv/ *adj.* 倾听的

apology /əˈpɒlədʒi/ *n.* 道歉

situation /ˌsɪtʃuˈeɪʃn/ *n.* 处境

explanation /ˌekspləˈneɪʃn/ *n.* 解释

intend /ɪnˈtend/ *v.* 打算

advisable /ədˈvaɪzəbl/ *adj.* 明智的

training /ˈtreɪnɪŋ/ *n.* 训练

dissatisfied /dɪsˈsætɪsfaɪd/ *adj.* 不满意的；不高兴的

potential /pəˈtenʃl/ *adj.* 潜在的

inclined /ɪnˈklaɪnd/ *adj.* 倾向于；有……意向的

argument /ˈɑːgjumənt/ *n.* 争吵

superior /suːˈpɪəriə(r)/ *n.* 上级

remedy /ˈremədi/ *n.* 补救

interrupt /ˌɪntəˈrʌpt/ *v.* 打断；中断

understanding /ˌʌndəˈstændɪŋ/ *n.* 理解

sympathy /ˈsɪmpəθi/ *n.* 同情

swift /swɪft/ *adj.* 迅速的

measure /ˈmeʒə(r)/ *n.* 措施

unfriendly /ʌnˈfrendli/ *adj.* 不友好的

memory /ˈmeməri/ *n.* 记忆

Useful Expressions

rather than 与其……倒不如……

be good for ... 对……有益

pay attention to ... 注意……

in many cases 在很多场合下

do harm to ... 给……带来损害

be disappointed with ... 对……失望

be prepared to do sth. 准备（愿意）做某事

intend to do sth. 打算做某事

keep sb. informed of sth. 随时告知某人某事

take measures to do sth. 采取措施做某事

be inclined to do sth. 倾向于；偏重；有意

be satisfied with ... 对……感到满意

in the short run 从短期来看

take actions to do sth. 采取行动做某事

be careful about ... 小心对待……

complain about ... 抱怨……；投诉……

sth. is wrong with ... 出了毛病（问题）

lend an attentive ear to ... 倾听……

carry out 执行；完成

词汇、课文资源

词汇、课文自测

微课

课堂练习

English for Hotel Services
酒店服务英语

General Expressions
基本交际用语

思政园地 / 二十大精神学习专栏

Learning Objectives

· *To get familiar with the occasions on which general expressions are used;*

· *To understand how the general expressions are used on each occasion;*

· *To master the new words and professional terms concerned;*

· *To improve reading ability through learning the text;*

· *To develop team spirit and self-study ability through learning activities;*

· *To receive education in ideological and political theories through course learning.*

Teaching Arrangements

节次	教学内容	自主学习资源	自主学习自测	课堂教学视频	课堂练习
L 1	General Expressions	词汇、课文资源	词汇、课文自测	微课	课堂练习

General expressions are necessarily and generally used by the hotel staff during the *course* of providing services to express daily *communications*, attitudes, and feelings / *emotions*. Specifically, the hotel staff uses general *expressions* for making greetings, bidding farewells, giving thanks, making apologies, giving wishes, giving *comforts*, giving congratulations, giving compliments, making

基本交际用语，是指酒店员工在完成对客服务过程中所普遍使用的日常用语，主要用来表达日常交际、表达态度及表达情绪情感。具体来说，主要有问候、道别、感谢、道歉、祝愿、宽慰、祝贺、恭维、请求、允许、提供服务、提供指引、提醒、应答、打电话等等。

requests, giving permissions, offering services, giving directions, giving reminders, making responses, making telephones, and so on.

7.1 Making Greetings

Greeting is a must for a hotel worker, which shows that you see guests, care about them, and are ready to offer help to them if they need. A polite and *energetic* greeting will give guests a good impression about the hotel.

1) Good morning (afternoon / evening), Sir (Madam / Miss).

早上好（下午 / 晚上好），先生（女士 / 小姐）。

2) How do you do?
您好!

3) Hello / Hi!
您好!

问候对酒店员工而言是非常重要的。你的问候表明你看到了宾客，重视他们并且会在他们有任何需要时提供帮助。一个礼貌且热情的问候会使宾客对酒店留下好的印象。

1) 最常用的打招呼用语。中午 12 点以前用 "Good morning."；12 点到下午 6 点之间用 "Good afternoon."；6 点以后用 "Good evening."。"Sir" 是用来称呼不知道姓名的男性宾客；"Madam" 是用来称呼不知道姓名的女性宾客，"Miss" 是用来称呼未婚女性。和熟识的客人问候时可省去 "Good"。其他的称谓如："Mr. Lee"（李先生）、"Mrs. Wu"（吴太太）、"Prof. Smith"（史密斯教授）、"Dr. James"（詹姆斯博士）等。

2) 这是比较正式的打招呼用语，只能用于初次见面，回答时仍说："How do you do?"。

3) 非正式的打招呼用语，比较随便。在酒店行业中尽量少用，只有对非常熟悉的宾客才可以用。美国

4) How are you?

您好吗？

5) Are you feeling better now?

你现在感觉好点了吗？

6) Glad / Nice / Pleased to see you.

见到您很高兴。

7) Welcome to our hotel.

欢迎来到我们的酒店！

8) I hope you will enjoy your stay with us.

希望您入住愉快。

人较随和，喜欢用"Hi."。

4) 用于和认识的宾客打招呼，回答说："Fine, thank you, and you?"或 "Not bad." 等。

5) 用来问候生病或不适的宾客，表示对宾客健康状况的关心。

6) 用来和熟识的宾客打招呼。如果加上宾客的姓氏，宾客会很高兴，因为你记住了他的名字，说明他在这里受到了重视，也体现了你服务时的细心。和初次见面的宾客打招呼说："Glad to meet you."。

7) 这句话用得非常多，可以变换出许多句子。比如中餐厅员工可以说："Welcome to the Chinese Restaurant!"。依此类推。也可以只说："Welcome."。"欢迎您再次光临"可用 "Hope to see you again."。

8) 还可以说："I hope you will have a good time here. / I hope you will have a pleasant stay in our hotel."。

7.2   Bidding Farewells

Saying goodbye includes "Goodbye," "Thank you," "Have you had a good stay here?" "We are looking forward to your coming again." and "Have a nice trip home." which makes a guest feel that you really care about him or her, and will leave a guest with a good final impression.

1) Good bye, thank you for having stayed with us!

与宾客的道别语包括"再见""谢谢您""您住店愉快吗""希望再来""一路平安"等。这些话会让宾客感受到你真挚的关心，会给宾客留下一个良好的最终印象。

1) "Thank you for staying with us!"多用在宾客入住酒店时或住店

再见，谢谢入住！

2) Did you enjoy your stay here with us?

您住店愉快吗？

期间，表示"谢谢入住"。

2) 餐厅服务员在宾客就餐后离开餐厅时常可说："Did you enjoy your meal?"（您喜欢这里的食物吗？）。

3) Hope to see you again soon.

希望不久再见到您！

3) 还可以说："We look forward to seeing / serving / receiving you again."。

4) Goodbye, and have a *pleasant* flight!

再见，祝您（坐飞机）旅行愉快！

4) 在宾客离开要去机场时，千万不要说"Good luck to you!"，否则会引起宾客的不快。因为近来飞机事故频发，宾客总是想讨个吉利。

5) Good night.

晚安！

5) 晚间告别用语，注意："Good evening."是晚间问候用语。

7.3　Giving Thanks

Thanks should be given to someone who offers help or *kindness* to you. And usually, you are *replied* by saying "you are welcome," which is a polite way of showing that your thanks are accepted.

1) Thank you (very much).

（非常）感谢。

接受了对方的帮助或对方对你有善意的举动时要表示感谢，通常对方回答"不客气"，表示对方接受了感谢。

1) 最常用的感谢用语。还可用"Many thanks." 或 "Thanks a lot."。后面常可以接"for"短语表示原因，如："Thank you for staying in our hotel / your understanding / your nice words."。

2) I really *appreciate* your help.

非常感谢您的帮助。

2) 比 "Thank you." 更能表达感激之情。还可用 "I really can't thank you enough." 或 "I really can't thank you too much."。

153

3) You are welcome.

不客气。

3) 这句话用来回答表示感谢的话，后面常可加上"It's my pleasure."（我很乐意。）/ "Please don't mention it."（不值一提。）/ "It's not a problem."（不成问题。）/ "It's the least I can do."（小事一桩。）。

7.4　Making Apologies

An apology is a polite way to show that you are sorry for your *error* or mistake. Saying "I am sorry" may not *mend* anything but it will show the guest that you care. Apologies should be made in a special occasion where you fail to hear guests clearly. Once this happens, you do need to ask guests for *repetition*. Otherwise, you don't know what the guests want and can't offer help guests want. What's worse, the guests will feel that you are *indifferent* to them.

1) Excuse me.

对不起，请原谅。

道歉是你为自己的失误或错误表示抱歉的一种礼貌方式。道一声"对不起"，虽不能挽回错误，但会让宾客感受到你的诚意。在没有听清楚宾客的说话时，也要道歉。一旦发生这种情况，一定要请求对方重复，否则，你就无法了解对方的需要，也就无法为对方提供所需要的帮助，更会让对方认为你对他们漠不关心。

1) 常用在给宾客添麻烦时或有事要离开或打断和宾客的谈话时。假如宾客正在用餐，这时有电话找他，你过去和宾客讲的第一句话应该是"Excuse me."。宾客起身接电话之前也会和一起用餐的朋友说"Excuse me."。还有许多场合，例如需要引起对方注意时做了一件令人尴尬的事（如打喷嚏、咳嗽或打嗝），打断宾客谈话，为宾客上菜时，进客房之前，请宾客让路，在服务时中途退场，等等。

2) Pardon / Excuse me; I need to get through.

2) 用在有宾客挡道时。

对不起，借过一下。

3) Sorry to have kept you waiting.

对不起，让您久等了。

4) I am sorry for the *delay* / my *misunderstanding*.

对不起，我延误 / 误解了。

5) Sorry to interrupt / disturb you.

对不起，打扰了。

6) We *regret* your *discomfort*. / We (do) apologize for any *inconvenience*.

我们对您的不适表示遗憾。

7) I am *terribly* sorry. It's my *fault*.

对不起，是我的错。

8) Please *forget* it.

请不要放在心上。

3) 这句话常用在让宾客等待之后。让宾客等待总不是一件愉快的事，所以要记住说这句话，不然对方会认为你没有礼貌。

4) 此句式还可用 "apologize for" 结构，如："I do apologize for my carelessness."（对于我的粗心大意我非常抱歉。）。

5) 此句用在给宾客带来不便之前表示遗憾或歉意。注意："interrupt" 强调的是打断别人的讲话或动作，"disturb" 强调的是"妨碍，扰乱"。

6) "Sorry" 或 "apologize" 后接讲话人自己的失误，而 "regret" 后接给对方造成的不便或不满意的结果。"regret" 后面还可接 that 从句，如："I regret that you didn't enjoy your stay here."（很遗憾，您在这里。住得不满意。）。

7) 向宾客表示歉意，并勇于承认过错，会减少宾客的愤怒并得到谅解。在表示歉意之后，常常还会接一些"补救"之类的话，如："We feel awfully sorry about this. I will take care of it / look into the matter / get someone to fix the problem right away."（实在抱歉，我即刻处理此事 / 调查此事 / 派人解决这个问题。）。

8) 用在回答对方的道歉时，以显示你的宽宏大量。另外，还可以说："It doesn't matter. / It's nothing. / That's all right. / Never mind. / That's OK. / Not at all. / No matter." 等。

9) *I beg* your *pardon*? / Pardon?

对不起，请再说一遍好吗？

9) 类似的有："I am sorry, but I didn't hear that."（对不起，我没听清楚。）；"I am afraid I didn't quite hear / understand what you said."（我恐怕没听清你的话。）；"Could you say it again, please?"（请再说一遍，好吗？）。

7.5 Giving Wishes

Giving wishes can make a guest feel happy, make a closer *psychological* distance between you and the guest, and even give a guest a good impression. Wishes can be given at the time when the guest is first met, when the guest is seen off, and when the guest has a special occasion.

一句祝福的话能够让宾客感觉愉悦，拉近与宾客之间的心理距离，更会给宾客留下美好的印象。祝福语可用在初见宾客、送别宾客，以及宾客的重要时刻。

1) Have a good rest.

好好休息！

1) 这句话用在宾客将要回房间休息时。

2) Have a good time.

祝您过得愉快！

2) 常用在宾客启程前或入住后。句中省去了"I hope you ..."，其中，"time" 可变换成 "day / holiday / weekend / trip / stay" 等。

3) All the best!

祝您万事如意！

3) 告别时的祝愿语。句子可以用 "in sth." 或 "with sb." 来扩展。如 "All the very best in your new position!"，或 "All the best with your family!"，还可以说 "Wish you every success."（祝您一切顺利。）。

4) I hope that you enjoy your business trip to Shaoxing.

4) 祝愿宾客商旅顺利，宾客自然高兴。此句还可用 "I hope

祝愿您在绍兴的商务之旅愉快！

5) We wish you a pleasant flight back.

祝您归途愉快！

6) I hope you will soon feel better / get it over.

希望您很快就能好转 / 恢复。

7) We wish you a pleasant stay in our hotel.

愿您在我们酒店过得愉快！

8) Please give my best wishes / *regards* / love to your wife / daughter.

请代我向您的妻子 / 女儿表示良好的祝愿。

9) A happy new year / A *merry* Christmas to you!

祝您新年 / 圣诞快乐！

10) Happy birthday / anniversary!

生日快乐 / 周年快乐！

11) Here's to you / yours / your health / your success!

为您 / 您的家人 / 您的健康 / 您的成功干杯！

12) Let me, on behalf of our general manager Ms. Li, wish you a happy *journey*.

我谨代表我们的总经理李女士，祝您旅途愉快。

everything goes well with your business trip to Shaoxing."。

5) 用在宾客离店去机场的情景中，给宾客留一个美好的最后印象。

6) 用在得知宾客身体不适时，自然会使宾客觉得自己被关心。

7) 比较正式的祝福语，前台在为宾客办完入住手续后常用这句话。还可说"I hope you will enjoy your stay with us."。离店时，可以说"I hope you have enjoyed your stay with us."。

8) 通过攀谈了解宾客的家人情况，在宾客离店时，请宾客代为传达问候或祝愿，会让宾客对你本人和酒店产生好感。此句还可用"Please remember me to your wife / daughter."。

9) 用在适逢特殊节日时。宾客回答时常用"Thank you. And I wish you the same! / And you too."或"Thanks. And the same to you."。

10) 用在适逢宾客的纪念日时。此句还可用"Many happy returns of the day!"。

11) 用在祝酒时。还可用"Let's drink to / propose a toast to our friendship!"（让我们为友谊干杯！）。

12) 用在代表上司向宾客祝酒时。

7.6　Giving Comforts, Congratulations, and Compliments

When guests meet with difficulty, *frustration*, *hopelessness*, or *clumsiness*, giving them words of comfort and giving them a helping hand will make them feel warm for being given much care here. Giving congratulations to guests who have good and happy events or certain *achievements* will make them happy because of their joys being *shared*. Every person from any country enjoys receiving compliments. So what you should remember is not to *skimp* on compliments when communicating with guests.

得知宾客遇到困难、挫折、失落或行为笨拙时，给予安慰并提供帮助会使得宾客觉得住在这里被关心、被重视，而感到温暖。得知宾客有非常高兴的事或取得某种成功，向宾客表示祝贺，使宾客因喜悦被人分享而感到快乐。任何一个国家的人都喜欢别人的称赞，所以与宾客交往时不要吝啬恭维话。

1) Don't worry (about it). Everything will be OK.

别（为此）担心，一切会好的。

1) 类似的有："There is no point in worrying about it."（用不着为此担心。）; "Please take your time; there is no hurry."（请慢慢来，别着急。）。

2) My *hearty* congratulations!

衷心祝贺您!

2) 类似的有："Many congratulations on your marriage."（恭喜你们喜结良缘。）; "Congratulate you on your winning the special gift of our hotel."（祝贺您赢得我们酒店的特别礼物。）; "Let me congratulate you on your achievements."（请允许我为您取得的成就表示祝贺。）; "Please accept my heartiest congratulations."（请接受我最衷心的祝贺。）。

3) It's very nice of you.

您真好!

3) 类似的有："You look great / handsome / beautiful / young and smart."（您看起来很精神 / 很帅 / 很漂亮 / 又年轻又精干。）; "You have a nice shirt!"（您的衬衣真好

看！）；"Your hair is very nice!"（您的头发真好！）。

7.7 Making Requests

The hotel staff will always offer services to guests, at the same time, guests will always ask for services from the hotel staff. Providing guests with help means that you are responding to their requests. The staff should do their best to meet guests' needs and make sure they are happy and comfortable by responding to guests' requests in an efficient, polite, and helpful way. The *patterns* guests usually use to ask for requests from you are: "I would like … / Could you ...? / May I have ...? / Please do …, will you? / Do you mind if I ...?"

1) Can / Will you tell me the way to the Chinese Restaurant?

能告诉我怎么去中餐厅吗？

2) I would like to order a taxi.
我想订一辆出租车。

除了酒店员工主动提供服务外，宾客也常常向酒店员工提出服务请求。为宾客提供帮助就意味着对他们的需求做出回应，员工应尽力满足宾客的需求，做到"迅速、礼貌、有效"，以确保他们感到愉快和舒适。宾客常用"我想……／你能……吗？／我可以……吗？／请帮忙……（好吗）？／你是否介意……？"来请求你给予帮助。

1) 更委婉的说法是："Could / Would you please tell me the way to the Chinese Restaurant ... ?"。

2) 表示"我想要（做）某事"还可有多种表达方式，如："I would like a bath soap."（我想要浴皂。）；"I need more shampoo."（请再拿点洗发液来。）；"I feel like having a cup of coffee."（我想要一杯咖啡。）；"May I have a wake-up call tomorrow morning?"（我想订明早的叫早服务。）。

3) Please do me a *favor* and call me a taxi.
请帮我叫辆出租车。

3) 更委婉的说法有："Would you please do me a favor and call me a taxi?"。其他表达方式还有："Would you please do me a favor to

4) Do you mind helping me with the Internet connection?

您介意帮我连接网络吗？

call me a taxi? / Would you please do me the favor of calling me a taxi? / Would you please favor me by calling me a taxi?"。

4) 其他表达方式有："Do you mind if you can help me with the Internet connection? / Would you mind if you could help me with the Internet connection?"。

7.8　Giving Permissions

A person, when he / she wants to do something, must consider whether it will bring any inconvenience to others, and any *violation* of relevant laws. In such occasions, *consents* and permissions should be obtained. Asking for permissions is the *reflection* of a nation's *civilization*, as well as a person's *moral character*. You should give permissions in a graceful, *modest*, and courteous way, try to satisfy guests without any violation of laws, and politely refuse any request not permitted by law.

1) Do you mind if I open the window?

我把窗子打开，您介意吗？

一个人想要做某事时，必须考虑到会不会给别人带来不便，是不是违反法律等问题。这时就要征得对方同意或请求允许。请求允许反映了一个人的品德素质和一个国家的文明程度。给予允许要有风度，要谦和、礼貌，在不违反法律的前提下尽量满足宾客，一些不在法律许可范围之内的要求，要委婉拒绝。

1) 这是请求允许的说法。更委婉的说法有："Would you mind if I could use your toilet?"（我想用一下您的洗手间，可以吗？）；"Would you mind my making your bed now?"（我现在替您整理床铺，您介意吗？）；"Could I have your passport?"（请出示您的护照。）。

2) As you wish / like.

2) 这是表达同意或允许的方

随您的便。

3) I'm sorry, but that's not *allowed*.
对不起，这是不允许的。

式。类似的有："If you like."（如果您喜欢的话。）；"I don't mind, just as you like."（我不介意，就随您便吧。）；"Feel free to do that."（尽管去做吧。）；"Go ahead."（去做吧。）。

3) 这是表达拒绝的方式。更委婉的说法有："I'd rather you didn't."（您最好不要做。）；"I am afraid (you can) not."（恐怕不行。）。

7.9 Offering Services

When a guest arrives at the hotel, especially for the first time, you are required to treat the guest kindly after greeting and offer him / her services to help with check-in, direction, and baggage. It is a must for you to make the guest feel welcome as if he / she were at home. Besides, you should say "Excuse me," or "Pardon me" in a polite way before offering services in case of any disturbance or *interruption* to the guest.

宾客到达酒店，特别是第一次到达酒店后，你在问候宾客之后应当友善对待宾客，主动为宾客提供帮助和服务，如帮助办理入住、指路、提送行李等。要用非常礼貌的方式让宾客觉得自己很受欢迎，大有宾至如归的感觉。另外，给宾客提供帮助往往会打断宾客，你需要有礼貌地先说一声 "Excuse me." 或 "Pardon me."。

1) What can I do for you?
我能为您做点什么？

2) Is there anything else I can do for you?
还有什么别的能为您效劳的吗？

1) 表达愿意向宾客提供即时帮助。常用的还有："May / Can I help you?"（要我帮您吗？）；"Would you like any help?"（需要帮忙吗？）"Is there anything I can do for you?"（有什么能为您效劳的吗？）。

2) 此句用在给予宾客某个帮助之后。

3) Just call me whenever you are in trouble.

如有困难随时给我打电话。

4) Let me take you to your room.

让我来送您去房间吧。

3) 告知宾客有困难就找你，可以显示出你是热心好客的，还可以反映出酒店服务人员的高素质。类似的表达还有："Just let me know if you need any help / if there is anything I can do for you."（需帮助请告知。）；"I would be happy to help you."（我会很乐意为您效劳。）。

4) 向宾客提供明确具体的帮助。再如："Excuse me, would you like some water?"（请原谅，您要喝点水吗？）；"Pardon me; you are wanted on the phone."（请原谅，有电话找您。）。

7.10 Giving Directions

Guests arrive at the hotel and they usually don't know the place well. If they want to go to a place outside the hotel, they always ask you to give directions. You are required to offer a polite, kind, and patient help. The sentence patterns guests use to ask for directions are: "Is there ... nearby? / Can you tell me where ... is? / Please tell me how to go to ..." If you are asked about the location of a certain facility of the hotel, you must, by the hotel rules, take the guest there. If you are too busy to take the guest there, you must *arrange* for someone else to do so.

1) Is there a bank nearby?

附近有银行吗？

宾客来到酒店，通常对这里是不了解的。如果他们要去酒店外的某个地方，都会要求你给他们指示方向。你要礼貌、热情、耐心地给予帮助。宾客常用"附近有……吗？/ 你能告诉我……在哪儿吗？/ 请告诉我怎么去……?"等提出请求。如果你遇到宾客询问酒店范围内的某营业场所在哪里，按酒店规定你要直接带领宾客去各营业点，假如你不能带领，你要安排其他同事带领前往。

1) 这是宾客请求指引的句子。其他表达方法有："Can you tell me where the nearest post office

is?"（能告诉我最近的邮局在哪儿吗？）；"Could you tell me where the Chinese Restaurant is?"（请问中餐厅在哪？）；"Could you tell me how I can get to the swimming pool?"（请问我怎么去游泳池？）；"Could you tell me which is the way to the work-out room?"（请问哪条是去健身房的路？）；"Please tell me how to go to the bookstore."（请告诉我去书店怎么走，好吗？）。

2) Walk *straight* ahead.

一直往前走。

2）指引时，务必准确地指明路线，切不可含糊不清。其他表达方式有："Turn left / right at the first crossing."（在第一个十字路口往左 / 右转。）；"It's fifty meters ahead on the right across the cinema."（就在前面50米处，路的右边，电影院的对面。）；"Take the lift to the third floor. The lift is on the right of the Front Desk."（乘电梯到三楼。电梯在前台的右边。）。

3) May I show you there?

我可以带您去吗？

3）按酒店规定，员工在指引时，应尽可能做到陪同。其他表达方式还有："This way, please!"（请这边走！）；"Follow me, please!"（请跟我来！）。

4) The doorman will show you the way to the banquet hall.

应接员将领您去宴会厅。

4）如不能亲自陪同时，则要安排他人陪同。

5) There is a washroom at the end of the corridor.

5）当你亲自带领宾客去某个地方时，要记得在路上向宾客介绍走廊尽头是洗手间。

酒店的各项设施，如："Here is our Chinese restaurant."（这是我们的中餐厅。）; "There is a smoking room nearby the lift."（电梯边有吸烟室。）。

6) Here we are. Wish you a pleasant stay in our hotel.

我们到了。祝您住得愉快。

6) 亲自把宾客送到时，别忘了说"到了"，并祝愿他住店愉快。

7.11　Giving Reminders

Giving reminders is an extremely personalized service, which is also the duty and responsibility of a hotel. A reminder can make the guest free from some *unnecessary* trouble, prevent the guest from delaying important matters, ensure the safety of the guest and his property, and also maintain a good public order of the hotel.

1) Please don't leave anything behind.

请不要遗忘您的物品。

2) I'd like to remind you of your date this evening.

我想提醒您今晚有约会。

3) Watch / Mind your steps!

注意台阶，请走好！

4) Please don't smoke here.

提醒是一种极其人性化的服务，是酒店的义务和责任。一句提醒可以帮助宾客减少一些不必要的麻烦，避免宾客耽误重大事情，保证宾客人身和财物的安全，也能保持酒店的公共秩序。

1) 宾客离店时，提醒其不要遗留什么行李物品。

2) 有些酒店提供重要事项提醒服务，以防宾客耽误重要事情。此句还可用："Please remember (to do) sth." 或 "Please don't forget (to do) sth."。

3) 宾客行动时，提醒其注意身体安全，使宾客有温馨的被体贴的感觉。类似的还有："Be careful."（小心。）; "Take care!"（多保重!）; "Don't hurry."（别匆忙。）; "Take it easy."（请慢点儿，别着急。）; "Mind you head."（小心碰头。）; "Wet floor."（小心滑倒。）。

4) 有时为了保持良好的公共秩

请不要抽烟。

序，需要提醒宾客注意一些规定，通常会以标语牌的形式张贴在公共场所。类似的有："No smoking!"（不许抽烟！）；"Don't park here / No parking here!"（不许停车！）；"Don't spit / No spitting!"（不许吐痰！）。

7.12　Making Responses

Making responses is just giving answers to guests' requests, questions, enquires, needs, etc. Much attention, when responses are made, should be paid to where the dialogue takes place, what the dialogue is about, and how the cultures *differ* from each other.

1) You are welcome.

不客气。

应答就是对宾客的各种请求、提问、询问、需求等做出回答。应答时要注意对话的场合、内容及文化差异。

1) 应答表示"感谢"的话。类似的有："Not at all!"（不用谢！）；"My pleasure!"（这是我的荣幸！）；"Don't mention it!"（不用介意！）；"At your service!"（愿意效劳！）。

2) That's all right.

这没什么。

2) 应答表示"道歉"的话。类似的有："It doesn't matter."（没关系。）；"Never mind."（不要紧，没关系。）；"Let's forget it."（没事的。）。

3) Thank you. / Many thanks.

多谢！

4) The same to you!

同样祝福您！

5) I am glad you like it / say so!

很高兴您能喜欢 / 这样说！

6) Just a moment / Wait a moment, please.

3) 应答表示提醒、祝愿、帮助的话。

4) 应答表示祝愿、祝福的话。

5) 用在宾客接受你的帮助或对你的服务表示称赞时。

6) 应答宾客的要求，请求宾客

请稍等。

7) Immediately, madam / sir.

马上就来，女士／先生。

8) Sorry, I am not sure. If you wait a minute, I will try to find it out.

对不起，我不太肯定。请稍等一会儿，我马上去查找。

9) I am afraid it is *against* hotel regulations / policy.

恐怕这有违酒店规定。

10) That sounds like a good idea.

主意不错。

11) I don't think it is a good idea.

我不认为这是好主意。

12) Certainly.

当然。

13) I am terribly sorry; we don't have any envelopes now.

对不起，我们现在没有信封了。

14) Go ahead, please.

请吧。

15) Sorry to keep you waiting; I will see to it right away.

抱歉，让您久等了。我马上查办。

16) Here is / are your ...

这是您的……

17) Thank you for telling me; I *assure* you it won't happen again.

谢谢您告诉我，我保证不会再发生这样的事。

允留片刻，好让你去做宾客要求做的事。

7) 表示能满足宾客要求，立刻为宾客提供所要求的服务。

8) 对宾客的询问没有把握时的应答语。

9) 不能满足宾客的要求时的应答语。还可以说："I am awfully sorry; we are not allowed to do this."。

10) 对宾客的建议表示赞许时的应答语。

11) 对宾客的建议表示反对时的应答语。

12) 对宾客的请求或询问表示肯定的应答语。还可以用："Of course." 或 "No problem."。

13) 在不能满足宾客的购物要求时，常用该句式。也可以说："We have sold out all the envelopes."。

14) 用在允许宾客的请求或要求时。

15) 用在宾客催促时。

16) 用在宾客购买、点菜、索取某物，而向宾客呈递时。

17) 用在宾客投诉时。还可以说："I will speak to our manager about it; please accept our apologies."。

18) There must have been some mistakes. I do apologize.

一定是出错了，实在对不起。

18) 用在自己发生过失时。

19) I am sorry to hear that. I hope you will be better soon.

听到这个消息，我很遗憾。希望您能很快好起来。

19) 用在了解到宾客的不幸消息时。

20) I am glad to hear that.

听到这个消息，我很高兴。

20) 用在得知宾客有喜事时。

7.13 Making Telephones

Telephone is an important tool with which guests communicate with the hotel and the hotel's personnel. Telephone expressions have the *specificity* of their own. So the hotel staff should *master* the basic telephone expressions in order to facilitate the communication with guests.

电话是宾客与酒店及员工进行信息交流的重要工具。电话用语具有其特殊性，因此员工要掌握基本的电话用语，保持与宾客畅通的信息交流。

1) You are wanted on the phone, Mr. Bellow.

贝罗先生，有您的电话。

1) 用在通知宾客接电话时。

2) Who is speaking, please?

请问您是谁?

2) 不应说 "Who are you?"。

3) This is housekeeping (speaking). May I speak to Mr. Robert?

房务中心。我找罗伯特先生。

3) 不应说 "I am housekeeping speaking."。

4) Is that Mr. Johnson (speaking)?

您是约翰逊先生吗?

4) 不应说 "Are you Mr. Johnson speaking?"。

5) I'll *switch* you to Room 1128.

我马上给您接 1128 房间。

5) 用在总机替宾客转接电话时。

6) What number are you calling?

请问对方是什么电话号码?

6) 问宾客需要转接什么号码。如是找人电话，可问"Who would you like to talk to?"（请问受话人姓名?）。

7) (Could you) *hold* the line, please?

请稍等一会儿好吗？

8) Sorry, he is not in at the moment.

对不起，他这会儿不在。

9) Would you like to leave a message?

您需要留言吗？

10) Sorry, I have dialed the wrong number.

对不起，我打错电话了。

11) Sorry, you have got the wrong number.

对不起，您打错电话了。

12) Good morning, *Rainbow* Hotel, May I help you?

早上好，彩虹酒店，有什么可以为您效劳？

13) Thank you for calling.

感谢您的来电。

7) "hold the line" 表示 "别挂断电话"。用在转接电话或叫人接电话时。

8) 还可以说 "Sorry, nobody answered."（对不起，没人在 / 无人接电话。）。

9) 当对方要找的宾客不在时，不要忘了提醒宾客要不要留言。

10) 因打错电话而表示歉意。

11) 用在对方拨错电话时。还可以用 "Sorry, there is nobody by Thomson here."（对不起，没有叫汤姆森的人。）。

12) 前台接线员习惯用语。电话铃声响三下，接线员拿起电话便说这句话。

13) 挂断电话时的礼貌用语。

Vocabulary

course /kɔːs/ *n.* 过程

emotion /ɪˈməʊʃn/ *n.* 情绪

comfort /ˈkʌmfət/ *n.* 安慰

pleasant /ˈpleznt/ *adj.* 令人愉快的

reply /rɪˈplaɪ/ *v.* 回复；回答

error /ˈerə(r)/ *n.* 过失

repetition /ˌrepəˈtɪʃn/ *n.* 重复

delay /dɪˈleɪ/ *n.* 耽搁；延误

communication /kəˌmjuːnɪˈkeɪʃn/ *n.* 交流；交际

expression /ɪkˈspreʃn/ *n.* 语句；表达方法

energetic /ˌenəˈdʒetɪk/ *adj.* 充满活力的；热情的

kindness /ˈkaɪndnəs/ *n.* 善意；友好的行为

appreciate /əˈpriːʃieɪt/ *v.* 感激

mend /mend/ *v.* 改进；修补

indifferent /ɪnˈdɪfrənt/ *adj.* 漠不关心的

misunderstanding /ˌmɪsʌndəˈstændɪŋ/ *n.* 误会；误解

regret /rɪˈɡret/ v. 遗憾

inconvenience /ˌɪnkənˈviːniəns/ n. 不便

fault /fɔːlt/ n. 过错；缺点

beg /beɡ/ v. 恳求

psychological /ˌsaɪkəˈlɒdʒɪkl/ adj. 心理的

merry /ˈmeri/ adj. 愉快的；欢乐的

frustration /frʌˈstreɪʃn/ n. 挫折

clumsiness /ˈklʌmzinəs/ n. 笨拙

share /ʃeə(r)/ v. 分享

hearty /ˈhɑːti/ adj. 衷心的

favor /ˈfeɪvə(r)/ n. 恩惠；帮忙；支持

consent /kənˈsent/ n. 同意；赞成

civilization /ˌsɪvəlaɪˈzeɪʃn/ n. 文明

character /ˈkærəktə(r)/ n. 品质

allow /əˈlaʊ/ v. 允许

arrange /əˈreɪndʒ/ v. 安排

unnecessary /ʌnˈnesəsəri/ adj. 不必要的；多余的

differ /ˈdɪfə(r)/ v. 不同；区别

assure /əˈʃɔː(r)/ v. 确保

master /ˈmɑːstə(r)/ v. 掌握；精通

hold /həʊld/ v. 使保持（某状态）

discomfort /dɪsˈkʌmfət/ n. 不适

terribly /ˈterəbli/ adv. 非常地

forget /fəˈɡet/ v. 忘记

pardon /ˈpɑːdn/ n. 原谅

regard /rɪˈɡɑːd/ n. 问候；致意

journey /ˈdʒɜːni/ n. 旅行

hopelessness /ˈhəʊpləsnəs/ n. 失落；绝望

achievement /əˈtʃiːvmənt/ n. 成就；成绩

skimp /skɪmp/ v. 舍不得给

pattern /ˈpætn/ n. 句型；句式

violation /ˌvaɪəˈleɪʃn/ n. 违反；违背

reflection /rɪˈflekʃn/ n. 反映

moral /ˈmɒrəl/ adj. 道德上的

modest /ˈmɒdɪst/ adj. 谦虚的

interruption /ˌɪntəˈrʌpʃn/ n. 打扰；中断

straight /streɪt/ adv. 直接地

against /əˈɡeɪnst/ prep. 违背

specificity /ˌspesɪˈfɪsəti/ n. 特殊性

switch /swɪtʃ/ v. 转接；接通

rainbow /ˈreɪnbəʊ/ n. 彩虹

Useful Expressions

during the course of ... 在……过程中

be glad to do sth. 很高兴做某事

apologize to sb. for sth. 因某事向某人道歉

look into ... 调查……

wish sb. sth. 祝愿某人某事

give regards/wishes/love to sb. 向某人表示祝愿

remember me to sb. 代我向某人问好

propose a toast to sth. 为某事干杯

have a pleasant flight 飞行愉快

be indifferent to sb. 对某人漠不关心

get ... over 克服……；恢复

drink to sth. 为某事干杯

on behalf of sb. 代表某人

skimp on ... 吝啬……

take one's time 不用着急

congratulate sb. on sth. 恭喜某人某事

do one's best to do sth. 尽力做某事

feel like ... 想要……

feel free to do sth. 随意做某事

do sb. a favor (to do sth.) 帮助某人（做某事）

do sb. the favor (of doing sth.) 帮助某人（做某事）

favor sb. by doing sth. 帮助某人做某事

be required to do sth. 必须做某事

be in trouble 有困难

make sb. free from ... 使某人免于……

arrange for sb. to do sth. 安排某人做某事

differ from ... 不同于……

sound like ... 听起来像……

be allowed to do sth. 被允许做某事

sell out 售完

词汇、课文资源

词汇、课文自测

微课

课堂练习

Chapter Eight

Situational Expressions
情景交际用语

思政园地／二十
大精神学习专栏

Learning Objectives

· *To get familiar with the situations in which the hotel staff offers services in English;*

· *To understand the expressions in each situation;*

· *To master the new words and professional terms concerned;*

· *To improve reading ability through learning the text;*

· *To develop team spirit and self-study ability through learning activities.*

Teaching Arrangements

节次	教学内容	自主学习资源	自主学习自测	课堂教学视频	课堂练习
L 1	8.1.1 Room Reservationist	词汇、课文资源	词汇、课文自测	微课	课堂练习
L 2	8.1.2 Registration Clerk	词汇、课文资源	词汇、课文自测	微课	课堂练习
L 3	8.1.3 Concierge	词汇、课文资源	词汇、课文自测	微课	课堂练习
L 4	8.1.4 Information Clerk	词汇、课文资源	词汇、课文自测	微课	课堂练习
L 5	8.1.5 Cashier	词汇、课文资源	词汇、课文自测	微课	课堂练习
L 6	8.1.6 Business Secretary 8.1.7 Operator 8.1.8 Salesperson	词汇、课文资源	词汇、课文自测	微课	课堂练习
L 7	8.2.1 Floor Attendant 8.2.2 Housemaid	词汇、课文资源	词汇、课文自测	微课	课堂练习
L 8	8.3 Restaurant Staff	词汇、课文资源	词汇、课文自测	微课	课堂练习
L 9	8.4 Management	词汇、课文资源	词汇、课文自测	微课	课堂练习

Situational expressions are those frequently and necessarily used by the hotel staff through different stages and different situations while carrying out their guest services. In the hotel, situational expressions are mainly and mostly used by those who provide face-to-face services to guests. They include all the personnel of hotel operations, and, of course, are *rarely inclusive* of the personnel of hotel administrative groups. The *so-called* situations are all *episodes* making up the whole process of providing guest services in the guest cycle.

情景交际用语，指的是酒店员工在完成对客服务过程中的各个不同阶段、不同场景里所常用的必要的交际用语。在酒店里，使用情景交际用语的主要是那些直接从事对客服务的酒店各经营部门的员工，当然也很少有酒店职能部门的员工。所谓情景，指的是开展入住流程中各种对客服务的全过程中的所有片段。

8.1　Front Office Staff

8.1.1　Room Reservationist

Distance-call reservation

1) Sunflower Hotel, Advance Reservations. Good morning. Can I help you?

2) Would you like a single room or a double room?

3) Would you like a room with bath or shower?

4) Would you like breakfast?

5) How long do you intend to stay?

6) Could you tell me your arrival time and departure time?

7) OK, there will be some available for those days. I can book you a single room with shower from the 26th to the 30th.

预订员

长途电话预订

1) 向日葵酒店预订部。早上好。我能为您做什么吗？

2) 您想要单人房还是双人房？

3) 您想要浴缸的还是淋浴的房间？

4) 您想订早餐吗？

5) 您准备住多久？

6) 请告诉我抵店时间和离店时间。

7) 好的。那几天有空房。我可以为您预订一间26日至30日的带淋浴的单人间。

8) Could you tell me your name, please? And how do you spell it, please?

9) Would you please say it again?

10) May I have your telephone number?

11) (Confirm) Crichton Robert. A single room with bath from the afternoon of July 26th to the morning of July 30th, without breakfast. Am I right?

12) You know it is the high season in this area. We can only hold the confirmed booking till 18:00. You can guarantee the booking by credit card now.

13) I will just need your credit card number, and I will take care of the rest.

14) OK, we look forward to your staying with us.

Group reservation

15) Could you tell me for which dates you want to book the rooms, sir? And how many people are there in your party?

16) What kind of rooms would you like to have? We have single rooms, double rooms, suites, and deluxe suites.

17) Yes, we can confirm 10 double rooms for 20 people from July 26th to 30th.

18) Yes, the current rate is $50 per night. But there is a 10 percent discount for group reservation. We also have some *reduction* for children. In addition, we offer complimentary breakfasts to tour guides.

19) Our hotel is one of the best hotels in

8) 请问您贵姓？请问怎么拼呢？

9) 您能再说一遍吗？

10) 请告诉我您的电话号码。

11)（确认）克里奇顿·罗伯特，7月26日下午到7月30日上午，带浴间的单人房一间，不含早餐，对吗？

12) 您知道，现在我们这里是旅游旺季，我们只负责将确认的订房保留到下午6点。您可以现在先用信用卡担保。

13) 请您告诉我您的信用卡号，其他我会办妥的。

14) 好的，我们期盼您的光临。

团队预订

15) 先生，您想订哪几天的？与您一起有几个人？

16) 您想要什么样的房间？我们有单人间、双人间、套间和豪华套间。

17) 可以，我们确认从7月26日至30日供20人使用的10个双人间。

18) 是的，现行价格是每晚50美元。但是对于团队预订，房价可以打九折。我们也有儿童优惠价。此外，导游的早餐是免费的。

19) 我们酒店是绍兴最好的酒

Shaoxing, and this is the lowest price.

20) Sorry, we don't have reduction for children on room rate, but our Western restaurant has a 40% discount for children.

21) By the way, how will they be arriving? Will they be coming by air?

22) Could you give me the flight number and the arrival time so that we can arrange an airport bus?

23) Yes, we have various conference halls, but please hold on, and I will get you through to the sales manager.

Face-to-face reservation

24) Sir, when will you be coming, and how long will you be staying?

25) We can confirm a room from the 20th to the 25th, but after the 25th, we can't guarantee you a room. We usually have a high occupancy in such *peak* seasons. If you don't mind, we can put you on a waiting list or find you a room in a nearby hotel.

26) Yes, we have special rooms and perfect facilities for the convenience of the *disabled* people. You will be satisfied.

27) Lastly, how will you be paying, in cash, by *check*, or by credit card?

28) This is our hotel card; the telephone number of our hotel is 88689188.

Reservation refusal

29) Unfortunately, we are fully booked for the 21st.

店之一。这也是最低的价格了。

20) 对不起，我们的房价没有给儿童特别优惠，但是在我们的西餐厅儿童可以享受 6 折优惠。

21) 顺便问一下，他们怎么来？乘飞机吗？

22) 请告诉我航班号及到达时间，以便我们安排机场大巴。

23) 是的，我们有各种类型的会议厅。请稍等，我帮您接通会议销售经理。

店堂预订

24) 先生，你什么时候到达，要住几天？

25) 我们可以确定 20 日至 25 日有一间房，但是 25 日以后，我们不能保证。在这高峰期，我们的入住率很高。如果您不介意的话，我们可以把您排入住店等候单或给您在附近酒店安排一个房间。

26) 是的，为了残障人士的便利，我们有专用客房和完善的设施。您会感到满意的。

27) 最后一个问题，您打算怎样付款，是现金，支票还是信用卡？

28) 这是我们酒店的名片，我们酒店的电话是 88689188。

谢绝预订

29) 遗憾的是 21 日的客房全部订满。

30) We won't be able to guarantee you a room for May 6th.

31) I am afraid our hotel is fully booked for those dates.

30) 我们不能保证 5 月 6 日给您一个房间。

31) 对不起，我们酒店那几天的客房全部订满了。

Vocabulary

situational /ˌsɪtʃuˈeɪʃənl/ *adj.* 情景的

inclusive /ɪnˈkluːsɪv/ *adj.* 包含在内的

episode /ˈepɪsəʊd/ *n.* 片段

peak /piːk/ *adj.* 最高峰的

check /tʃek/ *n.* 支票

rarely /ˈreəli/ *adv.* 很少地

so-called /ˈsəʊ kɔːld/ *adj.* 号称的；所谓的

reduction /rɪˈdʌkʃ(ə)n/ *n.* 折扣；优惠

disabled /dɪsˈeɪbld/ *adj.* 有残疾的

Useful Expressions

be inclusive of ... 包括……

get sb. through to sb. 帮某人接通某人（电话）

for the convenience of ... 为了……之便

by the way 顺便说一下

guarantee sb. sth. 保证某人某物

词汇、课文资源

词汇、课文自测

微课

课堂练习

8.1.2　Registration Clerk

Making registration

1) Good afternoon, welcome to our hotel. May I help you?

2) May I have your name, sir, please?

3) Do you have a reservation with us? And whom is the reservation by?

4) Just a minute, I will check the arrival list.

登记员

住宿登记

1) 下午好，欢迎光临。我能为您做点什么？

2) 请问你叫什么名字？

3) 您有预订吗？是以谁的名字订的房？

4) 请稍等，我查一下到客通知单。

5) Which country do you come from? Show me your passport, please. We need it for registration.

6) Would you please fill out this form while I prepare your key card for you?

7) You can *skip* that. I will put in the room number for you later on.

8) Let me have a look ... name, address, nationality, *forwarding* address, passport number, place of *issue*, signature, and date of departure. Oh, here, sir. You forgot to put down the date of your departure. Let me fill it in for you. You are leaving on ... ?

9) Could you sign here please, sir?

10) Now everything is in order. And here is your key, Mr. Johnson. Your room number is 1420. It is on the 14th floor and the room rate is $80 per night. Here is your key card with the information on your booking, the hotel services, and the hotel rules and regulations on it. Please make sure that you have it with you all the time. You need to show it when you sign for your meals and drinks in the restaurants and bars. You also need to show it when you collect your key from the information desk.

11) And these are your breakfast coupons, with which you can enjoy complimentary breakfast from 6:30 to 8:30 at the buffet restaurant on the first floor.

12) And now if you are ready, Mr. Johnson, I will call the bellboy, and he will take you to your room.

13) If you need help, please call 6605. We are always at your service. Hope you enjoy your stay with us.

5) 您是从哪个国家来的？请出示您的护照？我们登记需要它。

6) 请您把这个表格填一下，我为您准备房卡。

7) 这个您不用填，房号我马上帮您填。

8) 让我看看，姓名、地址、国籍、转投、护照号码、发照地点、签名、离店日期。噢，这儿，先生。您忘了填写离店日期了。我来帮您补上吧，您离店日期是……？

9) 先生，请在这儿签字。

10) 所有手续都好了。给您房间钥匙，约翰逊先生。您的房间号是1420，在第14层，每天房费80美元。这是您的出入证，上面有您的房间信息、酒店服务项目及本店的规章制度。请务必随身携带它。在餐厅和酒吧里吃饭或喝酒后记账时您得出示它，您到服务台取房间钥匙时也得出示它。

11) 这些是您的早餐券。您可以在六点半至八点半到一楼自助餐厅享用免费早餐。

12) 约翰逊先生，如果您现在准备好了，我这就让服务员送你去房间。

13) 如果您有什么需要，请致电6605，我们随时为您服务。希望您在这儿过得愉快。

Receiving a walk-in guest

14) Would you like to check in? Here is a brochure of our hotel, and this is a room tariff *table*.

15) What kind of room do you like?

16) Just a moment, I will check if there is a room available. Yes, we have a single room available.

17) The single room is 398 yuan per night. It's about 55 US dollars. An extra bed costs 200 yuan. The room rate includes breakfast.

18) (You are our VIP.) We can give a 40% discount; it's the lowest discount.

19) How many nights would you like to stay?

20) Please give me $60 for deposit. As a hotel policy, we require one day's room charge as deposit for guests without reservation.

21) Here is your welcome card, room key, and breakfast coupons. Complimentary breakfast is served from 6:00 to 9:00 on the first floor.

Refusing a walk-in guest

22) I am sorry, madam. We don't have any vacancy at the moment. You could try the Sunflower Hotel if you like.

23) I am sorry, but all the standard rooms are sold out. Shall I find a room in a nearby hotel for you?

24) There are some rooms available in the Sunflower Hotel. I write down the name of the hotel, and you can show it to the taxi driver. It takes about 10 minutes to get there by taxi. The taxis are right outside the hotel. Just go out by the front entrance and the doorman will take care of you.

过客接待

14) 您要住店吗？给您我们的酒店手册和房价表。

15) 您要哪一种房间？

16) 请稍等，我检查一下有没有空房。可以，我们有一间单人房。

17) 单人房398元，约55美元。加床另收200元。房价包含早餐。

18)（您是我们的贵宾。）我们可以给您打六折，这是最低折扣。

19) 您预计住几晚？

20) 请交押金60美元。根据酒店规定，对于没有预订的客人，我们要加收一天的房费作为押金。

21) 这是您的出入卡、房卡及早餐券。从6点到9点，您可以在一楼享受免费早餐。

谢绝过客

22) 对不起，女士。我们现在没有空房。如果您愿意，可以去向日葵酒店试试。

23) 对不起，所有标间都已住满。我帮您在附近酒店要个房间怎么样？

24) 向日葵酒店有空房。我把酒店的名字写下来，您将纸条出示给司机就可以了。打的去那里约需10分钟。出租车就在酒店外面，您从正门出去，门童会招呼您的。

Extending stay

25) May I know your name and your room number?

26) How many more nights would you like to stay?

27) Please wait a moment; I will have to check the computer records (or the booking situation).

28) Sorry, the rooms are very heavily booked; you will have to check out before twelve o'clock.

29) Yes, sir, I am very glad that we will be able to accept your *extension* request. But I am afraid that it will be necessary for us to ask you to change rooms for the last two nights. You see, we have already let your room to another gentleman. Is this *acceptable* to you?

30) When would you like to move tomorrow? The new *occupant* will be checking in a little after twelve.

31) You may keep the room till 2:00 p.m., if you wish. But you have to check out before two o'clock.

32) You may keep the room until six o'clock in the afternoon, but I am afraid I have to *charge* you a half day's room rate according to the hotel policy.

33) According to hotel regulations, the checkout time is 12:00. If you leave after 2:00 p.m., you have to pay half of the day's *rent*. If you leave after 6:00 p.m., you have to pay the full rent.

Changing room

34) Oh, dear. I am very sorry to hear that. Let me see if I can find you a quieter room. Here is a

延房

25) 请告诉您的名字和房号。

26) 您要续住几晚？

27) 请稍等，我要检查一下电脑记录（或预订状态）。

28) 对不起，房间预订比较紧张，你必须在 12 点之前结账。

29) 好的，先生，我很高兴我们能够接受您的延房请求。但恐怕我们有必要请您最后两晚换个房间。您看，我们已经把您的房间预订给了另一位先生，请问您能同意吗？

30) 您明天什么时候搬房？新房客 12 点以后就会入店。

31) 如果您愿意，可以将房间保留到下午 2 点。您必须在下午 2 点之前退房。

32) 您可以保留房间到下午 6 点，但根据酒店规定，需要加收半天的房费。

33) 酒店规定，退房时间是中午 12 点，如果下午 2 点以后走，您需要加付半天房租；如果晚上 6 点以后走，您就需要加付一天的房租。

换房

34) 哎呀，真抱歉。我看看能不能给您找一个安静点儿的房间。

better one, but it is two floors higher up. Do you mind moving two floors up, Mr. Johnson? Please give me a call when you are ready to move, and I will send you a bellboy to help you with your luggage. And please remember to bring your key card down to the reception desk so that I can change the room number on it.

35) I am sorry, sir. It is our fault. We'll make the change for you. You booked two *adjoining* rooms. But if you would like to take a seat for a few minutes I will see what I can do. It won't take long. I *promise* you.

这里有一个比较好一点儿的，但要再上两层楼。往上再搬两层，您介意吗，约翰逊先生？您准备好搬的时候，请给我一个电话，我会派服务员去帮您搬行李。还有，请记着把出入证拿来，好让我在上面把房号改过来。

35) 对不起，先生，是我们的错。我们可以给您换个房间。你订的是两个相邻房。请您坐几分钟，我想想办法。不会太久，我向您保证。

Vocabulary

skip /skɪp/ *v.* 跳过；省略

issue /ˈɪʃuː/ *n.* 发行；发放

extension /ɪkˈstenʃn/ *n.* 延长

occupant /ˈɒkjəpənt/ *n.* 住客

rent /rent/ *n.* 租金

promise /ˈprɒmɪs/ *v.* 做出保证

forwarding /ˈfɔːwədɪŋ/ *n.* 转送

table /ˈteɪbl/ *n.* 表；表格

acceptable /əkˈseptəbl/ *adj.* 合意的；可以接受的

charge /tʃɑːdʒ/ *v.* 收费

adjoining /əˈdʒɔɪnɪŋ/ *adj.* 毗邻的

词汇、课文资源

词汇、课文自测

微课

课堂练习

8.1.3　Concierge

Bellman in front of the hotel

1) (After opening the door of the car for the guests) Good evening, sir and madam. Welcome to our hotel. I am the bellman. Please let me open the *trunk* and take out your baggage for you.

2) (After looking at the name on the baggage tags) Mr. James, you have got four pieces of baggage *altogether*, right?

3) The registration desk is straight ahead. The doorman will show you there.

Parking valet in front of the hotel

4) Madam, this is not a *parking* place; please drive a bit ahead and park your car in line with other cars.

5) Sir, would you like me to park your car?

6) Please give me your key to the car; I can park it in the parking place for you.

7) Sir, this is the key to your car; your car has been properly parked. Hope you will have a good time in our hotel.

Porter at the entrance to the hotel

8) Sir, are these your *pieces* of baggage? May I take them for you?

9) How many pieces of baggage have you got? Two *suitcases* and one bag. Is that right?

10) Please wait a moment; I will *fetch* a baggage *cart*.

礼宾员

应接员在酒店门前

1)（替客人打开车门之后）女士和先生，晚上好。欢迎来到我们酒店。我是应接服务生。请让我帮您打开车厢取出行李吧。

2)（看了行李标签上的名字之后）詹姆斯先生，您一共有四件行李，对吗？

3) 登记处就在前面，门童会带您去的。

代客停车员在酒店门前

4) 女士，这里不能停车。请往前开一点，与其他车并排停放。

5) 先生，要我替您停车吗？

6) 请把车钥匙给我，我替您把车停在停车处。

7) 先生，这是您的车钥匙。车已停好。希望您在这里会很开心。

行李员在门厅入口处

8) 先生，这些是您的行李吗？我来帮您提吧。

9) 您共有几件行李？2 只箱子和 1 个包，对吗？

10) 请稍等，我去拿行李车。

11) Is there anything *valuable* or *breakable* in your luggage?

12) Don't worry, sir. I will take care of your baggage while you register. After that, I will take you to your room. Your luggage will be sent up at once.

Baggage clerk at the baggage area

13) Good evening, sir. I am glad to take care of your baggage.

14) Sir, would you like to have your baggage deposited here?

15) Is there anything valuable or breakable in your bag? According to regulation, we don't accept foods, *combustibles*, valuables, or breakables.

16) You have three items, one bag and two cases. Is that right? Please sign here.

17) Here is your baggage card. Please keep it.

18) Sir, are you here for your baggage? Please give me your baggage card.

19) Excuse me. May I have your baggage number?

20) Is this the correct number of your bags?

Porter taking a guest to the room

21) Sir, may I look at your room card? Oh, your room is on the 14th floor. I will show you there. Your baggage will be sent up soon. Please follow me.

22) We will take the lift to the fourteenth floor. The lift is right ahead over there.

23) After you please. Watch your head and your feet.

11) 您的行李中有贵重物品或易碎品吗？

12) 先生，不用担心。您登记的时候，由我来照看您的行李。登记好了，我会陪同您去房间。您的行李很快就会送上去的。

行李寄存员在行李区

13) 晚上好，先生。我很高兴为您照看行李。

14) 先生，您想寄存行李吗？

15) 您的包里有贵重物品或易碎品吗？根据规定，食品、易燃品、贵重物品和易碎品都不给予保管。

16) 您寄存3件物品，是1只包和2只箱子，对吗？

17) 这是行李牌，请收好。

18) 先生，您是来取行李吗？请您把行李牌给我。

19) 劳驾，请告诉我您的行李号。

20) 您的行李数目对吗？

行李员陪同客人去客房

21) 先生，请让我看一下您的房卡。噢，您的房间在14楼。我带您去。您的行李马上就送上来。请跟我来。

22) 我们乘电梯去14楼吧。电梯就在前面那个地方。

23) 请进，请小心碰头，当心脚下。

24) Certainly, sir. It is my duty to introduce to you our hotel's services. Our hotel is located on South Jiefang Road in the south of Shaoxing City. It is a first-rate hotel ideal for both business and leisure *traveler*s. There are over 500 rooms and suites in the hotel. We have four Chinese restaurants, one deluxe Western restaurant, large and small banquet halls and convention halls, two bars, one 24-hour cafe, and many recreation facilities. In addition, we have a lot of services at guests' convenience. For example, we have post service at the front desk; the business center is next to the lobby shop; you can get your money changed at the cashier's counter; there are some local products on sale in the lobby shop. Oh, please remember: the breakfast time is from 6:30 a.m. to 9:00 a.m. in the Western restaurant, and the business center opens from 7:30 a.m. to 11:30 p.m.

25) Here we are, madam. The floor attendant will show you to your room, and I will get your luggage up to your room by the baggage lift. See you later.

Porter delivering baggage to the room

26) (After pressing the door bell or three knocks on the door) Madam, may I come in?

27) I have got your baggage here. Where shall I put them?

28) Please check your baggage. If there is nothing wrong, I will have to leave. Wish you a good rest after the tiring journey.

Porter taking baggage down to the lobby

29) Please wait in your room; I will come soon.

24) 当然可以，先生。向您介绍我们酒店的服务是我的责任。我们酒店坐落在绍兴城南人民南路，是商务和休闲客人的理想处所。我们共有各类客房500多间套。我们有4个中餐厅，1个豪华西餐厅，大小宴会厅和会议室，2个酒吧，1个24小时咖啡厅，还有许多康乐设施。此外，我们还有许多便客服务。例如，前台有邮政服务；商务中心在大堂商场隔壁；你可以在收银处兑换外币；大堂商场有一些地方特产出售。噢，请记住：早餐是在西餐厅，时间是上午6点半到9点；商务中心的营业时间是上午7点半到晚上11点半。

25) 女士，我们到了。楼层服务员会领您去房间。我乘行李电梯把您的行李拿上来。一会儿见。

行李员送行李到客房

26)（按门铃或敲门三下之后）女士，我可以进来吗？

27) 我把您的行李拿来了，我把它们放在哪儿呢？

28) 请您核对一下行李。如果没有什么差错的话，我得先走了。您旅途劳累，请好好休息。

行李员拿行李到大堂

29) 请在房间里稍等，我马上

就来。

30) Excuse me, sir. Do you need my help with your baggage?

31) Have you *packed* up all your things? Please don't leave anything behind.

32) Let's take the lift down to the lobby.

33) No worry, Miss. I will take care of your baggage while you are checking out.

Bellman outside the entrance

34) Excuse me. Shall I carry the suitcase for you?

35) Could I carry these bags to your taxi?

36) Thanks for your coming; please *drop* in again. Wish you a god journey back.

Concierge booking restaurant for the guest

37) Hello, the Concierge Desk. What can I do for you?

38) Could you please tell me your name and your room number?

39) Which kind of food do you prefer, the Chinese food or the Western food?

40) What kind of seat would you like, a quiet one or a near-the-window one?

41) Please wait a while. I will get in *touch* with the Food Service Department.

42) Hello, Miss Chen? This is the Concierge Desk. We have booked you a table near the window at 8:00 p.m. in the 4th Chinese restaurant. The table number is five. Hope you will like it.

43) You are welcome. Hope you will enjoy a good dinner tonight.

30) 劳驾，先生。您需要我帮您拿行李吗?

31) 您的所有东西都拿好了吗? 请不要遗留下什么物品。

32) 我们乘电梯去大堂吧。

33) 别担心，小姐。您结账时，由我来看管您的行李。

应接员在大厅入口处外边

34) 劳驾，我替您拿箱子好吗?

35) 让我把这几个包送到出租车上吧。

36) 谢谢您的光临，欢迎下次再来。祝您一路顺风。

礼宾员代客订餐厅

37) 您好，礼宾部，能为您效劳吗?

38) 请告诉我您的姓名和房号，好吗?

39) 请问您想吃中餐还是西餐?

40) 请问您想要一个什么样的座位，安静的还是靠窗的?

41) 请稍等，我与餐厅部联系一下。

42) 您好，陈小姐吗? 这是礼宾部。我们已为您在第四中餐厅订了一个 8 点钟的临窗座位，是 5 号桌。希望您能喜欢。

43) 不用谢。希望您今晚用餐愉快。

Concierge arranging transportation

44) Hello, Mr. James. I think you are going out. Can I help you?

45) To the Book Store? It is a bit far from here. Shall I call a taxi for you? It's about 15 minutes by taxi.

46) Most taxi drivers do not speak English. It is helpful that you have your destination written in Chinese.

47) When you return to the hotel, please show this hotel card to the taxi driver.

48) That's nothing. Wish you a good *ride*.

Concierge booking tickets for guests

49) Good morning, Mr. Smith. Can I help you?

50) I am sorry, but we usually book air tickets 3 days in advance.

51) Sorry to tell you that it is the busy season for traveling now, and all tickets are booked up.

52) I wonder if you would like to go there by train instead.

53) How many tickets do you need? And when do you want to leave?

54) OK, two tickets for Shanghai at eight tomorrow morning. Am I right?

55) The hotel's *shuttle* bus takes guests between the *station* and the hotel every 30 minutes with the first bus at 6:30 in the morning. Wish you a good trip.

56) Please tell me how many tickets you want, for what film, and when it begins.

礼宾员安排交通

44) 您好，詹姆斯先生。您是要出去吗？可以为您做些什么？

45) 去书店？离这儿有点远。我可以帮您叫辆出租车吗？打的约15分钟路程。

46) 大多数出租车司机都不会英语，把您要去的目的地用中文写下来，会给您不少帮助。

47) 当您要返回酒店时，请向出租车司机出示一下酒店名片。

48) 不用谢。祝您愉快。

礼宾员帮客人订票

49) 早上好，史密斯先生。能为您效劳吗？

50) 对不起，我们预订机票通常需要提前3天。

51) 对不起，现在是旅游旺季，所有机票都订完了。

52) 不知道您想不想乘火车？

53) 您要几张票？什么时候出发？

54) 好的，两张明早8点去上海的票，对吗？

55) 我们酒店的班车每30分钟往返于车站和酒店接送客人，首班车是早上6点半。祝您旅途愉快。

56) 请告诉我您想要几张票，看什么电影，什么时间看。

57) OK, two tickets for *Kung Fu* at 4:00 p.m. tomorrow. Here are your tickets.

58) We have many *spot* tickets available. Please tell me how many of you will go to what spots.

57) 好的，两张《功夫》的票，明天下午 4 点，对吗？给您票。

58) 我们有很多景点的门票可售。请告诉我你们有几个人，要去哪些地方。

Vocabulary

trunk /trʌŋk/ *n.*（汽车后部的）行李厢

parking /ˈpɑːkɪŋ/ *n.* 停车

suitcase /ˈsuːtkeɪs/ *n.* 手提箱

cart /kɑːt/ *n.*（行李）车;（购物）车

valuable /ˈvæljuəbl/ *adj./n.* [pl.] 贵重的 / 贵重东西

breakable /ˈbreɪkəbl/ *adj./n.* [pl.] 易碎的 / 易碎物品

combustible /kəmˈbʌstəbl/ *n.* 易燃物

pack /pæk/ *v.* 收拾行李

touch /tʌtʃ/ *n.* 接触;联系

shuttle /ˈʃʌtl/ *n.* 穿梭班车

spot /spɒt/ *n.* 景点;地点

altogether /ˌɔːltəˈgeðə(r)/ *adv.* 总共

piece /piːs/ *n.* 件

fetch /fetʃ/ *v.* 取来

traveler /ˈtrævələ(r)/ *n.* 旅行者

drop /drɒp/ *v.* 访问

ride /raɪd/ *n.* 旅行

station /ˈsteɪʃn/ *n.* 车站

Useful Expressions

at one's convenience 在某人方便之时

get in touch with ... 联系……

词汇、课文资源　　词汇、课文自测　　微课　　课堂练习

8.1.4　Information Clerk

Posting mails

1) Would you like your mail sent by *airmail* or *surface* mail?

2) *Normally*, it takes about one month for an ordinary mail letter to reach America while airmail takes one week.

3) In that case, I would recommend sending it by airmail.

4) You need to pay 8.4 yuan for an airmail *abroad*.

5) What does this *parcel* contain? Can you open it for our inspection, please?

6) Do you want to register this letter?

7) Could you fill out the form, please?

8) May I have your letter *weighed*?

9) Your letter is *over-weighted* and you have to pay six yuan more.

10) We have FedEx and DHL, which one would you *prefer*?

11) Here is the FedEx waybill, would you please fill it out?

12) You need a box to send these in.

13) It is 9:00 p.m. now, and the FedEx will send someone to pick up your express mail tomorrow.

14) Here is your *change* and your *receipt*.

Introducing scenic spots

15) Have you ever been to Hangzhou? If not, I am very pleased to *suggest* that you visit the West Lake and the Lingyin *Temple*, the main *attractions* in Hangzhou. They are often visited by foreign guests.

问讯员

寄邮件

1) 您需要寄航空信还是平信？

2) 平信到美国约1个月才能到，航空邮件到达美国需要1个星期。

3) 这样的话，我推荐选择航空邮件。

4) 寄到国外的航空信要8元4角。

5) 这个包裹里包的什么东西？能请您打开让我们检查一下吗？

6) 您想寄挂号信吗？

7) 请填上这张单子，好吗？

8) 我可以称一下您的信吗？

9) 您的信超重了，需要再付6元钱。

10) 您需要用联邦快递还是敦豪快运？

11) 这是联邦快递包裹单，您填一下好吗？

12) 寄这些物品需要一个箱子。

13) 现在已是晚上9点，联邦快递明天会派人过来取您的快件。

14) 这是您的零钱和收据。

介绍景点

15) 您去过杭州吗？要是没有，我很高兴地建议您去看一看西湖和灵隐寺。它们是杭州的两个主要景点，常有外国人去那里游玩。

16) They are of typical Chinese style. You will particularly be *impressed* by the fine art of *architecture* there.

17) It is one of the most famous lakes in China. It has a long history.

18) What's more, the construction of the bridge is magnificent. I think it is a good place worth visiting.

Giving directions

19) Good morning, Mrs. Li. I *wonder* if I can do something for you.

20) Yes, the Luxun's *Former Residence* is not far from here. You can walk there. I can show you on the map. You see, this is our hotel. It is located here on South Jiefang Road. And the Luxun's Former Residence is located here between Zhongxin Road and Jiefang Road. Just go out of the hotel, turn right, and then take a right turning at the second traffic lights. Walk fifty meters ahead, and then you will see it. You can not *miss* it.

21) The East Lake is a bit far from here. I suggest you take a taxi or a No.1 bus there. It is about 20 minutes by taxi. The bus stop is just on the *opposite* side of the street in front of the hotel.

Answering enquiries

22) Yes, of course. You are more than welcome to do so. What is it?

23) The business center is on the left of the lobby.

24) Sauna center is on the 3rd floor.

25) Well, if you want to try the typical Shaoxing dishes, there is no other place in the whole

16) 它们具有典型的中国特色。尤其是，您会被那里美妙的建筑艺术折服。

17) 它是中国最著名的湖泊之一，已有数百年的历史。

18) 而且，桥的构造是非常精美的。我想这是一个值得一去的好地方。

指引

19) 早上好，李女士。有什么事情可以为您效劳？

20) 可以，鲁迅故里离这儿不远。您可以步行过去。我可以在地图上指给您看。您瞧，这里是我们酒店，在解放南路上。这就是鲁迅故里，位于中兴路与解放路之间。走出酒店，往右拐，在第二个红绿灯处往右拐，往前走 50 米，您就会看到了。您不会错过的。

21) 东湖离这儿有点远。我建议你打的去或乘 1 路车去。打的需要 20 分钟。车站就在酒店门前马路的对面。

回答询问

22) 当然可以，非常欢迎。是什么事儿？

23) 商务中心在大堂左侧。

24) 桑拿中心在 3 楼。

25) 噢，如果您想尝一尝正宗的绍兴菜，保您满意的全城哪儿也

city that will please your appetite better than the Shaoxing Chinese Restaurant. It serves very good local dishes. You may try there.

26) It's located on Jiefang Road in the town center. It's quite a distance from here. I suggest that you take a taxi there. Twenty yuan is enough to cover it.

27) The nearest shopping center has top-quality Chinese handcrafts.

28) If you want to go shopping, you can go to the nearby shopping mall. There you can buy some Chinese *stuff* and souvenirs.

29) You can get the money changed at the cashier's counter.

30) It takes about 20 minutes by taxi to Shaoxing Railway Station. The charge is about 15 yuan. Please give this slip to the taxi driver and he'll take you there.

31) The business time is from 8:30 a.m. to 9:00 p.m.

32) Breakfast is in the Sunshine Western Restaurant on the first floor.

33) Our hotel is about 7 km from the bus / train station.

34) I am sorry that we have no such service available in our hotel.

Handling messages

35) Do you have an *appointment* with Mr. Johnson?

36) Do you know which room he is staying in then?

比不上绍兴菜馆。那里的地方菜特好，您不妨去那里试试。

26) 它在市中心的解放路上，离这儿有一段路程，建议您打的去，20 元足够了。

27) 最近的购物中心有上乘的中国手工艺品出售。

28) 如果您想购物，你可以去酒店附近的购物商场。那里您可以买到一些中国特色的东西和纪念品。

29) 您可以去收银处兑换钱。

30) 打的去绍兴火车站约 20 分钟 15 元。请把这纸条给司机，他会送您去的。

31) 营业时间从早上 8 点半到晚上 9 点。

32) 用早餐在一楼阳光餐厅。

33) 我们酒店距汽车站 / 火车站 7 千米。

34) 对不起，我们酒店不提供这样的服务。

处理留言

35) 您与约翰逊先生有预约吗？

36) 那么您知道他住哪个房间吗？

37) That's OK. Let me check with the computer and find it out for you.

38) Sorry to have kept you waiting. Mr. Johnson is in Room 1402. Let me call him in his room first. I am sorry, sir. Nobody answered. Would you like to leave a message for him?

39) Would you please leave your name and telephone number? I will inform the guest to call you back.

40) So you are David from ABC Company. And you'd like to *invite* Mr. Johnson to dinner at 8 on Saturday evening. You also would like him to call your office between 9 and 10 tomorrow. Is that all? OK. I will make sure that he gets the message.

41) Good evening, Mr. Johnson. Here is a message from a David for you.

42) Mr. Johnson, a *certain* Miss Lin is here to see you.

43) Miss Lin, Mr. Johnson wants you to wait for him in the coffee garden. He said he would come down and meet you in a *couple* of minutes.

44) I am sorry. There is no guest with that name.

45) Sorry, Mr. Li has already checked out this morning.

46) I am terribly sorry, Miss. But I can't tell you the guest's room number without his permission.

47) Excuse me; are you looking for Mr. Johnson? He has something urgent to deal with. He has left a message for you. Here you are.

37) 那好，让我查一下电脑，帮您找一找。

38) 对不起让您久等了。约翰逊先生在 1402 号房间。我先替您给他房间打个电话。对不起，先生。没人。您想给他留言吗?

39) 请您留下您的姓名和电话，我会通知客人给您回电的。

40)（确认留言）您是 ABC 公司的戴维。您想邀请约翰逊先生共进晚餐，时间是周六晚 8 点。您想让他明天 9 点到 10 点间给您办公室打电话。是这些吗? 好的，我保证他收到您的留言。

41) 晚上好，约翰逊先生，有一位叫戴维的先生给您留了言。

42) 约翰逊先生，这里有一位林小姐想要见您。

43) 林小姐，约翰逊先生让您在咖啡厅等他。他说他过几分钟就下来见您。

44) 对不起，这里没有叫这个名字的客人。

45) 对不起，李先生今早已经退房了。

46) 对不起，没有客人的同意，我们不能把房间号码告诉您。

47) 劳驾，您是找约翰逊先生吗? 他有点急事要处理。他给您留了言。在这儿。

Vocabulary

airmail /ˈeəmeɪl/ *n.* 航空邮寄

normally /ˈnɔːməli/ *adv.* 正常地；通常

parcel /ˈpɑːsl/ *n.* 包裹

over-weighted /ˌəʊvəˈweɪtɪd/ *adj.* 超重

change /tʃeɪndʒ/ *n.* 零钱

suggest /səˈdʒest/ *v.* 建议

attraction /əˈtrækʃn/ *n.* 向往的地方

architecture /ˈɑːkɪtektʃə(r)/ *n.* 建筑（学）

former /ˈfɔːmə(r)/ *adj.* 旧时的；以前的

miss /mɪs/ *v.* 错过

stuff /stʌf/ *n.* 东西

invite /ɪnˈvaɪt/ *v.* 邀请

couple /ˈkʌpl/ *n.* 三两个；几个

surface /ˈsɜːfɪs/ *n.* 表面；平面

abroad /əˈbrɔd/ *adv.* 在海外；到海外

weigh /weɪ/ *v.* 称重

prefer /prɪˈfɜː(r)/ *v.* 更喜欢

receipt /rɪˈsiːt/ *n.* 收据；收条

temple /ˈtempl/ *n.* 寺庙

impress /ɪmˈpres/ *v.* 使有印象

wonder /ˈwʌndə(r)/ *v.* 想知道

residence /ˈrezɪdəns/ *n.* 住宅；住处

opposite /ˈɒpəzɪt/ *adj.* 对面的

appointment /əˈpɔɪntmənt/ *n.* 约会

certain /ˈsɜːtn/ *adj.* 某一个（些）

Useful Expressions

be far from ... 离……远

no other ... 别无其他……

have an appointment with ... 与……有约

more than ... 不只是……；非常……

词汇、课文资源

词汇、课文自测

微课

课堂练习

8.1.5　Cashier

Exchanging foreign currency

1) Do you want to change some US dollars into RMB?

2) Can I have your passport, please? We need information as to your name, which country's

收银员

兑换外币

1) 您想把美元换成人民币？

2) 请出示您的护照。我们需要您的姓名、护照签发国和护照号码

passport you are holding, and your passport number for both accounting and foreign exchange control purposes.

3) All the rates of exchange are on the board there. According to today's exchange rate, every US dollar in cash is *equivalent* to 6.8 yuan. It is exactly the same as the bank gives.

4) We don't charge a service fee. It is a *courtesy* service that we provide for our guests.

5) How much would you like to change?

6) Would you please complete this form with your name, passport number, and room number?

7) What *denominations* would you like? We have 100 yuan *bills*, 50 yuan bills, 20 yuan bills, 10 yuan bills, and 5 yuan bills.

8) Here is your receipt. Please keep it. You need to show it at the *customs* when you want to *convert* the Chinese currency you couldn't spend into your own currency.

9) Please keep the exchange *memo*. You can change it back at the Bank of China or at the airport exchange office.

Settling bills

10) Would you like to *vacate* your room / check out now?

11) Just a moment, please. May I have your name, room number, and room card?

12) Here is your bill. That *totals* $665. Please check it and sign here.

13) This is an *itemized* bill. So it is easy to *spot* a mistake if there exists one.

等信息，这是出于记账的需要，也是为了外汇管制。

3) 所有的兑率信息都在那个牌子上。根据今日汇率，1 美元兑换 6.28 元。这和银行的汇率一样。

4) 我们不收服务费。这是我们为客人提供的一项免费服务。

5) 您要换多少钱？

6) 请您在这张表单上填上您的姓名、护照号码及房间号码，好吗？

7) 您想要什么面额的？我们有 100 元币、50 元币、20 元币、10 元币和 5 元币。

8) 这是收据，请保留。当您要在海关把没用完的人民币兑回成本币时须出示此收据。

9) 请留好兑换水单。您可以在中国银行或机场兑换处换回本币。

结账

10) 您现在要退房吗？

11) 请稍等。请告诉我您的名字和房号，并把房卡给我？

12) 这是您的账单，合计 655 美元。请您核对一下，并签名。

13) 这是明细账单，如有错账很容易发现。

14) One towel was *dyed*, so we have to charge you 10 yuan.

15) Did you take a cola from the mini-bar? That charge is for drinks taken from the mini-bar.

16) Your *overseas* telephone call is included in the bill. This sum is for the IDD call you made in your room.

17) Oh, I am sorry, sir. I forgot to explain that to you. This one here is an *allowance* slip. You see, we made a mistake in your bill and *overcharged* you $12. So we had to write an allowance slip and *deduct* $12 from your bill.

18) There might be something wrong with the bill. I do apologize for my mistake. Let me give you another receipt.

19) It is our mistake. We will deduct this charge. I am sorry to cause you so much trouble. I will be more careful next time.

20) Sorry, according to the rule of our hotel, without the receipt of deposit, we can not *refund* your balance, but if you really lost the receipt of deposit, we need you to provide a receipt to prove that you have got the balance back.

21) I'm sorry, but could you let me know why you didn't tell us but signed the bill at that time if you think it is wrong?

Receiving payment

22) How would you like to settle your bill, in cash or by credit card?

14) 您房间的毛巾被染色了，我们要向您收取 10 元。

15) 请问您用过房间迷你吧里的可乐吗？那笔钱是您从房间迷你吧里取用饮料的费用。

16) 您的国际长途电话费用包括在这个账单里。这一笔就是您房间里的国际长途电话费用。

17) 对不起，先生。我忘了跟您解释了。这一张是更正单。您看，我们在您的账单上出了错，多收了 12 美元。所以我们必须开一个更正单，把这 12 美元减掉。

18) 账单可能有误。我为失误向您道歉。我重新开一张收据。

19) 是我们的工作出现了失误，这项收费我们会为您取消。对不起给您带来这么多麻烦。下次我会更加仔细。

20) 对不起，按酒店规定，没有押金单我们不能退给您余款，但如果您真的把押金单丢了，我们需要您提供一份收条证明您本人已收到余款。

21) 冒昧问一下您，您认为账单不对，当时却没有提出疑问，还在账单上签名确认，是有什么苦衷吗？

收款

22) 您准备以何种方式付账，付现金还是刷卡？

23) What kind of credit card have you got?

24) Sorry, I am afraid it's not allowed. We don't accept this kind of credit card.

25) I can't decide; I have to ask the manager.

26) We accept VISA® card, MASTERCARD®, AMERICAN EXPRESS® card, JCB card, and DINERS CLUB® card.

27) Since the amount *exceeds* 5,000 yuan, we have to ask for the approval *code*.

28) Sorry we don't accept personal checks. But we can accept traveler's check.

29) Sign here please. Thank you, sir. Here is your copy of the *voucher*, this is your receipt, and this is your card.

30) May I *present* you a little souvenir?

23) 您用哪种信用卡?

24) 对不起,恐怕这是不允许的。我们不接受这种信用卡。

25) 我决定不了,我要请示一下经理。

26) 我们接受维萨卡、万事达卡、美国运通卡、日财卡和大来卡。

27) 超过 5000 元,我们必须向发卡行取得授权。

28) 抱歉,我们不接受私人支票。但我们可以接受旅行支票。

29) 请在这里签字。感谢您,先生。这一联是您的收款单,这是您的收据,这是您的卡。

30) 请接受我们的一点小礼物。

Vocabulary

equivalent /ɪˈkwɪvələnt/ *adj.* 等于的;等价的

courtesy /ˈkɜːtəsi/ *adj.* 好意的(行为);免费的

customs /ˈkʌstəmz/ *n.* 海关

memo /ˈmeməʊ/ *n.* 公务便单;备忘录

total /ˈtəʊtl/ *v.* 总计;共计

spot /spɒt/ *v.* 认出

overseas /ˌəʊvəˈsiːz/ *adj.* 海外的

overcharge /ˌəʊvəˈtʃɑːdʒ/ *v.* 多收费

refund /ˈriːfʌnd/ *v.* 退款

code /kəʊd/ *n.* 密码;代码

present /prɪˈzent/ *v.* 赠送

denomination /dɪˌnɒmɪˈneɪʃn/ *n.* 面额

bill /bɪl/ *n.* 钞票

convert /kənˈvɜːt/ *v.* 兑换

vacate /veɪˈkeɪt/ *v.* 空出;让出

itemize /ˈaɪtəmaɪz/ *v.* 分条开列

dye /daɪ/ *v.* 染色

allowance /əˈlaʊəns/ *n.* 体谅;谅解

deduct /dɪˈdʌkt/ *v.* 扣除

exceed /ɪkˈsiːd/ *v.* 超出;超过

voucher /ˈvaʊtʃə(r)/ *n.* 凭证

Useful Expression

be equivalent to 等于

词汇、课文资源

词汇、课文自测

微课

课堂练习

8.1.6 Business Secretary

1) Yes, sir. We have comprehensive communication facilities and secretarial assistance *catering* to the needs of all our business guests.

2) Please wait for about five minutes. I will serve you then.

3) Do you want to have the contract typed or copied?

4) How many copies of this contract would you like?

5) We will charge 5 yuan a page for typing, and 1 yuan a page for copying.

6) It will take about 10 minutes to do so.

7) Your copies are ready. You should pay 10.5 yuan in all.

8) Here is your change and your receipt; please keep it safe.

9) Do you need fax service? Where do you want to fax it to?

10) Can you show me your passport and give me the fax number?

11) Here is your fax record, sir. Would you please sign here?

商务中心秘书

1) 是的，先生。我们提供齐全的通信设施和秘书服务，足以满足商务客人的需求。

2) 请等5分钟，我就为您服务。

3) 这份合同，您想打印还是复印？

4) 您这份合同需要复印几份？

5) 我们打印收费每页5元，复印每页1元。

6) 大概需要10分钟吧。

7) 您要复印的东西好了。您一共需要付10元5角。

8) 这是您的零钱和发票，请收好。

9) 您需要传真服务吗？请问传到哪里？

10) 请出示一下您的护照，并告诉我传真号码。

11) 这是您的传真记录，请在这里签名好吗？

12) The fee is 15 yuan altogether. Do you want it charged to your room account?

13) OK, would you sign here please? It will be on your account.

14) Please don't worry. Just leave your room number, and we will send it up to your room as soon as your fax comes in.

15) Do you want to get it translated into English?

16) The translation fee is 0.3 yuan per word by target language.

17) You can use the Internet here. The charge for using the Internet is 20 yuan for one hour, and the least charge is for 30 minutes.

18) The business center takes all kinds of booking, but we will charge you a 5% service fee.

19) You can have your ticket before ten o'clock this evening.

8.1.7 Operator

1) The Sunflower Hotel. Good morning. Can I help you?

2) Whom would you like to speak to please?

3) I am sorry, sir. There is no guest with this name in Room 1818.

4) All right, sir. Would you like me to get you through to the Information? They can help you to check it out. Hold on please.

5) Hold on please. I will get the *receptionist* to speak to you.

6) One moment please. I will get you through to his room.

12) 费用总共 15 元，您想记在房账上吗？

13) 那好，请您在这儿签字。这将记在您的账上。

14) 别担心，请留下您的房号，一收到您的传真，我们就给您送上去。

15) 您想把它译成英文吗？

16) 翻译费用按目的语计算每词 3 角。

17) 您可以在这里上网。上网收费 20 元每小时，半小时起收。

18) 商务中心代办各种预订事宜，但我们要收取 5% 的服务费。

19) 今晚 10 点以前，您可以拿到票。

总机接线员

1) 向日葵酒店。早上好。您有什么事吗？

2) 请问您找哪位？

3) 对不起，先生。1818 房间没有叫这个名字的客人。

4) 这样吧，我帮您转接问讯处，请他们帮您查找。请不要挂机。

5) 请不要挂机，我帮您找接待员与您通话。

6) 请稍等，我帮您转接到他的房间。

7) The line is busy, would you wait for one moment or call back later?

8) I am sorry, he has already checked out.

9) Sorry, nobody answers. Would you like to leave a message?

10) May I have your name? How to spell please?

11) Sorry I didn't catch, I beg your pardon?

12) May I repeat your message?

13) I ensure that he gets your message as soon as he comes back.

14) Could you tell me your room number? We will ask somebody to see it.

15) I will ask a *repairman* to your room now.

16) I will let the assistant manager call back.

17) You can make an IDD call from your room, first, please dial 9, then 00, the country area, and the telephone number. For outside call, please dial 9 first, and then the number you want. For room to room call, you can direct dial the room number.

18) For further information, please contact the Reception 6605.

19) What number are you calling? Maybe you have dialed the wrong number.

20) Thank you for your advice! Sorry for the inconvenience caused. Please accept my apology.

21) At what time would you like us to call you tomorrow morning?

7) 电话占线，您是等一会呢还是待会儿再打过来？

8) 对不起，他已经退房了。

9) 对不起，电话无人接听，需要留言吗？

10) 请告诉我您的名字，好吗？怎么拼？

11) 对不起我没听清，请再讲一遍好吗？

12) 我可以重复一下您的留言吗？

13) 我保证他一回来我就把您的留言给他。

14) 请问您的房号是多少？我会让服务员过来看一下。

15) 我现在就让维修人员到您的房间。

16) 我会让大堂副理打电话过来。

17) 您可以从房间里拨打国际长途。先拨 9，然后拨 00，再拨国家代码及电话号码。外线电话，先拨 9，再拨你所需的号码。房间之间通话，可以直接拨房号。

18) 需要更多信息，请打电话到接待处 6605。

19) 您所拨的号码是什么？您可能拨错号码了。

20) 感谢您的忠告！非常抱歉给您带来不便。请接受我的道歉。

21) 您想让我们明天早上什么时候叫醒您？

22) OK, so we will wake you up at five o'clock tomorrow morning. Good night. Have a good sleep.

8.1.8 Salesperson

1) Yes, sir. The local newspapers rate our arcade as one of the best shops here.

2) We have a very efficient packing and shipping system.

3) You may use the credit card or pay RMB here.

4) I'd like to recommend an item like this to you. It is of typical Chinese style.

5) We have many local foods of high quality here. They are all popular with foreign guests.

6) Do you want it packed for posting?

7) The case is 20 yuan, and the *postage* is 20 yuan. You should pay 40 yuan in all.

8) What do you think of the one with a *heart-shaped precious* stone? I think this one looks better on you than that one. What's more, it is in the newest fashion this year.

9) You have made a good choice. It is the best quality product.

10) Sorry, madam. They are all first-class products. We hold a reasonable one-price policy. We are not allowed to change the price at *will*.

22) 好的。我们明天早上 5 点叫您。晚安。祝您睡个好觉！

销售员

1) 是的，先生。当地报纸将我们评为这里最好的商店之一。

2) 我们有非常高效的包装递送系统。

3) 您可以用信用卡或人民币支付。

4) 您买个这样的如何？这是经典的中国式样。

5) 我们有各式高品质土特产，很受外宾喜欢。

6) 您想把它包装起来邮寄吗？

7) 盒子 20 元，邮寄费 20 元。您总共应付 40 元。

8) 您看这件带心形宝石的怎么样？我认为这件戴在您身上比那件好看。而且，这是今年最流行的。

9) 您真有眼光，这是最好的品质。

10) 对不起，女士。这些都是一流的商品。我们坚持合理的一口价，不允许随意变更价格。

Vocabulary

cater /ˈkeɪtə(r)/ *v.* 满足

repairman /rɪˈpeəmæn/ *n.* 修理工

heart-shaped /ˈhɑːt ˈʃeɪpt/ *adj.* 心形的

will /wɪl/ *n.* 意志

receptionist /rɪˈsepʃənɪst/ *n.* 接待员

postage /ˈpəʊstɪdʒ/ *n.* 邮费

precious /ˈpreʃəs/ *adj.* 宝贵的

Useful Expressions

in all 总共

at will 随意地

rate ... as ... 评……为……

词汇、课文资源　　　　词汇、课文自测　　　　微课　　　　课堂练习

8.2　Housekeeping Staff

8.2.1　Floor Attendant

Guiding guests to their rooms

1) Good afternoon, sir! Welcome to the 6th floor. I am the attendant. May I help you?

2) What's your room number, please? Can I look at your room card?

3) I will show you. Follow me, please.

4) Here we are. This is your room. May I have your room key, please? I will open it for you.

5) Sorry, the *password* of the key has been

楼层服务员

引客进房

1) 先生，下午好。欢迎来到 6 楼。我是服务员。有什么需要服务吗？

2) 您的房号是多少？我看一下您的房卡。

3) 我带您去。请这边走 / 请跟我来。

4) 我们到了。这是您的房间，请您把房间钥匙给我。我帮您开门。

5) 对不起，这个钥匙的密码

invalid. I will go to the front desk to check it, please wait a moment.

6) We don't accept *tips* in our hotel. Thank you all the same.

Introducing the room facilities

7) Please place the key card here for *electricity*. The electricity works only when the key card is kept inserted.

8) This is the bathroom. You should turn the faucet to the left for hot water and to the right for cold water. Please feel free to use all the shampoo and conditioner. Every item with a price on it is used for a fee, and those with no price are complimentary.

9) This room is a non-smoking *queen-size* one. You can change the air temperature by adjusting the *thermostat*. Guests are not allowed to use iron or electric *heaters* in their rooms.

10) Complimentary amenities in the room include 2 bottles of water and ... The Internet use is free of charge. The items in the mini-bar are charged if used. Here is the price sheet for room extras. Any extra fee will be charged to your account.

11) This is the TV set. You can use 10 *channels* for free, and you should pay extra for programs on other channels.

12) The safe is in the *wardrobe*. Valuables should be deposited at the cashier's counter.

13) The laundry bag and the laundry list are in the wardrobe. If you need laundry service, please put your clothes in this bag and fill out the laundry list.

已经失效了，我到总台刷一下，请稍等。

6) 我们酒店里不收小费。谢谢您。

介绍房内设施

7) 请把房卡插在这里取电。只有将房卡插在里面才能取电。

8) 这是浴室。要热水，将龙头向左，要冷水，将龙头向右。洗发液和护发素，请自便使用。凡标有价格的物品都是有偿使用的。没有标价的物品是免费使用的。

9) 这个房间是大床间，房内不能抽烟。要调节气温，可以调节温控器。宾客不能在房间里使用熨斗或电热器。

10) 房间内的免费用品有两瓶水和……上网不需额外付费。使用迷你吧物品是要收费的。这是房间里额外收费用品价目单。任何额外付费都会记在您的账上。

11) 这是电视，可以免费收看10个频道，其他频道的节目是要额外付费的。

12) 保险箱在衣橱里，贵重物品请在收银处寄存。

13) 洗衣袋和洗衣单在衣柜内。如需干洗服务，请把衣服放在这个包里，并填写洗衣单。

14) If you want a morning call service, you may tell the operator your room number and your time.

15) If you want to have breakfast in your room tomorrow, this is the door-knob menu. Just check the items you would like for breakfast. Mark down the time, and hang it outside your door before you go to bed tonight. We have a very good room service.

16) Please use this door *hanger*, if you don't want to be disturbed.

17) Please use the door-knob cards or call us for more services. For other facilities, please look at the Hotel Service Guide in the *drawer* of the desk.

18) When you check out, please call number 6032 and we'll help you with your luggage immediately. I hope you will enjoy your stay.

8.2.2　Housemaid

Doing *chamber* service

1) Housekeeping. May I come in?

2) Good morning, sir. Did you call for service?

3) Good afternoon, sir. I am sorry to disturb you. May I clean the room now?

4) When would you like me to do your room, sir?

5) Would you like me to make your bed now?

6) If you need to have your room cleaned, put the "To be cleaned" card on the door.

14) 如果您想要叫早服务，可以把您的房号和时间告知总机。

15) 如果您明天想在房间里用早餐，这是门餐牌，请在上面标出您需要的早餐，并注明时间，睡觉前将其挂在门外，我们会提供优良的送餐服务。

16) 如果不想被打扰，请用这个门吊钩。

17) 如需更多服务，请用门把上的卡片或给我们打电话。有关其他服务设施，请参阅书桌抽屉内的服务指南。

18) 如果您要退房，请打电话6032，我们会马上帮您运送行李的。希望您在这里住得愉快。

客房服务员

做客房服务

1) 客房部的，可以进来吗？

2) 早上好，先生，是您需要服务吗？

3) 下午好，先生。对不起打扰了。我现在可以打扫房间吗？

4) 您要我什么时候给您整理房间，先生？

5) 您需要我现在就给您整理床铺吗？

6) 如果需要清洁服务，请把"清洁"牌挂在门上。

Adding room amenities

7) I am sorry that your *flask* is empty. I will go and get you another flask that is full at once. I will be right back.

8) I am not really sure, sir. But I will try and see if I can get you a pair of larger ones.

9) I will fetch you some more right away. Is four enough?

10) I am sorry I didn't notice they were too *damp*, sir. I will bring you some dry ones immediately.

Offering on-call service

11) Anything the matter, sir?

12) Let me adjust the air conditioner for you. It is a bit hot in the room.

13) Yes, sir. The hotel provides free shoe shining service for guests. All that you have to do is place your shoes to be shined outside your door before you go to bed and the night porter will collect them. The shoes will be shined and returned to your doorstep early the next morning.

14) I am sorry, sir. The hotel does not have a shoe shining machine. But we do provide *compact* shoe *shiners* for our guests. They are in the drawer of the night *stand*.

15) I am sorry, madam. The television isn't working. I will send for a repairman right away.

16) I see. I will report to the Maintenance. We apologize for the inconvenience. Anything else, sir?

添加客房用品

7) 很抱歉，您的水壶空了。我马上给您拿一壶满的来。我马上就回来。

8) 我说不准，先生，不过我会想办法，看能不能给您弄双大点儿的来。

9) 我马上就给您拿来。四个够吗？

10) 对不起，先生，我原先没有注意到它们太湿了。我马上给您拿几条干的来。

提供随叫服务

11) 有问题吗，先生？

12) 我帮您调一下空调。房间里有点热。

13) 是的，先生。我们酒店为住在这里的宾客提供免费擦鞋服务。您只要在上床睡觉之前把要擦的鞋放在门外就行。夜班行李员会把您的鞋收走，次日一早将擦好的鞋送回来放在您的门口。

14) 对不起，先生。我们酒店没有擦鞋机，但是我们为宾客准备了盒式皮鞋刷，就放在床头柜的抽屉里。

15) 对不起，女士。电视机坏了，我马上给您叫修理工。

16) 我知道了，我会报告维修部。给您带来不便，我们表示抱歉。别的有什么事吗，先生？

17) I am very sorry to hear that, but we will try our best to look for it for you. I will report it to my supervisor immediately; we'll let you know as soon as we find it.

18) Of course. Which brand would you prefer and how many packs? But I am afraid *cigarettes* must be paid in cash. The sum of money can't be charged to your account.

19) That's no trouble at all. I will fetch you some *postcards* as soon as possible.

20) Good evening, sir. Here is the *telegram* for you. It has just arrived. Oh, still here is your air ticket and your fax.

21) What kind of tea do you prefer? We have green tea, black tea, and *jasmine* tea. And how many cups do you want?

22) OK, three cups of green tea, and one cup of black tea, right? Please wait a moment.

Handling laundry

23) Have you got any laundry? Anything else?

24) The suit and shirt are to be dry-cleaned?

25) Have you filled out the laundry list? Would you like express service or normal service?

26) They will be ready tomorrow morning by normal service. Usually, it takes one day to have laundry done.

27) We will do our best to remove the *stain* but we can not guarantee the result.

28) Is it urgent? We have quick service; it only takes 4 hours. There is an extra charge of 50% for

17) 很遗憾听到这件事（失窃），我们会尽全力替您寻找。我马上报告我的上司，一有消息就通知您。

18) 当然。您想要什么牌子，几包？不过，香烟得付现金，不能记在账上。

19) 不客气，我尽快给您拿些明信片来。

20) 晚上好，先生。这是您的电报，刚到的。哦，还有，这里有您的机票和传真。

21) 您想要什么茶？我们有绿茶、红茶和茉莉花茶。您要几杯？

22) 好的。3 杯绿茶，1 杯红茶，对吗？请稍等。

收送衣物

23) 请问您要洗衣服务吗？还有其他要洗的吗？

24) 这件西服和衬衫是要干洗的吗？

25) 您填过洗衣单了吗？您要快洗还是普洗？

26) 普洗的话，这些衣服明天早上可以送回。通常情况下，需要一天才能洗好。

27) 我们会尽力去污，但不能保证效果。

28) 很急吗？我们还有快洗服务，只需 4 小时。加快服务需要加

quick service.

    29) Your laundry is back, sir.

收 50% 的额外费用。

    29) 先生，您送洗的衣服好了。

Vocabulary

password /ˈpɑːswɜːd/ *n.* 密码；口令

electricity /ɪˌlekˈtrɪsəti/ *n.* 电

thermostat /ˈθɜːməstæt/ *n.* 自动恒温器

channel /ˈtʃænl/ *n.* 频道

hanger /ˈhæŋə(r)/ *n.* 挂钩

chamber /ˈtʃeɪmbə(r)/ *n.* 房间

damp /dæmp/ *adj.* 潮湿的

shiner /ˈʃaɪnə(r)/ *n.* 擦拭工具

cigarette /ˌsɪɡəˈret/ *n.* 香烟

telegram /ˈtelɪɡræm/ *n.* 电报

stain /steɪn/ *n.* 污渍

tip /tɪp/ *n.* 小费

queen-size /ˈkwiːn saɪz/ *adj.* 大号的

heater /ˈhiːtə(r)/ *n.* 加热器

wardrobe /ˈwɔːdrəʊb/ *n.* 衣橱

drawer /drɔː(r)/ *n.* 抽屉

flask /flɑːsk/ *n.* 水壶

compact /kəmˈpækt/ *n.* 盒（式）

stand /stænd/ *n.* 架

postcard /ˈpəʊstkɑːd/ *n.* 明信片

jasmine /ˈdʒæzmɪn/ *n.* 茉莉

Useful Expressions

call for 需要

send for ... 派（人）请……

词汇、课文资源

词汇、课文自测

微课

课堂练习

8.3　Restaurant Staff

Taking reservations

    1) Rose Restaurant. Good morning. Can I help you?

订餐

    1) 早安，这里是玫瑰餐厅。能为您效劳吗？

2) May I have your name, sir, please?

3) I advise you to make a reservation as the restaurant is often full.

4) You'd like to book a table for four for Friday evening. Right? ... Certainly, sir, what time do you like your table?

5) For what time and how many persons?

6) What kind of table would you prefer, by the window or near the *corner*?

7) I'm sorry, but the tables by the window are all occupied.

8) We have received many *bookings* and I cannot guarantee a table by the window.

9) I can't guarantee anything, but I will try my best.

10) How about a table in the corner of the restaurant? It is a bit quiet.

11) And what is it going to be, Chinese food or Western food?

12) So, Mr. Johnson, a table for four for Friday evening, Western food at 7:00 p.m.

13) Two tables by the window for 16 persons at 8:00 p.m. on Mr. Johnson. Right?

14) Our service hours are 6:00 a.m. to 10:00 a.m. for breakfast, 11:30 a.m. to 2:00 p.m. for lunch, and 5:30 p.m. to 9:30 p.m. for dinner.

15) We are open until 12:00 p.m., but the last order for dinner is at 11:00 p.m.

16) Thank you for calling. We are looking

2）先生，您贵姓？

3）由于餐厅常常客满，您最好预订。

4）您想订一个星期五晚上的四人桌，是吗？……当然可以，先生。您想要什么时间？

5）什么时间？有几位？

6）您对座位有什么要求，靠窗的还是角落里的？

7）对不起，靠窗的座位全都有人了。

8）我们已接到许多预订，因而无法向您保证能有一个靠窗的座位。

9）我不能保证，但会尽力而为。

10）餐厅角落里的座位可以吗？那里有点安静。

11）您想吃中餐还是西餐？

12）（确认）约翰逊先生，星期五晚7点西餐四人桌一张。

13）（确认）今晚8点，约翰逊先生预订两张靠窗餐桌16位，对吗？

14）餐厅营业时间：早餐6点到10点，中餐11点30分到下午2点，晚餐下午5点30分到晚上9点30分。

15）我们营业到晚上12点，但最后点餐截至晚上11点。

16）感谢您打来电话，我们期

forward to your visit.

17) I'm sorry we have had all the tables booked out for this evening.

Seating guests

18) Good evening, ladies and gentlemen. Welcome to our restaurant.

19) I am the waitress here. I am always at your service.

20) May I have your name?

21) Have you got a reservation? How many people in your party, please?

22) Just a moment. I'll take a look at out reservation book. Yes, Mr. Dewey, a table for two, eight o'clock. Would you come this way, please?

23) Here is your table. Please take your seats. Your waiter will be right with you.

24) Sorry, sir. All the tables are taken. Would you mind waiting over there? We will have you seated as soon as we have one free.

25) I'd say (you will have to wait) at least 20 minutes, sir.

26) I'm sorry to have kept you waiting, sir and madam. Now we have a table for you. I will show you the way. Would you step this way, please?

27) Will this table be all right?

Taking orders

28) Good evening. Do you care for anything to drink before you order, gentleman?

29) What would you like to have, coffee or tea?

30) Would you like to start with a glass of beer?

31) Do you want an aperitif or order straight

待您的光临。

17) 抱歉，今晚的订满了。

引座

18) 晚上好，女士们、先生们，欢迎光临！

19) 我是这里的服务员。很高兴为您服务。

20) 请问您叫什么名字？

21) 您预订座位了吗？请问您几位？

22) 请稍候，我查一下我们的预订簿。对了，德威先生，二人桌，8 点到。请这边走。

23) 这是您的座位，请坐。服务员马上就来。

24) 对不起，先生，没有空位了，能请您坐在那边等一会儿吗？一有空位我们就为您安排。

25) 先生，恐怕（您得等上）至少 20 分钟。

26) 先生、女士，对不起，让二位久等了。现在有空位了，我带二位过去。请这边来。

27) 坐这张桌子好吗？

点菜

28) 先生，晚上好。点菜前要不要来点什么饮料？

29) 您要点咖啡还是茶？

30) 要不要先来一杯啤酒？

31) 来点餐前酒水还是直接

away?

32) Dinner or à la carte?

33) Are you ready to order, gentleman? Here is our menu.

34) Can I take your order now?

35) What would you like for your appetizer?

36) And what would you like to follow?

37) What kind of food would you like to have? We have Cantonese food, Hangzhou food, and Shaoxing food.

38) If you are interested in Chinese cuisine, could I recommend something to you? Today we have chicken noodle, tomato, and *clam chowder*. The *crisp* fish is wonderful tonight. The fish is very fresh. We also have some good seafood dishes. Would you like to try some?

39) Certainly. The T-bone *steak* is very good. I suggest you try that.

40) How do you like your steak cooked, *rare*, *medium*, or *well done*?

41) You don't know the course. I can explain it to you. It is *lamb* cooked with *herbs* and served with spaghetti.

42) I am sorry to tell you that the dish you have ordered has been sold out today. Would you like to order another one?

43) And what would your *vegetable* be?

44) What can I get you for dessert?

45) And would you like dessert or cheese?

46) You want it now or after dinner?

47) Do you want any drink first? How about

点菜？

32) 是套菜还是点菜？

33) 可以点菜了吗，先生？这是我们的菜单。

34) 先生，点好了吗？

35) 您要点什么样的开胃菜（头盘）？

36) 下一道您点什么呢？

37) 您想吃什么菜？我们供应粤菜、杭帮菜和绍兴菜。

38) 如果您对中国烹饪感兴趣，我给您推荐几种菜，好吗？今天有鸡肉面、番茄、文蛤杂烩汤。今晚的脆皮鱼不错，鱼也很新鲜。我们还有一些上好的海鲜，想来一点吗？

39) 当然，带骨牛排不错。我建议您点这个。

40) 您的牛排是要一分熟，五分熟，还是全熟？

41) 您不了解这道菜，我跟您解释一下。这是香草烹羊肉，配意式面条。

42) 对不起，您点的菜今天售完了，您可以换点别的吗？

43) 那么您点什么蔬菜呢？

44) 甜点给您上什么呢？

45) 您想要甜点还是奶酪？

46) 现在送来还是饭后送来？

47) 要不要先来点饮料？来点

some coffee or tea then? Would you like me to recommend?

咖啡或茶怎么样？需要我推荐吗？

48) Would you like bottled or canned, with ice or no ice?

48) 您要瓶装的还是罐装的？要不要加冰？

49) Lastly, what would you like for the main course? We have rice, *dumpling*, mini-bread, noodle, and so on.

49) 最后，您点什么主食？我们有米饭、饺子、刀切馒头、面条等等。

50) May I repeat your order?

50) 我可以复述一下您点的菜吗？

51) The dish will be ready in twenty minutes.

51) 您的菜要等 20 分钟。

Taking wine order

推销酒水

52) Good evening, gentlemen. Would you like to have some wine with your dinner?

52) 先生们，晚上好。你们要佐餐酒吗？

53) Your wine list, please. We have a good selection of Bordeaux wines and Californian wine.

53) 这是酒水单。我们有多种波尔多酒和加利福尼亚酒。

54) What about a bottle of Chateau Haut Lafitte? Many guests give high comments on it.

54) 来一瓶夏多奥拉菲特怎么样？许多宾客对它的评价很高。

55) When would you like your wine to be served, with the main dish or with the first course?

55) 您希望什么时候用酒，随主菜还是随头道菜。

56) OK. I will bring them to you right away.

56) 好了。我马上给您送来。

Serving dishes

餐间服务

57) Your fried *prawns* with pepper salt, sir.

57) 您的椒盐炸明虾，先生。

58) Is there anything the matter, sir?

58) 有什么不对吗，先生？

59) I am sorry you didn't enjoy it, sir. I'll return it to the kitchen and bring you one that's well cooked.

59) 先生，很抱歉您没吃好。我把它送回厨房，给您拿一盘烧熟的。

60) How is your steak this time, sir? ... I am glad you enjoy it.

60) 先生，这次牛排如何？……我很高兴您能喜欢。

61) Excuse me; may I take your plate away?

61) 打扰了，我可以撤掉这个盘子吗？

62) You should eat the food while hot.

62) 这道菜最好趁热吃。

63) Take care; the soup is very hot.

63) 小心，汤很烫。

64) I am very glad to tell you how to use *chopsticks*. You see. Please hold them like this. Please *separate* the chopsticks. *Rest* them between the *thumb* and the *forefinger*. Place the thumb on the right chopstick about a third of the way down. Rest the left chopstick on the little finger and the ring finger. Use the chopsticks by the middle finger and the forefinger. Only the chopsticks on the right should move. The chopstick *rest* is used to prevent the tips of chopsticks from being *polluted*.

65) Is the food to your *liking*? Can I tell you how the food is prepared?

66) Here are the dishes you ordered. Enjoy your supper. Just let me know if there is anything else I can do for you.

67) Since you are group guests, we've arranged a set menu for you. If you want to have extra food, you should also pay extra for it.

68) Do you want to pack them?

69) Can we come to clear up the tableware?

70) Are you satisfied with our service?

71) In our hotel, we don't accept tips. It is our *pleasure* to serve our guests well. Thank you all the same.

Taking the bill

72) Yes, sir, here is your bill. Please check it.

73) The charge is for one Gordon Dry, sir.

64) 我很高兴教您使用筷子。您看着。这样拿住筷子。先把筷子分开，把它们夹在拇指和食指中间，把拇指放在右边的筷子从下往上三分之一处。把左边的筷子放在小指与无名指上，用中指和食指使用筷子。注意只有右边的筷子移动。筷托是用来防止筷头弄脏的。

65) 这道菜合您的口味吗？我可以告诉您这道菜的烹饪方法。

66) 您点的菜齐了。请慢用。有什么别的需要，请及时告知。

67) 你们是团客，所以我们给你们安排了套餐，如要加菜，要额外付钱。

68) 您想打包吗？

69) 我们可以收拾餐具吗？

70) 您对我们的服务还满意吗？

71) 在我们酒店不收小费。服务好客人是我们的荣幸。还是谢谢您了。

结账

72) 是的，先生，这是您的账单。请核对。

73) 这笔是哥顿杜松子酒的费用，先生。

74) Sorry, sir. Just a minute. I will check it for you.

75) Terribly sorry, sir. There is a mistake on the bill. I have corrected it.

76) We will give you a 10% discount after 8:00 p.m. It's 850 yuan in total. Do you want to pay in cash or would you like to sign?

77) OK. Take your 900 yuan. Here is your change.

78) As you live in our hotel, you can sign your bill. Can I have a look at your room card? What's your room number, please?

79) Please fill in your room number and sign here.

80) Yes, it's fine. Thank you for your coming.

Serving in the bar

81) How many people altogether please?

82) Excuse me, sir. How would you like us to arrange the seats?

83) Excuse me; what can I get for you?

84) How would you like it, with or without ice (on the rocks or straight up)?

85) Please have a seat while we prepare.

86) The bar opens 24 hours a day. We have live music, floor performance, and some other *specials*, like Happy Hour from 10 to 12 at night.

Offering room service

87) Room Service. Good afternoon. Can I help you?

74) 对不起，先生。请稍等，我去核对一下。

75) 非常抱歉，先生。账单有误，我已改正了。

76) 晚上 8 点以后，您可以享受九折优惠。总共 850 元。请问您是要付现金还是要签单？

77) 好的。收您 900 元。这是找您的零钱。

78) 既然您住在我们酒店，您可以签单。我能看看您的房卡吗？请问您的房号是多少？

79) 请在这里填上房号并签字。

80) 可以了。谢谢您的光临。

酒吧服务

81) 一共几位？

82) 劳驾，先生，您想要我们怎么安排座位？

83) 劳驾，要我给您拿点什么吗？

84) 您想要加冰还是不加冰的？

85) 请坐一会儿，我们为您准备。

86) 酒吧 24 小时营业。我们提供现场音乐、现场表演和其他一些特别节目，如我们夜里 10 点至 12 点有欢乐时光（酒吧的减价时段）。

客房送餐

87) 这里是送餐部。下午好，您有什么事？

88) Yes, sir, no problem. So it is two *sandwiches* and a large *pot* of coffee. Is that all?

89) OK. No sugar, no cream, *straight* coffee, and very black. I will bring them to you right away. See you.

90) Room Service. May I come in?

91) Mr. Johnson? Here are your sandwiches and your coffee. The sandwiches are 8 yuan each and the coffee is 60 yuan. That comes to 76 yuan, plus 15% service. So the total is 87.4 yuan. And here is your bill.

92) If you want to have it charged to your account, please sign here.

93) Thank you for using room service. Goodbye.

88) 好的，先生，没问题。是两份三明治和一大壶咖啡，就这些吗？

89) 好，不放糖，不要奶油，清咖啡且很浓。我马上给您送到，再见。

90) 我是送餐的，可以进来吗？

91) 约翰逊先生吗？这是您要的三明治和咖啡。三明治每只 8 元，咖啡 60 元，加起来 76 元，加 15% 的服务费，总共 87 元 4 角。这是账单。

92) 如果您想把这笔消费记在账上，请在这里签字。

93) 感谢您使用送餐服务。再见。

Vocabulary

corner /ˈkɔːnə(r)/ *n.* 角落

clam /klæm/ *n.* 蛤肉

crisp /krɪsp/ *adj.* 脆的

rare /reə(r)/ *adj.* 煎得嫩的

well-done /ˌwel ˈdʌn/ *adj.* 烧熟的

herb /hɜːb/ *n.* 药草；香草

dumpling /ˈdʌmplɪŋ/ *n.* 饺子

chopstick /ˈtʃɒpstɪk/ *n.* 筷子

rest /rest/ *v.* 使放置在

forefinger /ˈfɔːfɪŋgə(r)/ *n.* 食指

booking /ˈbʊkɪŋ/ *n.* 预订

chowder /ˈtʃaʊdə(r)/ *n.* 杂烩

steak /steɪk/ *n.* 牛排

medium /ˈmiːdiəm/ *adj.* 中等熟度的

lamb /læm/ *n.* 羔羊肉

vegetable /ˈvedʒtəbl/ *n.* 蔬菜

prawn /prɔːn/ *n.* 明虾

separate /ˈseprət/ *v.* 把……分开

thumb /θʌm/ *n.* 拇指

rest /rest/ *n.* 台；架

pollute /pəˈluːt/ *v.* 污染；弄脏

pleasure /ˈpleʒə(r)/ *n.* 荣幸；高兴

sandwich /ˈsænwɪdʒ/ *n.* 三明治

straight /streɪt/ *adj.* 纯的

liking /ˈlaɪkɪŋ/ *n.* 喜欢；爱好

special /ˈspeʃl/ *n.* 特别（的东西）

pot /pɒt/ *n.* 壶

Useful Expressions

advise sb. to do sth. 建议某人做某事

start with ... 以……开始

give comment on ... 评论……

on the rocks（饮料）加冰的

care for ... 喜欢……

recommend sth. to sb. 向某人推荐某物

in total 总共

straight up（饮料）不加冰的

词汇、课文资源

词汇、课文自测

微课

课堂练习

8.4 Management

General Manager hosting guests	**总经理招待客人**
1) How do you do? Welcome to our hotel. May I say a few words to our distinguished guests?	1) 您好，欢迎光临本店。我想跟我们尊贵的客人说几句话。
2) On behalf of the management and staff of the hotel, I would like to *extend* the warmest welcome to you.	2) 我代表酒店管理层和全体员工，向你们表示最热烈的欢迎。
3) We hope that all our guests will make our hotel their "homes away from home" and feel comfortable and happy here.	3) 我们希望所有宾客都能把本店当成是"家外之家"，并在这里过得舒适、愉快。
4) For your information, we have many facilities catering to the needs of our guests.	4) 我很高兴地告诉你们，我们设施齐全，可以满足宾客的需要。
5) Any suggestion for improving our service is welcome.	5) 我们欢迎任何改进我们服务的意见和建议。

6) Here is a souvenir for every one of you. Allow me to present it to you as a *token* of our hotel's welcome. I hope you will enjoy your stay with us.

PR Manager making farewell speech

7) How I wish you could stay here a little longer!

8) On behalf of our General Manager, I wish to take this opportunity to express our *heartfelt* thanks and bid farewell to all of you. We appreciate your *cooperation* and understanding. I hope you like our hotel and our service.

9) We look forward to serving you again. Be sure to leave nothing behind but your smile and friendship.

Housekeeper giving birthday congratulations

10) Happy birthday to you Mrs. Smith. We knew it from your registration form. Today is your birthday. The birthday cake and the flowers are sent by our general manager. Here is his congratulation card. We all wish you will expect to have many happy *returns* of the day.

Sales Manager negotiating on price

11) We feel *honored* that you will favor us with your bookings. Here is a copy of our tariff. We have different rates for different periods of the year.

12) The room rate for a double room during the peak season is $100. For old customers like you, the prices are always *negotiable*, and we offer 10% commission to travel agencies.

13) We will send you a copy of *agreement*. If

6) 每位都有一份纪念品。请允许我将此赠送给你们以表示我们的欢迎。祝愿各位在本店住得愉快。

公关经理致离别辞

7) 衷心地希望你们能再待一段时间！

8) 我利用这个机会代表总经理向你们表示衷心的感谢和惜别。感谢你们的合作与理解。希望你们喜欢我们的酒店及我们的服务。

9) 我们希望你们再次光临。愿你们笑口常开，愿我们友谊常在。

客房部经理祝贺客人生日

10) 史密斯女士，生日快乐！我们从您的登记卡得知，今天是您的生日。我们的总经理让我送来生日蛋糕和鲜花，这是他的贺卡。我们祝您年年有今日，岁岁有今朝。

销售经理议价

11) 您在我们酒店预订房间，我们倍感荣幸。这是我们的价目表。我们的房价在一年中不同的时候是不一样的。

12) 旺季时，双人间是100美元。对于像您这样的老顾客，价格总是可以协商的。我们给旅行社的佣金是10%。

13) 我们将发一份协议给您。

you agree to the terms, please sign and return a fax copy to us.

14) We look forward to hosting your guests and hope to cooperate with you for a long time to come.

Managers handling complaints

15) I am very sorry, sir. But it is the hotel policy. May I arrange a room for you in a nearby hotel? Or would you mind settling in another hotel first and check with us tomorrow? There may be a *cancellation*.

16) I am terribly sorry, sir. Our *housemaids* have to make up those rooms first. Because the previous occupant has extended his checkout time, our housemaid is still making up the room. But we *insist* on providing clean and tidy rooms for our guests. It will be ready in a few minutes. We will inform you immediately when the room is ready.

17) I am sorry, sir. But because you check out at six o'clock, there is an extra half day charge. We have tried to contact you, sir. But you were not in your room.

18) I am terribly sorry for the mistake. We will pay for the damage. Could you buy a new one and give us the receipt? We will refund it.

19) I do apologize for it. I'll check with the maintenance department. I assure you that they will come within minutes. I can also assure you such things won't happen again. We'll take necessary *precautions*.

20) Well, I understand how you feel and we'll

如果您同意其条款，请签字并传真一份给我们。

14) 我们期待着接待您的客人，并希望长期合作。

经理处理投诉

15) 很抱歉，先生，但这是酒店的规定。让我替您在附近的酒店安排一个房间吧。或者，您先在其他酒店住下，然后明天再来看看好吗？或许会有宾客取消订房的。

16) 非常抱歉，先生。我们的服务员必须先整理已退的房间。因为上一位宾客延迟退房，所以我们的服务员还在整理房间。我们坚持提供整齐清洁的房间给宾客。数分钟后便会办妥。房间准备好后，我们会第一时间通知您。

17) 对不起，先生。由于您在下午6点才退房，所以我们要多收半天房租。我们试过联络您，但您不在房内。

18) 我对这个失误感到非常抱歉，酒店愿意赔偿一切损失。请您买一件新的，然后把收据给我们，以方便退还费用。

19) 我真诚地为此道歉，我会跟维修部核查，我向您保证他们会马上来的。我也可以向您保证，此类事件不会再发生了。我们会采取必要的预防措施。

20) 我理解您的心情。我们会

try to do our best to help you. But first please allow me to send a housemaid to your room and look for it again thoroughly just in case it is still there. If she finds it, we'll all be happy. If she doesn't, we'll turn the whole matter to the police. But I must say that the hotel can't hold responsibility for your loss. You should have locked your gold necklace away at the hotel's safety box. If you had read your key card carefully, you would realize that we specially warned you to do so. Our general manager is not in town. But I would be more than glad to get our deputy general manager for you if you like. But I am afraid that he will say the same thing. We have very clear instructions about valuables and we must follow them.

21) Please accept our apology. Do you wish to try something else, sir? It would be on the house, of course. Or I will return it to the kitchen right away and send you a hot one.

22) I deeply apologize, madam. Would you care to send this dress for dry cleaning? No charge, of course.

23) I am very sorry, sir. I am sure the waitress didn't mean to be rude. You see, she just started out as a waitress a week ago and doesn't understand English very well. She should have changed your steak.

尽最大努力帮助您。但是首先请允许我派一名客房服务员到您的房间里再彻底找一找，项链说不定还在房间里。如果找到了那就皆大欢喜。如果找不到，我们就把此事交给警方处理。但是我必须申明，我们酒店对项链的遗失不负有责任。您本应该把项链存在酒店的保险柜里。您要是好好地阅读了您的出入证须知的话，您就会知道我们特地告诫过您要这样做。我们总经理现在不在本市。但是如果您愿意的话，我很乐意去把我们的副总经理找来。但是恐怕他也会这么说的。我们对贵重物品有严格的规定，我们必须按规定办事。

21) 请接受我的道歉。您愿意尝试其他菜吗，先生？当然是免费的。或者，我立刻把早餐拿回厨房，再给您送上一份热的。

22) 我们深感抱歉，女士。您可以把这条裙子拿去干洗，一切费用由我们承担。

23) 非常抱歉，先生。我敢肯定那位服务员不是故意对您无礼。是这样的，她一星期前才开始做服务员工作，英语又不太好。她本该给您换一份牛排才是。

Vocabulary

extend /ɪkˈstend/ *v.* 提供；给予

heartfelt /ˈhɑːtfelt/ *adj.* 衷心的

return /rɪˈtɜːn/ *n.* 报答；回报

negotiable /nɪˈɡəʊʃiəbl/ *adj.* 可协商的

cancellation /ˌkænsəˈleɪʃn/ *n.* 取消

insist /ɪnˈsɪst/ *v.* 坚持

token /ˈtəʊkən/ *n.* 象征；标志

cooperation /kəʊˌɒpəˈreɪʃn/ *n.* 合作

honored /ˈɒnəd/ *adj.* 深感荣幸的

agreement /əˈɡriːmənt/ *n.* 协议

housemaid /ˈhaʊsmeɪd/ *n.* 女服务员

precaution /prɪˈkɔːʃn/ *n.* 预防措施

Useful Expressions

warn sb. to do sth. 警告某人做某事

would care to do sth. 想做某事

on the house 免费

词汇、课文资源

词汇、课文自测

微课

课堂练习

Chapter Nine

Hotel Application Forms
酒店应用表单

思政园地／二十
大精神学习专栏

Learning Objectives

· To get familiar with the application forms used for the staff to save labor in papaerwork;

· To understand the content, layout, and outfilling of each form;

· To master the new words and professional terms concerned;

· To improve reading ability through learning the text;

· To develop team spirit and self-study ability through learning activities;

· To receive education in ideological and political theories through course learning.

Teaching Arrangements

节次	教学内容	自主学习资源	自主学习自测	课堂教学视频	课堂练习
L 1	Hotel Application Forms	词汇、课文资源	词汇、课文自测	微课	课堂练习

The hotel application form, *namely*, refers to the *well-designed* and neatly-printed form used by the hotel staff and guests. The application of forms makes it easy and convenient for the staff to do their paperwork, thus saving them a lot of *labor*. In addition, forms can be *filed* as *data* for later use. In hotels, there are many varieties of application forms being often and frequently used. So it is also a must for the to-be staff to *grasp* the making and filling of forms. The forms selected in this chapter are the most commonly used in hotels.

酒店应用表单，顾名思义，是指由酒店客人和员工所使用的表格，它们设计精美、印刷整齐。表格的应用方便了员工的文字工作，节省了她们很多的劳力。此外，表格还可以作为资料存档备用。在酒店里经常使用各种各样的表格，所以未来的酒店员工应当掌握表格的缮制和填写。本章精选的表单则是酒店中最为常见的。

No. 1

RESERVATION APPLICATION
客房预订单

☐ New Booking 新预订

☐ *Amendment* 修改

☐ Cancellation 取消

Arrival Date 到店日期	Departure Date 离店日期	Confirmation Number 确认号		
Date Month Year 日 月 年	Date Month Year 日 月 年			
Guest Name 宾客姓名		Persons 人数	Arriving from 来自	
		Transportation Required 交通要求		
		☐ Yes 是	☐ No 否	
Surname First Name *Title* 姓 名 头衔		☐ Flight 飞机 ☐ Train 火车 ☐ Ship 轮船		
Type of Accommodation Required 房型要求		Rate 房价 ☐ *Commercial* Discount 商业折扣 ☐ Courtesy Discount 优惠折扣 ☐ Travel Agent Discount 旅行社折扣 ☐ Airline Discount 航空公司折扣		
Name of Applicant 申请人姓名	Phone No. 电话号码	*Remarks* 备注		
Firm/Business Address 公司地址				
Date of Application 申请日期 Date Month Year 日 月 年	Received by 预订员	Payment Instructions 付款指示		
		☐ Room 房费	☐ R/Transfer 接送	☐ Agent A/C 旅行社账户
		☐ A/B Fast 美式早餐	☐ Arr/Transfer 来店接送	☐ Airline A/C 航空公司账户
		☐ C/B Fast 欧陆式早餐	☐ Dept/Transfer 离店接送	☐ Company A/C 公司账户
		☐ Lunch 午餐	☐ All Expenses 所有费用	☐ Guest A/C 客户账户
		☐ Dinner 晚餐	☐ Clt Voucher 收代金券	

酒店服务英语 ｜ 第二部分

No. 2

RESERVATION CONFIRMATION
订房确认书

To 致：_____ From 由：Rsv Dept.of ××× Hotel

　　　　　　　　　　　　　　　　　　　××× 酒店预订部

Fax No. 传真：_____ Fax No. 传真：0086-575-88888888 ext.（转）330

Date 日期：_____ Rsv No. 预订单号：_____

Dear 尊敬的 _____，

　　Thank you for your interest in ××× Hotel. We are pleased to confirm your reservation details as follows:

　　感谢您对 ××× 大酒店的青睐，我们特对您的预订做如下确认：

Guest Name 客人姓名：_____

Check In 到店日期：_____ Check Out 离店日期：_____

Room Type 房间种类：_____ Room Amount 房间数量：_____

Room Rate 房间价格：_____ Payment 付款方式：_____

Bank 酒店开户行：_____ Accounts 账号：_____

Remarks 备注：_____

Breakfast 早餐情况：_____

　　　　　　　　　　　　Taken by 预订确认人：_____

　　All *reserved* rooms will be held until 6:00 p.m. of this very day unless prior arrangements are made. If there is anything unclear, please don't *hesitate* to contact us.

　　Best Regards!

　　* 如无特殊情况，预订客房将保留至当日下午 6 点。如有任何疑问，请致电联系。

　　祝商祺！

No. 3

RESERVATION CONFIRMATION
预订确认单

（店徽）

×××酒店

★★★★★

From 由：<u>×××酒店公关销售部</u>

Tel 电话：<u>0575-88888888-581</u>

Fax 传真：<u>0575-88888888-585</u>

Add 地址：<u>×××市×××路×××号</u>

TO 致送：_____

DATE 日期：_____

FAX 传真：_____

PAGE 页数：_____

Dear _____,

    Thank you for your interest in ×××Hotel. We are pleased to confirm your reservation details as follows:

    感谢您对×××酒店的青睐，今特对您的预订做如下确认：

Group Name / Guest Name 团名 / 宾客姓名：_____

Check In 到店日期：_____ Check Out 离店日期：_____

Room Arrangements 房间安排：_____

Room Rate 房间价格：_____

Payment 付款方式：_____

Bank 酒店开户行：<u>ICBC, YUECHENG BRANCH 工行越城支行</u>

Account 账号：<u>1211016009aaaaaaaaa</u>

Remarks 备注：_____

Breakfast 早餐情况：_____

If there is anything unclear, please don't hesitate to contact us. Best Regards!

以上确认如有任何疑问，请致电联系，祝商祺！

Confirmed by 确认人：_____

No. 4

REGISTRATION FORM OF TEMPORARY RESIDENCE
临时住宿登记表

(Please Use Block Letters 请用正楷填写)

Name in English 英文姓名	Family Name 姓	Given Name 名
Sex 性别	Date of Birth 出生日期	
Name in Chinese 中文姓名	Nationality 国籍／籍贯	Where from 从何处来
Place of Work 工作处所	Occupation 职业	Where to 住何处去
Host Organization 接待单位	*Subject* of Stay 停留事由	Arrival Date 抵店日期
No. of *Certificate* 证件号码	Type of Certificate 证件种类	Departure Date 离店日期
Visa No. 签证号码	Type of Visa 签证种类	Visa Date of *Validity* 签证期限	Issued by 签证机关

Permanent Address 永久住址

Room No. 房号	Form of Payment 结算方式	Credit Cards 信用卡	
Room Rate 房价	□Cash 现金 □Company Account 公司账户 □Agent Account 代理账户 □Others 其他	□AMERICAN EXPRESS® 美国运通卡 □VISA® 维萨卡 □DINERS CLUB® 大来卡 □MASTERCARD® 万事达卡 □JCB 日财卡 □GREAT WALL 长城卡	Check Out Time Is 12:00 *Sharp.* 退房时间是中午 12 时整 Guest Signature 宾客签名
Clerk's *Initial* 职员签名	Remarks 备注		□Foreigner 外宾 □*Resident* from HK, Macao, or Taiwan 港、澳、台宾客 □Overseas Chinese 华侨 □*Resident* from the Chinese Mainland 内地（大陆）宾客

220

No. 5

REGISTRATION FORM OF RESIDENCE (GROUP)
团体人员住宿登记表

Name of Group   Date   Year   Mon   Day   Till   Mon   Day

团队名称   日期   年   月   日   至   月   日

Room No. 房号	Full Name 姓名	Sex 性别	Date of Birth 出生年月	Profession or Occupation 职业	Nationality 国籍	Passport No. 护照号码

Where from and to 何处来何处去	Received by 接待单位

No. 6

ROOM/RATE CHANGE SLIP
房间及房费更改条

Name 宾客姓名＿＿＿＿＿＿＿＿＿＿＿＿＿   Dept. Date 离开日期＿＿＿＿＿＿＿＿＿＿＿＿

From 由   Room No. 房号＿＿＿＿＿   To 转至   Room No. 房号＿＿＿＿＿＿＿＿

From 由   Rate 收费＿＿＿＿＿＿＿   To 改为   Rate 收费＿＿＿＿＿＿＿＿＿＿

Date 日期＿＿＿＿＿＿＿＿＿＿＿＿＿＿   Time 时间＿＿＿＿＿＿＿＿＿＿＿＿＿＿

Clerk 经手人＿＿＿＿＿＿＿＿＿＿＿＿   Bell Boy 行李员＿＿＿＿＿＿＿＿＿＿

Remarks 备注 ＿＿＿＿＿＿＿＿＿＿＿＿＿＿＿＿＿＿＿＿＿＿＿＿＿＿＿＿＿＿＿＿＿＿

CC 抄送：

Housekeeping; Information; Deposit; Cashier; Reservation; Switchboard; Reception; Bellboy

  客房部；   咨询台；   寄存处；收银处； 预订处；   总机；   接待处；行李部

No. 7

PARCEL COLLECTION AND *DELIVERY* RECORD
包裹代收及派送记录表

Guest Name 宾客姓名	Room No. 房号	Pcs. 件数	Guest Signature 宾客签收	Tel No. 电话	Received by 经手人	Date/Time 日期/时间	Delivered by 派送人	Date/Time 日期/时间	Remarks 备注

No. 8

LUGGAGE DEPOSIT SLIP
行李寄存单

Date 日期 _____   Time 时间 _____

Name 姓名 _____

Pcs. 行李数目 _____

Room No. 房号 _____

Guest Signature 宾客签名 _____

Bellboy Signature 行李员签名 _____

NOTE THE FOLLOWING CONDITIONS

注意以下条件

The slip is issued upon receiving the property.

No fee is charged for the storage of the said property.

If the property represented by the slip is not called for within 6 months, the hotel may, at its option, sell it without notice at public or private sale.

The hotel is *authorized* to deliver property to any person presenting this slip without identification.

在收到行李时签出此行李寄存单。

所及行李的保存不收任何费用。

如果行李 6 个月未取，本酒店将会在不通知的情况下进行拍卖。

本酒店有权将行李交给任何持有此寄存单的人士而不需要身份辨识。

No. 9

Safety Deposit Box Services
贵重物品寄存单

Service Hours 服务时间 07:30–23:00			Box No. 箱号	
Room No. 房号	Name 姓名	*Specimen* Signature 签名式样	Date 日期	
Counter Signed 会签	Date 日期	Counter Signed 会签	Date 日期	

Note the following conditions:
请注意以下说明：
If this key is lost, you will be charged the cost for our replacing a new lock.
如遗失此钥匙，必须更换新锁，您须照价赔偿。
The hotel reserves the right to open the box and remove the contents, without *liability*, if the key is not *surrendered* to the Front Desk when you depart from the hotel.
如您退房离店时未能将此钥匙交回前台，本店有权自行开启并移出保存物品，不负任何责任。
I *hereby acknowledge* that all the property stored in the safety box has been safely *withdrawn therefrom*, and the liability of the said Hotel therefore is released.
我认可已取走所有存放物品，以后与酒店无关。
Guest Signature 宾客签名 _____ Room No. 房号 _____ Date 日期 _____

No. 10

SAFETY DEPOSIT BOX ACCESS RECORD
保险箱开启记录

Date 日期	Time 时间	Guest Signature 宾客签名	Employee Signature 员工签名

I (We) hereby surrender this box and return the key *herewith*. All the contents were taken in good order and condition.

兹特承认保险箱钥匙已交回，箱内财物完好且已全部提取。

I hereby *certify* that I have examined this Safety Deposit Box immediately after the *patron* had surrendered the key. And I found that all contents have been removed.

兹特证明上述保险箱在宾客交回钥匙后，箱内所有物品，都已提取。

Date 日期 _____ Time 时间 _____
Guest Signature 宾客签名 _____

Date 日期 _____ Time 时间 _____
Front Desk Employee Signature
总台员工签名 _____

No. 11

EXCHANGE MEMO
外汇兑换水单

No. _____

Nationality 国籍 _____　　　　　Passport / ID No. 护照 / 身份证件号码 _____

Date 日期 _____

Name & Signature 姓名及签字 _____

Address / Hotel 住址 / 酒店 _____

Amount in Foreign Currency 外币币别及金额	Less Discount 扣贴息	*Net* Amount 净额	Rate 牌价	Net Amount in RMB Yuan 实付人民币金额
Particulars 详情				

Business *Seal*　　　　　*Reviewed* by　　　　　Handled by

业务公章　　　　　　　复核　　　　　　　　经办

Please keep this carefully. The *unused* RMB Yuan can be *reconverted* into foreign currency according to his or her passport and the EXCHANGE MEMO when the holder leaves China within six months.

请妥善保存，在 6 个月内出境时可凭本人护照和此水单兑回外汇。

No. 12

LIST FOR DEPOSITING AND FETCHING ROOM KEY
房匙存取记录表

Room No. 房号 _____　　　　　Depositor 寄存者姓名 _____

Depositing Handler 寄存经手人 _____　　　　　Date / Time 日期 / 时间 _____

Taker 取匙者签名 _____

Fetching Handler 取匙经手人 _____　　　　　Date / Time 日期 / 时间 _____

Remarks 备注：_____

_____

No. 13

GUEST MESSAGE
住客留言条

Date 日期 _____

To 致 _____   Room No. 房号 _____

From 由 _____   Of _____

I Will Be   □ Inside the Hotel（在店内）

我将在   At 在 _____

                                □ Outside the Hotel（在店外）

                                At 在 _____

                                Tel No. 电话 _____

I Will Be Back at (Time) 我的回店时间 _____

Message 留言 _____

Cerk 经手人 _____   Guest Signature 宾客签名 _____

No. 14

VISITOR MESSAGE
访客留言条

Mr. / Ms. 先生 / 女士 _____ Room No. 房号_____

When you were out, 当您外出时,

Mr. / Ms. 先生 / 女士 _____

of 单位 _____ Telephone 电话 _____

□ Telephoned 有电话找您   □ Will call again 将再来电话   □ Please call back 请回电话

□ Came to see you 来访时您不在   □ Will come again 将再来看您

Message 留言 _____

_____

Clerk 经手人 _____   Date 日期 _____   Time 时间 _____

No. 15

×××AIRLINES TICKET OFFICE
BOOKING CARD
×××民航售票处
旅客购票单

No.

记录编号：

	Name 旅客姓名	Occupation 工作单位及职务	Nationality 国籍	Documentation 证件名称	ID Card/Passport No. 身份证件/护照号码	Ticket No. 客票号码
1						
2						
3						
4						
5						

Routing 航程	Flt. No. 航班号	Class 等级	Flight Date 乘机日期		Take-off Time 起飞时间
From 自					
To 至					

Willing or unwilling to purchase personal accident insurance? 是否意愿购买人身意外保险？

□Yes 是　□No 否

Remarks 备注

Contact 联系人	Residence 住址	Tel. No. 电话	Issuer 出票人	Issue Date 出票日期

No. 16

MINI-BAR CHARGE VOUCHER
客房小型酒吧账单

Dear Guest,

Please feel free to enjoy the facility of your Mini-Bar provided for your convenience. Your room attendant will collect this voucher daily and take it down to the Front Office Cashier for billing to your account. If you require any additional service, please call Room Service at Ext. 2578.

Should you have some drinks on the day of your departure, please hand in your last voucher to the Front Office Cashier at checkout time.

Thank you.

亲爱的贵宾：

希望您能尽情享受房内迷你吧里的饮品。客房部服务员将每日核对您所饮用的饮品数量，并把清单送到前厅收银处转入您的账目内。如您需要其他特别饮品服务，请拨分机 2578。

为了能准确地计算您的账目，请您在结账离店时，将此单带到前厅收银处。

谢谢！

Room No. 房号 _____ Date 日期 _____				
Item 品类	Inventory 点存	Consumed 耗量	Unit Price 单价（¥）	Sub-total 小计
Martell VSOP 金牌马爹利			30.00	
Seagram's Gin 施格兰金酒			28.00	
Smirnoff Vodka 皇冠伏特加酒			25.00	
Whiskey 威士忌			30.00	
Remy Martin 人头马			28.00	
Tsingtao Beer 青岛啤酒			8.00	
Coca-Cola 可口可乐			8.00	
Balsam Snappy 宝鲜粒粒橙			8.00	
Mango Juice 芒果汁			6.00	
Total 合计				
10% Service Charge 10% 服务费				
Grand Total 总计				

No. 17

LAUNDRY LIST
水洗衣物登记单

Name 姓名 _____ Room No. 房号 _____

Date 日期 _____ Guest Signature 宾客签名 _____

Guest Count 宾客核数	Hotel Count 酒店核数	Gentlemen 男士	Unit Price 价目（¥）	Amount 收费
		Sport shirt (2 pcs) 运动装（2件）	20.00	
		Pajamas (2 pcs) 睡衣（2件）	18.00	
		Trousers 西裤	20.00	
		Jacket 短外衣	20.00	
		Short Trousers 短西裤	15.00	
		Normal Shirt 衬衫	12.00	
		T-shirt T恤	12.00	
		Underpants 内裤	6.00	
		Undershirt 内衣	6.00	
		Socks (1 pair) 袜（1对）	6.00	
		Handkerchief 手帕	5.00	
		Jeans 牛仔裤	20.00	

Guest Count 宾客核数	Hotel Count 酒店核数	Ladies 女士	Unit Price 价目（¥）	Amount 收费
		Dress 衫裙	28.00	
		Coat 外衣	20.00	
		Sport Shirt (2 pcs) 运动装（2件）	20.00	
		Normal Shirt 衬衫	15.00	
		T-Shirt T恤	12.00	
		Skirt 短裙	12.00	
		Skirt-Pleated 有褶短裙	22.00	
		Scarf 围巾	10.00	
		Jeans 牛仔裤	20.00	
		Trousers 西裤	20.00	
		Stockings 袜	6.00	
		Handkerchief 手帕	5.00	
		Shorts 短裤	15.00	
		Pajamas (2 pcs) 睡衣（2件）	20.00	
		Brassieres 胸罩	6.00	
		Underwear 内衣	6.00	
		Underpants 内裤	6.00	
		Slips 衬裙	6.00	
Basic Charge 基本费				
Express Service Charge 特快服务费				
15% Service Charge 加收 15% 服务费				
Grand Total 总计				

Please tick.

请做标记。

□**Regular Service**

普通服务

Garments collected after 10:00 a.m. will be returned the next day except those marked "Express Service."

早上 10 点后不注明 "快洗" 的第二天送回。

□**Express Service**

特快服务

Garments will be returned within 4 hours from the time of collection. A surcharge of 50% is for this service. The last collection is 6:00 p.m.

衣服由收衣时间起 4 小时内送回，收费加 50%。最后收衣时间为晚上 6 点。

Special Instructions

特别要求指示

□Repairs 修补

□*Buttoning* 缝扣

□Stain Removing 去污

□Folded 叠

□Hangers 挂

□*Starching* 浆

Total Pieces 衣物件数

No. 18

DRY CLEANING & PRESSING LIST
干洗及净烫登记单

Name 姓名 _____   Room Number. 房号 _____

Date 日期_____   Guest Signature 宾客签名 _____

DRY CLEANING & PRESSING ONLY 干洗及净烫				
Guest Count 宾客核数	Hotel Count 酒店核数	Gentlemen 男士	Unit Price 价目（¥）	Amount 收费
		Suit (3 pcs) 礼服 / 西服（3 件） 48.00		
		Suit (2 pcs) 西服（2 件） 38.00		
		Overcoat 大衣 40.00		
		Jacket 短外衣 22.00		
		Sweater/Pullover 毛衣 20.00		
		Normal Shirt 衬衫 18.00		
		Trousers 西裤 20.00		
		Tie 领带 10.00		
		Vest 马夹 18.00		
PRESSING ONLY 净烫				
Guest Count 宾客核数	Hotel Count 酒店核数	Gentlemen 男士	Unit Price 价目（¥）	Amount 收费
		Suit (3 pcs) 礼服 / 西服（3 件） 24.00		
		Suit (2 pcs) 西服（2 件） 20.00		
		Overcoat 大衣 20.00		
		Jacket 短外衣 12.00		
		Sweater/Pullover 毛衣 10.00		
		Normal Shirt 衬衫 9.00		
		Trousers 西裤 10.00		
		Tie 领带 5.00		
		Vest 马夹 9.00		
Basic Charge 基本费				
Express Service Charge 特快服务费				
Service Charge 15% 加收 15% 服务费				
Grand Total 总计				

Please tick.
请做标记。

□**Regular Service**
普通服务
Garments collected after 10:00 a.m. will be returned the next day except those marked "Express Service."
早上 10 点后不注明"快洗"的第二天送回。

□**Express Service**
特快服务
Garments will be returned within 4 hours from the time of collection. A surcharge of 50% is for this service. The last collection is 6:00 p.m.
衣服由收衣时间起 4 小时内送回，收费加 50%。最后收衣时间为晚上 6 点。

Special Instructions
特别要求指示
□Repairs 修补
□Buttoning 缝扣
□Stain Removing 去污
□Folded 叠
□Hangers 挂
□Starching 浆

Total Pieces 衣物件数

No. 19

RESTAURANT STATEMENT
餐厅结账单

No.

编号：

Table 桌号	Waiter 经手人	Date 日期	PAX^① 宾客	
Qty. 数量	Details 品名			
Check Paid 结账				
Room No. or Credit Card No. 房号或信用卡				

Name 姓名 (in Block Letter 请写正楷)

Signature 签名

Please present your Welcome Card or Room Key for identification.

请出示欢迎卡或房匙以便入账之用。

① passengers (in the airline industry); persons or occupants (in hotel/resort accommodation) 乘客（航空业）；人或使用者（酒店／旅游膳宿）

No. 20

BABYSITTER REQUEST
保姆服务表

Guest Name 宾客姓名 _____   Date 日期 _____

Room No. 房号 _____

Dear Guest,

As requested by you, we have arranged for:

Name of Babysitter _____ to report to you

from _____ to _____ on _____ .

Kindly note that there is a minimum charge of 60 yuan for the first 2 hours of babysitting. A fee of 30 yuan is charged for each additional hour. If you *release* the babysitter after 11:00 p.m., please pay her a fee of 20 yuan for taxi *fare*. A payment should be made direct to the babysitter herself.

A request should be made in advance if your baby needs *feeding*, and an *additional* fee will be charged for the food. A fee of 5 yuan will be charged for your cancellation of such service if you inform us of it one hour before the fixed time.

The hotel holds no responsibility for any *consequence* caused by the babysitter's *carelessness* and *negligence*.

I fully accept the above terms and conditions.

亲爱的宾客：

根据您的要求，我们已为您提供保姆服务。具体事项如下：

姓名 _____

时间由 _____ 至 _____

保姆服务每小时收费 30 元人民币，每次服务不得少于 2 小时，如果您要求保姆晚上 11 点后离开，则需另付 20 元人民币出租车交通费。所有付款事宜直接与保姆本人联系。

如需给婴儿提供食物，请事先提出，费用另计；您在指定服务时间前一小时内取消这项服务，则需要付 5 元手续费。

本店将不负责由于保姆粗心或疏忽而引起的一切后果。

本人接受上述所有条款。

Housekeeper Signature 管家部签名 _____   Guest Signature 宾客签名 _____

No. 21

ROOM STATEMENT

住房结账单

	Room No. 房号
	Room Rate 房费
	Persons 客数
	Folio No. 账号
	Page No. 页数
	Arrival 到店
	Departure 离店
	Deposit 订金

Ref. Code 代号索引	Date 日期	Reference No. 单号	Description 摘要	Debits/Credits 金额
01 Room Rent 房屋出租				
02 Seafood Restaurant 海鲜楼				
03 Western Restaurant 西餐厅				
04 Room Service 送餐				
05 Bar Service 酒吧				
06 Karaoke 卡拉 OK				
07 Nightclub 夜总会				
08 Buffet 自助餐				
09 Mini Bar 客房迷你吧				
10 Recreation 康乐				
11 Beauty Service 美容				
12 Telephone Service 电话				
13 Convention Service 会议				
14 Transportation Service 交通				
15 Laundry Service 洗衣				
16 *Miscellaneous* 杂项				

Booked by 订房联络	I agree that my liability for this bill is not *waived* and agree to be held personally liable in the event that the indicated person, company, or association fails to pay for any part or the full amount of these charges.
Transferred to 转账索引	如转账无效，本人愿意承担账单所列尚未清付之最后欠额。
	Signature 签署人

Room No.

房号

Departure Date

离店日期

Cashier

收银员代号

680 ××× Rd, ×××, ××× P. R. China

中国 ××× 省 ××× 市 ××× 路 680 号

Tel 电话: 8888888   Fax 传真: 8885558   Zip Code 邮政编码: aaa000

No. 22

REQUEST FOR COMMENTS
意见表

Dear Guest,

Welcome to the ×××　Hotel. I, on behalf of the hotel's management and staff, sincerely wish you a most pleasant stay here.

We have always been *committing* ourselves to providing guests with top-quality service heart and soul and listening attentively to your valuable and *constructive* comments or suggestions about us. We would greatly appreciate it if you could complete this *questionnaire* with anything that you feel could make you a more comfortable stay here. We will surely recognize it as your utmost support and *encouragement* you give us.

Thank you for your *valued patronage*, and we are looking forward to serving you again soon.

Yours sincerely,

General Manager

××× Hotel

尊敬的宾客：

我谨代表酒店管理层和全体员工欢迎您下榻 ××× 酒店，并衷心祝愿您在本店住得愉快！

本酒店热切希望为您提供一流的服务，欢迎您多提宝贵意见。如果您能花点时间在这张意见表上填写或留下能使您住得更加愉快的意见与建议，这将是对我们莫大的支持和鼓励。

感谢您的惠顾，并热忱恭候您的再次光临。

××× 酒店总经理　谨启

□ □ □ □ □ □

Add 地址：680, ××× Rd, ×××, ×××, China 中国 ××× 省 ××× 市 ××× 路 680 号

Tel 电话：aaaa-8068688　　　　　　　Fax 传真：aaaa-8051028

××× Hotel ××× 大酒店

General Manager 总经理　收

Postal Code 邮政编码：aaa000

No. 23

GUEST QUESTIONNAIRE
宾客意见表

Guest Name 贵宾姓名 ＿＿＿＿＿＿＿　　　Profession 职业 ＿＿＿＿＿＿＿＿

Company Name 公司名称 ＿＿＿＿＿＿　　　Home Address 家庭住址 ＿＿＿＿＿＿

Country 国家 ＿＿＿＿＿＿＿＿＿＿　　　City 城市 ＿＿＿＿＿＿＿＿＿＿

Arrival Date 抵达日期 ＿＿＿＿＿＿＿　　　Room Number 房间号 ＿＿＿＿＿＿＿

Reservation Service 预订服务：　　　Efficient 效率高　　　　Poor 欠佳
　　　　　　　　　　　　　　　　　　☺　　　　　　　☹

The Reception Services Below 以下接待服务	Excellent 优	Satisfactory 满意	Poor 欠佳
Doorman 门童	☺	☺	☺
Porter 行李员	☺	☺	☺
Receptionist 前台服务员	☺	☺	☺
Cashier 收银服务员	☺	☺	☺
Telephone Operator 电话接线员	☺	☺	☺
Room Attendants 客房服务员	☺	☺	☺
Laundry / Dry-Cleaning 洗衣服 / 干洗服务	☺	☺	☺
Room-Cleaning / Room Requisites 客房清洁 / 客房用品	☺	☺	☺
Business Center 商务中心	☺	☺	☺

Please rate your experience with the following 请评价下列各项：

	Food & Beverage 食品、饮料			Service 服务		
	Excellent 优	Satisfactory 满意	Poor 欠佳	Excellent 优	Satisfactory 满意	Poor 欠佳
Seafood Restaurant 海鲜楼	☺	☺	☺	☺	☺	☺
Flavor Restaurant 明珠楼	☺	☺	☺	☺	☺	☺
Special Hall Restaurant 君悦楼	☺	☺	☺	☺	☺	☺
Blossom Garden 百花苑	☺	☺	☺	☺	☺	☺
Western Restaurant 西餐厅	☺	☺	☺	☺	☺	☺
Bar 酒吧	☺	☺	☺	☺	☺	☺
Coffee House 咖啡厅	☺	☺	☺	☺	☺	☺

Why have you chosen our hotel? 为何选择我店？

□ Previous Experience 曾经住过　　　□ Travel Agent Recommendation 旅行社推荐

□ Recommendation by Friend 朋友推荐　　　□ Airline Recommendation 航空公司推荐

□ Advertisement 广告　　　□ Direct Mail 直接函请

Others (Please Specify) 其他（请写明）＿＿＿＿＿＿＿＿＿＿＿＿＿＿＿＿＿

＿＿＿＿＿＿＿＿＿＿＿＿＿＿＿＿＿＿＿＿＿＿＿＿＿＿＿＿＿＿＿＿＿＿＿

＿＿＿＿＿＿＿＿＿＿＿＿＿＿＿＿＿＿＿＿＿＿＿＿＿＿＿＿＿＿＿＿＿＿＿

No. 24

STAFF PERFORMANCE APPRAISAL FORM
工作评估表

Name 姓名	Date 上工日期
Department 部门	Position 职位
Appraisal for 评估目的	☐ End of *Probation* 试用期满 ☐ *Annual Assessment* 年度评估

APPRAISAL: A—*Outstanding*; B—Good; C—*Average*; D—Below Average; E—Far Below Average

卓越超凡　优秀表现　一般水准　　尚要努力　　远离要求

Performance 工作表现	A	B	C	D	E	Personality 个性	A	B	C	D	E
Job Knowledge & Skills 知识与技能						General Attitude 态度					
Completion of Tasks 任务完成情况						*Maturity* 成熟度					
Accuracy of Work 工作准确程度						*Honesty* 诚实度					
Enthusiasm towards Job 工作热情						*Reliability* 信赖度					
HR with Guests 与宾客关系						*Receptiveness* to Criticism 接受批评					
HR with *Colleagues* 同事关系						Potential for *Growth* 潜质					
Punctuality of Attendance 到岗情况						*Ambition* 上进心					
Language Ability 语言能力						Acceptance of Responsibility 责任感					
Overall *Grading* 总评						Organization Ability 组织能力					
						Leadership 领导能力					
						Self-Starter 自发性					

Comments 意见

Date _____　　　　Dept. Head Signature _____　　　　Employee Signature _____

日期　　　　　　　　　　主管签名　　　　　　　　　　　　　员工签名

Vocabulary

namely /ˈneɪmli/ *adv.* 即；也就是

well-designed /ˈwel dɪˈzaɪnd/ *adj.* 精心设计的

labor /ˈleɪbə(r)/ *n.* 劳力

data /ˈdeɪtə/ *n.* 资料；数据

amendment /əˈmendmənt/ *n.* 修改

title /ˈtaɪtl/ *n.* 头衔

remark /rɪˈmɑːk/ *n.* 备注

hesitate /ˈhezɪteɪt/ *v.* 犹豫

subject /ˈsʌbdʒɪkt/ *n.* 事由

visa /ˈviːzə/ *n.* 签证

sharp /ʃɑːp/ *adv.* 整点

resident /ˈrezɪdənt/ *n.* 居民

authorize /ˈɔːθəraɪz/ *v.* 授权

liability /ˌlaɪəˈbɪləti/ *n.* 责任

hereby /ˌhɪəˈbaɪ/ *adv.* 特此；凭此

withdraw /wɪðˈdrɔː/ *v.* 取出

herewith /ˌhɪəˈwɪð/ *adv.* 以此

patron /ˈpeɪtrən/ *n.* 客人

particular /pəˈtɪkjələ(r)/ *n.* 详情；细节

review /rɪˈvjuː/ *v.* 复核

reconvert /ˈriːkənˈvɜːt/ *v.* 使恢复

documentation /ˌdɒkjumenˈteɪʃn/ *n.* 文件；证件

routing /ˈruːtɪŋ/ *n.* 路由（选择）

issuer /ˈɪʃuːə(r)/ *n.* 出票人

starch /stɑːtʃ/ *v.* 上浆

fare /feə(r)/ *n.* 车费

additional /əˈdɪʃənl/ *adj.* 附加的

carelessness /ˈkeələsnəs/ *n.* 粗心

miscellaneous /ˌmɪsəˈleɪniəs/ *n.* 杂项

commit /kəˈmɪt/ *v.* 承诺

file /faɪl/ *v.* 把归档

grasp /ɡrɑːsp/ *v.* 理解；把握

surname /ˈsɜːneɪm/ *n.* 姓

commercial /kəˈmɜːʃl/ *adj.* 商业的

reserved /rɪˈzɜːvd/ *adj.* 预订的

entry /ˈentri/ *n.* 入境

certificate /səˈtɪfɪkət/ *n.* 证书

validity /vəˈlɪdəti/ *n.* 有效性

initial /ɪˈnɪʃl/ *n.* 首字母

delivery /dɪˈlɪvəri/ *n.* 派送

specimen /ˈspesɪmən/ *n.* 样本

surrender /səˈrendə(r)/ *v.* 交出

acknowledge /əkˈnɒlɪdʒ/ *v.* 认可；承认

therefrom /ˌðeəˈfrɒm/ *adv.* 从此

certify /ˈsɜːtɪfaɪ/ *v.* 证明

net /net/ *adj.* 净值的；无虚价的

seal /siːl/ *n.* 印章

unused /ˌʌnˈjuːzd/ *adj.* 未用过的

insurance /ɪnˈʃʊərəns/ *n.* 保险

button /ˈbʌtn/ *v.* 缝扣

release /rɪˈliːs/ *v.* 放走

feed /fiːd/ *v.* 喂食

consequence /ˈkɒnsɪkwəns/ *n.* 后果

negligence /ˈneɡlɪdʒəns/ *n.* 疏忽；渎职

waive /weɪv/ *v.* 放弃；免除

constructive /kənˈstrʌktɪv/ *adj.* 建设性的

questionnaire /ˌkwestʃəˈneə(r)/ *n.* 调查问卷

valued /ˈvæljuːd/ *adj.* 受重视的

probation /prəˈbeɪʃn/ *n.* 试用期

assessment /əˈsesmənt/ *n.* 评估

average /ˈævərɪdʒ/ *adj.* 一般的；中等的

maturity /məˈtʃʊərəti/ *n.* 成熟（度）

honesty /ˈɒnəsti/ *n.* 诚实（度）

reliability /rɪˌlaɪəˈbɪləti/ *n.* 可靠（度）

receptiveness /rɪˈseptɪvnəs/ *n.* 感受性；接受（度）

colleague /ˈkɒliːg/ *n.* 同事

punctuality /ˌpʌŋktʃuˈæləti/ *n.* 准时

grading /ˈgreɪdɪŋ/ *n.* 等级

self-starter /self ˈstɑːtə(r)/ *n.* 自发性；主动精神

encouragement /ɪnˈkʌrɪdʒmənt/ *n.* 鼓励

patronage /ˈpætrənɪdʒ/ *n.* 光顾

annual /ˈænjuəl/ *adj.* 一年一度的

outstanding /aʊtˈstændɪŋ/ *adj.* 优秀的

completion /kəmˈpliːʃn/ *n.* 完成

accuracy /ˈækjərəsi/ *n.* 精确（度）

enthusiasm /ɪnˈθjuːziæzəm/ *n.* 热情

growth /grəʊθ/ *n.* 成长（性）

ambition /æmˈbɪʃn/ *n.* 上进心

leadership /ˈliːdəʃɪp/ *n.* 领导（力）

Useful Expressions

as follows 如下

be authorized to do sth. 有权做某事

reconvert ... into ... 把……兑回……

in block letter 用正楷

commit oneself to ... 致力于……

at one's option 由某人选择

surrender ... to ... 把……交（出）给……

hand ... in to ... 把……上交给……

heart and soul 全心全意地

词汇、课文资源

词汇、课文自测

微课

课堂练习

Chapter Ten

Food & Beverage Menus[①]
酒店餐饮菜单

思政园地／二十
大精神学习专栏

Learning Objectives

· *To get familiar with the types and contents of menus;*

· *To understand formations of dish names and methods of translating menus into English;*

· *To master the new words and professional terms concerned;*

· *To improve reading ability through learning the text;*

· *To develop team spirit and self-study ability through learning activities;*

· *To receive education in ideological and political theories through course learning.*

Teaching Arrangements

节次	教学内容	自主学习资源	自主学习自测	课堂教学视频	课堂练习
L 1	Food & Beverage Menus	词汇、课文资源	词汇、课文自测	微课	课堂练习

The menu is a list of dishes consisting of beverages and cold dishes, hot dishes and heavy courses, and snacks and fruits in a certain proportion and a certain order. The menu serves as a medium through which catering enterprises sell their catering services by way of introducing dishes and dish features to guests, and also a basis on which catering enterprises determine their service activities like

菜单是将酒水冷碟、热炒大菜、点心蜜果等三组食品按一定比例和程序编成的菜点清单，是餐饮企业向顾客介绍菜品及菜品特色，进而推销餐饮服务的媒介。在餐饮服务活动中，原料采购、厨务人员配备、菜品制作、成本控制、接待服务工作安排等都依据菜单确定。

---

① 本章内容选编自北京市人民政府外事办公室、北京市旅游局编写的《中文菜单英文译法》（中国旅游出版社 2008年版）。

material purchasing, kitchen staffing, food cooking, cost controlling, and reception scheduling. The menu reflects the level of a hotel's management and operation, and displays the cooking technology and culture of an age or an area the hotel belongs to. Moreover, the menu is also a unique form of advertising, and, therefore, it is usually well designed. This chapter deals with Chinese food menu, Western food menu, Wine list, and Drinks list.

菜单可以体现酒店的经营水平及管理水平，也可体现酒店所在那个时代、那个地区的烹调工艺和饮食文化。而且，菜单也是一则别开生面的广告，通常设计精美。本章提供的有中式菜单、西式菜单、酒单和饮料单。

10.1 Chinese Food

10.1.1 Cold Dishes 冷菜

1) *Marinated Jellyfish* and Chinese Cabbage

白菜心拌蜇头

2) *Mushrooms* with Duck *Webs*

白灵菇扣鸭掌

3) Shredded Tofu with *Sauce*

拌豆腐丝

4) *Sliced* Boiled Chicken (Served with Soy Sauce, *Ginger* Sauce or Ginger and *Scallion* Sauce)

白切鸡

5) *Tossed* Black and White *Fungus*

拌双耳

6) Bitter Melon in *Plum* Sauce

冰梅凉瓜

7) Iced Chinese *Broccoli* with *Wasabi*

冰镇芥蓝

8) Special Flavored Beef *Shank*

豆豉多春鱼

9) *Shishamo* in Black Bean Sauce

怪味牛腱

10) Ox Tongue in *Chili* Sauce

干拌牛舌

11) Preserved Eggs in Ginger Sauce

姜汁皮蛋

12) Pig Feet in Brown Sauce

酱香猪蹄

13) Traditional Beijing Bean *Paste*

老北京豆酱

14) Deep-Fried Peanuts *Pickled* in Vinegar

老醋泡花生

15) Pickled *Turnip* with Green Soy Bean

萝卜干毛豆

16) Lily Bulb in *Squash* Sauce

南瓜汁百合

17) Honey-Stewed BBQ Pork

蜜汁叉烧

18) Sweet and Sour Pickled Vegetables

酸甜泡菜

19) Roast *Suckling* Pig

乳猪拼盘

20) Crispy Celery

爽口西芹

21) Sliced *Kelp* in *Garlic* Sauce

蒜蓉海带丝

22) *Spiced* Smoked Dried Tofu

五香熏干

23) Salt Baked Chicken

盐焗鸡

24) Salted *Shrimp* Meat

盐水虾肉

25) Braised Goose Webs in Rice Wine Sauce

糟香鹅掌

26) Fresh Fruit Salad

水果沙拉

27) Jellyfish in Vinegar

米醋海蜇

28) Spiced Beef Shank

五味牛腱

29) Dried Tofu with Day Lily

黄花素鸡

30) Steamed Lotus Root Stuffed with *Glutinous* Rice

桂花糯米藕

31) *Spicy* Beef Tendon

麻辣牛筋

32) Liquor-*Saturated* Chicken

醉鸡

33) *Kidney* Beans in Coca-Cola

可乐芸豆

34) Fish *Aspic*

水晶鱼冻

35) Hot and Sour *Fern* Root Noodles

酸辣蕨根粉

36) Mixed Bitter Vegetables

拌苦菜

37) Honeyed Walnuts

琥珀核桃

38) Air-Dried Goose, Hangzhou Style

杭州风鹅

39) Goose Liver with Scallion and Chili Oil

葱油鹅肝

40) *Sausage* Stuffed with Salty Egg

龙眼风味肠

41) Hand-Shredded Eggplant with Chili Sauce

香辣手撕茄子

42) Fried Silver Fish with Peanuts

小鱼花生

43) Steamed Sliced Chicken with Ham

清蒸火腿鸡片

44) Smoked Salmon

熏马哈鱼

45) *Mashed* Eggplant with Garlic

拌茄泥

10.1.2 Hot Dishes 热菜

Pork 猪肉

46) Braised Pork *Cubes* with Tofu and Chinese Cabbage

白菜豆腐焖酥肉

47) Red-Cooked Pork with *Abalone*

鲍鱼红烧肉

48) Stewed Pork Cubes and Tofu Skin in Brown Sauce

百叶结烧肉

49) Steamed Rice Rolls with BBQ Pork *Intestines* and Vegetables

碧绿叉烧肥肠

50) Fried Pork with Chili Soy Sauce, Chaozhou Style

潮式椒酱肉

51) *Spare Ribs* with Bitter Melon, Chaozhou Style

潮式凉瓜排骨

52) Steamed Preserved Pork in Black Bean Sauce

豉油皇咸肉

53) Shredded Pork with Vegetables, Sichuan Style

川味小炒

54) Dongpo Pork

东坡方肉

55) *Griddle* Cooked Spare Ribs and Chicken

干锅排骨鸡

56) Gulaorou (Sweet and Sour Pork)

咕噜肉

57) Baked Pig Feet with Black Pepper

黑椒焗猪手

58) Roasted Crispy Suckling Pig

脆皮乳猪

59) Pan-Fried Pork *Fillet*

煎猪柳

60) Deep-Fried Spare Ribs with Spiced Salt

椒盐炸排条

61) Sautéed Shredded Pork in Sweet Bean Sauce

京酱肉丝

62) Baked Spare Ribs

焗肉排

63) Sautéed *Minced* Pork with Bean Sprouts in *Curry* Sauce

咖喱肉松焖大豆芽

64) Braised Pork, Mao's Family Style

毛家红烧肉

65) BBQ Spare Ribs with Pineapple

炭烧菠萝骨

66) Sweet and Sour Spare Ribs

糖醋排骨

67) Spare Ribs with Curry Sauce Served on a *Sizzling* Iron Plate

铁板咖喱酱烧骨

68) Sautéed Pork with Pepper, Hunan Style

湘味回锅肉

69) Yu-Shiang Shredded Pork (Sautéed with Spicy Garlic Sauce)

鱼香肉丝

70) Curry Pork

咖喱肉

71) Pork Tripe Stuffed with Meat

罗汉肚

72) Fried Shredded Pork Tenderloin in Soy Bean Paste Served with Pancake

酱爆里脊丝配饼

73) Soft-Fried Pork *Tenderloin*

软炸里脊

74) Stir-Fried Sliced Pork Tenderloin

滑熘里脊片

75) Quick-Fried Pork Intestines with Brown Sauce

软熘肥肠

76) Roasted Suckling Pig

烤乳猪

77) *Scrambled* Eggs with Pig Brains

蛋煎猪脑

78) Hot and Spicy Pork Chops

香辣猪扒

79) Steamed Preserved Pork Steamed in Bamboo Tube

竹筒腊肉

80) Spicy Pig Kidney

温拌腰片

Beef 牛肉

81) Sautéed Beef Fillet with Bell Peppers

彩椒牛柳

82) Boiled Beef

白灼肥牛

83) Sautéed Sliced Beef and Green Vegetable in *Oyster* Sauce

菜胆蚝油牛肉

84) Grilled Beef with Green Vegetable

菜心扒牛肉

85) Braised Oxtail in Chili Sauce, Sichuan Style

川北牛尾

86) Sautéed Beef Fillet in Chili Sauce, Sichuan Style

川汁牛柳

87) Stewed Beef *Brisket* with Tomato

番茄炖牛腩

88) Griddle Cooked Beef and Mushrooms

干锅黄牛肉

89) Pan-Fried Beef Ribs with Black Pepper

黑椒牛肋骨

90) Beef with Chili Grilled on Stone Plate

石烹肥牛

91) Sliced Beef in Hot Chili Oil

水煮牛肉

92) Crispy Beef Fillet

酥皮牛柳

93) Beef *Kebabs* Served on a Sizzling Iron Plate

铁板串烧牛肉

94) Steamed Beef Ribs in Black Bean

Sauce

豉汁牛仔骨

95) Grilled Beef with *Cumin*

孜然烤牛肉

96) *Tangerine*-Flavored Beef

陈皮牛肉

97) Dry-Braised Beef, Sichuan Style

干烧牛肉

98) Beef Fillet Braised in Iron wok

铁锅牛柳

99) Spicy Beef Tripe

麻辣牛肚

100) Pan-Fried New Zealand *Veal Chops*

香煎新西兰牛仔骨

101) Fried Beef with Scrambled Eggs

清蛋牛肉

102) Tasty and *Refreshing* Beef Tripe

爽口碧绿百叶

103) Braised Beef *Tendon*, Home Style

家常烧蹄筋

Lamb 羊肉

104) Sautéed Sliced Lamb with Scallion

葱爆羊肉

105) Braised Lamb Chops with Carrots

红焖羊排

106) Roast Lamb Tenderloin

烤羊里脊

107) Stewed Lamb Leg

卤酥羊腿

108) Lamb and Tofu Skin in *Casserole*

支竹羊肉煲

109) Fried Lamb Chops Wrapped in

Paper

纸包风味羊排

110) Dried Lamb with *Truffles*

干羊肉野山菌

111) Grilled Lamb Chops

手扒羊排

112) Roasted Lamb

烤羔羊

113) Boiled Lamb, Mongolian Style

蒙古手抓肉

114) Hot Pot, Mongolian Style

涮羊肉

115) Lamb Spine Hot Pot

羊蝎子

Poultry and Eggs 禽蛋类

116) Sautéed Chicken with Hot and Green Pepper

巴蜀小炒鸡

117) Grilled *Mustard* Flavored Chicken Breast

扒芥香鸡胸

118) Braised Chicken in Hot Spicy Sauce, Sichuan Style

川味红汤鸡

119) Crispy Chicken

脆皮鸡

120) Deep-Fried Chicken with Chili Pepper

当红炸子鸡

121) Stewed Chicken in Scallion and Black Bean Sauce in Casserole

干葱豆豉鸡煲

122) Kung Pao Chicken

宫保鸡丁

123) Pan-Fried Chicken with Ginger and Scallion

姜葱霸皇鸡

124) Steamed Chicken with Lily Flowers and Fungus

金针云耳蒸鸡

125) Salt Baked Chicken, Hakka Style

客家盐焗鸡

126) Hand-Shredded Chicken

飘香手撕鸡

127) Roast Chicken Kebabs

烧鸡肉串

128) Chicken, South China Style

江南百花鸡

129) Sautéed *Diced* Chicken with Chili Pepper, Sichuan Style

四川辣子鸡

130) Chicken with Black Bean Sauce Served on a Sizzling Iron Plate

铁板豆豉鸡

131) Dry-Braised Chicken in Chili Sauce

干烧鸡

132) Special Flavored Shredded Chicken

怪味鸡丝

133) Chicken Braised in Sweet and Sour Sauce

糖醋鸡块

134) Honey-Stewed Chicken with Ginger *Shoots*

蜜糖子姜鸡

135) Red-Cooked Chicken, Daokou Style

道口烧鸡

136) Smoked Chicken

熏鸡

137) Spiced Chicken

五香鸡

138) Boiled Chicken with *Sesame* and Spicy Sauce

芝麻鸡

139) Beggar's Chicken (Baked Chicken)

叫花鸡

140) A Chicken Prepared in Three Ways

一鸡三吃

141) Sliced Chicken with Chicken Livers and Ham

广州文昌鸡

142) Two-Colored Crispy Duck with Minced Shrimp Stuffing

脆皮鸳鸯鸭

143) Salt Baked Duck in Lotus Leaf

盐烤荷叶鸭

144) Smoked Duck, Sichuan Style (Served with Lotus-Leaf-Like Pancake)

四川樟茶鸭（配荷叶饼）

145) Salted Duck Egg

咸鸭蛋

146) Marinated Egg

卤蛋

147) Egg Preserved in Rice Wine

糟蛋

148) *Poached* Egg

荷包蛋

149) Scrambled Eggs with Shrimp Paste

虾酱炒鸡蛋

150) Stir-Fried Minced Pork and Quail Egg

鹌蛋炒碎肉

151) Steamed Egg *Custard*

蛋羹

Other Meats 其他肉类

152) Steamed *Bullfrog* with Chili Pepper

笼仔剁椒牛蛙

153) Sautéed Rabbit Leg with Hot Spicy Sauce

麻辣玉兔腿

154) Deep-Fried Rolls with Five Shreds Filling and Scorpion

炸五丝筒全蝎

155) Stir-Fried *Venison* with Black Pepper

皇宫煎鹿柳

156) Sautéed Eel with Duck Blood *Curd*

山城血旺

Mushroooms 菇菌类

157) Braised Yellow Fungus with Pea Sprouts

豆苗羊肚菌

158) Griddle Cooked Tea Tree Mushrooms

干锅茶树菇

159) Stewed *Assorted* Mushrooms with Lotus Root

荷塘焖什菌

160) Sautéed Abalone Mushrooms and Vegetables

三色鲍鱼菇

161) Assorted Mushrooms in Casserole

砂锅三菌

162) Deep-Fried Mushrooms

酥炸山菌

163) Boiled Assorted Mushrooms, Thai Style

泰式煮什菌

Abalone 鲍鱼类

164) Braised Sliced Abalone with Mushrooms

白灵菇扒鲍片

165) Steamed Abalone Rolls Stuffed with Minced Shrimp

百花鲍鱼卷

166) Abalone Sauce on Deep-Fried Rice Cake

锅巴鲍鱼

167) Steamed Sliced Abalone with Egg White

百花酿鲍片

168) Sautéed Shredded Abalone with Bean Sprouts

银芽炒鲍丝

Shark's Fins 鱼翅类

169) Shark's *Fin* Soup with Shredded Abalone

鲍参翅肚羹

170) Braised Assorted Mushrooms in Shark's Fin Soup

翅汤浸什菌

171) Sautéed Shark's Fin with *Crab* Meat and Bean Sprouts

桂花炒鱼翅

172) Stewed Shark's Fin with Fish *Maw* and Bamboo Fungus

花胶菜胆炖竹荪翅

173) Boiled Shark's Fin and Bird's Nest Served in Dragon Fruit

火龙燕液翅

Seafood 海鲜类

174) *Turbot* (Steamed, Steamed with Black Bean Sauce, Boiled)

多宝鱼（清蒸，豉汁蒸，过桥）

175) Assorted Seafood with *Vermicelli* in Casserole

海鲜粉丝煲

176) Fotiaoqiang (Steamed Abalone with Shark's Fin and Fish Maw in *Broth*)

佛跳墙

177) Simmered *Prawns* with Medicinal *Herbs*

药味炖生中虾

178) Three *Delicacies* with Egg White

芙蓉三鲜

Vegetables 蔬菜类

179) Sautéed Lily Bulbs and Seaweed in XO Sauce

XO 酱炒海茸百合

180) Poached Chinese Cabbage with Chestnuts

板栗白菜

181) Pan-*Seared* Green Chili Pepper

虎皮尖椒

182) Assorted Vegetable Salad

乡村大丰收

183) Yu-Shiang Eggplant (Sautéed with Spicy Garlic Sauce)

鱼香茄子

Tofu 豆腐类

184) Steamed Tofu with Vegetables

彩虹蒸豆腐

185) Sautéed Dried Tofu with Hot Peppers in Black Bean Sauce

豉香尖椒炒豆干

186) Deep-Fried Tofu

脆皮豆腐

187) Braised Japanese Tofu with Vegetables

红烧日本豆腐

188) Stewed Tofu with Preserved Vegetable and Minced Pork

榄菜肉碎炖豆腐

Bird's Nest Soup 燕窝类

189) Stewed Bird's Nest with Rock Sugar

冰花炖官燕

190) Braised Bird's Nest with White Fungus and Rock Sugar

冰糖银耳燕窝

191) Best Quality Bird's Nest Soup

一品燕窝

192) Bird's Nest Soup

王府清汤官燕

193) Stewed Bird's Nest with Egg White

冰花芙蓉官燕

Soups 羹汤煲类

194) Abalone, Shark's Fin and Fish Maw Soup

煲参翅肚羹

195) Minced Chicken and Fish Soup

龙凤羹

196) Stewed Shark's Fin with Crab *Roe*

蟹黄鱼翅羹

197) Duck in Aweto Soup

虫草鸭块汤

198) *Clam* Soup Simmered with Chinese *Wolfberry*

枸杞炖蛤

199) Creamy Duck and Mushroom Soup

鸭茸奶油蘑菇汤

200) Shanghai *Specialty* in Casserole

腌鲜砂锅

201) Stewed Lamb Chops and Turnip in Casserole

砂锅萝卜羊排

202) Steamed Pork with Preserved Vegetable in Casserole

梅菜扣肉煲

Rice and Noodles 主食

203) Eight Delicacies Rice

八宝饭

204) Stir-Fried Rice with *Bacon* and Assorted Vegetables

翡翠培根炒饭

205) Stir-Fried Rice with Diced Beef, Pepper and Garlic

黑椒香蒜牛柳粒炒饭

206) Rice with Spare Ribs

京都排骨饭

207) Stir-Fried Rice with Shrimp

虾仁炒饭

208) Noodles in Chicken Soup

鸡汤面

209) Japanese Noodle Soup with Seafood

海鲜乌冬汤面

210) Noodle Soup with Fish and Shrimp Balls

双丸汤面

211) Hand-Pulled Noodles with Marinated Chicken Leg

酱鸡腿拉面

212) Hand-Pulled Noodle Soup

拉面

213) Stir-Fried Rice Noodles

炒河粉

214) Steamed Rice Rolls with Pickled Vegetables and BBQ Pork

菜脯叉烧肠粉

215) Steamed Rice Rolls with Shrimps and Water Chestnuts

马蹄鲜虾肠粉

216) Stir-Fried Rice Noodles with Minced Pork

肉酱炒米粉

217) Stir-Fried Rice Noodles with Fish

and Pumpkin

金瓜鲔鱼炒米粉

Local Snacks 小吃

218) Jiaozi (Dumplings) Stuffed with Pork and Vegetables

菜肉饺子

219) Jiaozi Stuffed with Juicy *Scallop*

瑶柱灌汤饺

220) Jiaozi Stuffed with Duck Meat

四喜鸭茸饺

221) Jiaozi Stuffed with Seafood in Soup

海鲜汤饺

222) Baozi Stuffed with BBQ Pork

叉烧包

223) Pan-Fried Baozi Stuffed with Pork

生煎包

224) Baozi Stuffed with Red Bean Paste

豆沙包

225) Baozi Stuffed with *Taro* Bun

香滑芋茸包

226) Baozi Stuffed with Preserved Vegetable

雪菜包

227) Baked Scallion Pancake

葱油饼

228) Tuna Pancake

鲔鱼松饼

229) Deep-Fried Taro Pancake

芋头饼

230) Deep-Fried Corn Pancake

香脆贴饼子

231) Minced Pork and Fish Roe Pancake

饼香肉酱鱼子

232) Mushroom Shaomai

春菇烧卖

233) Shrimp Shaomai

鲜虾烧卖仔

234) Crispy Spring Rolls

脆皮春卷

235) Deep-Fried Spring Rolls with Sweet and Sour Sauce

酸甜炸春卷

236) Guotie (Pan-Fried Meat Dumplings)

锅贴

237) Guotie Stuffed with Pork

生煎锅贴

238) Deep-Fried Taro Cake

脆炸芋头糕

239) Water Chestnut *Jelly*

冻马蹄糕

240) Baked Fruit Cake

果皇糕

241) Mini Steamed and Deep-Fried Mantou

金银迷你馒头

242) Huajuan with Salt and Pepper

椒盐花卷

243) Huajuan with Scallion

小笼葱油花卷

244) Wotou with Black Rice (Steamed Black Rice Bun)

黑米小窝头

245) Assorted Seafood Congee

极品粥

246) Congee with Minced Pork and Preserved Egg

皮蛋瘦肉粥

247) BBQ Pork *Pastry*

叉烧酥

248) Pastry *Puff* Stuffed with Lotus Seed Paste and Egg *Yolk*

蛋黄莲蓉酥

249) Traditional Assorted Sweets, Beijing Style

京味什锦甜食

250) Bingtanghulu / Crispy Sugar-Coated Fruit (*haws*, *yam*, etc.) on a Stick

冰糖葫芦

10.2 Western Food

Appetizers, Starters, and Salads
头盘及沙拉类

251) Smoked *Salmon*

腌熏三文鱼

252) Caesar Salad

凯撒沙拉

253) Chicken Liver *Terrine* with *Morel*

鲜蘑鸡肝

254) Seafood Salad with Fresh Fruits

鲜果海鲜沙拉

255) Salad Nicoise

尼斯沙拉

Soups 汤类

256) Cream of Carrot Soup

奶油胡萝卜汤

257) Cream of *Asparagus* Soup

奶油芦笋汤

258) Mexican Chili Beef Soup

墨西哥辣味牛肉汤

259) Chilled *Avocado* Soup

牛油梨冻汤

260) Gazpacho

西班牙番茄冻汤

Poultry and Eggs 禽蛋类

261) Braised Goose Live in Red Wine

红酒鹅肝

262) Chicken Cordon Bleu

奶酪火腿鸡排

263) Braised Chicken with Red Wine

红酒烩鸡

264) Char-Grilled Chicken Breast

扒鸡胸

265) Scrambled Egg

熘糊蛋

Beef 牛肉类

266) Beef Stew

红烩牛肉

267) Grilled Rib-Eye Steak

扒肉眼牛排

268) Roast Sirloin Steak with Red Wine

西冷牛排配红酒少司

269) Braised Ox Tongue

烩牛舌

270) Osso Bucco

红烩牛膝

Pork 猪肉类

271) BBQ Spare Ribs

烧烤排骨

272) Smoked Spare Ribs with Honey

烟熏蜜汁肋排

273) Pork Piccatta

意大利米兰猪排

274) Pan-Fried Swiss Meat Loaf with *Pesto* Sauce

煎面包肠香草汁

275) Deep-Fried Spare Ribs

炸猪排

Lamb 羊肉类

276) Grilled Lamb Chops

扒羊排

277) Grilled New Zealand Lamb Chops

扒新西兰羊排

278) Roast Lamb Chops in Cheese and Red Wine

烤羊排配奶酪和红酒汁

Fish and Seafood 鱼和海鲜类

279) Grilled Salmon with *Lime* and Butter

三文鱼扒配青柠黄油

280) Grilled Red *Snapper* Fillet

煎红加吉鱼排

281) *Gratinated* Lobster in *Mornay* Sauce

奶酪汁龙虾

282) Deep-Fried *Squid* Rings

香炸西班牙鱿鱼圈

283) Gratinated *Mussels* with *Hollandaise* Sauce

荷兰汁青口贝

Noodles, Pasta, and Side Dishes

面、粉及配菜类

284) Macaroni with Seafood

海鲜通心粉

285) Cheese *Lasagna*

意大利奶酪千层饼

286) Roast Beef and Mushroom Pizza

烤牛肉蘑菇比萨

287) Cheese *Ravioli* in *Herbed* Cream Sauce

意大利奶酪馄饨

288) Stir-Fried Seafood Rice with Curry

咖喱海鲜炒饭

289) Chicken Burger

鸡肉汉堡包

290) Club Sandwich

俱乐部三明治

291) Mashed Potato

土豆泥

292) Braised Red Cabbage

烩红椰菜

Bread and Pastries 面包类

293) *Croissant*

牛角包

294) *Pita* Bread *Plain*

袋子包

295) Hard Roll

硬质面包

296) French *Baguette*

长法棍

297) Corn Bread

玉米面包

Cakes, Cookies, and Other Desserts

甜品及其他西点

298) Black Forest Cake

黑森林蛋糕

299) Strawberry Cheese Cake

草莓奶酪蛋糕

300) Italian Tiramisu

意大利提拉米苏

301) *Cranberry Muffin*

红莓松糕

302) Assorted Nuts Pie

干果派

303) *Macaroon*

蛋白杏仁甜饼

304) Lady Finger

手指饼

305) Chocolate Cookies

巧克力曲奇

10.3　Wines List

10.3.1　Chinese Alcoholic Drinks 中国酒

Yellow Wine 黄酒类

306) Caitan Huadiao Medium Sweet

陈年彩坛花雕

307) Shaoxing Huadiao (30 Years) Medium Sweet

绍兴花雕（30 年）

308) Nü'er Hong (12 Years)

女儿红（12 年）

309) Guyue Longshan

古越龙山

310) Qingci Huadiao (5 Years) Medium Sweet

青瓷花雕（5 年）

Liquor 白酒类

311) Beijing Chun

北京醇

312) Erguotou (56°)

二锅头（56 度）

313) Wuliangye (52°)

五粮液（52 度）

314) Xiaohutuxian (52°)

小糊涂仙（52 度）

315) Xiaojiaolou

小角楼

Beer 啤酒

316) Tsingtao Beer

青岛啤酒

317) Yanjing Beer

燕京啤酒

318) Snow Beer

雪花啤酒

319) Beijing Draft Beer

北京生啤

320) Harbin Beer

哈尔滨啤酒

Wine 葡萄酒

321) Changyu Castel (Year 1995)

张裕卡斯特干红（1995 年）

322) Changyu Sparkling Cider

张裕起泡酒

323) Great Wall Red Wine (Three-Star)

沙城长城干红三星

324) Xixia King Red Wine

西夏王世纪

325) Dynasty White Wine

王朝干白

10.3.2　Imported Wines 洋酒

Aperitif 开胃酒

326) Dubonnet

杜本内

327) Absinth

苦艾酒

328) Martini Dry, Italy

马天尼（干）

329) Pimm's No.1

飘仙 1 号

330) Cinzano Bianco, France

仙山露（半干）

Brandy 白兰地

331) Martell VSOP

马爹利 VSOP

332) Courvoisier XO, France

拿破仑 XO

333) Remy Martin XO

人头马 XO

334) Seagram's VO

施格兰 VO

335) Hennessy VSOP

轩尼诗 VSOP

Whisky 威士忌

336) Irish Whiskey

爱尔兰威士忌

337) Glenmorangie

格林莫瑞

338) Chivas Royal Salute

芝华士皇家礼炮

339) Long John

龙津

340) Famous Grouse (15 Years)

威雀威士忌（15 年）

Gin 金酒

341) Beefeater

必发达金酒

342) Gordon's

哥顿

343) Gibeys Special Dry Gin, London, England

基比路钻石金酒

344) Greenalls Original Dry Gin, London, England

健尼路金酒

Rum 朗姆酒

345) Bacardi Rum

百加得朗姆酒

346) Bacardi 151, Jamaica

百加得 151

347) Bacardi Light, Jamaica

百加得白朗姆酒

348) Captain Morgan Rum Dark

摩根船长（黑）

349) Dark Rum

黑朗姆酒

Vodka 伏特加

350) Zubrowka-Bison Brand Vodka, Poland

波兰祖布兰卡伏特加

351) Danzka Vodka, Denmark

丹麦伏特加

352) Finlandia Cranberry

芬兰酸蔓伏特加

353) Ketel One Vodka, Holland

荷兰伏特加

354) Absolut Kurrant Vodka, Sweden

瑞典伏特加（葡萄味）

Tequila 龙舌兰

355) Tequila Sauza

潇洒龙舌兰

356) Jose Cuervo Gold

豪帅快活金

357) Pepe Lopez Premiun Gold, Mexico

墨西哥雷博司金色龙舌兰

358) Sauza Tequila Blanco, Mexico

墨西哥索查银色龙舌兰

Liqueurs 利口酒

359) Baileys Irish Cream

百利甜酒

360) Crème de Menthe (Green)

薄荷酒

361) Crème de Cacao

可可甜酒

362) Blue Curacao

蓝橙

363) Sambuca

森布卡茴香酒

Sake 清酒

364) Sake

日本清酒

Beer 啤酒

365) Budweiser

百威啤酒

366) Grolsch

高仕啤酒

367) Corona

科罗娜啤酒

368) Heineken

喜力啤酒

369) Blue Ribbon

蓝带啤酒

Cocktails and Mixed-Drinks 鸡尾酒

370) Pink Lady

红粉佳人

371) B-52 (Baileys Kahlua, Cointreau)

轰炸机

372) Angel's Kiss

天使之吻

373) Bloody Mary (Vodka, Tomato Juice)

血玛丽

374) Singapore Sling

新加坡司令

Table Wine 餐酒

375) Red Wine

干红葡萄酒

376) Chateau Lafite Rothschild

拉菲古堡

377) Chateau Cos d'Estournel

埃思杜耐尔古堡

378) L. Jadot, Nuit Saint Georges

路易亚都酒庄 夜丘村

379) Gaja Sperss, Langhe

嘉雅酒庄 思波斯果园

380) Alion, Ribera del Duero

杜埃罗阿里安

381) Penfolds, Grange Bin 15 Shiraz

奔富酒庄 葛兰脂宾 15 西拉

382) Villa Maria, Cabernet Merlot

新玛利酒庄 赤霞珠 – 美乐

383) Almaviva, Maipo

费加罗之恋

384) Silver Oak, Cab-Sauv, Napa

银橡木酒庄 赤霞珠

385) Chateau De Meursault

摩梭古堡

386) Clos La Roquette, Chateauneuf-du-Pape

火箭酒庄 教皇新堡

387) Cervaro, Castello de Sala

萨拉古堡 芝华露

388) Rosemount, Roxburgh Chardonnay

玫瑰山庄 罗斯伯格 霞多丽

389) Villa Maria, Reserve Chardonnay

新玛利庄园 霞多丽特选

Champagne 香槟

390) Veuve Clicquot

黄牌香槟

391) Piper Heidsieck Brut

白雪香槟

392) Moet & Chandon Brut

酩悦香槟

393) Veuve Pelletier Brut

派拉蒂香槟

394) Crappa di Ca Marcanda Magari

曼歌果渣酒

Sherry 雪利酒

395) Cream Sherry

奶油雪利酒

396) Tio Pepe Dry

干雪利酒

397) Dry Sack

半干雪利酒

10.4 Drinks List

Mineral Water 矿泉水

398) Ice Dew Mineral Water

冰露矿泉水

399) Volcano Spring Mineral Water

火山泉矿泉水

400) La Vie Mineral Water

雀巢矿泉水

401) Watson's Spring Water *Distilled*

屈臣氏矿泉水

402) San Pellegrino Mineral Water

圣培露矿泉水

Coffee 咖啡

403) Blue Mountain Coffee

蓝山咖啡

404) *Instant* Coffee

速溶咖啡

405) Fresh *Ground* Coffee

现磨咖啡

406) Hazelnut Latté

榛子咖啡拿铁

407) Iced Peach Americano

蜜桃冰美式咖啡

408) Iced Strawberry Mocha

草莓冰摩卡咖啡

409) Coconut Coffee

椰香咖啡

Tea 茶

410) Green Tea

绿茶

411) Taiping Houkui Tea (Green Tea)

太平猴魁

412) Xihu Longjing Tea (Green Tea)

西湖龙井

413) Xinyang Maojian Tea (Green Tea)

信阳毛尖

414) Dahongpao Tea (Wuyi Mountain Rock Tea)

大红袍

415) Anxi Tieguanyin Tea (Oolong Tea)

安溪铁观音

416) Pu'er Tea

普洱

417) Earl Grey Tea

伯爵茶

418) Greengage Black Tea

梅子红茶

419) Chrysanthemum Tea

菊花茶

Tea Drinks 茶饮料

420) Iced Black Tea / Iced Green Tea

冰红（绿）茶

421) Iced Milk Tea

冰奶茶

422) Taro Milk Tea

芋香奶茶

423) Hot Lemon Tea

热柠檬茶

424) Iced Blueberry Tea

蓝莓冰茶

Juice 果蔬汁

425) Passion Fruit Juice

百香果汁

426) Melon and Lemon Juice

西柠蜜瓜汁

427) Huiyuan Pear Juice

汇源梨汁

428) Yam Juice

山药养生汁

429) Pineapple, Lemon, and Celery Juice

凤梨柠檬芹

Sodas 碳酸饮料

430) Coca-Cola / Coke

可口可乐

431) Coke/Sprite (Large)

大可乐 / 雪碧

432) Sprite

雪碧

433) Fanta

芬达

434) Ginger Ale

姜汁汽水

Mixed Drinks 混合饮料

435) Vodka & Sprite

伏特加雪碧

436) Vodka & Coke

伏特加可乐

437) Campari & Orange

金巴利橙汁

438) Peppermint Orange

绿薄荷橙汁

439) Fruit Punch

果汁宾治

Other Drinks 其他饮料

440) Fresh Milk

草原鲜奶

441) Chocolate Milkshake

巧克力奶昔

442) *Papaya* Milk with Egg Yolk

木瓜牛奶蛋黄汁

443) Carrot-Flavored Egg-Milk

胡萝卜蛋奶

444) Mint Julep Mixed with Sprite

雪利教堂

Ice 冰品

445) Banana and Orange *Blended* with Ice

香蕉柳橙搅滑冰

446) Lemon Blended with Ice

柠檬搅滑冰

447) Sorbet

冰沙

448) Parfait

巴菲

449) Sundae

圣代冰激凌

450) Green Tea Ice Cream

绿茶冰激凌

Vocabulary

marinate /ˈmærɪneɪt/ *v.* 腌制（肉）

mushroom /ˈmʌʃrʊm/ *n.* 蘑菇

sauce /sɔːs/ *n.* 酱汁；调味汁

ginger /ˈdʒɪndʒə(r)/ *n.* 姜

jellyfish /ˈdʒelifɪʃ/ *n.* 海蜇

web /web/ *n.* 蹼

slice /slaɪs/ *v.* 切片

scallion /ˈskæliən/ *n.* 葱

toss /tɒs/ v. 拌；震荡

plum /plʌm/ n. 梅子

wasabi /wəˈsɑːbi/ n. 日本芥末

shishamo n. 多春鱼

paste /peɪst/ n. 酱

turnip /ˈtɜːnɪp/ n. 萝卜

suckling /ˈsʌklɪŋ/ adj. 还在吃奶的（幼畜）

garlic /ˈɡɑːlɪk/ n. 大蒜

shrimp /ʃrɪmp/ n. 虾

spicy /ˈspaɪsi/ adj. 辛辣的

kidney /ˈkɪdni/ n. 肾；芸豆

fern /fɜːn/ 蕨菜

mash /mæʃ/ v. 把……捣成糊状

abalone /ˌæbəˈləʊni/ n. 鲍鱼

spare /speə(r)/ adj. 瘦的

griddle /ˈɡrɪdl/ n. 煎饼用的浅锅

mince /mɪns/ v. 绞碎

sizzle /ˈsɪzl/ v.（油煎）发出咝咝声

scramble /ˈskræmbl/ v. 炒；熘

brisket /ˈbrɪskɪt/ n. 胸肉

jelly /ˈdʒeli/ n. 果冻

cumin /ˈkʌmɪn/ n. 小茴香（子）；孜然

veal /viːl/ n. 小牛肉

refreshing /rɪˈfreʃɪŋ/ adj. 爽口的；提神的

casserole /ˈkæsərəʊl/ n.（有盖的）焙盘

mustard /ˈmʌstəd/ n. 芥末

shoot /ʃuːt/ n. 幼苗

poach /pəʊtʃ/ v. 水煮

bullfrog /ˈbʊlfrɒɡ/ n. 牛蛙

curd /kɜːd/ n. 凝乳

fin /fɪn/ n. 鱼翅

fungus /ˈfʌŋɡəs/ n. 木耳

broccoli /ˈbrɒkəli/ n. 西兰花；花椰菜

shank /ʃæŋk/ n. 小腿

chili /ˈtʃɪli/ n. 红番椒

pickle /ˈpɪkl/ v. 腌制（菜）

squash /skwɒʃ/ n. 南瓜

kelp /kelp/ n. 海藻；海草

spice /spaɪs/ v. 用香料调味

glutinous /ˈɡluːtənəs/ adj. 黏性的；胶状的

saturate /ˈsætʃəreɪt/ v. 浸透

aspic /ˈæspɪk/ n. 肉冻

sausage /ˈsɒsɪdʒ/ n. 香肠；腊肠

cube /kjuːb/ n. 方块状物；（肉）块

intestine /ɪnˈtestɪn/ n. 肠

rib /rɪb/ n. 肋骨

fillet /ˈfɪlɪt/ n. 无骨肉（鱼）片

curry /ˈkʌri/ n. 咖喱

tenderloin /ˈtendəlɔɪn/ n. 嫩腰肉

oyster /ˈɔɪstə(r)/ n. 蚝

scallop /ˈskɒləp/ n. 扇贝

kebab /kɪˈbæb/ n. 烤肉串

tangerine /ˌtændʒəˈriːn/ n. 橘子

chop /tʃɒp/ n. 排骨

tendon /ˈtendən/ n. 腱

truffle /ˈtrʌfl/ n. 野山菌；块菌

dice /daɪs/ v. 将……切成丁

sesame /ˈsesəmi/ n. 芝麻

custard /ˈkʌstəd/ n. 牛奶沙司；乳蛋糕；羹

venison /ˈvenɪsn/ n. 鹿肉

assorted /əˈsɔːtɪd/ adj. 各式各样俱全的

crab /kræb/ n. 蟹

maw /mɔː/ *n.* 动物的胃

vermicelli /ˌvɜːmɪˈtʃeli/ *n.* 通心粉细面条

prawn /prɔːn/ *n.* 对虾；明虾

delicacy /ˈdelɪkəsi/ *n.* 佳肴

roe /rəʊ/ *n.* 鱼卵；鱼子

wolfberry /ˈwʊlfberi/ *n.* 枸杞

bacon /ˈbeɪkən/ *n.* 培根；咸肉；熏肉

puff /pʌf/ *n.* 泡芙

haw /hɔː/ *n.* 山楂

salmon /ˈsæmən/ *n.* 三文鱼

morel /məˈrel/ *n.* 羊肚菌

avocado /ˌævəˈkɑːdəʊ/ *n.* 鳄梨

pesto /ˈpestəʊ/ *n.* 香蒜沙司；香蒜酱

snapper /ˈsnæpə(r)/ *n.* 鲷鱼

mornay /ˈmɔːneɪ/ *n.* 奶油蛋黄沙司

mussel /ˈmʌsl/ *n.* 淡菜；贻贝

lasagna /ləˈzɑːnjə/ *n.* 烤宽面（浇肉末茄汁）

ravioli /ˌræviˈəʊli/ *n.* 馄饨；（意式）方形饺

herbed /ˈhɜːbd/ *adj.* 用香草料调味的

pita /ˈpiːtə/ *n.* （中东地区和南美的）皮塔饼

baguette /bæˈget/ *n.* 法式长棍面包

muffin /ˈmʌfɪn/ *n.* 松饼

distill /dɪsˈtɪl/ *v.* 蒸馏

ground /ɡraʊnd/ *adj.* （食物）磨碎的

blend /blend/ *v.* 混合

turbot /ˈtɜːbət/ *n.* 比目鱼之一

broth /brɒθ/ *n.* 肉汤；清汤

herb /hɜːb/ *n.* 药草；香草

sear /sɪə(r)/ *v.* 使……干枯；烤焦

clam /klæm/ *n.* 蛤肉

specialty /ˈspeʃəlti/ *n.* 特色菜

pastry /ˈpeɪstri/ *n.* 面粉糕饼；馅饼皮

yolk /jəʊk/ *n.* 蛋黄

yam /jæm/ *n.* 山药

terrine /teˈriːn/ *n.* 肉糜

asparagus /əˈspærəɡəs/ *n.* 芦笋

gazpacho /ɡæzˈpætʃəʊ/ *n.* 西班牙凉菜汤

lime /laɪm/ *n.* 青柠

gratinate /ˈɡreɪtɪnət/ *v.* 使表面有一层浓汁

squid /skwɪd/ *n.* 鱿鱼

hollandaise /ˌhɒlənˈdeɪz/ *n.* 蛋黄奶油酸辣酱

croissant /ˈkrwæsɒ̃/ *n.* 新月形面包

plain /pleɪn/ *adj.* 素的

cranberry /ˈkrænbəri/ *n.* 小红莓

macaroon /ˌmækəˈruːn/ *n.* 蛋白杏仁甜饼干

instant /ˈɪnstənt/ *adj.* 速食的；即溶的

papaya /pəˈpaɪə/ *n.* 木瓜

词汇、课文资源

词汇、课文自测

微课

课堂练习

Appendix 附 录

术语

Learning Activities
（学习活动）

Chapter One Hospitality Basics
Lecture 1 Functions, Categories, and Ratings

Part I Word Study

*In this part, you are required to work by yourself selecting one word (in both **bold** and **italic** type) from the text to match its corresponding meaning. Read through the text carefully before making your choices. You can use **the self-study materials** we have provided or any reference book available as well as the Internet.*

No.	Explanations	Words
1	to have and please guests by providing foods, services, etc. 招待	
2	(of persons) standing above others in character or reputation 尊贵的	
3	management of lodging operations, food service operations, and other operations 酒店管理	
4	the act of providing a service in which people are housed temporarily 提供住宿	
5	the act of supplying food ready to eat, esp. for parties and banquets 提供餐饮服务	
6	way of spending free time in renewing health and spirits by enjoyment and relaxation 娱乐	
7	food prepared in a certain manner 菜肴	
8	a connection allowing access between persons or places 通信	
9	sth. designed to provide a particular convenience or service 设施	
10	a covered passageway with shops and stalls on either side 购物中心	
11	an object kept as a reminder of an event, trip, place, etc. 纪念品	
12	the business of providing services to tourists 旅游业；观光业	
13	effect on or communication with each other 互动交流；交际	
14	revenues over expenditures in a given period of time 收入	
15	the act of changing one thing for another thing 兑换	
16	pleasing to the senses of taste or smell 美味的；可口的	
17	the social act of getting together 聚会	
18	a formal dinner for many people in honor of a particular person or occasion 宴会	

Continued

No.	Explanations	Words
19	the scene of any event or action (esp. the place of a meeting) 会场	
20	the quality of being healthy 健康	
21	time available for ease and relaxation 休闲	
22	state of being an owner or the right of possession 所有权	
23	customers collectively 客户（总称）	
24	popular holiday center 度假胜地	
25	the service in which the clothes are washed and ironed 洗衣	
26	a manservant who acts as a personal attendant to his employer （照顾客人私人衣物的）服务员	
27	to improve the appearance of an area of land by changing the design and planting trees, flowers, etc. 美化景观	
28	an area of land or water where races are held 场地	
29	a place where games such as tennis are played 球场	
30	the act of using a room, building, or area of land, usually for a fixed period of time 入住率	
31	the money that an organization, etc. receives from its business 收入；所得	
32	to think about a problem or a situation and decide how you are going to deal with it 设法解决	
33	to change your behavior so that you can deal with a new situation better 迎合；顺应	
34	a set of rooms, esp. in a hotel 套房	
35	an arrangement in which several people own a holiday/vacation home together and each uses it at a different time of the year 分时使用度假房	
36	an apartment building in which each flat/apartment is owned by the person living in it but the building and shared areas are owned by everyone together （独立产权的）公寓	
37	the business of providing holidays and related services which are not harmful to the environment of the area 生态旅游	
38	a collection of information shown in numbers 统计数据	
39	a public building or room where people play gambling games for money 娱乐场；赌场	
40	management by overseeing the performance or operation of a person or group 监督；管理	
41	to increase or further improve the good quality, value, or status of sb./sth. 提高；增强	
42	to manage and organize the affairs of a company, an organization, a country, etc. 管理；执行	
43	a person who has an important job as a manager of a company or an organization 主管	
44	sb. who pays for goods or services 客户	
45	(of buildings) with full things needed for a particular purpose or activity 装备精良的	
46	to arrange people or things in groups according to their ability, quality, size, etc. 分级	
47	to make an action or a process possible or easier 使容易；使方便	
48	to place sb./sth. in a particular position on a scale in relation to similar people or things 定等级	
49	of services that are cheap and have no luxuries or extras 经济的	
50	low in price 廉价的；不贵的	

Part II Term Study

In this part, you are required to work by yourself writing out in Column B the Chinese meaning of each corresponding term in Column A. Read through the text carefully before

*completing this task. You can use **the self-study materials** we have provided or any reference book available as well as the Internet.*

No.	Column A	Column B
1	labor-intensive hospitality enterprise	
2	established standard	
3	office communication system	
4	hospitality industry	
5	tourism supplies	
6	external contact	
7	tourist destination	
8	tourism earnings	
9	foreign exchange earnings	
10	specialized venue	
11	center-city hotel	
12	golf course	
13	tennis court	
14	sales per room	
15	convention attendee	
16	occupancy rate	
17	lodging industry	
18	chain hotel	
19	all-suite hotel	
20	timeshare property	
21	condominium hotel	
22	seniors housing	
23	resort hotel	
24	extended-stay hotel	
25	economy/budget hotel	
26	casino hotel	
27	rating system	
28	the Ministry of Culture and Tourism	
29	economy service	
30	target market	

Part III Structure Study

*Work in class by yourself or in pairs. Look through the text and complete the following sentences with the correct forms of the words or phrases from the box. Then try to orally translate the sentences you have completed into Chinese. You can use **the self-study materials** we have provided or any reference book available as well as the Internet.*

A. as far as ... be concerned	B. stress an impact on	C. get the meaning of
D. be categorized by	E. make up	F. with the purpose of
G. focus efforts on	H. make ... public	I. fall into
J. make a contribution to	K. a wide selection of	L. provide ... with

1. This will help _____ the improving of service.

2. Chinese restaurants around the world often include _____ Cantonese dishes on the menu.

3. The Service Guide _____ us _____ all the information we need.

4. It is our duty to _____ protecting the environment.

5. Eco-hotels _____ low or no _____ the natural environment.

6. He returned to his homeland _____ serving his own people.

7. _____ the hotel functions _____, it can provide guests with safe and comfortable rooms and various delicious cuisines.

8. For a long time, we did not _____ these facts _____.

9. Business travelers _____ nearly half of the resort lodging market for large resort hotels with conference and convention facilities.

10. Hotels can _____ ownership as independent hotels and chain hotels.

Part IV Questions & Answers

In this part, you are required to read through the text carefully again, and discuss with your partners or group members on your short and brief answers to the questions upon the text before reporting your work to the class.

1. What are the basic hotel functions?

2. What can hotels be categorized into by location, ownership, or price?

3. What are the aims of rating hotels?

4. What are the hotel-rating systems currently applied in the world?

Lecture 2 Hotel Organization

Part I Word Study

*In this part, you are required to work by yourself selecting one word (in both **bold** and italic type) from the text to match its corresponding meaning. Read through the text carefully*

*before making your choices. You can use **the self-study materials** we have provided or any reference book available as well as the Internet.*

No.	Explanations	Words
1	a section of a large organization such as a government, business, university 部门；处；局	
2	connected with or involved in organizing the work of a business or an institution 行政的；管理的	
3	the activity or work done in an area of business or industry 经营	
4	a job, esp. an important one in a large organization 职位	
5	the act of making parts of sth., groups of people, etc. work together in an efficient and organized way 协调；协作	
6	to describe, draw, or explain sth. in detail 描绘；叙述	
7	things such as shopping centers or sports facilities that are provided for people's convenience, enjoyment, or comfort 便利设施	
8	a large and important unit or section of an organization 部门	
9	to deal with a situation, a person, an area of work or a strong emotion 处理；操作	
10	an arrangement for a seat on a plane or train, a room in a hotel, etc. to be kept for you 预订	
11	the department in a hotel, a hospital, an office building, etc. that is responsible for cleaning the rooms, etc. 管家	
12	detailed information on how to do or use sth. 指令	
13	the money that a person, a region, a country, etc. earns from work, from investing money, from business, etc. 收入	
14	any type of drink except water 饮料	
15	the right to sell sth. in a particular place（摊位）特许经营权	
16	a house, car, or piece of equipment that you can rent 租借	
17	a piece of work that sb. is asked to do and is paid for（业务）代办	
18	the activity of presenting, advertising and selling a company's products in the best possible way 营销推广	
19	the work involved in maintaining a good order and condition of the property 工程	
20	the work involved in keeping financial accounts 会计	
21	the work involved in protecting a country, building or person against attack, danger, etc. 安全	
22	a person who serves drinks behind a bar 酒保	
23	the activity and industry of showcasing things to people on television, in newspapers, on the Internet, etc. 广告	
24	to give things to a large number of people 分配；分布	
25	a piece of business that is done between people, esp. an act of buying or selling 事务；事项	
26	to find new people to join a company, an organization, the armed forces, etc. 招聘	
27	to direct sb./sth. towards a post, direction, etc. 定岗	
28	to form an opinion of the amount, value or quality of sth. after thinking about it carefully 评估	
29	to make sb. want to do sth., esp. sth. that involves hard work and effort 激励	
30	to give sth. to sb. because they have done sth. good, worked hard, etc. 给报酬	
31	to direct money, feelings, ideas, etc. towards a particular thing or purpose 集中（精力）；引导	
32	the quality of doing sth. well with no waste of time or money 效率	

Continued

No.	Explanations	Words
33	goods that are bought or sold; goods that are for sale in a shop/store 商品	
34	to arrange for sb. outside a company to do work or provide goods for that company 外包	
35	the act of keeping sth. in good condition by checking or repairing it regularly 维修；保养	
36	an official examination of business and financial records to see that they are true and correct 审计	
37	connected with cooking or food 烹饪的	
38	to provide a large meal, usu. for a special occasion, at which speeches are often made 设宴	
39	the activity of managing money, esp. by a government or commercial organization 财务	
40	to move sb. to a higher rank or more senior job 晋升	

Part II Term Study

*In this part, you are required to work by yourself writing out in Column B the Chinese meaning of each corresponding term in Column A. Read through the text carefully before completing this task. You can use **the self-study materials** we have provided or any reference book available as well as the Internet.*

No.	Column A	Column B
1	rooms division	
2	uniformed service	
3	revenue center	
4	cost center	
5	food & beverage division	
6	telecommunications department	
7	marketing and sales division	
8	human resources	
9	front office	
10	room service	

Part III Structure Study

*Work in class by yourself or in pairs. Look through the text and complete the following sentences with the correct forms of the words or phrases from the box. Then try to orally translate the sentences you have completed into Chinese. You can use **the self-study materials** we have provided or any reference book available as well as the Internet.*

A. arrange ... into ...	B. regardless of	C. take charge of
D. keep track of	E. split ... into ...	F. in operation
G. in line with	H. channel efforts to	I. be made up of
J. spread out		

1. I have ordered more dishes _____ what we decided yesterday.

2. He _____ the hospitality industry after graduation.

3. Our hotel _____ four managements and two operations.

4. The documents _____ four different levels by the importance.

5. Our hotel opens to anybody _____ religion or colour.

6. All the hotel facilities are _____ perfect _____.

7. The accounting division is responsible for _____ the business transactions that occur in the hotel.

8. Their chain hotels _____ across over one hundred cities.

Part IV Questions & Answers

In this part, you are required to read through the text carefully again, and discuss with your partners or group members on your short and brief answers to the questions upon the text before reporting your work to the class.

1. What are the two factors affecting a hotel's structure?

2. What is the hotel organizational structure like?

3. What is the linear functional system adopted in most hotels in China?

Lecture 3 Hotel Operating Models

Part I Word Study

*In this part, you are required to work by yourself selecting one word (in both **bold** and* *italic type) from the text to match its corresponding meaning. Read through the text carefully before making your choices. You can use **the self-study materials** we have provided or any reference book available as well as the Internet.*

No.	Explanations	Words
1	the act of a company's giving formal permission to sb. who wants to sell its goods or services in a particular area, or a government's giving formal permission to sb. who wants to operate a public service as a business 特许；出卖产销权	
2	involving doing sth. together or working together with others towards a shared aim 合作的；协作的	
3	(of sth., esp. property or equipment) used or let in exchange for rent or a regular payment 租用的	
4	to link a group, a company, or an organization very closely with another larger one 使隶属于	
5	the activity of presenting a brand to the public in a way that makes it easy for people to recognize or identify 品牌推广	

Continued

No.	Explanations	Words
6	expert knowledge or skill in a particular subject, activity, or job 专门技术（知识）	
7	money spent in doing a particular job, or for a particular purpose 费用；支出	
8	a book that tells you how to do or operate sth., esp. one that comes with a machine, etc. when you buy it 手册	
9	to agree to give sb. what they ask for, esp. formal or legal permission to do sth. 授予；许可	
10	a person or company that has been given a formal permission to sell goods or services in a particular area 特许经营人	
11	a company or an organization that gives sb. a formal permission to sell its goods or services in a particular area 授予特许者	
12	the opportunity or right to use sth. or to see sb./sth. 使用……之权利	
13	a company that sells a particular product 供应商	
14	a legal document giving official permission to do sth. 许可证	
15	to end; to make sth. end 终止	
16	to clean and decorate a room, building, etc. in order to make it more attractive, more useful, etc. 整修	
17	to remove or get rid of sth./sb. 消除	
18	a business project or activity, esp. one that involves taking risks 企业（项目）	
19	a business owned by two or more people who share the profits 合伙经营	
20	the condition in which a standard has been successfully established 标准化	
21	to state sth., esp. by giving an exact measurement, time, instructions, etc. 规定	
22	to accept advice, instructions, etc. and do what you have been told or shown to do 遵守	
23	the act of looking closely at sth./sb., esp. to check that everything is as it should be 检查；监督	
24	a condition in which everything is regular and unvarying 一致性	
25	somewhere to live or stay, often also providing food or other services 膳宿（服务）	
26	a statement, letter, etc. that shows that sth. is true, correct, or definite 确认；证实	
27	a room that is available in a hotel, etc. 空房	
28	that is not being used or is not needed at the present time 闲置的	
29	to promise to do sth. 保证	
30	commonly used or practiced; usual 习惯的；惯例的	

Part II Term Study

*In this part, you are required to work by yourself writing out in Column B the Chinese meaning of each corresponding term in Column A. Read through the text carefully before completing this task. You can use **the self-study materials** we have provided or any reference book available as well as the Internet.*

No.	Column A	Column B
1	franchising operations	
2	cooperative operations	
3	leased operations	

Continued

No.	Column A	Column B
4	management contract	
5	wholly-owned operations	
6	parent corporation	
7	central purchasing contract	
8	pooled advertising	
9	direct investment	
10	joint venture	

Part III Structure Study

*Work in class by yourself or in pairs. Look through the text and complete the following sentences with the correct forms of the words or phrases from the box. Then try to orally translate the sentences you have completed into Chinese. You can use **the self-study materials** we have provided or any reference book available as well as the Internet.*

A. be affiliated with	B. in return	C. in the name of
D. put up	E. grant access to	F. take over
G. have advantage over	H. result in	I. a couple of

1. She decided that I was the ideal person to _____ the Rooms Division.

2. They _____ the necessary capital to build the hotel with.

3. Only hotel VIPs _____ such facilities.

4. We're very glad to greet you _____ the Chinese people.

5. Our hotel _____ the multi-national corporation.

6. The hotel chains _____ individually owned and operated establishments.

7. The reform _____ tremendous change in the hospitality industry.

Part IV Questions & Answers

In this part, you are required to read through the text carefully again, and discuss with your partners or group members on your short and brief answers to the questions upon the text before reporting your work to the class.

1. What are the operating models commonly adopted in modern hospitality industry?

2. How do hotel chains operate and expand according to the text?

3. What are the advantages hotel chains have over individually-owned hotels?

Lecture 4 Hotel Guests, Guest Cycle, and Hotel Services

Part I Word Study

*In this part, you are required to work by yourself selecting one word (in both **bold** and **italic** type) from the text to match its corresponding meaning. Read through the text carefully before making your choices. You can use **the self-study materials** we have provided or any reference book available as well as the Internet.*

No.	Explanations	Words
1	things of no importance but daily use 杂物；日用品	
2	a part of sth. that is separate from the other parts or can be considered separately 部分	
3	an official group of people who have joined together for a particular purpose 协会；社团	
4	the act of telling sb. that sth. is good or useful or that sb. would be suitable for a particular job, etc. 推荐；建议	
5	to arrange with a hotel, restaurant, theater, etc. to have a room, table, seat, etc. on a particular date 预订	
6	a quantity of sth. or an amount of time that is considered as a single unit 团体；一组	
7	a business or an organization that provides a particular service esp. on behalf of other businesses or organizations 代理机构	
8	(of a place or situation) encouraging close, friendly relationships 舒适怡人的	
9	belonging to or for the use of a particular person or group; not for public use 私用的	
10	going about to look at places of interest 观光；游览	
11	a special right to do or say things without being punished 特权	
12	to move or to move sb./sth. to a new place to work or operate 搬迁	
13	lasting for a long time or for all time in the future; existing all the time 永久的	
14	sth. that is useful and can make things easier or quicker to do, or more comfortable 便利设施；便利品	
15	a small room or a space in a wall with a door that reaches the floor, used for storing things 衣帽间；储物间	
16	the act of asking questions in order to get some information 查询；询问	
17	to leave a place, esp. to start a trip 离开	
18	the written work that is part of a job, such as filling in forms or writing letters and reports 日常文书工作	
19	existing in large numbers 为数众多的	
20	to start doing a task or job 进行	
21	to travel to or around an area or a country in order to learn about it 考察	
22	a sum of money that is paid by sb. when they rent sth. and that is returned to them if they do not lose or damage the thing they are renting 押金	
23	listed or recorded officially 注册过的	
24	to cause sth. happen to you because of sth. you have done 招致；带来；引起	
25	a printed record of money paid, received, etc. 明细单	
26	a piece of paper that shows that goods or services have been paid for 收据	
27	to use machines and computers instead of people to do a job or task 使自动化	
28	to be connected with sth. using an interface（界面）接合	

Continued

No.	Explanations	Words
29	a statement about what will happen in the future, based on information that is available now 预报	
30	a written account of sth. that is kept so that it can be looked at and used in the future 记录	
31	to move from one place to another 转移；转送	
32	money available for a client to borrow 信用	
33	a piece of equipment, usually consisting of a keyboard and a screen that joins the user to a central computer system 终端	
34	agreement to, or permission for sth., esp. a plan or request 审批	
35	a book (or manuscript) consisting of large sheets of paper folded in the middle to make two leaves, esp. for accounting keeping（记账）本	
36	to make sth. begin 开始	
37	to transfer (entries) from one account book to another 登入（账）	
38	the process of testing the ability, quality or performance of sb./sth. esp. before you make a final decision about them 试用；试算	
39	the amount that is left after taking numbers or money away from a total 结余	
40	the act of preparing and sending bills to customers 结账；记账；编制账单	

Part II Term Study

*In this part, you are required to work by yourself writing out in Column B the Chinese meaning of each corresponding term in Column A. Read through the text carefully before completing this task. You can use **the self-study materials** we have provided or any reference book available as well as the Internet.*

No.	Column A	Column B
1	guest segment	
2	long-term stay guest	
3	corporate group	
4	travel agency	
5	sight-seeing trip	
6	peak season	
7	guest cycle	
8	tour operator	
9	tourist online service	
10	registered guest	
11	statement of charges	
12	thank-you note	
13	letters of confirmation	
14	daily expected arrival list	
15	revenue forecast list	
16	reservation record	
17	online credit authorization terminal	

Continued

No.	Column A	Column B
18	credit card approval	
19	electronic guest folio	
20	revenue outlet	
21	trial balance	
22	night auditor	
23	direct billing privilege	
24	guest history record	
25	catering service	
26	laundry service	
27	valuables deposit	
28	voice mail	
29	in-city travel	
30	beauty salon	

Part III Structure Study

*Work in class by yourself or in pairs. Look through the text and complete the following sentences with the correct forms of the words or phrases from the box. Then try to orally translate the sentences you have completed into Chinese. You can use **the self-study materials** we have provided or any reference book available as well as the Internet.*

A. in the business of	B. run into	C. transfer ... to ...
D. in general	E. be busy doing	F. in blocks
G. in addition to	H. a wide range of	

1. Mr. Jones works as a salesperson _____ selling conferences.

2. Those booking tables _____ get them at reduced rates.

3. Convention and association groups have a larger size, which can well _____ the thousands.

4. All the hotel employees _____ (prepare) for the large-scale conference in the coming week.

5. Guest purchases at different revenue outlets _____ appropriate guest accounts electronically.

6. In hospitality industry, there are _____ career opportunities open to young people.

Part IV Questions & Answers

In this part, you are required to read through the text carefully again, and discuss with your partners or group members on your short and brief answers to the questions upon the text before reporting your work to the class.

1. What are the guest segments making up the market for the hotel industry?

2. What are the top six factors for corporate individuals to base their choices of hotel on?

3. What is the fully-automated guest cycle?

Chapter Two Service Guide
Lecture 1 Hotel Profile, Welcome Speech, and Environment Commitment

Part I Word Study

*In this part, you are required to work by yourself selecting one word (in both **bold** and **italic** type) from the text to match its corresponding meaning. Read through the text carefully before making your choices. You can use **the self-study materials** we have provided or any reference book available as well as the Internet.*

No.	Explanations	Words
1	rich and superior in quality 豪华的；高级的	
2	produced or developed with a high level of skill and knowledge 尖端的；高级的	
3	very impressive or amazingly beautiful 令人眼花缭乱的	
4	to provide sb. with a room or place to sleep, live, or sit 供给住宿	
5	a thing that you must do as a formal or official part of a legal process, a social situation, etc. 程序；手续	
6	a small magazine or book containing pictures and information about sth. or advertising sth. 小册子；资料手册	
7	a description of sb./sth. that gives useful information 简介	
8	a promise to do sth. 承诺	
9	sth. that makes you think about or remember sb./sth. that you have forgotten or would like to forget 提醒；提示	
10	the character and atmosphere of a place 气氛	
11	a house built all on one level, without stairs 有凉台的房间；小屋	
12	a small tent used as a dressing room beside the sea or a swimming pool 平房小屋	
13	to furnish or equip 配备	
14	reminding you of sb./sth. 使人联想的	
15	the attractive and exciting quality that makes a person, a job, or a place seem special 魅力	
16	to give special importance to sth. 重点突出	
17	(of a person) pleased to welcome guests; generous and friendly to visitors 热情好客的	

Continued

No.	Explanations	Words
18	to get enjoyment from or take pleasure in 欣赏	
19	to eat a large amount of food, with great enjoyment 享受；享用	
20	(of sth.) having won a prize 应获奖的；一流的	
21	a restaurant serving grilled food 烧烤店	
22	to allow yourself to have or do sth. that you like 沉湎于；纵情于	
23	a public room in a hotel, club, etc. for waiting or relaxing in 休息室	
24	a trip to see or hunt wild animals 游览	
25	a short period of time that you spend doing one particular activity that you enjoy, but often too much of it 狂欢	
26	a person who is on vacation in a particular place 休假者	
27	a short holiday/vacation 短假	
28	to repair and paint an old building, a piece of furniture, etc. so that it is in good condition again 翻新	
29	to have a particular situation that affects you or happens to you 体验	
30	a thing that is added to sth. that is not usual, standard, or necessary and that costs more 额外的事物；另收费的东西	
31	to stick to, keep, or follow 遵守；坚持	
32	showing what you really think or feel 真诚的	
33	to fill with high spirits 使陶醉	
34	a pleasing combination of related things 和谐	
35	to travel between two places frequently 穿梭移动	
36	to say hello to sb. or to welcome them 迎接；恭候	
37	to become worse 恶化	
38	a series of planned activities that are intended to achieve a particular social, commercial, or political aim 运动；活动	
39	a small device that you press or move up and down in order to turn a light or piece of electrical equipment on and off 开关	
40	the act of buying and using products 消费；消耗	

Part II Term Study

*In this part, you are required to work by yourself writing out in Column B the Chinese meaning of each corresponding term in Column A. Read through the text carefully before completing this task. You can use **the self-study materials** we have provided or any reference book available as well as the Internet.*

No.	Column A	Column B
1	deluxe hotel	
2	registration formalities	
3	service guide	

No.	Column A	Column B
4	hotel profile	
5	welcome speech	
6	environmental commitment	
7	fire safety tip	
8	friendly reminder	
9	executive lounge	
10	wireless Internet access	
11	shopping spree	
12	family vacationer	
13	luxury lodging	
14	upscale extra	
15	winter resort	
16	greenhouse effect	
17	one-use item	
18	express service center	
19	safe disposal	
20	green consumption	

Part III Structure Study

*Work in class by yourself or in pairs. Look through the text and complete the following sentences with the correct forms of the words or phrases from the box. Then try to orally translate the sentences you have completed into Chinese. You can use **the self-study materials** we have provided or any reference book available as well as the Internet.*

A. an array of	B. go through	C. be reminiscent of
D. feast on	E. raise the bar on	F. abide by
G. take the lead in	H. be intoxicated with	I. in response to
J. be at service to do sth.	K. make an effort to do sth.	L. use up

1. More and more persons _____ quit smoking currently.

2. _____ their hospitality, we wrote a thank-you note.

3. These pictures _____ my work with Dongfang Hotel.

4. Café serves a diverse buffet with _____ salads, spaghetti, and fruits.

5. To address the problem, the hotel _____ food safety.

6. The hotel's software and hardware both _____ the hospitality industry locally.

7. Our staff always _____ make this your home away from home.

8. We _____ our eyes _____ the mountain scene atop the hotel building.

9. We shouldn't _____ the successes already won.

10. If you are in our hotel, you have to _____ our rules.

Part IV Questions & Answers

In this part, you are required to read through the text carefully again, and discuss with your partners or group members on your short and brief answers to the questions upon the text before reporting your work to the class.

1. What may be included in the Service Guide?

2. How can you prepare a Welcome Speech for a certain hotel?

3. What should we, as guests, do to respond to the Environment Commitment in the text?

Lecture 2 Hotel Rules and Regulations

Part I Word Study

*In this part, you are required to work by yourself selecting one word (in both **bold** and **italic** type) from the text to match its corresponding meaning. Read through the text carefully before making your choices. You can use **the self-study materials** we have provided or any reference book available as well as the Internet.*

No.	Explanations	Words
1	an official rule made by a government or some other authority 规章	
2	to create or prepare sth. carefully, giving particular attention to the details 制订	
3	intended to last for only a short time until sb./sth. more permanent is found 暂行的；暂时的	
4	a condition or an arrangement in a legal document 规定	
5	to do a piece of work, perform a duty, put a plan into action, etc. 执行；实行	
6	to protect sth./sb. from loss, harm, or damage; to keep sth./sb. safe 保卫；保障	
7	to show sth. or make sth. appear from somewhere 出示	
8	an official document that gives sb. the right to do sth., esp. for a limited period of time 许可证	
9	official papers or a document that can prove who you are 身份证明	
10	a person who makes deceitful pretenses 冒名顶替者	
11	a place where things can be stored 存储处	
12	easily able or likely to explode 爆炸的	
13	causing death or illness if swallowed or absorbed into the body 有毒的	
14	sending out harmful radiation 放射性的	

No.	Explanations	Words
15	involving risk or danger, esp. to sb.'s health or safety 危险的	
16	connected with a court, a judge, or legal judgement 司法的	
17	an official organization that is part of a larger organization and has a special purpose 机关；机构	
18	the area that surrounds the place you are in or are talking about 当地；本地	
19	the act of widespreading 传播	
20	sound or pictures that have been recorded on tape, video, etc. 录音录像制品	
21	a machine that is designed to do a particular thing in the home, such as preparing food, heating, or cleaning 电器	
22	to have or keep a particular power 保留	
23	to ask sb. questions about sth., esp. officially 询问	
24	to go against or refuse to obey a law, an agreement, etc. 违反	
25	done or happening as a normal part of a particular job, situation, or process 常规的；例行的	
26	an official examination of the facts about a situation, crime, etc. 调查	
27	connected with the punishment of people who break rules 惩戒的；纪律的	
28	a punishment for breaking a law, rule, or contract 处罚	
29	the state of being kept in a place, esp. a prison, and prevented from leaving 拘留	
30	a particular item or separate thing, esp. one of a set 物品	
31	an unpleasant smell in the air sensed by using the nose 气味	
32	all the buildings and land that it occupies in one place 室内；场地	
33	an amount of money 一笔款项	
34	action that makes you stop what you are doing, or that upsets the normal state that sth. is in 混乱	
35	a small meal or amount of food, usually eaten in a hurry 快餐	
36	a list of fixed prices that are charged by a hotel or restaurant for rooms, meals, etc., or by a company for a particular service 价目表	
37	a plan of action agreed or chosen by a political party, a business, etc. 政策；制度	
38	given free 免费赠送的	
39	a small piece of printed paper that you can exchange for sth. or that gives you the right to buy sth. at a cheaper price than normal 票券；优惠券	
40	(of payment) that will be paid back to you in certain circumstances 可退的	

Part II Term Study

*In this part, you are required to work by yourself writing out in Column B the Chinese meaning of each corresponding term in Column A. Read through the text carefully before completing this task. You can use **the self-study materials** we have provided or any reference book available as well as the Internet.*

No.	Column A	Column B
1	Fire Control Law of the People's Republic of China	
2	Interim Provisions on the Hospitality Industry Management	
3	Public Security Bureau	
4	personal security	
5	home-visit permit	
6	identification document	
7	key card	
8	judicial officer	
9	public affairs	
10	public security organ	
11	military unit	
12	rules and regulations	
13	routine room check	
14	disciplinary warning	
15	administrative detention	
16	lodging regulations	
17	check-in formalities	
18	assistant manager	
19	room tariff	
20	standard room	
21	business single room	
22	deluxe double room	
23	deluxe single room	
24	business suite	
25	extra bed	
26	service charge	
27	group rate	
28	room prepayment	
29	coupon holder	
30	half-day room user	

Part III Structure Study

*Work in class by yourself or in pairs. Look through the text and complete the following sentences with the correct forms of the words or phrases from the box. Then try to orally translate the sentences you have completed into Chinese. You can use **the self-study materials** we have provided or any reference book available as well as the Internet.*

A. in the depository of	B. prohibit ... from doing sth.	C. without prior notice
D. nothing but	E. in the locality of	F. present ... to ...
G. large sums of	H. for the sake of	I. reserve the right to do sth.

1. Few people are living _____ the resort hotel.

2. I fear that a prior engagement will _____ me _____ joining you in dinner.

3. They expended _____ money in maintaining the hotel.

4. The case is _____ the bellman.

5. We _____ lodge a claim for loss.

6. The hotel reserves the right to change the above room rates _____.

7. _____ safety, valuables, and large sums of cash money shall be stored in the depository of the hotel.

Part IV Questions & Answers

In this part, you are required to read through the text carefully again, and discuss with your partners or group members on your short and brief answers to the questions upon the text before reporting your work to the class.

1. What should we, as guests, do to respond to the Fire Safety Tips in the text?

2. What should we, as guests, do to respond to the Lodging Regulations in the text?

3. How much should a guest pay if he / she stays from 4:00 p.m. Monday to 4:00 p.m. Wednesday (Room rate: 260 yuan)?

Lecture 3 Front Office Services

Part I Word Study

*In this part, you are required to work by yourself selecting one word (in both **bold** and italic type) from the text to match its corresponding meaning. Read through the text carefully before making your choices. You can use **the self-study materials** we have provided or any reference book available as well as the Internet.*

No.	Explanations	Words
1	a van or small bus that takes people to and from an airport（用于接送的）中型客车	
2	a person in a hotel whose job is to help guests by giving them information, arranging theater tickets, etc. 礼宾	

Continued

No.	Explanations	Words
3	an extra telephone line connected to a central telephone in a house or to a switchboard in a large building 电话分机	
4	the system of money that a country uses 货币	
5	as large, fast, etc. as is possible, or the most that is possible or allowed 最大数的	
6	a book containing lists of information, usually in alphabetical order, for example people's telephone numbers or the names and addresses of businesses in a particular area 名录；指南	
7	the act or process of separating them so that they are no longer connected or linked in any way 断开	
8	the act of putting sth. in a wrong position 错放	
9	an extra amount of money that you must pay in addition to the usual price 附加费	
10	an amount of money that is taken off the usual cost of sth. 折扣	

Part II Term Study

*In this part, you are required to work by yourself writing out in Column B the Chinese meaning of each corresponding term in Column A. Read through the text carefully before completing this task. You can use **the self-study materials** we have provided or any reference book available as well as the Internet.*

No.	Column A	Column B
1	guest service manager	
2	airport transfer	
3	limousine rental	
4	DDD call	
5	IDD call	
6	wake-up service	
7	extended stay	
8	handling charge	
9	collect call	
10	the Ministry of Industry and Information Technology	

Part III Structure Study

*Work in class by yourself or in pairs. Look through the text and complete the following sentences with the correct forms of the words or phrases from the box. Then try to orally translate the sentences you have completed into Chinese. You can use **the self-study materials** we have provided or any reference book available as well as the Internet.*

A. be delighted to do sth.　　　　　　B. free of charge　　　　　　C. pay a visit to ...

D. be in use　　　　　　　　　　　　E. refer to

1. Could you tell me how long the hotel _____?

2. We can deliver meals to your room _____.

3. You may _____ the telephone guide if you want.

Part IV Questions & Answers

In this part, you are required to read through the text carefully again, and discuss with your partners or group members on your short and brief answers to the questions upon the text before reporting your work to the class.

1. What services does the front office offer according to the text?

2. What should a guest do if he / she wants to have a letter typed?

3. What should a guest do if he / she wants to extend his stay?

4. How does a guest make a call according to the telephone directory?

Lecture 4 Housekeeping Services

Part I Word Study

*In this part, you are required to work by yourself selecting one word (in both **bold** and **italic** type) from the text to match its corresponding meaning. Read through the text carefully before making your choices. You can use **the self-study materials** we have provided or any reference book available as well as the Internet.*

No.	Explanations	Words
1	to change sth. slightly to make it more suitable for a new set of conditions or to make it work better 调节	
2	the act of supplying fresh air and getting rid of dirty air 通风	
3	of or relating to a device that measures and controls the temperature of a machine or room, by switching the heating or cooling system on and off as necessary 温度调节装置的	
4	to fix equipment or furniture into position so that it can be used 安装	
5	to keep sth.; to continue to have sth. 保持；保留	
6	to put sth. into sth. else or between two things 插入	
7	that can be moved or pulled back into the main part of sth. 可伸缩的	
8	likely to decay or go bad quickly 易腐烂的；易变质的；易枯萎的	

Continued

No.	Explanations	Words
9	a person who takes care of babies or children while their parents are away from home and is usually paid to do this 临时保姆	
10	to demand or ask for sth. because you believe it is your legal right to own or to have it 认领	

Part II Term Study

*In this part, you are required to work by yourself writing out in Column B the Chinese meaning of each corresponding term in Column A. Read through the text carefully before completing this task. You can use **the self-study materials** we have provided or any reference book available as well as the Internet.*

No.	Column A	Column B
1	executive room	
2	high-speed Internet access	
3	daily routine	
4	thermostatic control switch	
5	multi-functional socket	
6	master switch	
7	magnetic key card	
8	VOD System	
9	Internal Movie Theater	
10	Lost and Found	

Part III Structure Study

*Work in class by yourself or in pairs. Look through the text and complete the following sentences with the correct forms of the words or phrases from the box. Then try to orally translate the sentences you have completed into Chinese. You can use **the self-study materials** we have provided or any reference book available as well as the Internet.*

A. of different styles   B. in advance   C. trust ... to ...

D. dispose of

1. If you need a babysitter, please contact the service center four hours _____.

2. She will have to _____ her pet _____ her neighbour's care while she is on holiday.

3. You did us a great favor by _____ that problem.

Part IV Questions & Answers

In this part, you are required to read through the text carefully again, and discuss with your partners or group members on your short and brief answers to the questions upon the text before reporting your work to the class.

1. What should a guest do if he / she finds the bed sheet dirty?
2. What should a guest do if he / she uses a 4-hour express laundry service?
3. What should a guest do if he / she needs a babysitter?
4. What should a guest do if he / she has a visitor?
5. What should a guest do if he / she has a medium-size pet?
6. What should the hotel do if a guest has left a necklace in the room?

Lecture 5 Food and Beverage Services

Part I Word Study

*In this part, you are required to work by yourself selecting one word (in both **bold** and **italic** type) from the text to match its corresponding meaning. Read through the text carefully before making your choices. You can use **the self-study materials** we have provided or any reference book available as well as the Internet.*

No.	Explanations	Words
1	a special food or product that is always very good in a particular place 特色（菜）	
2	showing or characterized by honor and integrity 尊贵的；体面的	
3	everything you can see when you look across a large area of land, esp. in the country 风景	
4	very pleasantly inviting 诱人的	
5	so good or impressive that nothing can be compared to it 无可比拟的	
6	known to be real and genuine and not a copy 纯真的；纯正的	
7	physical desire for food 胃口	
8	a menu having individual dishes listed with separate prices （照菜单）零点	
9	(of architecture) being or characteristic of the style in which ordinary people's houses are built in a particular region 民间风格的	
10	pasta in the shape of long thin pieces that look like string when they are cooked 意面	
11	to display or present its best advantage 展示	
12	one of the things from which sth. is made, esp. one of the foods that are used together to make a particular dish 成分；原料；配料	
13	a person who knows a lot about good food and wines and who enjoys choosing, eating, and drinking them 美食（家）	

Continued

No.	Explanations	Words
14	a shop/store or an organization that sells goods made by a particular company or of a particular type 店口；商店	
15	sweets/candy, chocolate, etc. 糕点；甜点	
16	good quality (grape) wine that was made in a certain year 葡萄（酒）	
17	a Chinese dish or meal consisting of small pieces of food wrapped in sheets of dough 点心	
18	of high quality 优质的	
19	a substance such as salt or pepper that is used to give flavor to food 调味品；佐料	
20	a drink usually made from a mixture of one or more strong alcoholic drinks and fruit juice 鸡尾酒	

Part II Term Study

*In this part, you are required to work by yourself writing out in Column B the Chinese meaning of each corresponding term in Column A. Read through the text carefully before completing this task. You can use **the self-study materials** we have provided or any reference book available as well as the Internet.*

No.	Column A	Column B
1	honorable guest	
2	à la carte	
3	takeaway outlet	
4	dim sum	
5	Chinese premium tea	
6	culinary condiment	
7	evening cocktail	

Part III Structure Study

*Work in class by yourself or in pairs. Look through the text and complete the following sentences with the correct forms of the words or phrases from the box. Then try to orally translate the sentences you have completed into Chinese. You can use **the self-study materials** we have provided or any reference book available as well as the Internet.*

A. in charge of	B. have a total of	C. pick up
D. on the go	E. combine ... with ...	F. place an emphasis on

1. The restaurant _____ the classic Cantonese cuisine _____ the creative Huaiyang cuisine.

2. The foreman here is _____ twenty workmen.

3. She, as a hotelier, had been _____ all day.

4. The hotel chains _____ ten thousand employees.

5. We should _____ our staff's social behavior.

Part IV Questions & Answers

In this part, you are required to read through the text carefully again, and discuss with your partners or group members on your short and brief answers to the questions upon the text before reporting your work to the class.

1. What services does the F&B offer in the hotel?

2. What should a guest do if he / she holds a Chinese wedding party of 300?

3. What should a guest do if he / she wants to enjoy a braised sliced abalone with mushrooms?

4. What should a guest do if he / she wants to have a buffet breakfast?

5. What should a guest do if he / she wants a takeaway?

6. What should a guest do if he / she wants a gift of culinary condiments for his / her friend?

7. What should a guest do if he / she wants to enjoy orchestra performance?

Lecture 6 Conference and Recreation Services

Part I Word Study

*In this part, you are required to work by yourself selecting one word (in both **bold** and italic type) from the text to match its corresponding meaning. Read through the text carefully before making your choices. You can use **the self-study materials** we have provided or any reference book available as well as the Internet.*

No.	Explanations	Words
1	that is easy to carry or to move 移动式的	
2	connected with or typical of the eastern part of the world, esp. China and Japan, and the people who live there 东方的	
3	working hard at sth. because it is very important to you 兢兢业业的；专注的	
4	a person who works in an office, working for another person, dealing with letters and telephone calls, typing, keeping records, arranging meetings with people, etc. 秘书	
5	a person who does a job that needs special training and a high level of education 专业人士	

Continued

No.	Explanations	Words
6	a small shop/store that sells fashionable clothes or expensive gifts 精品店	
7	a craft that requires skillful hands 手工艺品	
8	a game, an activity, etc. that provides entertainment and pleasure 娱乐（节目）	
9	a person whose job is to translate what sb. is saying into another language 口译人员	
10	having knowledge or skill in a particular job or activity 经验丰富的	

Part II Term Study

*In this part, you are required to work by yourself writing out in Column B the Chinese meaning of each corresponding term in Column A. Read through the text carefully before completing this task. You can use **the self-study materials** we have provided or any reference book available as well as the Internet.*

No.	Column A	Column B
1	multi-function room	
2	slide projector	
3	board meeting	
4	convention team	
5	service professional	
6	floor show	

Part III Structure Study

*Work in class by yourself or in pairs. Look through the text and complete the following sentences with the correct forms of the words or phrases from the box. Then try to orally translate the sentences you have completed into Chinese. You can use **the self-study materials** we have provided or any reference book available as well as the Internet.*

A. cover an area of	B. at maximum	C. a full set of

1. This in-hotel training course includes _____ lecture notes and exams with solutions.

2. This lobby hall holds seventy people _____.

3. The hotel _____ about 5,000 square meters.

Part IV Questions & Answers

In this part, you are required to read through the text carefully again, and discuss with your partners or group members on your short and brief answers to the questions upon the text before reporting your work to the class.

1. What facilities can be used for holding conferences?

2. In what place should a meeting of 60 be held?

3. In what place could conventioneers enjoy oriental charm?

4. What are the recreational services the hotel provides?

5. What should a guest do if he / she wants to enjoy a good night view of the harbor?

6. What should a guest do if he / she wants a gift of souvenir?

Chapter Three Hospitality Management
Lecture 1 Hotel Management

Part I Word Study

*In this part, you are required to work by yourself selecting one word (in both **bold** and italic type) from the text to match its corresponding meaning. Read through the text carefully before making your choices. You can use **the self-study materials** we have provided or any reference book available as well as the Internet.*

No.	Explanations	Words
1	the act or process of making plans for sth（制订）规划	
2	a time when a particular situation makes it possible to do or achieve sth. 机会	
3	the work or profession of an accountant 会计工作	
4	that gives sb. an advantage or a useful result 有利可图的；有益的	
5	to be in charge of sb./sth. and make sure that everything is done correctly, safely, etc. 指导	
6	to organize the different parts of an activity and the people involved in it so that it works well 协调；一致	
7	to provide people to work in a situation 员工安排；配置员工	
8	to control or be in charge of sb./sth. 指导	
9	to make sb. pleased by doing or giving them what they want 使满足	
10	progress in a job, social class, etc. 晋升	
11	living in a particular place 常住的	
12	the style in which the inside of a building is decorated 陈设；布置	
13	to find an acceptable solution to a problem or difficulty 解决	
14	to take or begin to have power or responsibility 承担	
15	a person who shares the ownership of sth. with others 共同所有者	

Continued

No.	Explanations	Words
16	a person who owns or manages a hotel 旅馆经营者	
17	to do things to help to make sth. successful 贡献	
18	to succeed in getting sth., usually after a lot of effort 获得	
19	past events which help explain why sth. is how it is 背景	
20	the series of jobs that a person has in a particular area of work, usually involving more responsibility as time passes 职业；生涯	

Part II Term Study

*In this part, you are required to work by yourself writing out in Column B the Chinese meaning of each corresponding term in Column A. Read through the text carefully before completing this task. You can use **the self-study materials** we have provided or any reference book available as well as the Internet.*

No.	Column A	Column B
1	hospitality management	
2	communications technology	
3	interpersonal skill	
4	sales and marketing skill	
5	finance and accountancy skill	
6	executive manager	
7	resident manager	
8	service norms	
9	routine spot check	
10	career advancement	

Part III Structure Study

*Work in class by yourself or in pairs. Look through the text and complete the following sentences with the correct forms of the words or phrases from the box. Then try to orally translate the sentences you have completed into Chinese. You can use **the self-study materials** we have provided or any reference book available as well as the Internet.*

A. hold the responsibility for	B. round the clock	C. see that ...
D. be linked to	E. range from ... to ...	F. on a ... basis
G. under the supervision of	H. take a ... seat	I. belong to

1. _____ all the doors are locked before you leave.

2. Room rates _____ £60 _____ £100.

3. Resident managers, in some large hotels, resolve problems _____.

4. Managers _____ ensuring that the rules are enforced.

5. Managers from all the departments are going to be meeting _____ regular _____.

6. In big hotels, each division operates by itself, but they all _____ each other tightly.

7. The division managers work _____ the top management.

Part IV Questions & Answers

In this part, you are required to read through the text carefully again, and discuss with your partners or group members on your short and brief answers to the questions upon the text before reporting your work to the class.

1. What are the duties of the hotel management?

2. What are the qualities an executive manager should have?

3. What is the routine work of a general manager?

4. How can you attain the position of manager?

Lecture 2 Hotel Human Resources Management

Part I Word Study

*In this part, you are required to work by yourself selecting one word (in both **bold** and italic type) from the text to match its corresponding meaning. Read through the text carefully before making your choices. You can use **the self-study materials** we have provided or any reference book available as well as the Internet.*

No.	Explanations	Words
1	always thinking of other people's wishes and feelings 考虑周到的	
2	showing kindness towards people and animals by making sure that they do not suffer more than is necessary 有人情味的	
3	to make or change sth. to suit the needs of the owner 使个性化	
4	to use your power, rights, or personal qualities in order to achieve sth. 行使	
5	how well or badly you do sth.; how well or badly sth. works 绩效	

Continued

No.	Explanations	Words
6	a judgement of the value, performance, or nature of sb./sth. 评估	
7	polite behavior that shows respect for other people 举止礼貌	
8	a person who makes a formal request for sth. esp. for a job, a place at a college or university, etc. 申请人	
9	to officially remove sb. from their job 开除	
10	moral principles that control or influence a person's behavior （职业）道德规范	
11	sth. that encourages you to do sth. 激励	
12	the fact of behaving in a way that you feel is right even though this may cause problems 凭良心	
13	of very little importance or size and not worth considering 可以忽略的；微不足道的	
14	sth. that you are trying to achieve 目标	
15	to organize and/or do a particular activity 实施；开展	
16	to find the size, quantity, etc. of sth. in standard units 测量	
17	advice, criticism, or information about how good or useful sth. or sb.'s work is 反馈	
18	the act of fixing value, or worth of 评估	
19	the rate at which a worker, a company, or a country produces goods, and the amount produced, compared with how much time, work, and money is needed to produce them 生产效率	
20	a person who is applying for a job 求职者	

Part II Term Study

*In this part, you are required to work by yourself writing out in Column B the Chinese meaning of each corresponding term in Column A. Read through the text carefully before completing this task. You can use **the self-study materials** we have provided or any reference book available as well as the Internet.*

No.	Column A	Column B
1	service enterprise	
2	customized service	
3	administrative function	
4	performance appraisal system	
5	salary system	
6	benefits system	
7	work ethics	
8	in-house training program	
9	on-the-job coaching	
10	career development program	

Part III Structure Study

Work in class by yourself or in pairs. Look through the text and complete the following sentences with the correct forms of the words or phrases from the box. Then try to orally *translate the sentences you have completed into Chinese. You can use **the self-study materials** we have provided or any reference book available as well as the Internet.*

A. be laid on as	B. put ... in the right job	C. keep a watchful eye on
D. stick around	E. in good conscience	F. give ... feedback on
G. care about	H. work on	I. work out

1. We have to _____ the progress of the case.

2. It is a must for us all to work _____.

3. The HR will _____ you _____ your performance.

4. A good HR division can help a hotel meet guests' expectations by _____ the right people _____.

5. The human resources management should _____ a special emphasis in hotels.

6. A clear progression plan to advance to higher levels can also be a good incentive for employees to _____.

7. You don't _____ anything but yourself.

Part IV Questions & Answers

In this part, you are required to read through the text carefully again, and discuss with your partners or group members on your short and brief answers to the questions upon the text before reporting your work to the class.

1. What are the administrative functions of the HR division?

2. How can we understand the importance of the human resources management?

3. How does the HR management carry out training programs?

4. What are the contents of a sound HR program according to Rocco M. Angelo and Andrew N. Vladimir?

Lecture 3 Hotel Finance Management

Part I Word Study

*In this part, you are required to work by yourself selecting one word (in both **bold** and *italic* type) from the text to match its corresponding meaning. Read through the text carefully*

*before making your choices. You can use **the self-study materials** we have provided or any reference book available as well as the Internet.*

No.	Explanations	Words
1	to provide money for a project 融资；提供资金	
2	the act of giving or delivering sth. to a number of people 分配	
3	to give sth. to sb., usually officially 开具（发票）	
4	a list of goods that have been sold, work that has been done etc., showing what you must pay 发票	
5	a person whose job is to keep an accurate record of the accounts of a business 记账员	
6	the continuous supply of sth. 流；持续供应	
7	(usually following a noun of bills, accounts, etc.) for which money has not yet been received 应收的	
8	the fact of a series of events being repeated many times, always in the same order 循环；周期	
9	the quality of affording gain or benefit or profit 盈利能力	
10	a statement of how much a piece of work will probably cost 估算	
11	a book in which a bank, a business, etc. records the money it has paid and received 分类账	
12	(bookkeeping) listing expenses, charges, transactions, etc. on the company's records 过账	
13	a period of time worked by a group of workers who start work as another group finishes 轮班；班次	
14	all the goods in a shop 库存；存量表	
15	to explain the meaning of sth. 解释	
16	to say what you think will happen in the future based on information that you have now 预测；预报	
17	to provide a computer or computers to do the work of sth. 使计算机化	
18	to make oneself subject to, bring upon oneself, or become liable to 引致；带来	
19	extremely important because a future situation will be affected by it 关键的；紧要的	
20	to make problems or difficulties disappear 消除（问题）；克服（困难）	

Part II Term Study

*In this part, you are required to work by yourself writing out in Column B the Chinese meaning of each corresponding term in Column A. Read through the text carefully before completing this task. You can use **the self-study materials** we have provided or any reference book available as well as the Internet.*

No.	Column A	Column B
1	finance management	
2	financing management	
3	investment management	
4	cost control	
5	revenue management	

No.	Column A	Column B
6	profit distribution management	
7	financial transaction	
8	staff manager	
9	financial accounting information	
10	cash flow	
11	bill payment	
12	accounts receivable	
13	cash flow management	
14	financial accounting report	
15	budget estimate	
16	cost estimate	
17	financial record	
18	capital inventory	
19	financial statement	
20	daily operating report	

Part III Structure Study

*Work in class by yourself or in pairs. Look through the text and complete the following sentences with the correct forms of the words or phrases from the box. Then try to orally translate the sentences you have completed into Chinese. You can use **the self-study materials** we have provided or any reference book available as well as the Internet.*

> A. give advice on   B. smooth out   C. be key in doing sth.
> D. bring ... into line with ...   E. result from   F. go through

1. He was _____ differences with other managers.

2. Many health problems _____ what you eat.

3. We need to modify that plan somewhat to _____ it _____ the others.

4. Sales promotion materials _____ (implement) hotel sales strategies.

5. The CFO is able to _____ managers _____ how to increase profits

Part IV Questions & Answers

In this part, you are required to read through the text carefully again, and discuss with your partners or group members on your short and brief answers to the questions upon the text before reporting your work to the class.

1. What are the administrative functions of the finance division?

2. What are the responsibilities of a CFO?

3. What are the responsibilities of the finance team?

4. What are the features of the hotel accounting?

Lecture 4 Hotel Engineering Management

Part I Word Study

*In this part, you are required to work by yourself selecting one word (in both **bold** and **italic** type) from the text to match its corresponding meaning. Read through the text carefully before making your choices. You can use **the self-study materials** we have provided or any reference book available as well as the Internet.*

No.	Explanations	Words
1	the cost or process of keeping sth. in good condition 维护；保养	
2	the act or process of sth. (esp. tools, machines, properties, etc.) becoming worse in quality, value, use, etc. 折旧	
3	to keep sth. in its original state in good condition 保持	
4	the impression that a person, an organization, or a product, etc. gives to the public 形象	
5	a reduction in the amount of time or money that is used or needed 节省开支	
6	to arrange sth. in groups according to features that they have in common 分类；归类	
7	the process of cooling or freezing (e.g. food) for preservative purposes 制冷	
8	to put (the air inside the room or house) into a better state 调节	
9	a thing of value, esp. property, that a person or company owns, which can be used or sold to pay debts 资产	
10	to include a large number or range of things 包含	
11	an extremely large number of sth. 极大数量	
12	a necessary or typical part of sth. 要素	
13	needing great effort and energy 费力的；艰苦的	
14	a state of being essentially equal or equivalent; equally balanced 相等	
15	used water and waste substances that are produced by human bodies, that are carried away from houses and factories through special pipes 污水	
16	intended to try to stop sth. that causes problems or difficulties from happening 预防的	
17	to praise sb./sth., usually publicly 嘉奖	
18	a service provided for the public, for example an electricity, water, or gas supply 公共设施	
19	to examine (a machine) and make any necessary repairs 维护	
20	management by watching the performance or operation of a person or group 监管	

Part II Term Study

*In this part, you are required to work by yourself writing out in Column B the Chinese meaning of each corresponding term in Column A. Read through the text carefully before completing this task. You can use **the self-study materials** we have provided or any reference book available as well as the Internet.*

No.	Column A	Column B
1	physical upkeep	
2	physical deterioration	
3	fire alarm	
4	equipment-asset management	
5	equipment operation and maintenance	
6	electrical distribution	
7	sewage and water system	
8	preventive maintenance	
9	scheduled maintenance	
10	electrical leak	

Part III Structure Study

*Work in class by yourself or in pairs. Look through the text and complete the following sentences with the correct forms of the words or phrases from the box. Then try to orally translate the sentences you have completed into Chinese. You can use **the self-study materials** we have provided or any reference book available as well as the Internet.*

> A. have an impact on   B. to a minimum   C. a myriad of
>
> D. see to   E. in the equation   F. behind the scenes
>
> G. be on-call to do sth.   H. be commended for   I. be expected to do sth.

1. Hotel clerks can only _____ (do) what is reasonable and practicable.

2. It is said the two hotels are good _____.

3. The general manager's speech _____ profound _____ everyone.

4. The hotel had three weeks to make _____ arrangements.

5. Office machinery is kept _____.

6. You go ahead with the formalities. I'll _____ the heavy luggage.

7. All the medical workers _____ (head) for the disaster area.

Part IV Questions & Answers

In this part, you are required to read through the text carefully again, and discuss with your partners or group members on your short and brief answers to the questions upon the text before reporting your work to the class.

1. Why is the physical upkeep of the hotel facilities so important?

2. What systems are the hotel facilities classified into?

3. What are the contents of the hotel engineering management?

4. How do the engineering workers perform their maintenance work?

Lecture 5 Hotel Security Management

Part I Word Study

*In this part, you are required to work by yourself selecting one word (in both **bold** and **italic** type) from the text to match its corresponding meaning. Read through the text carefully before making your choices. You can use **the self-study materials** we have provided or any reference book available as well as the Internet.*

No.	Explanations	Words
1	a person or thing that is likely to cause trouble, danger, etc. 威胁	
2	not wanted 不受欢迎的；讨厌的	
3	to go around an area or a building at regular times to check that it is safe and that there is no trouble 巡逻；巡查	
4	the act of carefully watching a person suspected of a crime or a place where a crime may be committed 监视	
5	having the practical knowledge or skills to do sth. 有资格的；称职的	
6	a document showing to the truth of certain stated facts 证书	
7	the act of stopping sth. bad from happening 预防	
8	fighting or a fight, esp. during a time of war 搏击；搏斗	
9	the work of investigating a crime in order to find out what has happened and who committed it 侦查	
10	the crime of stealing money or goods from a bank, shop/store, person, etc., often by using violence or threats 抢劫	
11	connected with or involving crime 违法犯罪的	
12	a person whose job is dealing with people arriving at or leaving a hotel 职员	
13	making you feel that sth. is wrong, illegal, or dishonest 可疑的	
14	a sudden serious and dangerous event or situation which needs immediate action to deal with it 突发情况	
15	the things that you own which can be moved, for example not land or buildings 财产；所有物	
16	very careful to notice any signs of danger or trouble 警惕的	

Continued

No.	Explanations	Words
17	a situation in which people, groups, or countries are involved in a serious disagreement or argument 冲突	
18	connected with the act of attacking sb./sth. 攻击性的	
19	the act of ensuring observance of or obedience to 执（法）	
20	the act of leaving a place in an orderly fashion esp. for protection 撤离；疏散	

Part II Term Study

*In this part, you are required to work by yourself writing out in Column B the Chinese meaning of each corresponding term in Column A. Read through the text carefully before completing this task. You can use **the self-study materials** we have provided or any reference book available as well as the Internet.*

No.	Column A	Column B
1	crime prevention	
2	crime detection	
3	response procedure	
4	emergency exit	
5	access control	
6	security professional	
7	law enforcement official	
8	closed-circuit television	
9	fire-fighting equipment	
10	evacuation plan	

Part III Structure Study

*Work in class by yourself or in pairs. Look through the text and complete the following sentences with the correct forms of the words or phrases from the box. Then try to orally translate the sentences you have completed into Chinese. You can use **the self-study materials** we have provided or any reference book available as well as the Internet.*

A. go through   B. keep sb. from doing   C. lay emphasis on
D. be familiar with   E. make sth. known to sb.   F. serve sth. to sb.
G. in a(n) ... voice   H. make rounds of   I. gain access to

1. The security staff _____ the premises every 30 minutes.

2. It is difficult for a non-resident to _____ the guestroom blocks.

3. His only thought was to _____ the guest _____ (harm).

4. The hotel was _____ a very difficult time.

5. We should _____ efficiency and fairness both.

6. The guest talked to the attendant _____ angry _____.

7. Reservations staff should _____ the procedures and related knowledge concerning reservation, sales, and reception.

Part IV Questions & Answers

In this part, you are required to read through the text carefully again, and discuss with your partners or group members on your short and brief answers to the questions upon the text before reporting your work to the class.

1. What is the job of the security staff?

2. What are the two important things that can ensure the safety?

3. What is the comprehensive security program according to Rocco M. Angelo and Andrew N. Vladimir?

Lecture 6 Hotel Marketing Management

Part I Word Study

*In this part, you are required to work by yourself selecting one word (in both **bold** and italic type) from the text to match its corresponding meaning. Read through the text carefully before making your choices. You can use **the self-study materials** we have provided or any reference book available as well as the Internet.*

No.	Explanations	Words
1	a plan that is intended to achieve a particular purpose 策略	
2	to find or discover sb./sth. 发现；找到	
3	to make a judgement about the nature or quality of sb./sth. 评估	
4	a quality or an ability that a person or thing has that gives them an advantage 优势	
5	the state or quality of being recognized or acknowledged 认知度；知名度	
6	the ability to measure very small changes 敏感性；感受性	
7	to control or influence how sth. happens 影响；决定	
8	to tell the public about a product or a service in order to encourage people to buy or to use it 广告；宣传	
9	to limit the size, amount, or range of sth. 限制	

No.	Explanations	Words
10	the reporting of news and sport in newspapers and on the radio and television 新闻报道	
11	a famous person 名人；社会名流	
12	a scene in a film/movie that is filmed continuously by one camera 镜头；画面	
13	connected with a charity or charities 慈善的	
14	sth. that is given to a person or an organization such as a charity, in order to help them 捐赠	
15	all the people who live in a particular area, country, etc. when talked about as a group 社区	
16	good or useful 正面的；积极的	
17	an increase in the amount or number of sth. that there is, or in the area that is affected by sth. 传播	
18	bad or harmful 消极的；负面的	
19	a way of behaving towards or dealing with a person or thing 对待	
20	the attention that is given to sb./sth. by newspapers, television, etc. 宣传	

Part II Term Study

*In this part, you are required to work by yourself writing out in Column B the Chinese meaning of each corresponding term in Column A. Read through the text carefully before completing this task. You can use **the self-study materials** we have provided or any reference book available as well as the Internet.*

No.	Column A	Column B
1	marketing research	
2	marketing strategy	
3	corporate image strategy	
4	marketing management	
5	prospective customer	
6	business promotion	
7	target customer group	
8	advertising strategy	
9	brand recognition	
10	business opportunity	
11	sports event	
12	advertising media	
13	direct advertising	
14	radio campaign	
15	television coverage	
16	television shot	
17	public relations management	
18	charitable donation	
19	community work	
20	damage control	

Part III Structure Study

*Work in class by yourself or in pairs. Look through the text and complete the following sentences with the correct forms of the words or phrases from the box. Then try to orally translate the sentences you have completed into Chinese. You can use **the self-study materials** we have provided or any reference book available as well as the Internet.*

A. distinguish ... from ...	B. have a sensitivity of	C. seek for
D. in the form of	E. restrict ... to ...	F. make ... aware of
G. maintain a(n) ... relationship with	H. take the form of	I. have trouble with

1. We _____ aware of the potential problems.
2. He _____ great _____ the overseas lodging market.
3. The hotel received a benefit _____ a tax reduction.
4. State-owned economy _____ state-owned enterprises in reality.
5. Every hotel _____ itself _____ others.
6. We have to _____ an experienced manager to fill the post.
7. The division managers seem to _____ good working _____ the top management.

Part IV Questions & Answers

In this part, you are required to read through the text carefully again, and discuss with your partners or group members on your short and brief answers to the questions upon the text before reporting your work to the class.

1. What are the contents of the hotel marketing management?
2. What are the activities of the sales & marketing division?
3. What are the functions of the sales & marketing division?

Chapter Four Rooms Division

Lecture 1 Front Office Department (4.1.1 Overview of Front Office Department)

Part I Word Study

*In this part, you are required to work by yourself selecting one word (in both **bold** and **italic** type) from the text to match its corresponding meaning. Read through the text carefully*

*before making your choices. You can use **the self-study materials** we have provided or any reference book available as well as the Internet.*

No.	Explanations	Words
1	an idea, a feeling, or an opinion that you get about sb./sth., or that sb./sth. gives you 印象	
2	the formal rules of correct or polite behavior in society or among members of a particular profession 礼仪	
3	a statement that sb. makes saying that they are not satisfied 投诉	
4	any type of vehicle that you can travel in or carry goods in 交通车辆	
5	to record your/sb.'s/sth.'s name on an official list 登记	
6	to pay the money that you owe 结算	
7	to do or have what is required or necessary 履行	
8	sth. that you think is more important than other things and should be dealt with first 重点；优先	
9	having a rank below a senior person and helping them in their work 副的；辅助的	
10	having less power or authority than sb. else in a group or an organization 下级的；次要的	

Part II Term Study

*In this part, you are required to work by yourself writing out in Column B the Chinese meaning of each corresponding term in Column A. Read through the text carefully before completing this task. You can use **the self-study materials** we have provided or any reference book available as well as the Internet.*

No.	Column A	Column B
1	formal education	
2	general knowledge	
3	equipment skill	
4	room status	
5	guest shuttling	
6	guest history record	
7	valuables deposit	
8	guest satisfaction	
9	guest expectation	
10	guest relations	

Part III Structure Study

*Work in class by yourself or in pairs. Look through the text and complete the following sentences with the correct forms of the words or phrases from the box. Then try to orally translate the sentences you have completed into Chinese. You can use **the self-study materials** we have provided or any reference book available as well as the Internet.*

A. act as	B. have contact with	C. have a demand for
D. be considered as	E. take place	F. be composed of
G. give access to	H. have control over	I. act in sb.'s place
J. on behalf of	K. hold responsibility for	L. on duty

1. The rooms division _____ the most frequent _____ guests.

2. Our hotel _____ the best in our locality.

3. The hotel has adapted these facilities to _____ wheelchair users.

4. Miss White _____ the operation of the front office department.

5. The lobby manager can handle complaints _____ the general manager when he is off duty.

6. John will _____ a deputy for me during my absence.

7. The houses of the hotel chiefly _____ wood.

8. Mr. Wang will _____ while I am out.

9. In recruiting, a hotel should _____ higher _____ work experience.

10. In big luxury hotels, a guest relations dean _____ special _____ establishing and maintaining good relationship with guests.

Part IV Questions & Answers

In this part, you are required to read through the text carefully again, and discuss with your partners or group members on your short and brief answers to the questions upon the text before reporting your work to the class.

1. What is the front office department composed of?

2. What are the major functions by the front office department?

3. What is the routine work of the front office department?

4. How can the rooms division ensure guest satisfaction?

5. What are the duties of the front office management?

Lecture 2 Front Office Department (4.1.2 Front Desk, 4.1.3 Room Reservations Desk)

Part I Word Study

*In this part, you are required to work by yourself selecting one word (in both **bold** and* *italic type) from the text to match its corresponding meaning. Read through the text carefully before making your choices. You can use **the self-study materials** we have provided or any reference book available as well as the Internet.*

No.	Explanations	Words
1	the leader of a group of people, esp. a sports team 领班；主管	
2	to make a formal judgement about the value of a person's work, usually after a discussion with them about it 考核；鉴定	
3	to set up on a firm or lasting basis 确定	
4	to give sb. sth. that they can use 分配	
5	empty, with nobody living there or using it 空闲的；没人住的	
6	an official examination of business and financial records to see that they are true and correct 审计；查账	
7	to bring into agreement 使一致；使相符	
8	to make sth. easier to do or understand 使简化；使简单	
9	to go with sb. to protect or guard them or to show them the way 护送；陪同	
10	a small shop/store, open at the front, where newspapers, drinks, etc. are sold 亭子	
11	to be equal to sth. to be sth. 相当于	
12	great skillfulness and knowledge of some subject or activity 掌握	
13	a clerk in the hospital who is in charge of reservation at desk 预订人员	
14	the use of the telephone as an interactive medium for promotion and sales 电话推销	
15	to tell a customer how much money you will charge them for a job, service, or product 报价	
16	to deal officially with a document, request, etc. 处理	
17	a formal (often written) request for sth., such as a job, permission to do sth. or a place at a college or university 申请表格；申请单	
18	furniture and appliances and other movable accessories that make a home (or other area) livable 陈设	
19	to refuse politely to accept or to do sth. 婉拒	
20	to change your opinions or plans, for example because of sth. you have learned 修改；修正	

Part II Term Study

*In this part, you are required to work by yourself writing out in Column B the Chinese meaning of each corresponding term in Column A. Read through the text carefully before completing this task. You can use **the self-study materials** we have provided or any reference book available as well as the Internet.*

No.	Column A	Column B
1	check-in registration	
2	information enquiry	
3	accounts settlement	
4	method of payment	

Continued

No.	Column A	Column B
5	direct billing	
6	night audit	
7	telemarketing personnel	
8	communication link	
9	reservation application	
10	room status	

Part III Structure Study

*Work in class by yourself or in pairs. Look through the text and complete the following sentences with the correct forms of the words or phrases from the box. Then try to orally translate the sentences you have completed into Chinese. You can use **the self-study materials** we have provided or any reference book available as well as the Internet.*

A. sign in	B. inform sb. of/about sth.	C. reconcile ... with ...
D. escort sb. to sp.	E. feel at home	F. on real time
G. make sure of	H. be divided into	

1. All the participants were required to _____ as they entered the hall to attend the meeting.

2. Waitresses are very friendly, which makes us _____.

3. As a hotel policy, a porter will _____ you _____ your room.

4. It was hard to _____ his career ambitions _____ the needs of his children.

5. With technology development, the reservation desk can, _____, be informed of the number and types of rooms available.

6. Reservationists must _____ guest reqirements.

Part IV Questions & Answers

In this part, you are required to read through the text carefully again, and discuss with your partners or group members on your short and brief answers to the questions upon the text before reporting your work to the class.

1. What are the sections the front desk is divided into in larger hotels?

2. What are in the charge of the front desk captain?

3. What are the duties of front desk agents?

4. What are the qualities necessary for a good reservationist?

5. What are the six stages of the reservation process?

Lecture 3 Front Office Department

(4.1.4 Reception Desk, 4.1.5 Information Desk, 4.1.6 Business Center)

Part I Word Study

*In this part, you are required to work by yourself selecting one word (in both **bold** and **italic** type) from the text to match its corresponding meaning. Read through the text carefully before making your choices. You can use **the self-study materials** we have provided or any reference book available as well as the Internet.*

No.	Explanations	Words
1	the quality of being at hand when needed 可用性	
2	a job that you do for sb. that involves going somewhere to take a message, to buy sth., to deliver goods, etc. 杂事；差事	
3	a person whose job is carrying people's bags and other loads, esp. at a train station, an airport or in a hotel 行李员	
4	to send a letter, package, or message somewhere 派遣；派件	
5	ability to work with skill 熟练；精通	
6	an object or a piece of equipment that has been designed to do a particular job 设备	
7	the act of giving or receiving official information about sth. 通知	
8	speaking or using several different languages 使用多种语言的	
9	a copy of a document, etc. made by the action of light on a specially treated surface 影印；复印	
10	to write or speak about sth./sb., esp. without giving much information 提起；提及	

Part II Term Study

*In this part, you are required to work by yourself writing out in Column B the Chinese meaning of each corresponding term in Column A. Read through the text carefully before completing this task. You can use **the self-study materials** we have provided or any reference book available as well as the Internet.*

No.	Column A	Column B
1	police regulations	
2	room availability	
3	in-hotel guest	
4	service hour	
5	guest folio	

Continued

No.	Column A	Column B
6	Whitney slip	
7	flight booking	
8	direct-dial multi-line telephone	
9	voice mail	
10	data port	

Part III Structure Study

*Work in class by yourself or in pairs. Look through the text and complete the following sentences with the correct forms of the words or phrases from the box. Then try to orally translate the sentences you have completed into Chinese. You can use **the self-study materials** we have provided or any reference book available as well as the Internet.*

A. hand/turn over ... to ...   B. in detail   C. introduce sth. to sb.

D. have a great proficiency in   E. explain sth. to sb.   F. assist sb. to do sth.

1. He _____ a letter of apology from the manager_____ the guest.

2. It is my duty to _____ our hotel's services _____ you.

3. Secretaries of the business center should _____ using various devices of the business center.

4. The cleaning and maintenance work of the public areas includes, _____, carpet cleaning, marble maintenance, equipment maintenance, and so on.

Part IV Questions & Answers

In this part, you are required to read through the text carefully again, and discuss with your partners or group members on your short and brief answers to the questions upon the text before reporting your work to the class.

1. How does the room clerk do his / her routine work?

2. What does the information clerk do as his / her routine work?

3. What are the qualities necessary for a good business secretary?

4. What services does the business center offer?

Lecture 4　Front Office Department (4.1.7 Cashier's Counter, 4.1.8 Concierge Desk)

Part I　Word Study

*In this part, you are required to work by yourself selecting one word (in both **bold** and **italic** type) from the text to match its corresponding meaning. Read through the text carefully before making your choices. You can use **the self-study materials** we have provided or any reference book available as well as the Internet.*

No.	Explanations	Words
1	to join things together into one; to be joined into one 整理（成一体）	
2	to officially ask sb. to write, make, or create sth. or to do a task for you 委托	
3	not yet paid, done, solved, etc. 未支付的	
4	to make a process happen more quickly 加快	
5	(of a place) quiet and private; not used or disturbed by other people 隐蔽的；僻静的	
6	to sign a document that has already been signed by another person, esp. in order to show that it is valid 会签	
7	to regard as untrustworthy, or to have no confidence in 怀疑；嫌疑	
8	(of money and goods for sale) made to look exactly like sth. in order to trick people into thinking that they are getting the real thing 假冒的	
9	a printed piece of paper that can be used instead of money to pay for sth., or that allows you to pay less than the usual price of sth. 凭证	
10	a person whose job is to serve or help people in a public place 侍者	

Part II　Term Study

*In this part, you are required to work by yourself writing out in Column B the Chinese meaning of each corresponding term in Column A. Read through the text carefully before completing this task. You can use **the self-study materials** we have provided or any reference book available as well as the Internet.*

No.	Column A	Column B
1	guest bills	
2	accounting statement	
3	money changer	
4	traveler's check	
5	outstanding balance	
6	occupancy report	
7	revenue report	
8	key drop	
9	sales voucher	

Continued

No.	Column A	Column B
10	transaction amount	
11	transaction date	
12	authorized credit limit	
13	signature panel	
14	summary sheet	
15	door attendant	
16	valet parking	
17	airport shuttling	
18	representatives-at-the-airport	
19	traffic control	
20	transportation personnel	

Part III Structure Study

*Work in class by yourself or in pairs. Look through the text and complete the following sentences with the correct forms of the words or phrases from the box. Then try to orally translate the sentences you have completed into Chinese. You can use **the self-study materials** we have provided or any reference book available as well as the Internet.*

A. report sth. to sb.	B. commission sb. to do sth.	C. remind sb. of sth.
D. in relief	E. go beyond	F. compare ... with ...

1. Have you _____ the accident _____ the police yet?

2. She simply welcomed him and _____ him _____ the last time they had met.

3. Money changers _____ (exchange) foreign currencies and cash traveler's checks or credit cards by the Bank of China.

4. According to the regulations, the amount of sales does not _____ the authorized credit limit.

5. The hotel building stood out _____ against the blue sky.

Part IV Questions & Answers

In this part, you are required to read through the text carefully again, and discuss with your partners or group members on your short and brief answers to the questions upon the text before reporting your work to the class.

1. What is the cashier's counter responsible for?

2. What are the clerks at the cashier's counter?

3. What is the safety deposit box?

4. What should a cashier do when a guest wants to pay by check?

5. What should a cashier do when a guest wants to pay by credit card?

6. What are the employees at the concierge?

Lecture 5　Front Office Department
(4.1.9 Hotel Lobby, 4.1.10 Telephone Operator)

Part I　Word Study

*In this part, you are required to work by yourself selecting one word (in both **bold** and **italic** type) from the text to match its corresponding meaning. Read through the text carefully before making your choices. You can use **the self-study materials** we have provided or any reference book available as well as the Internet.*

No.	Explanations	Words
1	feeling sure about your own ability to do things and be successful 自信的	
2	a person that you work with, do business with, or spend a lot of time with 伙伴	
3	to arrange and settle an agreement with sb. formally and finally 达成协议	
4	the selling of goods to the public, usually through shops/stores 零售	
5	the subject or main idea in a talk, piece of writing, or work of art 主题	
6	a person's understanding of a subject or of difficult facts 理解；把握	
7	the state of being alone and not watched or disturbed by other people 隐私	
8	to watch and check sth. over a period of time in order to see how it develops, so that you can make any necessary changes 监控	
9	clearly expressed or pronounced 发音清晰的	
10	the central part of a telephone system used by a company, etc., where telephone calls are answered and put through to the appropriate person or department 电话总机	

Part II　Term Study

*In this part, you are required to work by yourself writing out in Column B the Chinese meaning of each corresponding term in Column A. Read through the text carefully before completing this task. You can use **the self-study materials** we have provided or any reference book available as well as the Internet.*

No.	Column A	Column B
1	light snack	
2	retail outlet	
3	sundry store	
4	personal-care item	
5	travel convenience	
6	revenue stream	
7	call distribution	
8	dictation skill	
9	guest privacy	
10	emergency communication	

Part III Structure Study

*Work in class by yourself or in pairs. Look through the text and complete the following sentences with the correct forms of the words or phrases from the box. Then try to orally translate the sentences you have completed into Chinese. You can use **the self-study materials** we have provided or any reference book available as well as the Internet.*

A. call for sb. to do sth.	B. get to know	C. do a good business
D. on the contrary	E. regard ... as ...	F. be worth doing
G. show off	H. have a grasp of ...	I. a series of

1. _____ technical problems delayed the opening of the new hotel.

2. When you _____ him you'll find he is quite nice.

3. The hotel _____ owing to all the staff's efforts last year .

4. It's no trouble at all; _____, it will be a great pleasure to help you.

5. The manager soon _____ what was going on.

6. The guests regard shopping at high prices in such outlets as a story that _____ (show) off.

7. When a guest checks out, he / she will _____ the porter_____ (bring) his / her luggage downstairs.

Part IV Questions & Answers

In this part, you are required to read through the text carefully again, and discuss with your partners or group members on your short and brief answers to the questions upon the text before reporting your work to the class.

1. What are the front office sections in the lobby?

2. What are the functional areas in the lobby?

3. What kinds of outlets may there be in the lobby shopping area?

4. What are the qualities necessary for a telephone operator?

5. What is the routine work of a telephone operator?

Lecture 6 Housekeeping Department (4.2.1 Overview of Housekeeping Department)

Part I Word Study

*In this part, you are required to work by yourself selecting one word (in both **bold** and **italic** type) from the text to match its corresponding meaning. Read through the text carefully before making your choices. You can use **the self-study materials** we have provided or any reference book available as well as the Internet.*

No.	Explanations	Words
1	having a full array of suitable equipment or furnishings of high standard 设备完善的；配备齐全的	
2	not important or serious; not worth considering 琐碎的；不重要的	
3	the number of people present at an organized event 出勤（情况）	
4	tired and easily annoyed 疲惫的	
5	a list of people employed by a company showing the amount of money to be paid to each of them 工资单	
6	a person who is in charge of sb./sth. 主管人	
7	(of a seat, hotel room, house, etc.) empty; not being used 空置的	
8	to treat things that have already been used so that they can be used again 循环；再利用	
9	to state clearly and firmly that sth. must be done, or how it must be done 规定	
10	to protect sth. so that it is safe and difficult to attack or damage 妥善保管	

Part II Term Study

*In this part, you are required to work by yourself writing out in Column B the Chinese meaning of each corresponding term in Column A. Read through the text carefully before completing this task. You can use **the self-study materials** we have provided or any reference book available as well as the Internet.*

No.	Column A	Column B
1	bath tub	
2	bed sheet	
3	executive housekeeper	
4	assistant housekeeper	
5	room inspector	
6	specified procedure	
7	non-recycled inventory	
8	pre-determined fee	
9	administrative support	
10	payroll procedure	

Part III Structure Study

*Work in class by yourself or in pairs. Look through the text and complete the following sentences with the correct forms of the words or phrases from the box. Then try to orally translate the sentences you have completed into Chinese. You can use **the self-study materials** we have provided or any reference book available as well as the Internet.*

A. on a large scale   B. what's more   C. respond to

D. follow up   E. log ... in ...   F. issue ... to ...

G. work through

1. The hospitality industry is developing _____.

2. Details of the expense then _____ the computer.

3. The waiter can speak English, and _____, he speaks it very well.

4. The general manager required them to _____ the matter until they got results.

5. Work permits _____ only 5% of those who applied for them.

Part IV Questions & Answers

In this part, you are required to read through the text carefully again, and discuss with your partners or group members on your short and brief answers to the questions upon the text before reporting your work to the class.

1. What is the Housekeeping responsible for?

2. What are the sections under the Housekeeping?

3. What are the responsibilities of the executive housekeeper?

4. What are the employees under the executive housekeeper?

5. What are the duties of the assistant housekeeper?

Lecture 7 Housekeeping Department

(4.2.2 Housekeeping Center, 4.2.3 Laundry, Linen, and Public Areas)

Part I Word Study

*In this part, you are required to work by yourself selecting one word (in both **bold** and **italic** type) from the text to match its corresponding meaning. Read through the text carefully before making your choices. You can use **the self-study materials** we have provided or any reference book available as well as the Internet.*

No.	Explanations	Words
1	a relationship between two organizations or different departments in an organization, involving the exchange of information or ideas 联络	
2	to formally or officially tell sb. about sth. 通知；报告	
3	the way that sb./sth. looks on the outside; what sb./sth. seems to be 相貌	
4	showing calm control rather than emotion 有节制的	
5	the way that you think and feel about sb./sth.; the way that you behave towards sb./sth. that shows how you think and feel 态度	
6	the quality of being open and truthful 真诚	
7	goods that are intended to be used fairly quickly and then replaced 消费品	
8	a reception room in an inn or club where visitors can be received 会客室	
9	happening fairly often and regularly 定期的	
10	(of a person) polite, well-educated, and able to judge the quality of things; having the sort of manners that are considered typical of a high social class 优雅的	

Part II Term Study

*In this part, you are required to work by yourself writing out in Column B the Chinese meaning of each corresponding term in Column A. Read through the text carefully before completing this task. You can use **the self-study materials** we have provided or any reference book available as well as the Internet.*

No.	Column A	Column B
1	liaison & coordination center	
2	floor master key	
3	guest consumables	

Continued

No.	Column A	Column B
4	infant care	
5	personalized service	
6	targeted service	
7	laundry management rules	
8	equipment maintenance	

Part III Structure Study

*Work in class by yourself or in pairs. Look through the text and complete the following sentences with the correct forms of the words or phrases from the box. Then try to orally translate the sentences you have completed into Chinese. You can use **the self-study materials** we have provided or any reference book available as well as the Internet.*

A. undertake no task of	B. face to face	C. be placed into
D. make an introduction of	E. bid farewell to	F. leave ... undone

1. I will have to stay longer to deal with something _____.
2. The housekeeping center _____ receiving guests.
3. I went into the room and found myself _____ with him.
4. The general manager has come to _____ all his colleagues.
5. The floor attendant _____ detailed _____ the room amenities to the guests.

Part IV Questions & Answers

In this part, you are required to read through the text carefully again, and discuss with your partners or group members on your short and brief answers to the questions upon the text before reporting your work to the class.

1. What are the responsibilities of the housekeeping center?
2. What are the qualities necessary for room attendants?
3. What are the categories of guest services?
4. What are the responsibilities of the Laundry, the Linen, and the Public Area?

Lecture 8 Housekeeping Department (4.2.4 Room Description, 4.2.5 Room Cleaning)

Part I Word Study

*In this part, you are required to work by yourself selecting one word (in both **bold** and **italic** type) from the text to match its corresponding meaning. Read through the text carefully before making your choices. You can use **the self-study materials** we have provided or any reference book available as well as the Internet.*

No.	Explanations	Words
1	a strong metal box or cupboard with a complicated lock, used for storing valuable things in, for example, money or jewelry 保险箱	
2	far away from places where other people live 远程的	
3	the basic systems and services that are necessary for a country or an organization to run smoothly, for example buildings, transport, and water and power supplies 基础设施	
4	a person, an object, an event, etc. that represents a more general quality or situation 象征；标志	
5	the most important or famous; in a position at the front 最重要的	
6	to go in search of 追求	
7	a group of things that are organized or placed in a particular order or position; the act of placing things in a particular order 布置	
8	a thing that makes sth. look more attractive on special occasions 装饰品	
9	(of a process, a business, or an activity) producing enough profit to continue 节约的；经济的	
10	to have enough money or time to be able to buy or to do sth. 花费得起	
11	to fill sth. with food, books, etc. 配备	
12	reduced in volume by pressure 压缩的	
13	using a system of receiving and sending information as a series of the numbers one and zero, showing that an electronic signal is there or is not there 数字的	
14	(of sth.) that can be used again 可（多次）重复使用的	
15	to make clean, not likely to cause health problems 使卫生	
16	to interrupt sb. when they are trying to work, sleep, etc. 打扰	
17	to obey rules, laws, etc. 遵守	
18	(of sth.) made dirty or polluted 污染的；弄脏的	
19	having holes or cracks that allow liquid or gas to escape 出现裂缝的；泄漏的	
20	to make sth. full again by replacing what has been used 补充；再装满	

Part II Term Study

*In this part, you are required to work by yourself writing out in Column B the Chinese meaning of each corresponding term in Column A. Read through the text carefully before completing this task. You can use **the self-study materials** we have provided or any reference book available as well as the Internet.*

No.	Column A	Column B
1	guest service	
2	room extra	
3	rental amenities	
4	interior design	
5	furniture arrangement	
6	double room	
7	twin room	
8	triple room	
9	standard suite	
10	deluxe suite	
11	presidential suite	
12	special floor	
13	sewing kit	
14	reusable item	
15	room code	
16	Early Cleaning	
17	Late Checkout	
18	occupied clean room	
19	vacant clean room	
20	check-out room	

Part III Structure Study

*Work in class by yourself or in pairs. Look through the text and complete the following sentences with the correct forms of the words or phrases from the box. Then try to orally translate the sentences you have completed into Chinese. You can use **the self-study materials** we have provided or any reference book available as well as the Internet.*

A. account for	B. base one's choice upon	C. as a rule
D. take ... into account	E. have ... in mind	F. be in normal operation
G. stock ... with ...	H. on request	I. keep a record of
J. interfere with	K. give ... a thorough cleaning	L. be for rent

1. _____, I don't go to the office on Saturday morning.

2. In China, the area of a hotel's guestrooms usually _____ over 60% of its total construction area.

3. Fund is a basic safeguard to make the hotel go _____.

4. All the staff should always _____ the needs of guests.

5. Comfort seems to be the last thing travelers _____.

6. These non-charge-based amenities are available _____ in our hotel.

7. As to check-out rooms, room attendants should _____ them _____ as soon as possible.

8. Guests often _____ the most basic requirements: clean, comfortable, convenient, and safe.

9. The minibar in each room _____ food and water, which are charge-based.

10. Upon finishing the room cleaning, room attendants should _____ their work with "OC" for occupied clean rooms and "VC" for vacant clean rooms.

Part IV Questions & Answers

In this part, you are required to read through the text carefully again, and discuss with your partners or group members on your short and brief answers to the questions upon the text before reporting your work to the class.

1. What should a guest be informed of when he / she checks in?

2. What are the principles for room design?

3. What are the categories of guestrooms?

4. What amenities may a guestroom be stocked with?

5. What are the major tasks of Room Cleaning?

6. What are the room codes used for Room Cleaning?

7. What should a room attendant observe while doing room cleaning?

8. What are the procedures for room cleaning?

Chapter Five Food & Beverage Division
Lecture 1 Overview of Food & Beverage Division
(5.1.1 Food & Beverage Management, 5.1.2 Food & Beverage Facilities)

Part I Word Study

*In this part, you are required to work by yourself selecting one word (in both **bold** and italic type) from the text to match its corresponding meaning. Read through the text carefully before making your choices. You can use **the self-study materials** we have provided or any* *reference book available as well as the Internet.*

No.	Explanations	Words
1	most important; main 首要的；主要的	
2	great in amount, size, importance, etc. 可观的；相当大的	
3	to get sth. from sth. 获得	
4	giving useful information 传播信息的	
5	the act of doing a piece of work, performing a duty, or putting a plan into action 执行；履行；实施	
6	an administrative division of some larger or more complex organization 下属部门	
7	a professional cook, esp. the most senior cook in a restaurant, hotel, etc. 主厨	
8	the process of keeping places clean and healthy, esp. by providing a sewage system and a clean water supply （环境）卫生	
9	a message that you write which gives information in a formal or definite way 书面意见；（情况）说明	
10	to consider in detail in order to discover essential features or meaning 分析研究	
11	the opinion that people have about what sb./sth. is like, based on what has happened in the past 声誉	
12	serving to set in motion, willingly without being forced 主动的	
13	feeling or showing a lot of excitement and interest about sb./sth. 热情的	
14	showing that you think about and care for other people 体贴的；周到的	
15	the ability or qualities necessary to do sth. 能力	
16	the ability of recovering easily and quickly from unpleasant or damaging events 应变	
17	the ability to make yourself do sth., esp. sth. difficult or unpleasant 自律	
18	the act of working with another person or group of people to create or produce sth. 合作	
19	designed for a particular person or thing; connected with a particular person or thing 个性化的	
20	to emphasize sth., esp. so that people give it more attention 突出	
21	the act of making sth. available to the public 发行；发表；发布	
22	a popular way of behaving, doing an activity, etc. 时尚	
23	an outdoor meal or party when food is cooked outdoors on a grill or an open fire 烤肉；烧烤	
24	a strong desire to know about sth. 好奇	
25	to produce sth. again; to make sth. happen again in the same way 重现	
26	a series of performances of music, plays, films/movies, etc., usually organized in the same place once a year; a series of public events connected with a particular activity or idea 节日	
27	(of sth.) for which one can afford money for 支付得起的；不算太贵的	
28	seeming exciting and unusual because it is connected with foreign countries 异国的	
29	a refined quality of gracefulness and good taste 典雅	
30	very typical of sth. or of sb.'s character 显示特色的	

Part II Term Study

In this part, you are required to work by yourself writing out in Column B the Chinese meaning of each corresponding term in Column A. Read through the text carefully before

*completing this task. You can use **the self-study materials** we have provided or any reference book available as well as the Internet.*

No.	Column A	Column B
1	entertainment facilities	
2	conference facilities	
3	work efficiency	
4	informative communication	
5	authority execution	
6	purchasing steward	
7	executive chef	
8	chief steward	
9	service basics	
10	job knowledge	
11	non-dining time	
12	high consumer	
13	press conference	
14	news release	
15	fashion show	
16	academic conference	
17	theme restaurant	
18	food festival	
19	themed event	
20	buffet reception	

Part III Structure Study

*Work in class by yourself or in pairs. Look through the text and complete the following sentences with the correct forms of the words or phrases from the box. Then try to orally translate the sentences you have completed into Chinese. You can use **the self-study materials** we have provided or any reference book available as well as the Internet.*

> A. be derived from   B. decide on   C. of a higher level
>
> D. vary by   E. in essence   F. be characteristic of
>
> G. full of imagination   H. enable sb. to do sth. I. be made up of

1. The guest group _____ very young children.

2. A considerable income can _____ the services provided by the food & beverage division.

3. The Mallorcan (马略卡岛) landscape _____ windmills (风车).

4. The executive chef _____ the items on the menus and coordinates preparation of the food and beverage.

5. Our menu content may _____ season.

6. A theme restaurant, _____, sells a certain cultural theme.

7. The software _____ you _____ (access) the Internet in seconds.

Part IV Questions & Answers

In this part, you are required to read through the text carefully again, and discuss with your partners or group members on your short and brief answers to the questions upon the text before reporting your work to the class.

1. What does the food & beverage division cover?

2. What are the sub-divisions under the food & beverage division?

3. What are the staff members of the food & beverage division?

4. What are the qualities necessary for the food & beverage staff?

5. How do you understand the "SERVICE" standards?

6. What catering facilities does a big hotel have?

Lecture 2 Food Service Department
(5.2.1 Food Service Management, 5.2.2 Food Service Cycle)

Part I Word Study

*In this part, you are required to work by yourself selecting one word (in both **bold** and **italic** type) from the text to match its corresponding meaning. Read through the text carefully before making your choices. You can use **the self-study materials** we have provided or any reference book available as well as the Internet.*

No.	Explanations	Words
1	to check that sth. is true or accurate 核实	
2	to make objects or activities of the same type have the same features or qualities 使标准化	
3	(of a person) who receives a good training 训练有素的	
4	a waiter who manages wine service in a hotel or restaurant 斟酒服务员	
5	to take goods, letters, etc. to the person or people they have been sent to; to take sb. somewhere 传送	
6	a type of food considered to be very special in a particular place 精致；精美	

Continued

No.	Explanations	Words
7	the feeling that you can trust, believe in, and be sure about the abilities or good qualities of sb./sth. 自信；信心	
8	a greater interest in or desire for sb./sth. than sb./sth. else 喜好	
9	eating/serving no meat or fish or (often) any animal products 素食的	
10	a date that is an exact number of years after the date of an important or special event 周年纪念日	

Part II Term Study

*In this part, you are required to work by yourself writing out in Column B the Chinese meaning of each corresponding term in Column A. Read through the text carefully before completing this task. You can use **the self-study materials** we have provided or any reference book available as well as the Internet.*

No.	Column A	Column B
1	food server	
2	cash payment	
3	signed bill	
4	booking register	
5	table service	
6	credit slip	

Part III Structure Study

*Work in class by yourself or in pairs. Look through the text and complete the following sentences with the correct forms of the words or phrases from the box. Then try to orally translate the sentences you have completed into Chinese. You can use **the self-study materials** we have provided or any reference book available as well as the Internet.*

A. charge ... to an account B. be on the first level C. be on a par with
D. fall short of E. with confidence F. guide sb. to a place

1. Both hotels _____ in the city.
2. They _____ the calls _____ their credit-card _____.
3. The food & beverage division may _____ its goals this month.
4. The clerk representative spoke _____ from the heart.
5. A guest usually demands that the service from the food & beverage division _____ that from other divisions in the hotel.

Part IV Questions & Answers

In this part, you are required to read through the text carefully again, and discuss with your partners or group members on your short and brief answers to the questions upon the text before reporting your work to the class.

1. What are the responsibilities of the food service manager?

2. What are the staff members under the food service manager?

3. What should the top-class restaurant service be like?

4. How does the restaurant reservationists take reservations?

5. How does the restaurant captain take orders?

6. Can you cite some examples to illustrate the table service standards?

Lecture 3 Food Service Department
(5.2.3 The Chinese Food, 5.2.4 The Western Food)

Part I Word Study

*In this part, you are required to work by yourself selecting one word (in both **bold** and **italic** type) from the text to match its corresponding meaning. Read through the text carefully before making your choices. You can use **the self-study materials** we have provided or any reference book available as well as the Internet.*

No.	Explanations	Words
1	(in a restaurant or at a formal meal) the main dish of the meal or a dish served before the main course 主菜	
2	a drink, usually one containing alcohol, that people sometimes have just before a meal 开胃酒	
3	how food or drink tastes 风味	
4	typical of a country or culture that is very different from modern Western culture and therefore interesting for people in Western countries 民族特色的	
5	to cook sth. slowly, or allow sth. to cook slowly, in liquid in a closed dish （用文火）炖	
6	to fry meat or vegetables quickly and then cook it slowly in a covered dish with a small amount of liquid 烩	
7	to cook sth. in hot fat or oil （油）煎	
8	to cook thin strips of vegetables or meat quickly by stirring them in very hot oil 用旺火煸；炒	
9	to cook vegetables or meat quickly in very hot oil in a shorter time 爆炒	
10	to cook food in oil that covers it completely 炸炒	
11	to cook sth. by keeping it almost at boiling point 煨	
12	to fry food quickly in a little hot fat 快炒；煸	

No.	Explanations	Words
13	to cook food, esp. meat, without liquid in an oven or over a fire 烤	
14	to place food over boiling water so that it cooks in the steam 蒸	
15	to cook food by pouring very hot liquid over it or by dipping it into and then taking it out of very hot liquid 灼	
16	to cook food by coating it with sth. sweet 蜜汁；用糖煮	
17	to cook food by quick-boiling in hot water 汆	
18	to add salt, pepper, etc. to food in order to give it more flavor 调味	
19	to cook food over a fire, esp. outdoors（在烤架上）烤；铁扒	
20	to cook meat or fish under direct heat or over heat on metal bars, esp. by burning coal（用碳）烧	

Part II Term Study

*In this part, you are required to work by yourself writing out in Column B the Chinese meaning of each corresponding term in Column A. Read through the text carefully before completing this task. You can use **the self-study materials** we have provided or any reference book available as well as the Internet.*

No.	Column A	Column B
1	regional distribution	
2	food materials	
3	high-end consumption	
4	service cycle	
5	table wine	

Part III Structure Study

*Work in class by yourself or in pairs. Look through the text and complete the following sentences with the correct forms of the words or phrases from the box. Then try to orally translate the sentences you have completed into Chinese. You can use **the self-study materials** we have provided or any reference book available as well as the Internet.*

A. lay down   B. be popular with   C. be recognized as

D. be themed with   E. see off

1. She _____ her knife and fork and pushed her plate away.

2. She raised her head to _____ the guest, with her eyes full of tears.

3. These artistic handicrafts _____ very _____ foreign guests.

4. The cafe-style Western restaurants _____ traditional or trendy European & American cultures and arts.

Part IV Questions & Answers

In this part, you are required to read through the text carefully again, and discuss with your partners or group members on your short and brief answers to the questions upon the text before reporting your work to the class.

1. What are the Chinese dishes generally categorized into?
2. What are the skills necessary for waiters/waitresses in a Chinese restaurant?
3. What do Western foods mainly include?
4. How are the foods served in Western restaurants?
5. What skills should Western restaurant waiters/waitresses have?
6. What is the service cycle in Western restaurants?

Lecture 4 Other Subordinate Departments
(5.3.1 Beverage Service Department, 5.3.2 Catering Department)

Part I Word Study

*In this part, you are required to work by yourself selecting one word (in both **bold** and **italic** type) from the text to match its corresponding meaning. Read through the text carefully before making your choices. You can use **the self-study materials** we have provided or any reference book available as well as the Internet.*

No.	Explanations	Words
1	needing a lot of effort, money, or time to succeed but intended to achieve impressive results 隆重的	
2	a large important organization that has a particular purpose, for example, a university or bank 社会事业机构	
3	a message saying that you are happy about their good luck or success 祝贺	
4	to show that a day or an event is important by doing sth. special on it 庆祝	
5	a marriage ceremony, and the meal or party that usually follows it 婚礼	
6	a collection of information stored together in a box, esp. on a particular person or subject 档案	
7	a series of actions that are always performed in the same way, esp. as part of a religious ceremony 仪式	
8	to be very good at doing sth. 善于	

No.	Explanations	Words
9	relating to or characteristic of art or artists 艺术的	
10	of or relating to the activity or business for which you are trained 职业的	

Part II Term Study

*In this part, you are required to work by yourself writing out in Column B the Chinese meaning of each corresponding term in Column A. Read through the text carefully before completing this task. You can use **the self-study materials** we have provided or any reference book available as well as the Internet.*

No.	Column A	Column B
1	live entertainment	
2	government organ	
3	public institution	
4	food production	
5	guest-satisfaction-tracking survey	
6	dining ritual	
7	occupational habit	

Part III Structure Study

*Work in class by yourself or in pairs. Look through the text and complete the following sentences with the correct forms of the words or phrases from the box. Then try to orally translate the sentences you have completed into Chinese. You can use **the self-study materials** we have provided or any reference book available as well as the Internet.*

> A. represent as much as   B. excel in

1. She is one of the employees who _____ sales in the catering department.

2. Catering sales can _____ 50% of a hotel's total food and beverage sales.

Part IV Questions & Answers

In this part, you are required to read through the text carefully again, and discuss with your partners or group members on your short and brief answers to the questions upon the text before reporting your work to the class.

1. What are the responsibilities of the beverage manager?

2. What are the types of various bars?

3. How are banquets categorized?

4. What are the procedures of banquet selling?

5. What are the preparations for banquets?

6. What are the qualities necessary for the banquet staff?

Lecture 5 Other Subordinate Departments
(5.3.3 Room Service Department, 5.3.4 Culinary Department,
5.3.5 Purchasing Department)

Part I Word Study

*In this part, you are required to work by yourself selecting one word (in both **bold** and italic type) from the text to match its corresponding meaning. Read through the text carefully before making your choices. You can use **the self-study materials** we have provided or any reference book available as well as the Internet.*

No.	Explanations	Words
1	drinks and small amounts of food that are provided or sold to people in a public place or at a public event 茶点	
2	to give information in writing 写明	
3	an act of taking sth. away from a place; an act of bringing things together into one place 取走	
4	to cut or tear sth. into small pieces 切丝	
5	a mixture of raw vegetables such as lettuce, tomato, and cucumber, usually served with other food as part of a meal 冷盘	
6	a man whose job is to take care of passengers on a ship, an aircraft, or a train and who brings them meals, etc. 管事	
7	the act of taking sth. that is offered 接受	
8	(of food) to become bad so that it can no longer be eaten 变质	
9	a detailed description of how sth. is, or should be, designed or made 规格	
10	to take the skin off fruit, vegetables, etc. 剥皮；削皮	

Part II Term Study

In this part, you are required to work by yourself writing out in Column B the Chinese meaning of each corresponding term in Column A. Read through the text carefully before

*completing this task. You can use **the self-study materials** we have provided or any reference book available as well as the Internet.*

No.	Column A	Column B
1	central kitchen	
2	primary-processing cook	
3	dish-shredding and dish-fixing cook	
4	salad cook	
5	dish-cooking cook	
6	pastry cook	

Part III Questions & Answers

In this part, you are required to read through the text carefully again, and discuss with your partners or group members on your short and brief answers to the questions upon the text before reporting your work to the class.

1. What are the responsibilities of the room service manager?

2. What are the procedures of the room service?

3. What are the two main difficulties for the room service?

4. What are the staff members under the executive chief?

5. How does the Culinary operate?

6. What are the responsibilities of the chief steward?

7. How does the Purchasing operate?

Chapter Six Convention, Recreation, and Complaints
Lecture 1 Convention and Recreation
(6.1.1 Convention Service, 6.1.2 Recreation Service)

Part I Word Study

*In this part, you are required to work by yourself selecting one word (in both **bold** and **italic** type) from the text to match its corresponding meaning. Read through the text carefully before making your choices. You can use **the self-study materials** we have provided or any reference book available as well as the Internet.*

No.	Explanations	Words
1	polite words or good wishes, esp. when used to express praise and admiration 恭维	
2	an award or official statement giving public praise for sb./sth. 赞赏	

Continued

No.	Explanations	Words
3	to arrange for sth. official to take place 主办	
4	a formal meeting or series of meetings of a court, a parliament, etc.; a period of time when such meetings are held 会议	
5	a class at a university or college when a small group of students and a teacher discuss or study a particular topic（大学）研讨班	
6	the ability to understand or to do sth. 能力	
7	the number of workers needed or available to do a particular job 人力	
8	pleasant; friendly and easy to like 友善的；和蔼的	
9	the way in which the parts of sth. such as the page of a book, a garden, or a building are arranged 安排；布置	
10	to get sth. useful from a situation 得益；获利	
11	(of sth.) with value added to a product, or a service 增值的	
12	the act of organizing an event to which others are invited and make all the arrangements for them 主持	
13	to show, express, make clear, or be a sign of 反映	
14	physical exercises intended to make the heart and lungs stronger, often done in classes, with music 有氧运动	
15	ways of resting and enjoying yourself; time spent resting and enjoying yourself 消遣；放松	
16	a person who trains a person or team in sport 教练	
17	to care for sb./sth. 照料；养护	
18	a person whose job is to teach sb. a practical skill or sport 教员；指导者	
19	a person who is employed at a beach or a swimming pool to rescue people who are in danger in the water 救生员	
20	a person who shows other people the way to a place, esp. sb. employed to show tourists around interesting places 向导	

Part II Term Study

*In this part, you are required to work by yourself writing out in Column B the Chinese meaning of each corresponding term in Column A. Read through the text carefully before completing this task. You can use **the self-study materials** we have provided or any reference book available as well as the Internet.*

No.	Column A	Column B
1	service business	
2	sponsoring organization	
3	reception capacity	
4	common practice	
5	convention division	
6	conference attendant	
7	venue layout	

Continued

No.	Column A	Column B
8	sponsoring party	
9	value-added service	
10	etiquette model hosting	
11	simultaneous interpretation	
12	PR presentation writing	
13	health and fitness center	
14	exercise equipment	
15	extra-pay service	
16	local snack bar	
17	band playing	
18	floor show	
19	professional athlete	
20	riding instructor	

Part III Structure Study

*Work in class by yourself or in pairs. Look through the text and complete the following sentences with the correct forms of the words or phrases from the box. Then try to orally translate the sentences you have completed into Chinese. You can use **the self-study materials** we have provided or any reference book available as well as the Internet.*

A. be bound to do sth.	B. run to	C. set up
D. direct sb. to sp.	E. accord with	F. profit from
G. bring in	H. give lessons to sb.	

1. The two sides agreed to _____ a commission to investigate claims.

2. By the conditions of our agreement we _____ (do) as we are doing.

3. The hearts of our people _____ those of yours.

4. Many resort hotels hire professional athletes to _____ guests in tennis, golf, and skiing.

5. I have three part-time jobs, which _____ about £14,000 a year.

6. A hotel can _____ the rentals of conference facilities to the sponsoring party, and many value-added services provided by the convention division.

Part IV Questions & Answers

In this part, you are required to read through the text carefully again, and discuss with your partners or group members on your short and brief answers to the questions upon the text before reporting your work to the class.

1. Why do hotels provide convention services?
2. What are the types of convention?
3. What are the features of convention services?
4. What is the common practice of convention service in big hotels?
5. What are the qualities necessary for conference attendants?
6. What are the responsibilities of the chief steward?
7. What recreational facilities do you think a big hotel may provide?
8. What are the employees under the recreation manager?

Lecture 2 Complaints

Part I Word Study

*In this part, you are required to work by yourself selecting one word (in both **bold** and *italic* type) from the text to match its corresponding meaning. Read through the text carefully before making your choices. You can use **the self-study materials** we have provided or any reference book available as well as the Internet.*

No.	Explanations	Words
1	existing or done for a good reason 合理的；有道理的	
2	to prevent sth. bad from happening 回避；避免	
3	a person complaining a lot about his / her problems or about things he / she does not like 抱怨者	
4	a fault in sb.'s character, a plan, a system, etc. 不足；缺点	
5	being careful that every detail of sth. is correct 严谨的；一丝不苟的	
6	upset because sth. you hoped for has not happened or been as good, successful, etc. as you expected 感到失望的	
7	to annoy, worry, or upset sb.; to cause sb. trouble or pain 打扰；烦扰	
8	rude and offensive; criticizing rudely and unfairly 辱骂的；出言不逊的	
9	a person of higher rank, status, or position 上级	
10	a way of dealing with or improving an unpleasant or difficult situation 补救	
11	listening or watching carefully and with interest 倾听的	
12	to say or do sth. that makes sb. stop what they are saying or doing 打断；中断	

No.	Explanations	Words
13	all the circumstances and things that are happening at a particular time and in a particular place 处境	
14	the feeling of being sorry for sb.; showing that you understand and care about sb.'s problems 同情	
15	an official action that is done in order to achieve a particular aim 措施	
16	sensible and a good idea in order to achieve sth. 明智的	
17	not happy or satisfied with sb./sth. 不满意的；不高兴的	
18	that can develop into sth. or be developed in the future 潜在的	
19	tending to do sth.; likely to do sth. 倾向于；有……意向的	
20	a word or statement saying sorry for sth. that has been done wrong or that causes a problem 道歉	

Part II Structure Study

*Work in class by yourself or in pairs. Look through the text and complete the following sentences with the correct forms of the words or phrases from the box. Then try to orally translate the sentences you have completed into Chinese. You can use **the self-study materials** we have provided or any reference book available as well as the Internet.*

> A. be satisfied with   B. be good for   C. in the short run
>
> D. take actions to do sth.   E. be careful about   F. do harm to
>
> G. complain about   H. be prepared to do sth.   I. lend an attentive ear to
>
> J. keep sb. informed of sth.   K. in many cases   L. be inclined to do sth.

1. Negative complaints may not _____ the hotel's business in the short run.

2. When you talk directly to complainers, they will tell you what they not _____.

3. _____, revenues will increase and profits will improve.

4. Guests should _____ their possessions and not leave them lying around.

5. We need to _____ (prepare) for the event in our hotel.

6. _____, regulations alone will not work.

7. The guest _____ being kept waiting long in the lobby.

8. When complaints occur, employees should _____ (handle) them.

9. While handling complaints, the hotel staff should always be ready to _____ what the guest has to say.

10. Please _____ us _____ the status of guestrooms.

Part III Questions & Answers

In this part, you are required to read through the text carefully again, and discuss with your partners or group members on your short and brief answers to the questions upon the text before reporting your work to the class.

1. Why should hotels welcome complaints?

2. What should the hotel staff do while handling complaints?

Chapter Seven General Expressions
Lecture 1 General Expressions (7.1–7.13)

Part I Word Study

*In this part, you are required to work by yourself selecting one word (in both **bold** and **italic** type) from the text to match its corresponding meaning. Read through the text carefully before making your choices. You can use **the self-study materials** we have provided or any reference book available as well as the Internet.*

No.	Explanations	Words
1	the way sth. develops or should develop 过程	
2	the activity or process of expressing ideas and feelings or of giving people information 交流；交际	
3	a strong feeling such as love, fear, or anger; the part of a person's character that consists of feelings 情绪	
4	a feeling of not suffering or worrying so much; a feeling of being less unhappy 安慰	
5	having or needing a lot of energy and enthusiasm 充满活力的；热情的	
6	to be grateful for sth. that sb. has done; to welcome sth. 感激	
7	a mistake, esp. one that causes problems or affects the result of sth. 过失	
8	the act of doing or performing again 重复	
9	having or showing no interest in sb./sth. 漠不关心的	
10	a situation in which sth. does not happen when it should; the act of delaying 耽搁；延误	
11	a situation in which a comment, an instruction, etc. is not understood correctly 误会；误解	
12	trouble or problems, esp. concerning what you need or would like yourself 不便	
13	the responsibility for sth. wrong that has happened or been done 过错；缺点	
14	connected with a person's mind and the way in which it works 心理的	
15	used to send good wishes to sb. at the end of a letter, or when asking sb. to give your good wishes to another person who is not present 问候；致意	
16	the fact that sth. is preventing sth./sb. from succeeding 挫折	
17	a thing that sb. has done successfully, esp. using their own effort and skill 成就；成绩	
18	to try to spend less time, money, etc. on sth. than is really needed 舍不得给	

No.	Explanations	Words
19	permission to do sth., esp. given by sb. in authority 同意；赞成	
20	a state of human society that is very developed and organized 文明	
21	concerned with principles of right and wrong behavior 道德上的	
22	the qualities and features that make a person, groups of people, and places different from others 品质	
23	not talking much about your own abilities or possessions 谦虚的	
24	the act of saying or doing sth. that makes sb. stop what they are saying or doing 打扰；中断	
25	to plan or organize sth. in advance 安排	
26	to make sth. certain to happen 确保	
27	the quality of being specific rather than general 特殊性	
28	showing friendly feelings for sb. 衷心的	
29	unskillfulness resulting from a lack of training 笨拙	
30	happy and cheerful 愉快的；欢乐的	

Part II Term Study

*In this part, you are required to work by yourself writing out in Column B the Chinese meaning of each corresponding term in Column A. Read through the text carefully before completing this task. You can use **the self-study materials** we have provided or any reference book available as well as the Internet.*

No.	Column A	Column B
1	general expression	
2	daily communication	
3	psychological distance	

Part III Structure Study

*Work in class by yourself or in pairs. Look through the text and complete the following sentences with the correct forms of the words or phrases from the box. Then try to orally translate the sentences you have completed into Chinese. You can use **the self-study materials** we have provided or any reference book available as well as the Internet.*

A. during the course of	B. look forward to	C. be indifferent to
D. get ... over	E. give regards/wishes/love to	F. wish sb. a ... birthday
G. skimp on	H. do one's best to do sth.	I. mind doing sth.

1. We should not _____ the suffering of others.

2. I _____ her a happy _____.

3. We are certain that he will _____ his illness.

4. We _____ your staying with us.

5. They had to _____ everything to send their sons to college.

6. _____ your brother _____ when you see him.

7. Helmets (头盔) must be fastened _____ cycling.

Part IV Role Playing

Work in pairs or groups after class. Compose and act out the dialogues in the following situations. Present your work by using videos.

Situation 1: The hotel employee greets a repeat guest in the lobby in the morning.

Situation 2: The hotel employee greets an in-hotel guest in the hallway, wanting to know how his trip is going.

Situation 3: The hotel employee bids farewell to the guest who is leaving and wants to make sure that she has had a good stay in the hotel.

Situation 4: The hotel employee says goodbye to a repeat guest and makes sure that he has had a good stay in the hotel and is coming back soon.

Situation 5: The hotel employee expresses thanks to the guest who is leaving and commenting on the good services he has received during the stay.

Situation 6: The hotel employee expresses thanks to the guest who informs that the toilet is broken.

Situation 7: The hotel employee makes apologies to a guest who becomes quite angry because he doesn't like the food.

Situation 8: The hotel employee makes apologies to a guest who is not satisfied with the room cleaning.

Situation 9: The hotel employee greets and offers services to a walk-in guest who doesn't need help.

Situation 10: The hotel employee offers help to a guest who is looking for her lost earring.

Situation 11: The hotel employee offers his assistance to the guest who seems lost while going to the conference room.

Situation 12: The hotel employee has to interrupt the guest who is talking with her friends in the lobby bar to inform her that there is an important call for her at the Front Desk.

Situation 13: The guest of Room 1818 walks up to the Front Desk and makes a request of a wake-up call at 5:30, for he is leaving for Beijing tomorrow morning. The clerk Lily handles the request.

Situation 14: The guest of Room 1818 comes back from the shopping mall, and asks for helping with her shopping bags. The bellman Li Dong handles the request.

Situation 15: The guest of Room 1818, Mr. Smith, wants two bottles of mineral water to his room. The housemaid Lily handles the request.

Situation 16: The guest of Room 1818, Mr. Smith, needs help turning off the vent of the bathroom. The housemaid Lily handles the request.

Situation 17: The guest wants to know the service hours of the restaurant, the check-out time of the hotel, and the best time for him to leave for the airport to catch the ten-o'clock plane. Lily gives the answers.

Situation 18: The guest calls the operator from the railway station wanting to know how to get to the hotel. Lily tells the location of the hotel.

Situation 19: The guest in the lobby area wants to know the nearest Ladies or Gentlemen's room. Lily gives the direction.

Situation 20: The guest complains that the food is too cold. The waitress Lily handles the complaint.

Situation 21: The guest complains about having been kept waiting too long. The restaurant manager handles the complaint.

Situation 22: The guest is unhappy with the room service for the reason that the food arrives very late, besides, the food is cold. The captain of the Room Service handles the complaint.

Situation 23: The General Manager delivers a speech to welcome a large tour delegation from Australia.

Chapter Eight Situational Expressions
Lecture 1 Front Office Staff (8.1.1 Room Reservationist)

Part I Word Study

*In this part, you are required to work by yourself selecting one word (in both **bold** and*

italic type) from the text to match its corresponding meaning. Read through the text carefully

*before making your choices. You can use **the self-study materials** we have provided or any reference book available as well as the Internet.*

No.	Explanations	Words
1	(of or relating to circumstances and things) that are happening at a particular time and in a particular place 情景的	
2	including a wide range of people, things, ideas, etc. 包含在内的	
3	used to introduce the word that people usually use to describe sth. 号称的；所谓的	
4	an event, a situation, or a period of time in sb.'s life, a novel, etc. that is important or interesting in some way 片段	
5	an amount of money by which sth. is made cheaper 折扣；优惠	
6	used to describe a time when the greatest number of people are doing sth. or using sth. 最高峰的	
7	unable to use a part of your body completely or easily because of a physical condition, illness, injury, etc. 有缺陷的	
8	a printed form that you can write on and sign as a way of paying for sth. instead of using money 支票	

Part II Term Study

*In this part, you are required to work by yourself writing out in Column B the Chinese meaning of each corresponding term in Column A. Read through the text carefully before completing this task. You can use **the self-study materials** we have provided or any reference book available as well as the Internet.*

No.	Column A	Column B
1	situational expression	
2	Advance Reservations	
3	high season	
4	confirmed booking	
5	current rate	
6	a 10 percent discount	
7	group reservation	
8	complimentary breakfast	
9	high occupancy	
10	waiting list	

Part III Structure Study

*Work in class by yourself or in pairs. Look through the text and complete the following sentences with the correct forms of the words or phrases from the box. Then try to orally translate the sentences you have completed into Chinese. You can use **the self-study materials** we have provided or any reference book available as well as the Internet.*

| A. be inclusive of | B. guarantee sb. sth. | C. get sb. through to sb. |
| D. by check | E. in cash | F. for the convenience of |

---

1. All prices _____ delivery.

2. Mary could hardly _____ herself _____ Jack because the line was busy.

3. We have provided seats _____ our customers.

4. How would you like to settle your bill, _____ or by credit card?

5. The ticket will _____ you free entry.

Part IV Role Playing

Work in pairs or groups after class. Compose and act out the dialogues in the following situations. Present your work by using videos.

Situation 1: A girl walks into the hotel and books for her boss Mr. Black one king-size bed room on a smoking floor for a week.

Situation 2: The reservationist Lily handles a telephone reservation, by George Clinton through the number 0044-0156-899800, of a double room with the room rate of 180 dollars per night from June 22 to June 25.

Situation 3: Wang Ling telephones the Hongxing Hotel to book 20 standard rooms from May 8 to May 15 for a coming tour group. But at that time there will be only 15 standard rooms and 10 junior suites (普通套房) available, and there will be five more standard rooms available from May 10. The standard room is 150 dollars per night and the junior suite is 180 dollars per night. According to the hotel rules, a discount of 10 percent in the rate of junior suite is given for the group reservation.

Situation 4: Mary handles the cancellation of Mr. Black's May-20 telephone reservation of 10 standard rooms from June 1 to June 7.

Lecture 2 Front Office Staff (8.1.2 Registration Clerk)

Part I Word Study

*In this part, you are required to work by yourself selecting one word (in both **bold** and **italic** type) from the text to match its corresponding meaning. Read through the text carefully before making your choices. You can use **the self-study materials** we have provided or any* *reference book available as well as the Internet.*

No.	Explanations	Words
1	to leave out sth. that would normally be the next thing that you would do, read, etc. 跳过；省略	
2	the act of sending on to another destination 转送	
3	the act of supplying or making available things for people to buy or use 发行	
4	an extra period of time allowed for sth. 延长	
5	that sb. agrees is of a good enough standard or allowed 合意的；可以接受的	
6	a person who lives or works in a particular house, room, building, etc. 住客	
7	an amount of money that you regularly pay so that you can use a house, etc. 租金	
8	to tell sb. that you will definitely do or not do sth., or that sth. will definitely happen 做出保证	
9	a list of facts or numbers arranged in a special order, usually in rows and columns 表；表格	
10	to ask an amount of money for goods or a service 收费	

Part II Term Study

*In this part, you are required to work by yourself writing out in Column B the Chinese meaning of each corresponding term in Column A. Read through the text carefully before completing this task. You can use **the self-study materials** we have provided or any reference book available as well as the Internet.*

No	Column A	Column B
1	arrival list	
2	forwarding address	
3	place of issue	
4	breakfast coupon	
5	walk-in guest	
6	room tariff table	
7	welcome card	
8	booking situation	
9	extension request	

Part III Structure Study

*Work in class by yourself or in pairs. Look through the text and complete the following sentences with the correct forms of the words or phrases from the box. Then try to orally translate the sentences you have completed into Chinese. You can use **the self-study materials** we have provided or any reference book available as well as the Internet.*

A. put down	B. later on	C. at one's convenience
D. be in order		

1. You forgot to ＿＿＿＿＿＿＿＿＿ the date of your departure in the form.

2. When everything ＿＿＿＿＿＿＿＿＿, I will ask a porter to take your baggage to your room.

3. Can you telephone me ＿＿＿＿＿＿＿＿＿ to arrange a meeting?

Part IV　Role Playing

Work in pairs or groups after class. Compose and act out the dialogues in the following situations. Present your work by using videos.

Situation 1: Lily handles the registration for Black Smith and his wife. The reservation, under Black Smith, was a double room for three nights. Black Smith fills in the registration form, makes the payment by American Express® Card, gets the key card and breakfast coupons and then goes to their room of 1618 accompanied by a bellman.

Situation 2: Lily checks in a walk-in guest, Black Smith, a regular guest in the hotel. He hasn't made reservation and wants to stay in the room facing south which he stayed last time. Lily expresses sorry for the unavailability of the room and recommends him Room 2818 with the same rate. Black Smith goes through the registration and goes to his room by himself with light luggage.

Situation 3: Lily refuses a walk-in guest, who wants a standard room for one night. Because all standard rooms have been sold out and the guest refuses a junior suite, Lily advises him to find a room in a nearby hotel and tells him the name of and the way to the hotel.

Situation 4: Black Smith approaches to the Front Desk for extending the stay till 2:00 p.m. Lily checks the booking situation and sees that the room he is staying in has been sold out and that the new guest will arrive at 4:00 p.m. So Lily accepts the guest's extension request but reminds him that he should leave before 2:00 p.m., or half the day's rent is charged if he checks out later than 2:00 p.m.

Situation 5: Black Smith didn't sleep well last night because of the noise from the air conditioner. He comes to the Front Desk for changing a room. Lily checks the reservation record and finds him a room of the same kind but two floors higher. Black Smith agrees and Lily arranges for a bellman to help Black Smith with the luggage.

Lecture 3 Front Office Staff (8.1.3 Concierge)

Part I Word Study

*In this part, you are required to work by yourself selecting one word (in both **bold** and **italic** type) from the text to match its corresponding meaning. Read through the text carefully before making your choices. You can use **the self-study materials** we have provided or any reference book available as well as the Internet.*

No.	Explanations	Words
1	a covered space at the back or front in which you put luggage or other things（汽车后部的）行李厢	
2	the act of stopping a vehicle at a place and leaving it there for a period of time 停车	
3	to go to where sb./sth. is and bring them/it back 取来	
4	sth. of value 贵重东西	
5	(sth.) likely to break; easily broken 易碎的／易碎物品	
6	able to begin burning easily 可燃物；易燃物	
7	to put clothes, etc. into a bag in preparation for a trip away from home 收拾行李	
8	the act of communicating with sb., esp. by writing to them or telephoning them 接触；联系	
9	a plane, bus, or train that travels regularly between two places 往返移动之物	
10	a particular area or place 景点；地点	

Part II Role Playing

Work in pairs or groups after class. Compose and act out the dialogues in the following situations. Present your work by using videos.

Situation 1: A guest arrives at the hotel in a taxi with many pieces of luggage. The bellboy Li Dong walks up to the taxi, helps take out three pieces of luggage from the trunk, brings a luggage cart, shows the guest to the Front Desk for checking in, accompanies the guest to her room on the 18th floor after registration, introduces dining and recreational facilities during the lift flight, opens the door of Room 1818 and the air conditioner for the guest, introduces the use of the room amenities, and says goodbye to the guest.

Situation 2: A guest, after three days' stay, checks out in the morning. The bellboy Li Dong is called to the guest's room to help with the luggage. Li Dong knocks on the door, greets the guest, makes sure that the guest has got everything ready and that nothing is left, helps with the luggage, makes sure that the guest had a good stay during the lift, carries the luggage into a taxi waiting outside while the guest checks out, bids farewell to the guest, wishes her a good journey back, and hopes for her coming again.

Situation 3: Li Dong receives a guest, who is named Joan Smith on her first tour trip to the city, at the airport. He parks his car in the parking lot, waits for and greets her, makes self introduction, helps with the luggage to the car, chats with her about the climate, scenic spots, transportation facilities, and so on … on the way back to the hotel, and leaves the guest with Li Ming waiting all the time at the entrance and wishes the guest a good stay in the hotel.

Situation 4: Li Dong is called to book two tickets for the concert to be held at 7:00 p.m. at the City Theater for Robert, the guest of Room 1818, takes the ticket to the room, and tells something important about the concert and the tickets.

Lecture 4　Front Office Staff (8.1.4 Information Clerk)

Part I　Word Study

*In this part, you are required to work by yourself selecting one word (in both **bold** and **italic** type) from the text to match its corresponding meaning. Read through the text carefully before making your choices. You can use **the self-study materials** we have provided or any reference book available as well as the Internet.*

No.	Explanations	Words
1	used to refer to a substance, material, group of objects, etc. when you do not know the name, when the name is not important or when it is obvious what you are talking about 东西	
2	sth. that is wrapped in paper or put into a thick envelope so that it can be sent by mail, carried easily 包裹	
3	to measure how heavy sb./sth. is, usually by using scales 称重	
4	to like one thing or person better than another; to choose one thing rather than sth. else because you like it better 更喜欢	
5	the money that you get back when you have paid for sth. giving more money than the amount it costs 零钱	
6	a piece of paper that shows that goods or services have been paid for 收据；收条	
7	an interesting or enjoyable place to go or thing to do 向往的地方	
8	to have an emotional or cognitive impact upon 使有印象	
9	any address at which you dwell more than temporarily 住宅；住处	
10	a formal arrangement to meet or visit sb. at a particular time, esp. for a reason connected with their work 约会	

Part II Term Study

*In this part, you are required to work by yourself writing out in Column B the Chinese meaning of each corresponding term in Column A. Read through the text carefully before completing this task. You can use **the self-study materials** we have provided or any reference book available as well as the Internet.*

No.	Column A	Column B
1	surface mail	·
2	ordinary mail letter	
3	express mail	

Part III Structure Study

*Work in class by yourself or in pairs. Look through the text and complete the following sentences with the correct forms of the words or phrases from the box. Then try to orally translate the sentences you have completed into Chinese. You can use **the self-study materials** we have provided or any reference book available as well as the Internet.*

A. pick up	B. more than	C. be far from
D. have an appointment with	E. leave a message for sb.	F. inform sb. to do sth.

1. Your ten percent _____ being acceptable.

2. They were _____ glad to help us.

3. Hello, I _____ Mr. Parker. My name is Dashan.

4. Would you please leave your name and telephone number? I will _____ the guest _____ (call) you back.

5. The FedEx will send someone to _____ your express mail tomorrow.

Part IV Role Playing

Work in pairs or groups after class. Compose and act out the dialogues in the following situations. Present your work by using videos.

Situation 1: The information clerk Lily receives a guest with the name Rose Smith, who posts an express mail. She asks the guest to open the big envelope for a check, asks the guest to fill out a form, tells the guest the charge and the time to be picked up, and tells the guest that the charge will be put on her room account.

Situation 2: Lily receives a guest who wants to know something about the nearby scenic spots. She tells something about two key scenic spots, the ways to go and the transportation tools to use.

Situation 3: Lily gives directions to a guest who wants to the East Lake. She tells the guest something about the location, the route, the distance and transportation tips.

Situation 4: Lily receives a guest who wants to buy some specialties for her friends. She gives some tips about what to buy, where to buy them, and the open hours.

Lecture 5　Front Office Staff (8.1.5 Cashier)

Part I Word Study

*In this part, you are required to work by yourself selecting one word (in both **bold** and **italic** type) from the text to match its corresponding meaning. Read through the text carefully before making your choices. You can use **the self-study materials** we have provided or any reference book available as well as the Internet.*

No.	Explanations	Words
1	equal in value, amount, meaning, importance, etc. 等于的；等价的	
2	a unit of value, esp. of money 面额	
3	the government department that collects taxes on goods bought and sold and on goods brought into the country, and that checks what is brought in 海关	
4	to change or make sth. change from one form, purpose, system, etc. to another 兑换	
5	a short official note that is sent by one person to another within the same company or organization 公务便单；备忘录	
6	to leave a building, seat, etc., esp. so that sb. else can use it 空出；让出	
7	to see or notice a person or thing, esp. suddenly or when it is not easy to do so 认出	
8	to allow sb. to behave in a way that you would not usually accept, because of a problem or because there is a special reason 体谅；谅解	
9	to take away money, points, etc. from a total amount 扣除	
10	to be greater than a particular number or amount 超出；超过	

Part II Term Study

*In this part, you are required to work by yourself writing out in Column B the Chinese meaning of each corresponding term in Column A. Read through the text carefully before completing this task. You can use **the self-study materials** we have provided or any reference book available as well as the Internet.*

No.	Column A	Column B
1	foreign exchange control	
2	exchange rate	
3	courtesy service	
4	exchange memo	
5	itemized bill	
6	allowance slip	
7	approval code	

Part III Structure Study

*Work in class by yourself or in pairs. Look through the text and complete the following sentences with the correct forms of the words or phrases from the box. Then try to orally translate the sentences you have completed into Chinese. You can use **the self-study materials** we have provided or any reference book available as well as the Internet.*

> A. be equivalent to   B. deduct ... from

1. Eight kilometers roughly _____ five miles.
2. We made a mistake in your bill and overcharged you $12. So we had to _____ it _____ your bill.

Part IV Role Playing

Work in pairs or groups after class. Compose and act out the dialogues in the following situations. Present your work by using videos.

Situation 1: Lily exchanges five hundred US dollars into RMB with denominations of 100 yuan and 50 yuan for an American guest with the passport number ×××××××. The exchange rate is 1 dollar equivalent to 6.35 yuan, and no service fee is charged. She asks the guest to keep the receipt or exchange memo because it must be shown when he wants to convert the remaining RMB back into his own currency.

Situation 2: Lily settles bills for a guest who checks out. She checks the key card, calls the floor attendant to check the room, asks the guest to check the itemized bills and the total charge and sign the bill if they are correct. The guest finds a mistake of 10 yuan, and Lily explains that it is the charge for the dyed towel. Lily asks the guest in what way and by what credit card to have the bill settled, hands over the voucher and receipt to the guest, gives a small gift to the guest, and says goodbye to the guest.

Lecture 6 Front Office Staff（8.1.6 Business Secretary, 8.1.7 Operator, 8.1.8 Salesperson）

Part I Word Study

*In this part, you are required to work by yourself selecting one word (in both **bold** and **italic** type) from the text to match its corresponding meaning. Read through the text carefully before making your choices. You can use **the self-study materials** we have provided or any reference book available as well as the Internet.*

No.	Explanations	Words
1	to provide the things that a particular type or person wants, esp. things that you do not approve of 满足	
2	a person whose job is to deal with people arriving at or telephoning a hotel, an office building, a doctor's surgery, etc. 接待员	
3	the cost of sending a letter, etc. by post 邮费	
4	(of sth.) shaped like a heart 心形的	
5	rare and worth a lot of money 宝贵的	
6	the ability to control your thoughts and actions in order to achieve what you want to do; a feeling of strong determination to do sth. that you want to do 意志	

Part II Term Study

*In this part, you are required to work by yourself writing out in Column B the Chinese meaning of each corresponding term in Column A. Read through the text carefully before completing this task. You can use **the self-study materials** we have provided or any reference book available as well as the Internet.*

No.	Column A	Column B
1	secretarial assistance	
2	fax service	
3	translation fee	
4	target language	
5	one-price policy	

Part III Structure Study

*Work in class by yourself or in pairs. Look through the text and complete the following sentences with the correct forms of the words or phrases from the box. Then try to orally translate the sentences you have completed into Chinese. You can use **the self-study materials** we have provided or any reference book available as well as the Internet.*

A. cater to	B. on one's account	C. rate ... as
D. be in fashion	E. at will	F. in all

1. _____, some 15 million people live in the selected areas.

2. He told us that we could wander around _____.

3. The show _____ a success by critics and audiences.

4. We have many facilities _____ the needs of our guests.

5. If you want the bill _____ your room _____, please sign here.

Part IV Role Playing

Work in pairs or groups after class. Compose and act out the dialogues in the following situations. Present your work by using videos.

Situation 1: The in-hotel guest of Room 1818, Black Smith, comes to the Business Center to have a contract copied. He wants the materials sent to No. 2 Meeting Room in ten minutes. Lily receives the guest, makes two black and white copies of each in A4, charges the total fee of 50 yuan (1 yuan per page × 50) to the guest's room account, and sends the material to the meeting room on time.

Situation 2: Mr. Blake, the in-hotel guest in Room 1818, comes to the Business Center to have a Spanish interpreter arranged for tomorrow's trade talks with a Spanish textile company. The guest wants an interpreter who knows textile well and has trade-talk experience. The interpreter should come to discuss with the guest not later than two o'clock this afternoon. Lily receives the guest, negotiates about the charge at 450 yuan per hour, contacts a translation company to arrange one because the hotel has no suitable Spanish interpreter, and promises to inform the guest as soon as possible after the interpreter is chosen. The guest agrees about the charge, chooses to charge the payment to his room account, shows out his room card, and fills out a form.

Situation 3: John Smith, the hotel guest of Room 1818, calls the operator Lily about how to make an international call. Lily suggests that it be cheaper to call from the guestroom than through the operator, tells the guest the dialing methods, and also refers the guest to the Service Guide.

Situation 4: Mr. Smith, the guest of Room 1818, comes to the shopping arcade of the hotel to look for a present related to Chinese culture for his wife. Lily, the shop assistant, shows the guest around, talks about his wife's hobby and interest, recommends Chipao to him, persuades him to accept the suggestion by giving him a detailed explanations of Chinese silk, offers him many articles to choose from, declines the guest's request of a discount by using the shop rules, settles the bill, charges the expense to the room account, and wraps up the article for the guest.

Lecture 7 Housekeeping Staff (8.2.1 Floor Attendant, 8.2.2 Housemaid)

Part I Word Study

*In this part, you are required to work by yourself selecting one word (in both **bold** and **italic** type) from the text to match its corresponding meaning. Read through the text carefully before making your choices. You can use **the self-study materials** we have provided or any reference book available as well as the Internet.*

No.	Explanations	Words
1	a series of letters or numbers that you must type into a computer or computer system in order to be able to use it 密码；口令	
2	a small amount of extra money that you give to sb., for example sb. who serves you in a restaurant 小费	
3	larger than a standard size but not as big as king-size 大号的	
4	a band of radio waves used for broadcasting television or radio programs 频道	
5	a room used for the particular purpose that is mentioned 房间	
6	a small flat box with a mirror, containing powder that women use on their faces 盒（式）	
7	a message sent by telegraph and then printed and given to sb. 电报	
8	a dirty mark on sth., which is difficult to remove 污渍	
9	a piece of equipment or furniture that you use for holding a particular type of thing 架	
10	a device that measures and controls the temperature of a machine or room, by switching the heating or cooling system on and off as necessary 自动恒温器	

Part II Term Study

In this part, you are required to work by yourself writing out in Column B the Chinese *meaning of each corresponding term in Column A. Read through the text carefully before completing this task. You can use **the self-study materials** we have provided or any reference book available as well as the Internet.*

No.	Column A	Column B
1	chamber service	
2	normal service	
3	quick service	
4	extra charge	

Part III Structure Study

*Work in class by yourself or in pairs. Look through the text and complete the following sentences with the correct forms of the words or phrases from the box. Then try to orally translate the sentences you have completed into Chinese. You can use **the self-study materials** we have provided or any reference book available as well as the Internet.*

A. call for   B. send for

1. There is no need to _____ the general manager.

2. The situation _____ prompt action.

Part IV Role Playing

Work in pairs or groups after class. Compose and act out the dialogues in the following situations. Present your work by using videos.

Situation 1: Mr. Blake, the new guest of Room 1818, walks out of the lift to the 18th floor. The floor attendant Lily sees him, greets him, opens the door for him, introduces room facilities to him, informs him which are used for a fee or free of charge, explains to him how to use the safety, the bathroom, the air conditioner, TV programs, and door knob menu, and tells him to call at 6666 if he needs cleaning service, turn-down service, laundry service, and other services.

Situation 2: The housemaid Lily wants to give a cleaning, but the guest of Room 1818 happens to be sleeping and to have forgotten to put up "DND." Lily says sorry to the guest and tells him to put up "Clean Card" on the door if he needs room cleaning.

Situation 3: Mr. Blake, the new guest of Room 1818, calls the housemaid Lily to add towels because the towels in the room are a bit wet.

Situation 4: Mr. Blake, the new guest of Room 1818, calls the housemaid Lily to buy some newspapers and deliver them to the room. The guest wants the expense charged to his room account, but Lily says it is not allowed because there are no such rule in the hotel and insists on the guest's paying in cash.

Situation 5: Mr. Blake, the new guest of Room 1818, calls the housemaid Lily to collect laundries for a quick service. Lily comes to the door, knocks on the door, collects the laundries, asks the guest to fill out the laundry list, and tells him the charge for quick service and the time to deliver back.

Lecture 8 Restaurant Staff

Part I Word Study

*In this part, you are required to work by yourself selecting one word (in both **bold** and **italic** type) from the text to match its corresponding meaning. Read through the text carefully before making your choices. You can use **the self-study materials** we have provided or any reference book available as well as the Internet.*

No.	Explanations	Words
1	an arrangement that you make in advance to buy a ticket to travel somewhere, go to the theater, etc. 预订	
2	a thick soup made with fish and vegetables 杂烩	
3	(of food) pleasantly hard and dry 脆的	
4	(of meat) cooked for only a short time so that the inside is still red 煎得嫩的	
5	(of meat) cooked until there is just a little pink meat inside 中等熟度的	
6	(of meat) cooked until there is no pink meat left inside 烧熟的	
7	either of a pair of thin sticks that are used for eating with, esp. in some Asian countries 筷子	
8	to support sth. by putting it on or against sth. 使放置在	
9	the feeling that you like sb./sth.; the enjoyment of sth. 喜欢；爱好	
10	not mixed with water or anything else 纯的	

Part II Term Study

*In this part, you are required to work by yourself writing out in Column B the Chinese meaning of each corresponding term in Column A. Read through the text carefully before completing this task. You can use **the self-study materials** we have provided or any reference book available as well as the Internet.*

No.	Column A	Column B
1	main dish	
2	the first course	
3	live music	
4	floor performance	
5	Happy Hour	

Part III Structure Study

*Work in class by yourself or in pairs. Look through the text and complete the following sentences with the correct forms of the words or phrases from the box. Then try to orally translate the sentences you have completed into Chinese. You can use **the self-study materials** we have provided or any reference book available as well as the Internet.*

A. start with	B. recommend sth. to sb.	C. give comment on
D. on the rocks	E. straight up	F. in total

1. I _____ the hotel _____ all my friends.

2. Well, maybe it would be easier to _____ a smaller problem.

3. She _____ helpful _____ my work.

4. These products, _____, account for about 80% of all our sales.

5. I ordered a Scotch _____ instead of a cola straight up.

Part IV Role Playing

Work in pairs or groups after class. Compose and act out the dialogues in the following situations. Present your work by using videos.

Situation 1: Mr. Blake in Room 1818 wants to book a table by the south window in the hall for five at 18:00. The restaurant reservationist Lily handles and confirms the reservation.

Situation 2: Lily, at the entrance to the restaurant hall, sees five guests coming, greets them, and seats them at the table reserved under Mr. Blake of Room 1818.

Situation 3: Lily sees five guests seated at the table, and walks up to help them order foods. She serves tea to the guests, introduces the characteristics of Chinese dishes and the special foods the restaurant provides, asks the guests what dishes they like, helps them to tick four dishes, one soup, and four bowls of rice on the menu, confirms orders with the guest, and asks the guests to drink some tea and wait for a short while before the orders are served.

Situation 4: After the dish orders are taken, Lily walks up to the table and takes wine orders.

Situation 5: Lily serves Chinese dishes to a table for five. She brings dishes, asks the guests how they like the dishes, answers their questions about the way of cooking, helps settle the bill, and packs up the remaining.

Situation 6: The clerk Lily of the Room Service receives an order, from Mr. Blake of Room 1818, for two sandwiches and a large pot of coffee. She brings the orders, knocks at the door, greets the guest, names what the guest has ordered, asks the guest to check whether they are what he has ordered, settles the bill, wishes the guest to enjoy the food, and says goodbye to the guest.

Lecture 9　Management

Part I　Word Study

*In this part, you are required to work by yourself selecting one word (in both **bold** and **italic** type) from the text to match its corresponding meaning. Read through the text carefully before making your choices. You can use **the self-study materials** we have provided or any reference book available as well as the Internet.*

No.	Explanations	Words
1	to offer or give sth. to sb. 提供；给予	
2	sth. that is a symbol of a feeling, a fact, an event, etc. 象征；标志	
3	showing strong feelings that are sincere 衷心的	
4	the act of thanking sb. or paying them for sth. they have done 报答；回报	
5	(of sb.) who feels respected 深感荣幸的	
6	that you can discuss or change before you make an agreement or a decision 可以协商的	
7	to demand that sth. happens or that sb. agrees to do sth. 坚持	
8	sth. that is done in advance in order to prevent problems or to avoid danger 预防措施	
9	an arrangement, a promise, or a contract made with sb. 协议	
10	the fact of doing sth. together or of working together towards a shared aim 合作	

Part II　Structure Study

Work in class by yourself or in pairs. Look through the text and complete the following sentences with the correct forms of the words or phrases from the box. Then try to orally *translate the sentences you have completed into Chinese. You can use **the self-study materials** we have provided or any reference book available as well as the Internet.*

> A. warn sb. to do sth.　　　　B. on the house　　　　C. would care to do sth.

1. I wonder whether he _____ (come) with us.
2. The landlord gave us a drink _____.
3. He _____ Billy _____ (keep) away from drugs.

Part III Role Playing

Work in pairs or groups after class. Compose and act out the dialogues in the following situations. Present your work by using videos.

Situation 1: The PR manager, on behalf of the General Manager, makes a farewell speech to a trade-talk delegation from the US.

Situation 2: The F&B manager, on behalf of the General manger, congratulates to Mr. Blake on his sixtieth birthday.

Situation 3: The sales manager negotiates on price with the representative of a conference group.

Situation 4: The Housekeeping manager handles a complaint of necklace missing in the room.

Chapter Nine Hotel Application Forms

Part I Word Study

*In this part, you are required to work by yourself selecting one word (in both **bold** and **italic** type) from the text to match its corresponding meaning. Read through the text carefully before making your choices. You can use **the self-study materials** we have provided or any reference book available as well as the Internet.*

No.	Explanations	Words
1	(of sth.) that has been well planned and made 精心设计的	
2	to put and keep documents, etc. in a particular place and in a particular order so that you can find them easily; to put a document into a file 把……归档	

Continued

No.	Explanations	Words
3	facts or information, esp. when examined and used to find out things or to make decisions 资料；数据	
4	a small change or improvement that is made to a law or a document; the process of changing a law or a document 修改	
5	a word in front of a person's name to show their rank or profession, whether or not they are married, etc. 头衔	
6	sth. that you say or write which expresses an opinion, a thought, etc. about sb./sth. 备注	
7	to be slow to speak or act because you feel uncertain or nervous 犹豫	
8	an act of going into or getting into a place 入境	
9	a thing or person that is being discussed, described, or dealt with 事由	
10	an official document that may be used to prove that the facts it states are true 证书	
11	a stamp or mark put in your passport by officials of a foreign country that gives you permission to enter, pass through or leave their country 签证	
12	the state of being legally or officially acceptable 有效性	
13	the act of taking goods, letters, etc. to the people they have been sent to 派送	
14	to give official permission for sth., or for sb. to do sth. 授权	
15	a small amount of sth. that shows what the rest of it is like 样本	
16	the state of being legally responsible for sth. 责任	
17	to give up sth./sb. when you are forced to 交出	
18	to accept that sth. is true 认可；承认	
19	to take money out of a bank account 取出	
20	to state officially, esp. in writing, that sth. is true 证明	
21	a person who uses a particular shop/store, restaurant, etc. 客人	
22	a fact or detail esp. one that is officially written down 详情；细节	
23	to carefully examine or consider sth. again, esp. so that you can decide if it is necessary to make changes 复核	
24	the act of choosing a way to follow from one place to another 路由（选择）	
25	an arrangement with a company in which you pay them regular amounts of money and they agree to pay the costs, for example, if you die or are ill/sick, or if you lose or damage sth. 保险	
26	a person who issues sth. (checks, invoices, bills, etc.) 出票人	
27	to let sb./sth. come out of a place where they have been kept or trapped 放走	
28	a result of sth. that has happened 后果	
29	the failure to give sb./sth. enough care or attention 疏忽；渎职	
30	many different kinds of things that are not connected and do not easily form a group 杂项	
31	to choose not to demand sth. in a particular case, even though you have a legal or official right to do so 放弃	
32	to promise sincerely that you will definitely do sth., keep to an agreement or arrangement, etc. 承诺	
33	a written list of questions that are answered by a number of people so that information can be collected from the answers 调查问卷	
34	the support that a person gives a shop/store, restaurant, etc. by spending money there 光顾	

Continued

No.	Explanations	Words
35	a time of training and testing when you start a new job to see if you are suitable for the work 试用期	
36	extremely good; excellent 优秀的	
37	a strong feeling of excitement and interest in sth. and a desire to become involved in it 热情	
38	willingness or readiness to receive (esp. impressions or ideas) 感受性；接受（度）	
39	the quality or habit of doing sth. or arriving somewhere at the right time 准时	
40	the quality of persons being able to work on their own and make their own decisions without needing anyone to tell them what to do 自发性；主动精神	

Part II Term Study

*In this part, you are required to work by yourself writing out in Column B the Chinese meaning of each corresponding term in Column A. Read through the text carefully before completing this task. You can use **the self-study materials** we have provided or any reference book available as well as the Internet.*

No.	Column A	Column B
1	application form	
2	reservation application	
3	confirmation number	
4	payment instruction	
5	reservation confirmation	
6	temporary residence	
7	host organization	
8	place of entry	
9	subject of stay	
10	forms of payment	
11	room change	
12	parcel collection	
13	luggage deposit	
14	specimen signature	
15	net amount	
16	depositing handler	
17	personal accident insurance	
18	charge voucher	
19	guest count	
20	hotel count	
21	express service charge	
22	regular service	
23	restaurant statement	

Continued

No.	Column A	Column B
24	room statement	
25	guest questionnaire	
26	direct mail	
27	performance appraisal	
28	end of probation	
29	annual assessment	
30	punctuality of attendance	

Part III Structure Study

*Work in class by yourself or in pairs. Look through the text and complete the following sentences with the correct forms of the words or phrases from the box. Then try to orally translate the sentences you have completed into Chinese. You can use **the self-study materials** we have provided or any reference book available as well as the Internet.*

A. at one's option

D. reconvert ... into ...

G. commit oneself to

J. without liability

B. be authorized to do sth.

E. in block letter

H. for later use

K. feel free to do sth.

C. surrender ... to ...

F. heart and soul

I. without notice

L. bill ... to one's account

---

1. Write your name and address _____ or in capital letter.

2. The unused RMB Yuan can _____ foreign currency when the holder leaves China within six months.

3. The room rate is subject to change _____.

4. Please _____ (enjoy) the facility of your Mini-Bar provided for your convenience.

5. We have always been _____ providing guests with top-quality service.

6. If the property represented by the slip is not called for within 6 months, the hotel may, _____, sell it at public or private sale.

7. The hotel reserves the right to open the box and remove the contents, if the key not _____ the Front Desk when you depart from the hotel.

8. The hotel _____ (deliver) property to any person presenting this slip without identification.

9. We must serve the guests _____.

10. The rest of the meat can be salted down _____.

Part IV Translation Work

Work in groups in class. Translate the following application forms into English. Present your work in class.

(1)
订房单

□紧急		
□订房	□更改	□取消

姓名

_____

姓	名
_____	_____

到店日期	离店日期
_____	_____

原定到店日期	原定离店日期
_____	_____

交通

_____

房间数量	房间类别	房价	服务代号
_____	_____	_____	_____

备注

_____

_____

订房者	电话／电传／传真
_____	_____

公司名称

_____

接受订房者	日期	接受取消者	日期
_____	_____	_____	_____

(2)
团体资料

团名						团号		
本地代理					旅行社			
到店日期		离店日期		唤醒时间			用餐时间	
全陪		房号			会务组		房号	

房类	房数	房价	小计	房租分析	人数
双人房				国籍分析	客类
单人房				订房分析	客源
套房					
贵宾套房				备注:	
加床					
总计					
旅行社				付账方式:	
免费					
陪同					
总计					
房号				宾客签名:	

(3)
商务中心服务单

No.

贵客姓名   日期

_____   _____

说明					金额
传真　　传真号码　　目的地　　时间　　每分钟收费					
其他					
				现金额	¥
收款员　　账项编号　　　日期　　　　时间　　　　房号　　　金额					
请勿在以上空格内填写					

经手人   宾客签名

_____   _____

(4)
宴会预订单

宴会名称						
预订者		单位			联系方式	
预订时间		宴会时间：由＿＿＿＿＿＿至＿＿＿＿＿＿				
宴会类别		宴会场地				
宴会形式		收费标准				
预订人数 （席数）		最低人数 （席数）				
订金		其他费用＿＿＿＿＿＿　租金＿＿＿＿＿＿				
结账方式		注意事项				
预订单 发送日期		发送人				

菜单与临时酒吧（或会议茶水服务）：

宴会布置（贵宾室布置）：

宴会指示牌横幅：

台型设计摆放：

花草布置：

工程装潢：

(5)
康娱部顾客访问登记表

尊敬的宾客：

非常感谢您的光临；您的意见是对我们莫大的支持和鼓励；请您在我们的顾客访问登记表上留下您的宝贵建议；我们热忱恭候您的再次光临！

您对下列服务如何评价？

项目	优	满意	欠佳
总台接待			
保龄球馆			
男子浴区			
女子浴区			
风味餐厅			
二楼康乐			
美容室			
足部护理区			
保健中心			
四楼棋牌室			
健身房			
六楼 KTV 包厢			
商场			

其他建议（请写明）

_____

宾客姓名　　　　　　　　　职业　　　　　　　　　日期

访问人

Chapter Ten　Food & Beverage Menus

Part I Word Study

*In this part, you are required to work by yourself selecting one word (in both **bold** and **italic** type) from the text to match its corresponding meaning. Read through the text carefully before making your choices. You can use **the self-study materials** we have provided or any reference book available as well as the Internet.*

No.	Explanations	Words
1	to leave meat or fish, before cooking it, in a mixture of oil, wine, spices, etc., in order to make it softer or to give it a particular flavor 腌制（鱼、肉等）	
2	to cut sth. into pieces 切片	
3	to shake or turn food in order to cover it with oil, butter, etc. 拌；摇匀；翻动	
4	to preserve food in vinegar or salt water 腌制（菜）	
5	(of a baby or young animal) that is still drinking milk from its mother 还在吃奶的（幼畜）	
6	to add spice to food in order to give it more flavor 用香料调味	
7	having a strong taste because spices have been used to flavor it 辛辣的	
8	to cut food, esp. meat, into very small pieces using a special machine 绞碎	
9	to make the sound of food frying in hot oil（油煎）发出咝咝声	
10	to cook an egg by mixing the white and yellow parts together and heating them, sometimes with milk and butter 炒；熘	
11	to cut meat, vegetables, etc. into small square pieces 将……切成丁	
12	to cook food, esp. fish or egg, gently in a small amount of nearly boiling water 水煮	
13	to burn the surface of sth. in a way that is sudden and powerful 使……干枯；烤焦	
14	to cook food, coated or covered with a layer of thick soup or juice 做使表面有一层浓汁	
15	to remove impurities from 蒸馏	
16	to mix two or more substances together 混合	
17	(of food) that can be made quickly and easily, usually by adding hot water 速食的；即溶的	
18	of various different sorts 各式各样俱全的	
19	the part that grows up from the ground when a plant starts to grow; a new part that grows on plants or trees 幼苗	
20	making you feel less tired or hot 爽口的；提神的	

Part II Term Study

*In this part, you are required to work by yourself writing out in Column B the Chinese meaning of each corresponding term in Column A. Read through the text carefully before completing this task. You can use **the self-study materials** we have provided or any reference book available as well as the Internet.*

No.	Column A	Column B
1	beverages and cold dishes	
2	dishes and heavy courses	
3	dish feature	
4	material purchasing	
5	kitchen staffing	
6	reception scheduling	

Part III Activity

Work in pairs or groups in or after class. Translate the following dishes into English. Present your work in class or online in PowerPoint.

No.	Dishes	Translations
1	夫妻肺片	
2	桂花糯米藕	
3	三丝木耳	
4	白菜豆腐焖酥肉	
5	回锅肉片	
6	米粉扣肉	
7	雪菜炒肉丝	
8	酱爆里脊丝配饼	
9	芽菜回锅肉	
10	蚂蚁上树	
11	菜胆蚝油牛肉	
12	川汁牛柳	
13	姜葱爆牛肉	
14	三彩牛肉丝	
15	尖椒香芹牛肉丝	
16	香煎新西兰牛仔骨	
17	小炒黑山羊	
18	大煮干丝	
19	干葱豆豉鸡煲	
20	龙凤琵琶豆腐	